Reading Melanie Klein

The psychoanalytic thought of Melanie Klein has experienced a renaissance in the humanities and has become increasingly influential in literary, cultural and political theory. The essays in *Reading Melanie Klein* reflect the most innovative work on Kleinian thought in recent years and respond to the upsurge of interest in her work with vigorous and challenging re-readings of the central tenets of Klein's thinking. The book features material which appears here for the first time in English, and several newly written chapters.

Reading Melanie Klein reassesses Klein's relation to the more well-known works of Freud and Lacan and challenges the long-held claim that her psycho-analysis is both too normative and too conservative for critical consideration. The essays address Klein's distinctive readings of the unconscious and phantasy, her tenacious commitment to the death drive, her notions of anxiety, projection and projective identification and her challenge to Freud's Oedipus complex and theories of sexual difference. The authors demonstrate how it is possible to rethink the basis of Kleinian theory, and show how her psychoanalysis can engage in powerful and productive dialogue with diverse disciplines such as politics, ethics and literary theory.

This timely collection is an invaluable addition to the scholarship on Melanie Klein and provides a catalyst for further debate not only within the psychoanalytic community but also across social, critical and cultural studies.

Lyndsey Stonebridge is a lecturer in English at the University of East Anglia. She is author of *The Destructive Element: British Psychoanalysis and Modernism* (1998). **John Phillips** is a lecturer in English at the National University of Singapore.

Contributions from: Leo Bersani; Harold N. Boris; Judith Butler; Adèle Covello; Mary Jacobus; Melanie Klein; Juliet Mitchell; Laura Mulvey; John Phillips; J.-B. Pontalis; Jacqueline Rose; Hanna Segal; Lyndsey Stonebridge; Barbro Sylwan; Maria Torok; Eli Zaretsky.

Reading Melanie Klein

Edited by Lyndsey Stonebridge
and John Phillips

London and New York

First published 1998 by Routledge
11 New Fetter Lane, London EC4P 4EE

Simultaneously published in the USA and Canada
by Routledge
29 West 35th Street, New York, NY 10001

© 1998 John Phillips and Lyndsey Stonebridge for the collection as a whole

Typeset in Times by Keystroke, Jacaranda Lodge, Wolverhampton
Printed and bound in Great Britain by TJ International Ltd, Padstow, Cornwall

British Library Cataloguing in Publication Data
A catalogue record for this book is available from the British Library

Library of Congress Cataloging in Publication Data
Reading Melanie Klein / edited by Lyndsey Stonebridge and
John Phillips.
    p. cm.
    Includes bibliographical references and index.
    1. Klein, Melanie. 2. Psychoanalysis. I. Phillips, John, 1956–   .
    II. Stonebridge, Lyndsey, 1965–   .
BF109.K57R43 1998
150.19'5'092—dc21   97–47651
                                                                   CIP

ISBN 0–415–16236–X (hbk)
ISBN 0–415–16237–8 (pbk)

Contents

Illustrations

Contributors

Leo Bersani is Professor of French at the University of California, Berkeley. He is the author, most recently, of *Homos* (1995) and, with Ulysse Dutoit, of *Arts of Impoverishment: Beckett, Rothko, Renais* (1993) (both from Harvard University Press). His latest book *Caravaggio's Secrets*, also written in collaboration with Ulysse Dutoit, was published in 1997 by MIT Press.

Harold N. Boris was born in 1932 and died in 1996. He was a respected practising analyst but did not go through official analytic institute training. Although he cannot be categorised in terms of any specific school, he has been described as neo-Kleinian and his work has clear affinities with that of Wilfred Bion. Boris has published numerous articles on psychoanalysis, and his books include *Sleights of Mind: One and Multiples of One* and *Envy* (both from Jason Aronson, 1994). A special issue (September, 1997) of the *Journal of Melanie Klein and Object Relations* was devoted to Boris's work.

Judith Butler is Chancellor's Professor of Rhetoric and Comparative Literature at the University of California, Berkeley. She is the author of *Subjects of Desire: Hegelian Reflections in Twentieth Century France* (Columbia University Press, 1997), *Gender Trouble: Feminism and the Subversion of Identity* (Routledge, 1990), *Bodies That Matter: On the Discursive Limits of 'Sex'* (Routledge, 1993), *Excitable Speech: A Politics of the Performative* (Routledge, 1996) and *The Psychic Life of Power* (Stanford University Press, 1997).

Adèle Covello was born in Italy and was a medical doctor, psychiatrist and psychoanalyst in Paris until her death in 1995. She published widely on psychoanalysis and psychoanalytic history. Her last papers included 'Ferenczi: avenir d'une illusion pédagogique' (*Bulletin du Collège des Psychanalystes*, no. 6, 1983) and 'Lettres de Freud: du scénario de Jones au diagnostic sur Ferenczi' (*Cahiers Confrontation*, no. 12, 1984).

Mary Jacobus is Anderson Professor of English and Women's Studies at Cornell University. She has written two books on Wordsworth, and is the author of *Reading Woman: Essays in Feminist Criticism* (Columbia University Press,

1986) and *First Things: The Maternal Imaginary in Literature, Art and Psychoanalysis* (Routledge, 1996). She is also the editor of *Women Writing and Writing about Women* (Croom Helm, 1979) and, with Evelyn Fox-Keller and Sally Shuttleworth, *Body/Politics: Women and the Discourses of Science* (Routledge, 1989). Her forthcoming book, *Objects – Lost and Found: Psychoanalysis and the Scene of Reading*, based on the Clarendon Lectures, will be published in Oxford in 1999.

Juliet Mitchell is Lecturer in Gender and Society at the University of Cambridge, Fellow of Jesus College, Cambridge and a practising psychoanalyst. She is the author of many articles on literature, feminist theory and psychoanalysis. Her books include *Woman's Estate* (Pantheon, 1972), *Psychoanalysis and Feminism* (Allen Lane, 1973), *The Rights and Wrongs of Women* (co-edited with Ann Oakley, Penguin, 1976) and *Women: The Longest Revolution* (Virago, 1984). She is the editor of *The Selected Melanie Klein* (Penguin, 1986) and, with Jacqueline Rose, of *Feminine Sexuality: Jacques Lacan and the école freudienne* (Macmillan, 1982).

Laura Mulvey is the Postgraduate Programme Co-ordinator at the British Film Institute, London. Her essays have been collected in two volumes, *Visual and Other Pleasures* (Macmillan, 1989) and, most recently, *Fetishism and Curiosity* (BFI, 1996). She has written the monograph on *Citizen Kane* for the BFI Monograph Series (BFI, 1992).

John Phillips lectures in English and Critical Theory at the National University of Singapore. He has published on literature, philosophy and psychoanalysis and is the author of a forthcoming book on Critical Theory.

J.-B. Pontalis is a full member and training analyst of the French Psychoanalytic Association, and founder of the *Nouvelle Revue de Psychanalyse*. He is the author, with Jean Laplanche, of *The Language of Psycho-Analysis* (Hogarth, 1973). Recent books include *Après Freud* and *Love of Beginnings*, trans. James Greene and Marie-Christine Réguis (Free Association Books, 1993).

Jacqueline Rose is Professor of English at Queen Mary and Westfield College, University of London. She has published widely on literary criticism, psycho-analysis, feminism and politics. She is the author of *The Case of Peter Pan, or The Impossibility of Children's Fiction* (Macmillan, 1984), *Sexuality in the Field of Vision* (Verso, 1986), *The Haunting of Sylvia Plath* (Virago, 1991), *Why War? – Psychoanalysis, Politics, and the Return to Melanie Klein* (Basil Blackwell, 1993) and *States of Fantasy* (Clarendon Press, 1996).

Hanna Segal qualified in medicine at the Polish Medical School in Edinburgh before training under Melanie Klein and becoming a psychoanalyst in 1947. She became a training analyst in the British Psycho-Analytical Society in 1951. She has served as President of the British Society and Vice-President of the International Psychoanalytic Association. She is the author of *Introduction* *to the Work of Melanie Klein* (Hogarth, 1973), and many of her articles have been collected in *The Work of Hanna Segal* (Aronson, 1981; Free Association Books, 1986).

Lyndsey Stonebridge is Lecturer in English at the University of East Anglia. She is the author of *The Destructive Element: British Psychoanalysis and Modernism* (Macmillan, 1998).

Barbro Sylwan was born in Sweden and has worked as a psychoanalyst in Paris since 1968. She is an associate member of the *Société Psychanalytique de Paris*. Her publications on the history and theory of psychoanalysis include 'Sous le sein de Georg Brandes: le cachet de Melanie Klein Reizes' (*Cahiers Confrontation*, no. 8, 1982), 'An "untoward event" ou la guerre du trauma. De Breuer à Freud, de Jones à Ferenczi' (*Cahiers Confrontation*, no. 12, 1984) and '"Freud & Co." Marchands de Manchester. A propos de la mort de Philipp Freud et de ses effets' (*Cahiers Confrontation*, no. 18, 1987).

Maria Torok has been an analyst in Paris since the 1950s. She is the author, with Nicolas Abraham, of *The Shell and the Kernel: Renewals of Psychoanalysis* (Chicago University Press, 1994) and *The Wolf Man's Magic Word* (University of Minnesota Press, 1986). She has most recently collaborated with Nicholas Rand on *Questions for Freud: The Secret History of Psychoanalysis* (Harvard University Press, 1998). She also wrote the general introduction with Nicolas Abraham for the French edition of Melanie Klein's collected essays.

Eli Zaretsky is Professor of History at the University of Missouri, Columbia, Visiting Professor at the New School for Social Research in New York, and Visiting Scholar at the Institut für die Wissenchaft von Menschen in Vienna. He is the author of *Capitalism, the Family and Personal Life* (Pluto, 1986), a work that was translated into sixteen languages, and the editor of William I. Thomas and Florian Zananiecki's *The Polish Peasant in Europe and America*. He is currently completing an overall history of psychoanalysis, *Psychoanalysis, Modernity and Personal Life*, which will be published by Alfred J. Knopf.

Acknowledgements

The idea for this collection goes back to our graduate classes with Jacqueline Rose at the University of Sussex in the late 1980s. Our first debt is to Jacqueline for her suggestions, support and, not least, for the example of her own work on Melanie Klein. Our second is to our contributors for their articles, hard work and patience. We would also like to thank Elizabeth Bott Spillius and the Melanie Klein Trust, John Forrester, René Major, Adam Phillips and Nicholas Rand for their generous assistance. John Phillips would like to thank the Faculty of Arts and Social Sciences at the National University of Singapore for granting study leave to finish the project, and Gilbert W. Adair for patient and constructively critical responses to this editor's material. Lyndsey Stonebridge would like to thank the School of English and American Studies at the University of East Anglia for granting her leave to finish this project, and Linda Allen, Mary Ahl and Aggie Sirrine at the Society for Humanities, Cornell University whose patience and computer competence eased the nightmare of intercontinental editing.

In addition, the editors would like to thank the following for their permission to include copyright material in this book:

Chapter 1, Introduction to Melanie Klein by Juliet Mitchell, from *The Selected Melanie Klein*, Penguin 1991. Reproduced courtesy of the Melanie Klein Trust, Juliet Mitchell, The Hogarth Press and with the permission of The Free Press, a Division of Simon & Schuster © 1986 by Juliet Mitchell.

Chapter 3, Melanie Mell by Herself by Maria Torok, Barbro Sylwan and Adèle Covello, from *Geopsychanalyse: Les Souterrains de l'Institution*, ed. René Major, *Cahiers Confrontation*, Paris, 1981.

Chapter 4, The Question Child by J.-B. Pontalis, from *Frontiers of Psychoanalysis: Between the Dream and Psychic Pain*, trans. Catherine and Phillip Cullen, The Hogarth Press, 1981. Reproduced courtesy of Random House UK.

Chapter 5, 'Tea Daddy': Poor Mrs Klein and the pencil shavings by Mary Jacobus, from *Women: A Cultural Review*, Vol. 1, No. 2 (Summer 1990) pp. 160–80. Reproduced courtesy of Oxford University Press.

Chapter 6, Tolerating Nothing by Harold N. Boris, from *Contemporary Psychoanalysis*, Vol. 23, No. 3 (July 1987) pp. 351–66. Also published in *Envy*, Aronson, 1994, pp. 21–32.

Chapter 7, Negativity in the Work of Melanie Klein by Jacqueline Rose, from *Why War? Psychoanalysis, Politics and the Return to Melanie Klein*, Blackwell, 1993, pp. 137–90.

Chapter 11, A Psychoanalytic Approach to Aesthetics by Hanna Segal, from *Delusion and Artistic Creativity*, Free Association Books, 1986. Originally published in *New Directions in Psychoanalysis*, Tavistock, 1955.

Chapter 12, Death and Literary Authority: Marcel Proust and Melanie Klein by Leo Bersani, from *The Culture of Redemption*, Cambridge, Mass.: Harvard University Press. Copyright © 1990 by the President and Fellows of Harvard College.

Chapter 13, Notes on *Citizen Kane* by Melanie Klein. Reproduced courtesy of the Melanie Klein Trust and *Psychoanalytic Inquiry*.

Editors' note

We have retained the original citation style of contributors wherever possible, although bibliographical references to the works of Sigmund Freud and Melanie Klein have been standardized for clarity. Similarly, contributors' spellings of key psychoanalytic terms have been retained, to reflect authorial nuances.

Introduction

Lyndsey Stonebridge and John Phillips

I

In 1927 Ernest Jones, Melanie Klein's early advocate in Britain, wrote to Freud to tell him about the recently successful analysis of his children. This letter is famous for Jones's injudicious criticism of the work of Freud's own daughter, Anna, which, he suggests, is premature and limited by her 'imperfectly analysed resistances.' Tellingly, Jones fails to mention the name of his own children's analyst – Melanie Klein. Unable to name Klein as Freud's theoretical inheritor in the analysis of children, Jones, in a logic familiar to psychoanalysis, turns to attack the 'rightful' heir. Jones' and Freud's subsequent correspondence on Klein covers many of the same issues that the contributors to this book discuss: the early super-ego, the primacy Klein gives to the role of phantasy, the genesis of guilt and female sexuality, for example, all figure. The tone of the letters – the muted charges of legitimacy and illegitimacy that simmer between the lines – also rehearses that popular psychoanalytic parlour game in which analysts act out the very theory they are supposed to be debating or opposing. Masters of psycho-analysis both, neither Freud nor Jones seems quite able to master the affects that Klein's work produces.[1] The same might be said for Edward Glover and Melitta Schmideberg (Klein's own daughter). Their opposition to Klein's work, as the recently published proceedings of the Controversial Discussions attest, was to culminate in behaviour which, while not of course psychotic, certainly seemed to drive some a little mad.[2] And so it goes on. As Mary Jacobus argues here, the brutality that Lacan objects to in Klein can also be found in his own critical discourse. For some readers and analysts, it seems, Melanie Klein has always been hard to swallow.

While it is true to say that it is often what is most 'unmasterable' in or about Klein that proves to be most intriguing, troubling, repeatable or (in the case of many contributors to this volume) most critically productive, it is just as important to stress that others have mastered her work or, at the very least, worked with its effectiveness as a theory and a practice. Many practising analysts might be surprised to hear of a 'return to Klein.' Klein's relative marginalization in humanities studies is not mirrored in British psychoanalysis where her legacy is contested but secure. Indeed, one of the strangest things about the current return to Klein in the case of British literary and cultural studies is the sense that you don't really have to go very far to find her. This is not only because Kleinianism continues to be practised as a therapy but because, as Eli Zaretsky argues in his essay, Klein's work, alongside that of others in the British psychoanalytic movement, played a crucial part in the formation of British modernity. Her theory of object relations, he suggests, sketches out a psychoanalysis of 'the potentially democratic character of collective activity.' Some of us perhaps won't be surprised to find that the origins of this democratic character are of a violent, even psychotic, nature (as John Phillips argues below). Contemporary Kleinian analysts have continued to uncover the morbid formations that haunt modern life and often with a critical and analytic verve equal to Klein's. The essays collected in the two-volume collection *Melanie Klein Today: Developments in Theory and Practice* testify to this and, with contributions by Elizabeth Bott Spillius, Betty Joseph, Herbert Rosenfeld and Wilfred Bion (to name but a few), demonstrate both the richness of Kleinian theory and practice and the extent to which it has developed.[3] In fact, the best 'readers' of Klein are those extraordinary thinkers who read – really read – and then transformed or departed from her work: Wilfred Bion, Donald Winnicott and W.R.D. Fairbairn. Neither has the task of reading Klein over the last fifty years been left to Kleinian analysts. Her ideas found a new and powerful force in Adrian Stokes's art writing (who not only knew how to read Klein, but art too).[4] Likewise, sociologists, philosophers and literary critics have found much in Klein's work that can be applied to their fields.[5]

None of the contributors to this collection is really attempting to apply Kleinian theory – except, of course, Klein herself, and Hanna Segal, who both applies and transforms Kleinian aesthetics. As John Phillips explains below, they are reading her in a different way. If some of our contributors seem blind to the contexts and traditions of contemporary Kleinianism this is not because it is considered unimportant (far from it), but because they are starting from a different place. The reasons for the current return to Klein among theorists and critics in the humanities are varied. In part, more people have started to read Klein in the past decade simply because her work and reputation have become more prominent generally. In the late 1980s Nicholas Wright's play *Mrs Klein* and Phyllis Grosskurth's biography put Klein on the cultural stage on both sides of the Atlantic.[6] In 1986 Juliet Mitchell's edited selection not only made Klein's most important essays available to the general reader but provided a much-needed lucid introduction to her work – which is why we have reprinted it here. More recently, Pearl King and Riccardo Steiner's meticulous scholarship means that we now have a full account of the Controversial Discussions.

Along with a general opening up of the psychoanalytic archives, much of the impetus behind the current return to Klein comes from feminism (Virago's decision to republish her work in the late 1980s is obviously crucial here).[7] But while some feminists have turned to Klein's matricentric version of psychic development as a way of exploring a positive alternative to Freud's and Lacan's 'phallicism,' others have been repelled by the uncomfortable proximity between mother-love and matricide in her work, not to say with the theory's not so latent heterosexism.[8] For others still, however, Klein's version of early Oedipal life provides a language to talk about those areas of psychic experience that seem to resist socio-symbolic representation. The curious and unsettling corporeality of Klein's good, bad, part and whole objects testifies to a phantasy world lived on the margins of (and maybe in opposition to) the so-called successful resolution of the Oedipus complex and the ensuing discomfort of 'gendered representation.'[9] Why Klein herself produced such a violent and destructive vision of our maternal beginnings, and quite why we should be returning to this today, is another question. Reading Klein often feels like an attack on our own voyeurism as well as an invitation to peer into forbidden spaces (the inside of the mother's body no less). The interior spaces of the psyche that she describes so literally both compel because they are revealed, and appal because of what they reveal. The unconscious, for Klein, is somewhere where you fry your parents' kidneys.[10]

Klein, as many of the contributors to this book emphasize, seems to take us to the limits of what is imaginable about psychic life. For some, this is a return too far. But Klein is doing more than adding flesh to the gothic architecture of our modern minds. What is important about her work is not only what she demands we imagine (our own inhumanity), but the imperative in her work that insists upon the difficulty we have in imagining ourselves in the first place. That 'in the first place' is important. Readers of contemporary psychoanalytic theory should have no difficulty with the suggestion John Phillips makes below that reading Klein begins not by assuming that she assumes too much (a familiar charge against Klein), but with the recognition of 'an externality at the origin.' It's exactly the paradoxes of this kind of formulation about subjectivity that have motivated much current work in psycho-politics. Recent post-Lacanian criticism has tended to move away from a psychoanalysis of representation (the neurotic model of symptom formation that was so efficacious in the semiotic analysis of film and literature) and towards a consideration of what both resists and enables representation (and, in the case of Slavoj Žižek, ideology).[11] The return to Klein that these essays evidence has been accompanied in recent years by the 'return of the real' in much post-Lacanian work.[12] These 'returns' do not amount to the same thing (although remember that what Lacan admired about Britain in the war was both its psychoanalysts and its '*rapport véridique au réel*' – 'truthful relation to the real'[13]), but they do cross a similarly negative terrain. Reading Melanie Klein, in other words, need not necessarily be an alternative to post-Lacanian theory, but a different way of approaching the same problem. In the 1930s and 1940s it was Klein's daring analysis of the psychoses that incurred the wrath of many. At the end of the century, many theorists are trying to understand the psychic dynamics of a modernity that seems to demand that we are, somehow, psychotic. Klein's account of object relations, the schizoid mechanisms that, for her, determine our social being (loving and hating, annihilating and reviving, persecuted and persecuting), not only offers an account of our earliest relations with the mother but, as Teresa Brennan has argued, might also account for our paranoid relations to the world which we – in true paranoid fashion – have made for ourselves.[14] It is all the more fitting, therefore, that this collection should end with Klein's own analysis of one of the most powerful dramatizations of the melancholia of modernity's everyman, *Citizen Kane*. In this respect we need not so much to return to Klein as catch up with her. In terms of articulating the morbid formations that underpin contemporary social existence she, perhaps, had mastered us long before we found her unmasterable.

Lyndsey Stonebridge

II

What is at stake in reading Melanie Klein today?

One of the aims of this collection is to focus on what many see as a belated 'return' to the work of Melanie Klein in a field that has already been considerably influenced by developments in psychoanalysis. It is as if something has been missed and Klein somehow provides the clue to what that is. What, then, has provoked diverse humanities scholars to return to Klein – and to Klein's texts themselves – in search of new ways of working through a whole range of problems? In other words, what is to be gained for humanities scholarship in returning to and re-reading an early albeit influential practitioner of child analysis? In what ways are her texts anything other than either historical documents or source texts for training analysts?

First I want to address the question of reading per se. Most strands of post-war critical theory increasingly emphasize not only the central importance of *reading* but also its intractable difficulties. Reading, in its most basic and essential sense, involves an attempt to deal with a text as a mediation between reader and some otherwise absent meaning or intention. The text is a mediation because it represents something other than what it is. The ancient problem regarding this is that texts are notoriously unreliable and tend to be misunderstood as often as they are correctly understood. Various adventures in literary criticism and theory have, especially in the period since the Second World War, led to consistent yet often misunderstood conclusions. We find, for instance, that it is the unreliable, troublesome aspects of writing and language as mediating tools that allow them to work at all. Writing is possible only because it can be repeated in all kinds of contexts (in principle infinitely many) which in turn cannot but contribute to (add to and change) the essential significance of the thing being read. The main implication here is that there can be no single precise and eternally valid 'meaning' of a text independently either of a given context (what it means now) or of the permanent possibility of randomly determined future contexts (unimaginable future significations). No context can exhaust the meaning of a text but, because of that, *more or less* stable and determinate meanings and intentions are possible. Any attempt, however, to contain or exclude those other possibilities will inevitably lead to paradoxes. As a consequence a whole range of extremely sophisticated reading strategies have emerged that, while no longer looking for the definitive singular reading of a given text, are alert to the inevitable consequences that even minor and often unexpected changes in context have for a given reading. Hence in the humanities the notion of a 'return' suggested by this 'return to Melanie Klein' is not without precedent.

Psychoanalysis has played a major role in the post-war development of critical thinking, partly because it can be considered as having contributed in its own way to this kind of change of emphasis in the context of reading. It's helpful to think of psychoanalysis as having a speculative or philosophical significance that is independent of clinical practice, although the status of that significance – divorced, as it were, from the transference – is perpetually controversial. If this aspect of Klein has not been recognized historically, it is partly, I think, because mainstream critical theory has followed a trail that leads in a rather different direction. When Jacques Lacan adapted Ferdinand de Saussure's structural linguistics and grafted it neatly into Freud's *Interpretation of Dreams* he opened up a number of genuinely groundbreaking possibilities for critical thought. Lacan initially found a sympathetic audience among both structuralist thinkers, for whom language is the privileged element, and Marxist theorists who saw how Lacan's concepts of desire and the symbolic tie in with notions of ideology and interpellation. So Lacan offered arguments that could explain how a social (and moral) milieu that is historically determined could construct a gendered human subject who feels unique, singular and whole, in an environment that is naturalized and internalized as eternally fulfilling. Inevitable failures return as neuroses and psychoses (or at least a feeling of general inadequacy), thus suggesting a social or 'symbolic' cause for mental illness – symptoms of the disease known as capitalist history. Such explanations, because they are language-based, offer the promise of political change. Sexuality, gender and all forms of authority are determined historically on the basis of language regarded in its essential mode as an empty signifier. Against all this Klein's apparently normative and certainly heterosexist perspective appears less than attractive to a highly politicized and protean critical theory.

For some, however, Lacan's 'linguistic a priori' is less than satisfying. His formulations seem to offer little room for manoeuvre. Klein can thus be seen as theorizing a deeper determination, something at once more radical than and less assimilable to existing paradigms. In fact the precondition for infantile (and thus adult) development in Klein would seem to trouble all paradigms. It is a kind of negative a priori where experience begins with an inexplicable exterior at its very core.

Klein provides a route that goes under, or undercuts, Lacan's historical determination of gendered identification and the various myths of sexual difference, providing a yet deeper level of understanding. Klein's accounts of infantile development are independent of and ontologically prior to Oedipal and all linguistically based constructions. But Klein doesn't simply replace the father and his prohibition with an earlier maternal alternative, as is sometimes thought. Phantasy and the anxiety that provokes it are the proactive makers of the infant's world. The mother is the bland representative whose essence (such as it is) is precisely the unknowable outside, the one whose actions can neither be controlled nor mastered.

The 'Return to Klein' that the majority of these essays represent tends to focus on problem moments (of which there are many): Leo Bersani and J.-B. Pontalis each present a reading of the very early writing in order to expose difficulties for what is seen as an increasing conservatism and socially normative complicity in her later work; Lyndsey Stonebridge concentrates on the crucial and transitional reading of Freud's *Inhibitions, Symptoms and Anxiety* in *The Psycho-Analysis of Children*; Jacqueline Rose examines the Controversial Discussions that split the British Psycho-Analytical Society in 1944; and Judith Butler reads Klein's crucial essays on mourning and guilt. But Klein is always, beneath each of these problematizations, already a problem, because at the centre of Kleinian theory is the necessarily unmasterable and endlessly disruptive work of negativity, anxiety, alterity. As a consequence of this, there can be nothing in Klein's writing that doesn't offer something like the productive tensions that these contributors have settled upon.

Alongside these re-readings the collection includes indispensable essays (by Hanna Segal, Harold N. Boris and Klein herself) which demonstrate how the 'problems' of Klein are used and regarded as positive resources by those who work with her concepts every day. Boris, particularly, shows how the analyst, when faced with the unknowable, can learn to read it anyway, to recognize and learn about the unspeakable – to receive secret messages while at the same time maintaining their secrecy. This is less an interpretation of meaningful symbols than an acknowledgment of unspeakable, unsymbolizable emotions.

Torok et al., Stonebridge, Jacobus, Butler, Rose and Bersani each bring a sophisticated contemporary understanding of literary and critical theory to their readings, which does not, of course, mean a theoretical mastery, but does reveal how much a Kleinian aesthetics, as set out in this collection by Hanna Segal, has to offer. These creative and sophisticated readings, informed by a literary theory that is already practised in the hermeneutics of the unmasterable, find in Kleinian analysis a working out of the meaning of the unmasterable itself – the origin of meaning as death or negativity – but fleshed out and made obscene in a kind of phenomenological *epoche* that reduces the adult experience to its infantile core. The infant, or more generally, the child, is at the centre of the most controversial issues in relation to Kleinian analysis. Issues concerning education, the transmission of knowledge, the contested line between child analysis and abuse, are as current as ever. In Klein, however, there is a palpable sense in which speaking to the unconscious involves listening to the unconscious speak.

But the relationship between the adult and child is perhaps what is most difficult to read in Klein's writings. One of the controversial issues is the question of how much the infantile mechanisms, represented by paranoid anxiety and depressive guilt, remain in operation during adult life. The Kleinian answer is disturbing. The adult is never free of the infantile processes; there is no pure, rational, objective separation between epistemological and emotional life. Rather it is the infantile mechanisms that make all knowledge and judgement possible. What inhibits the acquisition of knowledge is also what makes the acquisition of knowledge possible. This formulation can make no sense in a context where knowledge is considered to be in principle complete, and ignorance a kind of absence in it that is just waiting to be filled. But Klein does not simply deny or restrict the possibility of achieving such a knowledge, putting obstacles in its way, as if something like a partial knowledge was possible but not a total one. Rather her texts offer a fundamental revision of the concept of knowledge itself, making knowledge and the unknowable functions, as it were, of the same principle. What is significant here is the concept of time. For classical science time is little more than a kind of spatiality extending backwards or forwards, a geometric compass that in theory (and thus in reality) one can plot. That is, time is ideally reversible and thus masterable.[15] One way to characterize the essays in this collection would be to view them through the question of time. What they reveal, I would argue, is that the most tenaciously difficult moments in Klein's writings involve attempts to engage with the problem of a temporality that cannot be charted at all, let alone reversed.

Accounts of the difference between Sigmund Freud and Melanie Klein often focus on the theoretical role of time. For Freud a symptom is always the return of a past that was created by repression (the return of the repressed). Klein on the contrary is apparently more interested in the perpetual present of infantile experience. Significantly, of course, the foundation of Klein's theory is in the pre-Oedipal child, who, in Freudian terms at least, is a child without memory, a child who has not acquired a history. In other words Klein is concerned only with the child's atemporal confrontation with the external world.[16] This is undoubtedly a useful distinction but I think that the concept of time in Klein's writing is more complex and interesting than the term 'atemporal' suggests. In distinguishing between the adult and the infant Klein puts into relief the strangeness of infantile experience. The sudden presences and abrupt absences that punctuate the infant's experience suggest a set of fixed coordinates that are constantly and unpredictably interrupted by unmasterable comings and goings, events that no past–present schema could comfortably chart. Klein shows us that the radical difference between infantile and adult experience has to do with the absence of history and historical time for the infant.

Klein's concept of phantasy, from the very beginning, involves an element that fissures, disturbs, disorganizes or displaces whatever spatial schema prevails at any moment. Each of the contributors to this collection, in different ways, can be seen to be addressing a disturbing negativity that is in some sense related to time but is reducible neither to historical (even Freudian) time nor to the pure atemporality of non-historical time.

Harold Boris begins his essay 'Tolerating Nothing' by quoting a poem by Carson McCullers which, for Boris, communicates a poetic sense of the 'presence of an absence,' which 'the no-thing' represents for patients who cannot tolerate negativity. The poem begins with the 'configured Hell' of a 'nothing' that 'is not blank.' The static existence of unrelated objects ('noticed clocks . . . malignant stars') is converted to 'agony immobilized' by the 'air between.' This 'air between' may be space or time, 'Or the joined trickery of both conceptions.' The poem ends with the rushing, screaming flux of an irrational temporality, the madness of time: 'While Time/The endless idiot, runs screaming round the world.' Boris does not provide a commentary on the poem – he doesn't need to; its terms resonate effectively with everything he has to say – but it is possible to link this particularly terrifying conception of time to his main issue, the difficulty that some patients have in tolerating anxiety caused by the negativity of the death drive. It is a powerful conception of time as that which the infant must learn to bear. But this is not a historical or developmental time; it is, rather, an exteriority that breaks into the agonizingly static horizon of spatial experience. The agony and the terror are permanent. But it is difficult to tell whether they are caused by empty space or endless time, for the spatial and temporal conceptions seem to be, again, functions of the same principle.

Such an incomprehensible aspect at the centre of meaning returns consistently in the essays collected here: in Stonebridge, as anxiety; in Rose, as negativity; in Pontalis, as the unmasterable unconscious against psychoanalytic theory; in Boris, as nothing; in Butler, as doubt. Each time this incomprehensible aspect is linked in some way to time, but time not on any of the models normally available (from Aristotle to Heidegger). Time is usually (oddly) only explicable by spatial models, which are thus reversible. But in Melanie Klein time is impossible, it is an unimaginable future that nonetheless determines development and writes an absolute past into the present before it has even arrived. It is externality at the origin, the outside in the inside. This concept of time is constituted entirely by contingency, externality and negativity and, while it is strictly speaking untheorizable, it orients and organizes so many of the theoretical formulations in Klein's writing. It is in this sense that we might take Rose's suggestion that 'Klein does theory otherwise.'

John Phillips

Notes

1 See *The Complete Correspondence of Sigmund Freud and Ernest Jones, 1908–1939*, ed. R. Andrew Paskauskas, Cambridge, Mass. and London: Belknap Press of Harvard University Press, 1993. My thanks to John Forrester for drawing my attention to these letters.

2 *The Freud–Klein Controversies: 1941–45*, eds Pearl King and Riccardo Steiner, London: Tavistock/Routledge, 1991. For an account of Klein's reception by the British Psycho-Analytical Society, see Pearl King, 'The Life and Work of Melanie Klein in the British Psycho-Analytical Society', *International Journal of Psycho-Analysis (IJPA)*, vol. 64, 1983.

3 *Melanie Klein Today: Developments in Theory and Practice* (2 vols), ed. Elizabeth Bott Spillius, London: Tavistock/Routledge, 1988. See also Donald Meltzer, *The Kleinian Development: Parts 1–3*, Perthshire: Clunie Press, 1978.

4 Adrian Stokes, *The Critical Writings of Adrian Stokes, Vols 1–3*, ed. Lawrence Gowing, London: Thames and Hudson, 1978.

5 Michael Rustin has maybe done the most to demonstrate Klein's relevance to social and political theory. See his 'A Socialist Consideration of Kleinian Psychoanalysis', *New Left Review*, 131, 1982; (with Margaret Rustin) 'Relational preconditions of socialism', in *Capitalism and Infancy*, ed. B. Richards, London: Free Association Books, 1984; and *The Good Society and the Inner World: Psychoanalysis, Politics and Culture*, London: Verso, 1991. See also Fred C. Alford, *Melanie Klein and Critical Social Theory: An Account of Politics, Art and Reason Based on her Psychoanalytic Theory*, New Haven, Conn.: Yale University Press, 1989 and (for a comparative view) N.J.H. Dent, *Rousseau: An Introduction to his Psychological, Social and Political Theory*, Oxford: Basil Blackwell, 1988. For recent examples of a Kleinian approach to literary interpretation, see Meg Harris Williams and Margot Waddell, *The Chamber of Maiden Thought: Literary Origins of the Psychoanalytic Model of the Mind*, London: Tavistock/Routledge, 1991, and Michael and Margaret Rustin, *Narratives of Love and Loss: Studies in Modern Children's Fiction*, London: Verso, 1987.

6 Phyllis Grosskurth, *Melanie Klein: Her World and Her Work*, London: Hodder & Stoughton, 1985.

7 In 1990 the second issue of the journal *Women: A Cultural Review* (vol. 1, no. 2, Summer) was dedicated to Klein's work and legacy. In the same year Janet Sayers published her *Mothering Psychoanalysis: Helene Deutsch, Karen Horney, Anna Freud and Melanie Klein*, London: Hamish Hamilton, 1990.

8 For an account of Klein's normative views on sexuality, see Noreen O'Connor, 'Is Melanie Klein the One Who Knows Who You Really Are?', *Women: A Cultural Review*, vol. 1, no. 2, Summer 1990.

9 Julia Kristeva's writing on early Oedipality was clearly important for setting a new agenda for Klein's work. See *Proust and the Sense of Time*, trans. with an introduction by Stephen Bann, New York: Columbia University Press, 1993, for a recent example of Kristeva's use of Kleinian motifs. Some of the most interesting feminist work on Klein has been in the field of art history. See Briony Fer, 'Bordering on Blank: Eva Hesse and Minimalism', *Art History*, vol. 17, no. 3, September 1994 and Mignon Nixon, 'Bad Enough Mother', *October*, 71, Winter 1995.

10 Melanie Klein, 'A Contribution to the Psychogenesis of Manic-Depressive States'(1935), *Love, Guilt and Reparation and Other Works, 1921–1945*, London: Virago, 1988, p. 208.

11 The translation of Lacan's seminars on ethics and the psychoses is important in this context (see *The Seminar of Jacques Lacan Book VII: The Ethics of Psycho-analysis*, trans. Dennis Porter, London: Routledge, 1992 and *The Psychoses: 1955–56*, trans. with notes by Russell Grigg, New York: Norton, 1993). See also Slavoj Žižek, *The Sublime Object of Ideology*, London: Verso, 1989 and *The Metastases of Enjoyment: Six Essays on Women and Causality*, London: Verso, 1994, and Joan Copjec, *Read My Desire: Lacan against the Historicists*, Cambridge, Mass.: MIT Press, 1994.

12 Cf. Hal Foster, *The Return of the Real: The Avant Garde at the End of the Century*, Cambridge, Mass.: MIT Press, 1996.

13 Jacques Lacan, 'La Psychiatre anglaise et la guerre', *Travaux et Interventions*, Paris: 1947, p. 294.

14 Teresa Brennan, 'The Foundational Fantasy', *History After Lacan*, London: Routledge, 1993, pp. 79–117. Klein is also a central figure in Gilles Deleuze's and Félix Guattari's postmodern classic, *Anti-Oedipus: Capitalism and Schizophrenia*, trans. Robert Hurley, Mark Seem and H.R. Lane, New York: Viking, 1984.

15 Notwithstanding protestations that science has moved on from this classical

conception, Jacqueline Rose's observations on Stephen Hawking's *A Brief History of Time*, in her contribution to this volume, reveal that the conception of time characteristic of classical physics remains intact in contemporary versions – although, as Rose shows, Hawking's explanation fades into fantasy at the very moment he speculates on the possibility of time's reversal. 'Close to naked singularities,' he writes, 'it may be possible to travel into the past.'

16 See Juliet Mitchell's section on 'Freud and Klein: Time Past and Future. Time Present' in this volume, pp. 25–28.

Chapter 1

Introduction to Melanie Klein

Juliet Mitchell

Editor's note:

In the following introduction Juliet Mitchell suggests that one aspect of Melanie Klein's importance lies in her ability to identify with what she observes in order to follow what is going on and then to describe it. It is this that provides such a powerful evocation of infantile experience in Klein's writings. But, more than that, Mitchell argues, what Klein identifies and describes bears directly on the very business of clinical observation and description. The analyst, no less than the struggling infant, must learn to engage with 'areas of confusion, fusion, lack of boundaries, of communicating without the differential structures of speech.' So for Klein, analysis must address aspects of the infant's experience that strictly cannot be articulated in theoretical language.

The chapter first appeared as the introduction to *The Selected Melanie Klein*, which Mitchell edited in 1986, and which, as a widely circulated single edition of Klein's key works, has helped to pave the way for the 'return to Klein' that we are witnessing today. Mitchell very carefully distinguishes between the ideas of Sigmund Freud and those of Klein in a way that denies the need to engage at length with their endlessly controversial differences. What is at stake here is not a question of orthodoxy but of what it is precisely that Klein contributes. Mitchell gives an eloquent account of the main principles of Freudian development by focusing on what in Freud has most relevance to Klein's own development – centrally, his theory of infantile sexuality and his account of the unconscious as 'a hypothetical area that is always unfathomable.' Mitchell also emphasizes the importance of Freud's later theories of the death drive and the super-ego, which were new to psychoanalysis when Klein was developing her own analytic technique, and which are crucially transformed notions in Klein's writings.

Mitchell's commentary on Klein is the ideal opening chapter for this collection, because in it she clearly sets out what is at stake in attempts to identify and describe the first few months of the infant's life. According to Klein, the mechanisms that govern those early experiences are the same ones used by adults in their daily encounters with the world. But Klein shows that when compared to adult psychic experience the world of the infant appears to be very different. It is Klein's insistence on this unmasterable difference that marks her out as a groundbreaking analyst.

So Mitchell's introduction, admirable as it is in its didactic role, is also rather more than that. It is an elaborate argument for the importance of Kleinian thought as an essential addition to classical psychoanalytic knowledge. In pointing out, for instance, that Klein's first paper records not a simple analysis of a child but a re-education of both child *and* mother (and analyst as it turns out), Mitchell is drawing attention to what is from the beginning already there in the infant, what is intrinsic to the infant and cannot be separated from its (or the adult's) experience of external reality. Parents, teachers and analysts must learn from this element in their attempts to engage with their charges (children, pupils, patients). So where Freud's account of the super-ego describes it as a vehicle for passing on traditional values and morality – a vehicle that inculcates the child's unconscious with a memory and a past – Klein insists on instinctual anxiety and the pre-Oedipal death drive as formative of the infant's rudimentary know-ledge, a knowledge that is without memory and without history, and which informs all subsequent knowledge and experience whatsoever. Mitchell's patient clarification of the Kleinian perspective qualifies two criticisms that are commonly made: first, she effectively defends Klein against the charge of reductive biologism – Klein does indeed talk of the biological instincts but as 'conditions' of being (anxiety, love and death) that promote phantasy – and, second, she shows that Klein does not deny the importance of outside agency when dealing with children (which was Anna Freud's charge); rather, Mitchell suggests, Klein transforms the notion of agency altogether. (JP)

Melanie Klein: her psychoanalytic heritage

Psychoanalysis starts but does not end with Freud. Yet his work remains the reference point, the still explosively creative point of departure or of return both for clinicians and for theorists. Melanie Klein started work as a psychoanalyst at the time of the First World War and died, still working, practising and developing her ideas, in 1960. In her first ten years as a psychoanalyst she was anxious to stress that her work was a direct and loyal extension of Freud's thinking. Gradually she acknowledged an occasional, important disagreement. By the second half of the 1930s, her contribution to psychoanalysis, though at least to her and her followers' minds remaining within a Freudian framework, was developing into an autonomous unit, a growing independent body.

To recount the many arguments as to where the ideas of Klein and Freud conform and where they differ would be tedious here. More important, in a brief introduction it would be misleading. It is for the new territories she explored and started to chart, not for the failures or successes of orthodoxy, that Melanie Klein should be acclaimed. What she did was new. She was an outstanding clinician and her ideas, despite problems with their presentation, represent an important new departure in the theory of mental processes. Yet, this having been said, her ideas, like all ideas, were not self-created; their context and their relationship to Freud's innovation are important.

In 1910 Melanie Klein, with her husband and two children, went to live in Budapest. There she discovered psychoanalysis. Probably in 1912, she started her analytic training with Sandor Ferenczi and became a member of the Hungarian Psychoanalytic Society. In 1921, she moved to Berlin and continued her psycho-analytic work there. From the beginning of 1924 until the summer of 1925, Karl Abraham was her analyst. Abraham's importance for Klein's work is always emphasized – both by herself and by her commentators. The period in Budapest with Ferenczi is mentioned only briefly. As far as conscious influence is con-cerned, this bias is undoubtedly correct – as regards unconscious influence, I am less sure. The Budapest Psychoanalytic Society, in the crucial years when Klein was there, was vibrant and inventive, a small, dynamic group of creative thinkers with Ferenczi at their centre. Sandor Ferenczi was a maverick. By contrast with Budapest, Berlin, though the world's most active psychoanalytic city, was more rivalrous and conscious of its intellectual proximity to Freud's Vienna. Karl Abraham's work is important, and interesting particularly on the period of earliest infantile development, but it never quite escapes from his reverence for Freud. Where Ferenczi loves, quarrels and bursts with ideas, Karl Abraham respects, smoothes things over and binds his new insights in a strait-jacket of dubious loyalty. Intellectually, consciously, there is no doubt that Melanie Klein owed most to Karl Abraham's encouragement and to his ideas. Spiritually, something of the freedom of Ferenczi and the excitement of Budapest seems to have found its unconscious echo in her. But ultimately more important than either Budapest or Berlin was Klein's move to England where she was most warmly welcomed. Once in England, her work became freer and more coherent. In July 1925 Klein's good friend Alix Strachey, with the help of her husband, James, arranged for Klein to lecture at the Institute of Psycho-Analysis in London. At Christmas, after an illness that had fluctuated for months, Abraham died. Early in 1926 Klein settled permanently in Britain.

In England analysts thought in ways similar to Klein's; she was not struggling with an ill-fitting coat. British empirical traditions, which privileged direct and careful observations and, at their best, an open-mindedness that resulted from the lack of a habit of reference to and reverence for an over-arching philosophical mode of thought, were not only congenial to a new investigator but in Klein's case coincided with her own propensities. In addition, although interest in child analysis was becoming strong on the continent, perhaps in London it was given added impetus by that aspect of English culture which had for three hundred years, and more emphatically since the Romantic poets and nineteenth-century novelists, put the determinative effect of childhood at the centre of its world-view. It was Wordsworth, not Freud, who first said that 'the child is father to the man.' Also, there was at the turn of the century in England an efflorescence of interest in the mother–child relationship. It was this relationship that was to dominate psychoanalysis in Britain until the present day. When she started work, Klein was a mother with young children.

The changing psychoanalytic background

1 Theory and therapy – free association and reconstruction; sexuality, the unconscious and psychic reality

By the beginning of the 1920s, psychoanalysis, though in no sense 'accepted,' was an established body of thought. The theory concerned the formative importance of early childhood. Therapeutically Freud and his adherents treated patients whose free associations led to their unconscious life and whose imagined histories were interpreted and reconstructed within a clinical session. Over time, Freud developed 'free association' as the fundamental rule of psychoanalysis. The patient says everything, however trivial or unpleasant, that comes to mind – this gives access to unconscious chains of associations, to the unconscious determinants of communication. In this way one's actions or the language of the body is squeezed into words. Instead, for instance, of getting locked out of one's home repeatedly or having a cramp in one's neck for which there is no physical explanation, one hears the chain of associations that leads to one having lost the key idea or to finding out what or who is a pain in the neck. In interpreting a dream, although symbolism may be important, access to its meanings is through the patient's free associations. A patient dreams of two cars crashing: in recounting the dream his first association is of the supermarket he had visited the day before; he had come out, seen a car like his own but in better condition, and, envious, hoped it would crash. Another patient with a similar dream-story thinks first how she hates travelling by car, she gets car-sick, she's suffering from morning sickness, she's frightened of giving birth . . . it's so violent . . . Between different individuals, a similar dream-image may have some symbolic aspects in common – but the particular history of the individual patient, discovered through his or her free associations, gives access to the particular meaning of the symbol and the wish.

This is why interpretations of dreams can only take place in an analytic setting. The dream of crashing cars immediately suggests a 'primal scene' (phantasies of parents in intercourse) – but it is useless to say this, for the many-layered meaning depends on the person's hitherto undiscovered history, past and present, which is reconstructed through associations to something that is latent in the unconscious.

Roughly speaking, during the first twenty years of this century the very diverse preoccupations of Freud's work can be subjugated to two central tenets: the formative importance of infantile sexuality and the existence of an unconscious mind that works on principles quite distinct from those of the conscious mind. These two discoveries come together in Freud's theory of the Oedipus complex and its destruction by the castration complex. Together these organize, and offer normative possibilities for the psychological expression of sexuality in human life. The structuring role of these complexes makes them for Freud the nuclei of the neurosis and the key tenets of psychoanalytic understanding.

Until the 1920s the term 'unconscious' had been used either loosely, as still it is today in non-psychoanalytic discussions, to describe everything which is not present to consciousness, or more strictly, and as the object of psychoanalytic inquiry, as a mental process, a system in its own right containing all that has been repressed from consciousness. Crudely speaking, within the Freudian unconscious there is a hypothetical area that is always unfathomable and which is produced by what is known as 'primal repression.' Then there is an area (whose testing-ground is the psychoanalytical clinical setting) produced by the restriction of the wishes of infancy and early childhood: by repression 'proper.' Repression proper acts on illicit or unacceptable wishes so that they disappear from consciousness to form an unconscious domain with its own laws, the so-called 'primary process.' The wishes are forgotten and the result is an amnesia that covers our earliest years.

In Freud's theory the same sexual energy that originally belonged to the wishes tries to push the ideas back into consciousness. If they manage to re-emerge from the unconscious, they do so in a form that is distorted by the marks of the prohibition on them. They come back not as direct wishes, but as hidden, disguised, displaced wishes represented in the symptoms of neuroses, in 'normal' slips of the pen or tongue, in dreams – these can be 'interpreted' and the history of the original wish reconstructed so that it is made more acceptable to consciousness. For the patient, at its centre, this is a painful and a brave endeavour.

The concepts of the Oedipus and castration complexes include the observation that the human infant is born with sexual drives which will only eventually – and then never in a final or absolute way – become dominated by genital urges. A primary relationship to the mother becomes culturally problematic at the stage or level when the child wants to occupy the place already filled by the father, when, in a phallic and hence competitive way, it wants to be everything for the mother, to have everything she needs to satisfy her and thus to have exclusive rights to her.

The forbidden wishes and all the phantasies connected with them constitute the core of what is called 'psychic reality.' This concept replaced Freud's first idea that some actual occurrence such as seduction in childhood caused the later production of neurotic symptoms. Unconscious processes completely replace external reality (with which they have no truck) by psychical reality. Psychical reality is not commensurate with an inner world in general or with all psychological productions; it is a hard core, a nugget, felt to be as real as the grass and the trees, as real as (and not unconnected with) the fact that one is born to two parents and is either a boy or a girl. Like other realities, with time and effort it can, if it is so wished, be modified to a degree. Historical reality both is and is not changed by new ways of seeing and experiencing – so too is psychical reality.

2 The ego, the object, life, death and anxiety

Freud developed psychoanalysis through an attempt to understand some inexplicable occurrence, a symptom, a dream, or an hysterical (not an organic) illness. In the years after the First World War other aspects of his work were being taken up, developed, and diverged from. Instead of the symptoms that indicated the primary process of a system of the unconscious, aspects of human relationships that determined the psychological dimension of character development started to come to the fore. In Vienna, interest increased in the agency that implemented the repression along with other defences. Eventually this led to the emergence of 'ego psychology,' which was vastly extended when it was transported by refugee analysts to North America. In Berlin, Abraham emphasized the significance of the earliest oral and anal experiences of the nursing baby and the toilet-trained infant. In Budapest, Ferenczi, back from work with war neurosis, was interested, among other things, in the present analyst–patient relationship and in working out a therapy that utilized it more actively. In London, an interest in children and their human environment and in the vicissitudes of 'normal' development led to a tendency known as 'object relations analysis.' The period prior to (or, speaking structurally, 'underneath') the Oedipus complex gained in theoretical and clinical importance.

Under the impact of clinical experience, speculative necessity and confrontation with colleagues' differing psychoanalytic theories, Freud's work itself was changing. Here, I shall select the new theories that are of relevance to Klein's thinking. In *Beyond the Pleasure Principle* (1920) (*SE*, XX) Freud subsumed the previous dominance of the sexual drive under a 'life drive' that, while still sexual (and hence not to be confused with Jungian notions), also included the urge for self-preservation. He introduced, in opposition to the life drive, the highly controversial speculation of a death drive, a force that strove to return the human being back into a state of inertia, of the inorganic. Clinically it is seen in masochism, in an unconscious sense of guilt, in the quality of driven-ness within the compulsion to repeat certain experiences and in the wish not to recover.

In 1923, in *The Ego and the Id* (*SE*, XIX), Freud introduced a new metapsychology. Though the division between unconscious, preconscious and conscious continues to be used by Freud after the twenties, it is superseded by a new topographical division of the mind: the id, the ego, the super-ego. All have unconscious parts and origins – the id is completely unconscious and inherits the characteristics of the previous system of the unconscious. Finally, in 1926, prompted explicitly by Otto Rank's argument that the nature and degree of the trauma of birth is causative of all future development, but also by a more general tendency of psychoanalytic work of which Klein's was an important part, Freud revised his understanding of the affectual state of anxiety. Earlier he had thought that when a sexual idea is repressed the idea becomes unconscious but the feelings are converted into anxiety. Now he argues that, although this does happen to a degree (particularly in what were known as the 'actual neuroses'), in most other cases the feeling of anxiety comes first and warns of the danger inherent in certain sexual desires and ideas. Freud's many revisions did not cancel out his earlier ideas: they are more like new layers on old rock – affecting it and changing its composition, but not annihilating it.

Freud's new ideas: division and the wearisome condition of humanity

In the 1920s Freud argued that the neonate is born with what is to become the id, the ego and the super-ego undifferentiated. The ego and the super-ego (in that order) are carved – never totally, never for ever – out of the id. The id (like the previous system of the 'unconscious') is the repository of ideational representatives of human drives and desires. The ego is the organized part of the mental structure. The super-ego is the protector and critic of this ego. While originating in the id, the super-ego takes its form from an internalization of particular external injunctions and prohibitions and of particular 'inherited' ones – of the world's *thou shalts* and *thou shalt nots*. Freud wrote:

> thus a child's super-ego is in fact constructed on the model not of its parents but of its parents' super-ego; the contents which fill it are the same and it becomes the vehicle of tradition and of all the time-resisting judgements of value which have propagated themselves in this manner from generation to generation.

> (*SE*, XX, 1923, p. 67)

The concepts of id, ego and super-ego are metapsychological descriptions – phenomenologically the distinctions may well not be perceived. (We shall see this lack of differentiation again later in Klein's observation of the proximity of conscious, preconscious and unconscious in the very young child.) Freud thought that the division into ego and id characterized humankind and was one of three factors that might well be causative of our unique (or exceptional) proclivity to neurosis.

Freud mentions certain preconditions which he saw as crucial for the unique development of the human psyche. The human baby is born prematurely. Its instincts are weak – it seems to have only a slight instinctual notion of how to avoid danger or to get satisfaction for its own needs from the outside. It is thus much more helpless and dependent on others for the satisfaction of its vital needs than even those mammals most closely related to human beings. When its caretaker (usually – but, more important, prototypically – its mother) satisfies the baby, she is 'at one' with it and hence not felt as separate. When, however, she is felt to fail to satisfy the baby's need, she (or her breast) is experienced as separate from the baby and hence as the first distinct psychological object. When she is thus perceived to be missing, two things happen. One is that the loss or the removal of the means whereby its needs are met make the baby feel anxious. Anxiety is an affectual state that warns the baby of a danger. The danger is not experienced directly but is apprehended as a danger on the model of a preceding danger that was actually experienced (a 'trauma' – such as birth). The second is that the baby re-creates the mother for itself, making the satisfaction she has represented seem now to be inside itself (for instance, by hallucinating a 'good feed'); it thus forms a separate area within itself – which in part becomes its ego (the ego is 'the precipitate of abandoned object cathexes').

For the prematurely born infant there is a perception of the danger of help-lessness and a signal of anxiety. The ego is formed on this bed of helplessness and anxiety. But the infant's helplessness relates to its inside as well as to its outside world. The internal needs and wishes, which are the instigators of the problem, themselves come to feel dangerous. Thus the ego which is being constructed has to cope with dangers from two directions: it develops means of avoiding external dangers and of rejecting internal ones that emanate from the id – these means are termed the ego's defences.

The biphasic nature of human sexuality is a further condition that Freud always felt was responsible for the predisposition of humankind to neuroses. In other mammals there seems to be a straightforward uninterrupted progression to sexual maturity; in humans amnesia overtakes infancy. The first phase is the efflorescent generalized sexuality of the infant (called 'polymorphously perverse'), then for a period sexuality is 'forgotten' and only latent, then it re-emerges in a second phase of ebullient sexuality in puberty and adolescence. This biphasic situation of infantile and then pubertal sexuality with a gap between them indicates the repression of infantile sexuality, the mark of the unconscious. Once again it suggests a division within the subject which seems to be the hallmark of the human being and which can be seen in an exaggerated version in the neurotic. It is through the exaggerations of the neuroses that normality can be seen.

Freud's work emphasizes the divisions that condition the human subject. He is concerned with the construction of different areas of mental life. There is one mind, but something divides it. For him the wearisome condition of humanity (in the words of the renaissance poet Fulke Greville), which produces both creativity and neurosis, is that we are born under one law yet to another bound. Human beings bring something with them, but the mind's divisions are set up by the encounter with the world, with the commands, phantasies and wishes of others – with humankind's culture, laws and prohibitions.

Melanie Klein: child analysis and the play technique

When Melanie Klein started to work with children she was not the first analyst to do so, but the field was a completely new one. When Freud had been working with adults in the first decades of the century, others joined him, coming together, submitting to the dominance of his ideas or parting in hostility. The different analysts who started to work with children after the First World War repeated his experience – but with a difference. For them there was a body of psychoanalytic theory already dominated by Freud's writings – their own theories had all to be contained within a reference to this work.

Klein started her psychoanalytic work with observations of a normal child – her first papers all show her applying basic psychoanalytic ideas to child development. Soon, Abraham was to encourage her to extend her observations into proper, full analyses of very young children. Klein always argued that, though there were differences in the mental apparatus of children and adults, the same psychoanalytic treatment could be applied to both.

It is Freud's early theories of sexuality and the unconscious that Klein uses in her first published paper. The first part she read originally in 1919 to the Hungarian Psychoanalytic Society and the second part to the Berlin Society in 1921. She discusses a later revised version of it in her retrospective essay on play technique. Klein describes the prophylactic treatment she carried out on a five-year-old boy, Fritz. Where, in the case of 'Little Hans,' his famous analysis of a childhood phobia, Freud talked to the father, Klein talks directly and listens to Fritz. But this was not a psychoanalysis – nor intended as such – but rather a re-education of mother and child using Freudian theories. Klein also watches what Fritz does. He was a late speaker and soon Klein was working with two-year-olds or with autistic children – if language is not available, something else must replace it. From this work Melanie Klein developed her 'play technique' – the central method of her analysis. In the consulting room, the child has access to general play materials – water, pencils, paper, etc. – and its own set of 'neutral' toys – small basic human figures, a train, a car and so on. How it deals with these toys and the whole analytic space is observed and interpreted. Although she did not, of course, use the technique with older children and adults, its use with very young and verbally disturbed child patients led to her insights into the earliest preverbal ways of communication and to her account of the phantasies and psychic contents of the neonatal and infantile mind.

Klein's own interests always centred on the very young child or the infant in the older child and in the adult, but her ideas led other analysts into working with psychotic conditions in which the patient may have no access to language or may not be able to use the normal structures of language.

Melanie Klein claimed that the play technique, as a technique for gaining access to the unconscious, was the complete equivalent of free association. She writes [in 'The Psycho-Analytic Play Technique' (1955) – Eds]:

> . . . the brick, the little figure, the car, not only represent things which interest the child in themselves, but in his play with them they always have a variety of symbolical meanings as well which are bound up with his phantasies, wishes, and experiences. This archaic mode of expression is also the language with which we are familiar in dreams, and it was by approaching the play of the child in a way similar to Freud's interpretation of dreams, that I found I could get access to the child's unconscious. But we have to consider each child's use of symbols in connection with his particular emotions and anxieties and in relation to the whole situation which is presented in the analysis; mere generalized translations of symbols are meaningless.
>
> (*Writings*, III, p. 137)

Play, like dream-thoughts, can be a manifest expression with a latent unconscious content. In using it, we have to consider each child's game in connection with its particular emotions and anxieties. When a child crashes a toy car into another, it may do so enthusiastically, nervously, lethargically, sadistically . . . We also have to note what it does before and after each action. In this way the interpretation of play and the understanding of the symbols, displacements and affects in their context are very similar to the interpretation of dreams or symptoms through the patient's free associations.

Melanie Klein: the baby and its world

I The ego's defences, the paranoid-schizoid and the depressive positions, normality and the psychoses

Observing and working in an intensive and extensive psychoanalytic practice with children and adults, Klein developed a model of mental development which she amended and amplified throughout her life. Simplifying somewhat, I would suggest that Klein's basic model is that the neonate brings into the world two main conflicting impulses: love and hate. In Klein's later formulations, love is the manifestation of the life drive; hate, destructiveness and envy are emanations of the death drive. The life drive and death drive are two innate instincts in conflict with each other. From the very beginning the neonate tries to deal with the conflict between these two drives, either by bringing them together in order to modify the death drive with the life drive or by expelling the death drive into the outside world. The baby brings with it the effects of these two instincts, its various impulses and a body with sensations and a primitive residual ego which is endangered by the baby's own impulses and which develops different, ever more mature mechanisms for dealing with them. Furthermore, the baby encounters a world which is both satisfying and frustrating. It exists from the start in a relationship to another person or part of that person (prototypically its mother and her breast). Gradually, its world becomes more complex and includes a father. The relationship between the ego and the impulses, drives and body-feelings on the one hand, and between these and the outside world on the other (represented by mother-and-father at first combined together), are the two poles whose interaction Klein describes.

Freud made the act of repression critical for the formation of that aspect of psychic life which psychoanalysis could decipher; it was the particular defence which constructed the unconscious whose manifestations could be understood in the distortions of neurosis. But Klein, along with a growing number of analysts, paid attention to the ego's earlier mechanisms of defence. There are many things the threatened infantile ego can do by way of protecting itself. It can, for instance, deny or repudiate unwelcome reality; but there are other mechanisms which, in the clinical setting of the relationship between the patient and the analyst, can be seen as communicating an experience that cannot be verbalized.

In this connection I would single out four mechanisms which are central to an understanding of Klein's work. *Splitting* – the ego can stop the bad part of the object contaminating the good part, by dividing it, or it can split off and disown a part of itself. In fact, each kind of splitting always entails the other. In *projection*, the ego fills the object with some of its own split feelings and experience; in *introjection*, it takes into itself what it perceives or experiences of the object. *Projective identification* was first described by Klein but has been developed much more fully by Kleinians subsequently. In this the ego projects its feelings into the object which it then identifies with, becoming like the object which it has already imaginatively filled with itself. The ego makes use of these defences to cope with the inner world and the constant interaction between inner and outer. Its own destructive feelings – emanations of the death drive – make the baby very anxious. It fears that the object on which it vents its rage (e.g. the breast that goes away and frustrates it) will retaliate. In self-protection it splits itself and the object into a good part and a bad part and projects all its badness into the outside world so that the hated breast becomes the hateful and hating breast. Klein describes this as the paranoid-schizoid position (see particularly 'Notes on Some Schizoid Mechanisms,' *Writings*, III). As developmentally the ego becomes able to take in the whole person, to see that good and bad can exist together in the same person, it continues to rage against the mother for the frustrations she causes, but now, instead of fearing retaliation, it feels guilt and anxiety for the damage it itself has done in phantasy. This Klein calls the depressive position. In overcoming this position the baby wishes to undo or repair the earlier phantasized destruction of the actual and the internalized mother. As it does so it also takes in the damaged and then restored mother, adding these new internalizations as part of the self's inner world. These two positions, the paranoid-schizoid and the depressive, develop in the first months of life, but they always remain as part of our personality, of our normal and our psychotic development.

We all use these mechanisms unconsciously as part of our daily lives; in psychoses, one or other of them takes over and dominates over any other form of communication. Perception of inner and outer reality can become so distorted that normal communication is impossible.

Every infant introjects, projects, splits its objects and hence its ego – excessive use of these defences is psychotic. In the normal course of events, every child does its best to repudiate undesirable parts of reality; severe repudiation is at the heart of psychosis. A difference of degree can become a difference of kind.

In a clinical setting all these defences and positions that Klein describes are discoverable in the present relationship between patient and analyst; they are primitive, preverbal or extra-verbal ways of communicating an experience, and they can be understood and put into words in an interpretation which can bring clarity and relief. A clear description of the practice is given in Klein's account of four-year-old Dick (see 'The Importance of Symbol Formation in the Development of the Ego' (1930), *Writings*, I).

2 Anxiety, symbolism, phantasy and the toy

Three concepts cover the area of Klein's observations: anxiety, symbolism and phantasy. All three work together – each is a condition or product of the others.

From the very beginning, Melanie Klein stressed the importance of anxiety as a diagnostic tool. An increase in anxiety, and its diminution, seemed to her to indicate that the analyst was getting near to the trouble. Even to a lay person, it is noticeable how a child becomes acutely anxious and then relieved if one touches on a secret, shameful problem. Klein, in conformity with Freud's first theories, thought anxiety was a transformation of frustrated or prohibited desire; later she saw it as the manifestation of the death drive. As her work developed, she specified types of anxiety. Each position has its appropriate anxiety – persecutory in the paranoid-schizoid position, depressive in the depressive position. The type of anxiety is thus the key to the level of the condition. Klein's work with child patients, her use of the play technique in particular, privileged symbolism. At first her understanding was that similar pleasures derived from different objects made the baby equate the objects symbolically. Soon she realized that this was a static model and she proposed that anxiety produced the movement within the development of symbol formation. Anxious lest its negativity destroy an object, the infant moves to another which thus relates symbolically to the one left behind. If, as in some psychotic conditions, no anxiety is expressed, then there is stasis and no, or severely reduced, symbol formation including language.

How the baby relates to the conjunction of its inner and outer worlds psychically is expressed in Klein's notion of phantasy. (The 'ph' spelling is used to indicate that the process is unconscious.) By later Kleinians and critics alike, phantasy is often seen as identical to Freud's concept of psychic reality. Klein herself was right to think it is not the same.

To see the distinction between them it is perhaps easiest to start with the observation that Freud's concept of a human drive is never as something that is equivalent to an animal instinct. A human drive initially has no object. As humans, probably because of our premature birth, we are weak in instincts. For Freud our drives take shape in relation to this weakness of our instincts and to the greatness of our dependence. But as humans we are, of course, also animals. An animal instinct knows and goes for its object – as a calf finds a nipple, or a chick follows a hen. Presumably we too have some residual animal instinct expressed in human terms. I would argue that the Kleinian concept of phantasy describes the human being's vast elaboration through perceptions and experience of this animal, biological instinct. Klein herself writes:

> My hypothesis is that the infant has an innate unconscious awareness of the existence of the mother. We know that young animals at once turn to the mother and find their food from her. The human animal is not different in that respect, and this instinctual knowledge is the basis for the infant's primal relation to his mother . . .
>
> (*Writings*, III, p. 248)

Kleinian 'phantasy' cannot be reduced to this, but this is its origin and in this it differs from Freud's concept of psychical reality, which is something not innate but produced by the peculiar conditions of the human being. In Klein's concept, phantasy emanates from within and imagines what is without, it offers an unconscious commentary on instinctual life and links feelings to objects and creates a new amalgam: the world of imagination. Through its ability to phantasize, the baby tests out, primitively 'thinks' about, its experiences of inside and outside. External reality can gradually affect and modify the crude hypotheses phantasy sets up. Phantasy is both the activity and its products.

It is in the light of the concept of phantasy that we must view Klein's major technical innovation in child analysis; the use of toys. A toy on the one hand is archetypal, but it can be used in various ways according to the individual's phantasy: a train can be cuddled like a baby as well as more obviously driven furiously into a tunnel/womb. A typical or archetypal toy such as Klein used is something that bridges the gap between an external object and the inner world. Toys represent the object of phantasy and of object relations. As Hanna Segal says, for Freud, the psychological object is the object of the drive and for Klein it is the object of the child, most importantly of the child's phantasy. A toy stands for this object. Klein moves the symbol into the consulting room and offers it to the child, senses its anxiety and discovers its phantasies.

I would suggest that the centrepoint of Klein's therapy is her understanding of anxiety; the key concept of her theory is not the system of the unconscious (the key concept of Freud's psychoanalysis) but 'phantasy.'

Freud and Klein: the unconscious and phantasy

When Klein started writing, Anton von Freund in Budapest said that she was only dealing with preconscious material: the sexual questions and answers were available to the child, but were just put out of mind – descriptively 'unconscious,' technically only 'preconscious.' In response, Klein gave interpretations to the child that went deeper. In particular, she talked of what could be assumed to be unknown: the father's role in coitus and procreation.

It is sometimes argued that Klein's concept of the unconscious conforms to Freud's notion of 'primal repression,' but it does not do so exactly. Primal repression in Freud's sense is something that happens in the individual's prehistory or in its taking in of human prehistory. For Klein, what is unconscious is the biological and affectual condition of the human being. In essence, by the time of her later writings, the unconscious is equivalent to the instincts: to the life drive and death drive and their affects. The unconscious exists as a condition and from it emerge preconsciousness and consciousness. The Kleinian unconscious is a container full of contents; it is not another system of thought; it does not have its own laws which would bear the mark of its construction. There are unconscious mechanisms, the unconscious ego's many defences, but not mechanisms of the unconscious as a system. Freud's system of the unconscious knows neither time nor contradiction, but works primarily through displacing, condensing or symbolizing different elements. In Klein's theory there is no clear distinction between what Freud called the primary process (the unconscious) and the secondary processes (the conscious and the preconscious). There is unconscious symbolism but not symbolism as a basic manifestation of the unconscious. The ego displaces and condenses but, though done unconsciously, these are not defining characteristics of 'an unconscious.' Klein's theory reflects her observation of children – the distinction between conscious, unconscious and preconscious is not sharp. Despite her response to Anton von Freund, Klein's concept of the unconscious is of something not dynamic but descriptive. It is not surprising that some eminent analysts who started work in Klein's footsteps, such as Wilfred Bion, rarely use the concept. In a way it has become uninteresting; after all, in what way can we say a baby phantasizing a breast is unconscious of it?

Klein's unconscious phantasy and Freud's unconscious as a mental area utterly distinct in its laws of operation from consciousness are different concepts. All Klein's interest, therapeutically and theoretically, is directed to finding the unconscious content of the phantasies and the work of the unconscious ego. As Klein's friend and colleague Susan Isaacs wrote: 'The primary *content* of all mental processes are unconscious phantasies. Such phantasies are the basis of all unconscious and conscious thought processes' (my italics). Klein is not concerned with how the unconscious as a mode of thought works. The content not the dream-work is central to her interpretation of dreams. This orientation towards phantasy contents and the ego's defences suggests there must be some differences between free association and the play technique.

Freud and Klein: time past and future, time present

In the 1880s Freud became increasingly struck by the psychological nature of physiological symptoms. The picture of the neuroses was confused, and, in conformity with scientific practice, his aim was to sort it out – while always realizing that the phenomena themselves and their clinical presentation would remain for ever confused.

The differentiating pattern that Freud first espoused divided the neuroses into two conditions: the 'actual' neuroses and the psychoneuroses. Throughout his life, Freud continued to be interested in the distinction, but he never fully developed it. Its use declined to the extent that it is hardly heard today. I am resurrecting it here to help me clarify an important difference that I find in the theories of Klein and Freud. The actual neuroses – anxiety attacks, neurasthenia, hypochondria and possibly the war neuroses – were psychological conditions provoked by contemporary, that is to say 'actual,' situations such as prolonged sexual abstinence, violence or persistent frustration.

In the 1890s Freud had advanced a crucial argument: the psychoneuroses, hysteria and the actual anxiety neurosis had much in common and were often found together, but, despite this, hysteria was a distinct structure with a determinant from the past. At first, perhaps as a reflection of the mixed presentation of the neuroses, Freud thought that an actual event (childhood seduction) had taken place in the past and had caused the trouble in the present. Freud's hysterical patients 'suffered from reminiscences.' The psychoneurosis of hysteria became more differentiated from the actual neuroses when he realized that it was an infantile sexual phantasy (a version of what he later called the Oedipus complex) that was its main determinant. The determining instance is no longer historically real; yet it is a case of the past, in a complex way, producing the present. As the existence or the significance of an actual past trauma was abandoned by Freud, the notion of a key phantasy formed in the past but operating by deferred action in the present replaced the notion of reminiscences. There is, however, never an absolute distinction – the important point is the 'pastness': 'Up to the present we have not succeeded in pointing to any difference in the consequences, whether phantasy or reality has had a greater share in these events of childhood' (*SE*, XVI, p. 370).

In brief, I would suggest that, through all its vicissitudes, Freud's theory revolves around the question of a past. Psychically speaking, there is no past until after the repression of Oedipal wishes by the castration complex. The castration complex destroys the phantasy of an eternally satisfying relationship with the mother, it introduces the command that the Oedipus complex be over and done with: if you accept it as past you will be able to have a new version (be a father in your turn with a woman of your own) in the future. (The theory's phallocentrism is outside the scope of this introduction.) The castration complex, bearing the injunction of human history, inaugurates history within the individual.

The clearly observed phenomenon of an amnesia that covers our infancy indicates the construction of memory. The paradox here is only apparent. Infancy is a perpetual present. This could be linked with the small child's extraordinary memory – which is not memory, but a continuous actuality. So too, because of the Oedipus and castration complexes only humans have yesterdays. As far as we can tell neither animals nor pre-Oedipal human infants divide time into future, past and present. Time for them would seem to be nearer to spatial relationships: here, there; come, gone; horizontal, punctuated duration rather than an historical, vertical temporal perspective.

By contrast with the psychoneuroses, the expressions of the actual neuroses are not over-determined by the complexity and multifacetedness of a person's history. They may use a physical weakness or an affective condition which may well exist in a person's past as well as in their present, or the trauma may be cumulative – but this past condition does not determine or give the pattern to the present situation. Repeated exposure to warfare may stir an individual's anxiety about their own aggression; persistent sexual frustration or seduction may provoke tabooed fantasies. What is produced in the actual neurosis is a hidden, probably hitherto unused, but nevertheless continuing possibility of the personality. 'Pastness' is unimportant.

Freud argued that the actual neuroses were the grain of sand around which the oyster produced the pearl of the psychoneuroses; Klein's work leads in another direction. From her observations of normal children she is led to an analysis of infantile development that finds the points of psychosis which at the present time, or repeated in the future because they are always current, will be echoed in a psychotic illness. At first, it looks as though we have here a parallel with Freud's work. It is often claimed that, where Freud found the child was father to the man, Klein found the infant gave birth to the child and adult. The resemblance between the two notions is illusory. Freud's historical imagination examines the present (the adult illness) and from it reconstructs a hypothetical past determinant. For Klein the past and the present are one.

Today the concept of actual neurosis has been replaced by the idea of psychosomatic illness. The shift preserves the bodily and affectual traits but loses the dimension of present time. Defining the actual neurosis in their *Language of Psycho-Analysis*, Laplanche and Pontalis end with this comment:

> It is worth noting that it is only the lack of satisfaction of the sexual instincts which is taken into consideration by Freud's theory. In attempting to understand the genesis of actual and psychosomatic symptoms we should be well advised to pay some attention too to the suppression of aggressiveness.
>
> (1964, p. 11)

Klein is not interested in psychosomatic illness, and when she started work actual neurosis was a current but soon to recede diagnosis. It is not one she makes use of. However, I suggest that her work finds the links between the psychology of the actual neurosis and the psychosis. From a particular perspective, in doing this she has already taken into account Laplanche and Pontalis's proposals – she has found an important place for the effects (one of which is aggressiveness) of the death drive.

The very nature of Klein's first observations makes the obsolete category of actual neurosis useful. Klein's first work was with inhibited children. Their difficulties resemble those of neurasthenics:

> The following characteristics proved in a number of cases and in a typical way to be inhibitions: awkwardness in games and athletics and distaste for them, little or no pleasure in lessons, lack of interest in any particular subject or in general, the varying degrees of so-called laziness.
>
> (*Writings*, I, p. 77)

In placing anxiety at the centre of the theoretical elaboration of the clinical picture Klein is once more dealing with present-day or persistent, potential actuality. The unanswered questions, the practice of masturbation once it is no longer acceptable, produce anxiety. The child of three or four is dealing with sexual or aggressive problems or hypochondriacal worries in the present. Where in Freud repression is a defence that creates a past and a symptom is a return of that past, Klein is appropriately more interested in the defences which have no such dimension of time past and with atemporal inhibitions of the ego, not with symptoms.

Although Klein worked often with latency children and later with adults, her innovation in theory and practice is with Freud's 'pre-Oedipal' child. By definition, the pre-Oedipal child, but also the psychotic, whether child or adult, has not negotiated the Oedipus complex, has not acquired a history. Klein's contribution is to chart an area where present and past are one and time is spatial, not historical. This area has all the characteristics of a descriptive unconsciousness, an unconscious that has not been constructed by repression.

This absence of historical time is evident both in Klein's innovations and in her omissions. Thus the concept of regression plays no role in Klein's theory. She has no explanation of infantile amnesia and she and her followers show an ever-decreasing interest in the castration complex. Her discovery of an early Oedipus complex is not of something overcome by an internalization of a prohibition but rather of an internal unconscious sociology of immediate object relations that are come to terms with through the activities and phantasies of the depressive position. Even experientially, what is depressing about depression (among other things) is that, though it may come and go, the sufferer from it has no sense of a past or hence of a future freedom. Klein's crucial concept of a 'position' speaks to this different, earlier, prehistorical sense of time – a position is a mental space in which one is sometimes lodged.

In the psychotherapeutic setting, the anxiety, the nature and contents of the phantasies, the mechanisms of their operation, all come into the present situation with the analyst. Because psychotic elements are present all the time in everyone and psychoses themselves are not regressed to, these states are potentially present all the time; they are not activated by the analytic situation – the analytic situation provides the space and the skills for their comprehension and their mitigation. The instances of our ego's earliest defences can be worked through in a particular type of transference that deals not with the past but with the 'here and now' – the total present of the relationship between analyst and analysand (see 'The Origins of Transference,' *Writings*, III pp. 48–56).

Whatever the shifts in Freud's theory, the central creation remains the same. Freud's psychoanalytic theory of the psychoneuroses is about the production of a psychic domain which is not reducible to either or both of two poles. If we imagine two overlapping triangles, the Freudian unconscious is at the apex of one whose two sides are the inner drives and the laws and history of the outer world; the psychoneuroses are at the apex of another whose base points are the bipolar opposition between sexuality and its prohibition.

Freud thought the ego could regress to early protopsychotic mechanisms, tunnel back to its beginnings – use the grain of sand; Klein, looking at the flat earth of infancy, the direct relationship between normality and psychosis, sees that past and present are one. Not surprisingly, in the clinical picture Klein finds what Freud finds – for instance, an Oedipus complex and a super-ego, both of which she places much earlier. In fact, though what Klein describes may be, as she asserts, the kernel of the later developments, they are not, I would suggest, even residually the same conceptions at the level of a theoretical understanding of them. In Klein these situations are all products of the ego's phantasized relations with its external world, they are not in any dynamic sense triangular structures; neither the 'combined parents' nor the 'father-inside-the-mother' that she proposes, constitute a different third term. Hence these key concepts do not describe another psychic domain.

Klein's model is a two-way process from inner to outer and back again. For Klein the construction of a third independent psychic structure does not arise. It does not arise because what she is observing, describing and theorizing is the very absence of history and of historical time.

Klein is not a scientific theorist in the nineteenth-century tradition. The great theorists of the nineteenth century – Darwin, Marx and Freud – explain the present by the past. The dominant sociological phenomenologies of the twentieth century, in which Klein participated, study lateral, horizontal, not vertical, relationships. But Klein is also observing something different from the neuroses: she is working with the prototypes of psychotic behaviours whose mechanisms, like those of the actual neuroses, may well be only bipolar oppositions.

Klein and Freud: mothers and fathers

Freud was always intent on differentiation. This was and is the scientific tradition: separation, categorization – Wordsworth's 'we murder to dissect.' (Recently it has been identified as 'masculine.' Certainly psychoanalysis itself could provide an explanation of why this might be so.) The clinical picture is always mixed but to Freud the theory must not echo this state of affairs. Early in his work, he wrote to his friend Fliess: 'In my opinion it is possible to deal with hysteria, freed from any admixture, as something independent; and to do so in every respect *except in that of therapeutics*' (*SE*, II, p. 261, my italics). The situation is muddled, the task of science is to sort it out – recognizing that such sorting is an imposition:

> We cannot do justice to the characteristics of the mind by linear outlines like those in a drawing or in a primitive painting, but rather by areas of colour melting into one another as they are represented by modern artists. After making the separation we must allow what we have separated to merge together once more.
>
> (*SE*, XII, p. 79)

It is always recognized that Klein's theory itself can be somewhat confused. It is held that the confusion arises because her theory is really more a descriptive phenomenology that sticks close to the complexity of her clinical material. Without doubt such an explanation is correct. Freud always thought of himself as a poor therapist, Klein was a superb clinician. But this distinction and this explanation raise more questions than they solve. To be a good clinician or even a good experimental scientist demands the ability to identify and to be intuitive on the basis of endlessly accumulated experience. The geneticist Barbara McClintock describes her work thus: 'I found that the more I worked with [the chromosomes] the bigger and bigger they got, and when I was really working with them, I wasn't outside, I was down there. I was part of the system. I was right down there with them, and everything got big ... it surprised me because I actually felt as if I were right down there and these were my friends' (cited in Keller, 1983, p. 117). Identification and intuition on the basis of accumulated experience are maternal characteristics – they are the mechanisms by which a mother comes to know the meaning of her baby's cry. (Masculine dissections are no more limited to men than maternal abilities for identification are limited to women.) Being a good clinician is not the same as being a good theoretician, but being good at identifying with what one observes in order to follow what is going on in something other than oneself and then describing it constitutes an intermediary level of conceptualization. This is Klein's achievement – but it is more than that. Just as Freud theorizes the construction of what scientific theory itself is about, so too, Klein identifies and describes what intuitive identification and clinical observation are about: areas of confusion, fusion, lack of boundaries, of communicating without the differential structures of speech.

Melanie Klein: the psychoses, the death drive and the ego

Klein effected a major shift within an important branch of psychoanalysis. She explored the borderland between the physiological and the psychological, seeing the one emanating from the other under the provocation of the external world. In doing so she effected a shift in interest from the neuroses to the psychoses. Concomitant with this is a change in the orientation from the effects of sexuality to the effects of the death drive.

In her early writings Klein is concerned with Freudian sexual explanations but there is an ever-increasing reference to the death drive as a given cause of mental development. Klein's concept of a death drive differs from Freud's, though once again, as both are psychoanalysts, the clinical material they are elucidating mostly looks the same. The question of a death drive in Freud's writing is highly complicated, but it is clear, and of relevance to Klein, that its manifestations (though for Freud always mixed with sexuality) relate to the ego, to the ego's struggle to preserve itself. From the very beginning it is the ego that interests Klein. She extends the concept to cover what would nowadays probably be called 'the self.' Everything in her early orientation, long before she accepted the notion of a death drive and when she was working within a Freudian framework of the Oedipus and castration complexes, can be seen to harbinger her later development. In starting work with the problems of the normal child she rediscovered an ego psychology that existed before Freud started psychoanalysis with his attempt to understand the neurotic symptom. Klein brought to her rediscovery the insights and techniques of Freud's psychoanalysis and thereby profoundly changed it. Psychoses or narcissistic neuroses are illnesses of the ego. Where Freud had proposed that, to produce the psychoses, the neuroses must be closed off or regressed from, Klein sees a spider's web of direct lines between normal ego development and psychosis. In Klein's theory the ego works with both the death and the life drive, fending off annihilation, moving towards integration; expressing envy, feeling gratitude. While in all senses using Freud's development of psychoanalysis, Klein changes the terrain and thereby changes the task.

References

SE Freud, Sigmund *The Standard Edition of the Complete Psychological Works of Sigmund Freud*, ed. and trans. James Strachey, London: Hogarth, 24 vols, 1953–74.

Writings Klein, Melanie *The Writings of Melanie Klein*: vol. I, *Love, Guilt and Reparation, and Other Works*; vol. II, *The Psycho-Analysis of Children*; vol. III, *Envy and Gratitude, and Other Works*; vol. IV, *Narrative of a Child Analysis*; London: Hogarth, 1975.

Klein, Melanie (1920) 'Der Familienroman in Statu Nascendi,' *Internationale Zeitschrift für Psychanalyse*.

—— (1955) 'The Psychoanalytic Play Technique: Its History and Significance,' *Writings*, III.

Keller, Evelyn (1983) *A Feeling for the Organism: The Life and Work of Barbara McClintock*, New York: Freeman.
Laplanche, Jean and Jean-Bertrand Pontalis (1964) *The Language of Psycho-Analysis*, New York: Norton, 1973.

Chapter 2

Melanie Klein and the emergence of modern personal life

Eli Zaretsky

Editor's note:

This essay reads Klein in terms of a chapter in the history of British modernity that she both represented and, in important ways, sustained and helped to transform. Zaretsky's argument here is an extension of the thesis he developed in his classic study, *Capitalism, The Family and Personal Life* (1976). First published in instalments in the journal *Socialist Revolution* (1973), and by Pluto Press in 1976, this hugely influential work was one of the first New Left responses to the Women's Movement. Zaretsky demonstrated how industrial capitalism had split the home and family from the economics of production. Only by comprehending the historical dynamics of this separation, he argued, can we fully understand the origins of women's oppression. At the same time, this division gave rise to what Zaretsky terms 'personal life' – a concept that is the product of capitalism ('proletarianization gave rise to subjectivity,' p. 61) and that also masks its effects (confirming 'the modern working class in its illusion of freedom and autonomy,' p. 140). We are not, however, simply the willing dupes of personal life. Part of the boldness of Zaretsky's book lay in its demand that the Left should give personal life its due – as a concept to be criticized and understood historically and, importantly, for the extent to which it can also transform social relations. Psychoanalysis is crucial in this account insofar as it both reflects the historical shift towards the promotion of the personal and, as the present essay demonstrates, also has the potential to redefine the psychic dynamics of social and democratic life. Reading Klein's work alongside key ideological and historical shifts in mid-century British modernity (shifts in ideas about personal autonomy, gender and the democratization of authority), Zaretsky shows how her work inaugurated a new interpersonal ethics. In contrast to Freud's moral and Kantian emphasis on the father, Klein's matricentric work promotes the concrete and relational aspects of personal life and so gives an account of 'the potentially democratic character of collective activity.' As Britain dismantles its welfare state and struggles to find new meanings for personal and collective life, one way to read Zaretsky's argument might be as a timely prompt to ask what kind of social and historical discourse a return to this aspect of Kleinian theory might produce today. (LS)

I   Introduction

Melanie Klein is probably the most important figure in the history of psychoanalysis after Sigmund Freud, yet her contributions are not widely understood.[1] The reason is that we have not yet historicized psychoanalysis itself: we lack the large social, cultural and intellectual frameworks that are necessary if we are to understand a thinker of her stature. The following article aims to historicize, contextualize and bring out the social context in which Klein's work developed, especially in the 1930s and early 1940s. It rests on three basic ideas.

First, I situate the history of psychoanalysis in the context of the shift from the family to 'personal life.' Historically, the family was the primary site organizing production and reproduction. As a result, the individual's sense of identity was rooted in their place in the family. This began to change in the nineteenth century. The separation of the family from the workplace – which is to say the rise of industrial capitalism – gave rise to the experience and the goal of personal life as distinct from the family. Personal identity became a problem and a project for individuals as opposed to something given to them by their place in the society. The rise of personal life did not mean the decline in the family's importance; indeed, in some ways it became more important, but now it was no longer the primary institution mediating between the individual and the society. Psychoanalysis, I contend, emerged as a theory and practice of personal life, its goal was *de*familialization, the freedom of the individual from paternal and maternal imagos.

Second, the rise of personal life changed the relation of culture to the individual. The premodern 'therapist' or shaman was effective because he or she could mobilize collectively shared symbols. Claude Lévi-Strauss has described the case of a shaman assisting in childbirth by calling for the assistance of the god Muu. As Lévi-Strauss notes, the effectiveness of the shaman does not depend on whether the god being called upon exists. What matters is that the sick woman, the shaman and the society all believe in it.[2] Modern personal life, by contrast, is characterized by the disjuncture between the cultural order and the intrapsychic world. Freud's insight, in contrast, for example, to Jung, was that the symbolism that organized the inner lives of modern men and women was largely personal, idiosyncratic, and often devoid of any apparent intersubjective meaning. Examples of such modern symbols included aimless humming, the repeated winding of one's watch, a repetitive rat fantasy, slips of the tongue, coughing, hallucinated 'clicks.' Such symbols could be 'interpreted' but there was no longer any culturally overarching symbolic whole into which to reintegrate them. Thus when Freud proclaimed in 1918, 'We refused to turn a patient who puts himself into our hands in search of help into our private property, to decide his fate for him, to force our own ideals upon him, and with the pride of the Creator to form him in our own image and see that it is good,' he was articulating a modern conception of freedom.[3]

Third, the rise of personal life coincided with the decline of traditional authority. Traditional authority had been family-centred. As production left the home, new centres and new forms of authority arose. Included among these were the professions, or what Michel Foucault termed the 'disciplines.' Psychoanalysis was a critique of traditional authority, yet one that itself became a profession or a discipine in the Foucaultian sense.

The account of Klein that follows is related to what I call the threefold promise of modernity, three interrelated aspirations first articulated in the Enlightenment: personal autonomy, gender justice and reconciliation, and the democratization of authority. I argue that personal life complicated the meaning of these Enlightenment ideals and I read psychoanalysis in terms of this complication. To characterize the original promises I refer to classic Enlightenment formulations: Kant on autonomy, meaning that individuals can only be bound by obligations they give to themselves; equality between men and women, captured in Mary Wollstonecraft's famous wish that the difference between the sexes be restricted to the sphere of sexual love; and finally, Locke's idea that politics be 'fatherless,' a sphere of freely contracting individuals rested upon the division between the public and the private. In the selection below, under the rubrics 'ego,' 'gender' and 'society,' I discuss Klein's complication and radicalization of these promises.

II The prehistory of the object relations perspective

The integration of psychoanalysis into the welfare state began in England during the 1930s, and culminated during World War II. At the centre of analytic thought during this period was the idea of ruptured connection. Along with the emphasis on the mother, British analysis developed a new view of 'the ego,' as ethically responsible, i.e., not reflecting upon universal considerations, but rather involved in concrete obligations to others. This ethic expressed a new attitude towards personal life and represented, in effect, a 'feminine' alternative to Freud – an ethic of care instead of an ethic of justice. The main terrain in which this 'relational' ego or self was envisioned was the terrain of personal life, a terrain of friends, colleagues and relations, not the narrowly conceived family any more. Not accidentally, Bloomsbury, with its ethic of transfamilial sociality, played an important role in the evolution of 'object relational' thinking. At the same time, the 'social' which had loomed in Freud's model in the form of the imaginary 'castrating father,' now was both specified and shrunken to the sphere of the interpersonal.

The history of this shift was intertwined with the third great conflict in the history of psychoanalysis, that between Melanie Klein and Anna Freud. Like its predecessor conflicts, Freud vs. Jung and Adler, and Freud vs. Rank and Ferenczi, this conflict took place during a great wave of analytic expansion. It differed from the earlier conflicts, however, in that Klein – the rebel – was the dominant voice, Anna Freud the critic. Beginning in the late 1920s and stretching into the 1950s, it eventually took the form of the struggle between 'object relations,' – Klein's legacy – and 'ego psychology,' as represented by Anna Freud. Klein's initiative, and the conflicts that swirled around her during the pre- and early history of the welfare state, dominates the history of US and British psychoanalysis until well into the 1950s; it also framed the issues that Jacques Lacan's post-World War II work addressed. The emergence of the object relations perspective thus structures a huge swathe of analytic history, comparable to its predecessors; the theory of the unconscious (1890–1914) and the structural theory (1919–1939).

Several features of the British context shaped the first stage in this history, which occurred before and during World War II. First, England was a relatively democratic society in contrast to Austria. One consequence was the apparent irrelevance of the Marxism associated with Reich. Keynes, for example, thought of economics in 'moral' or psychological terms, arguing that 'dangerous human proclivities can be canalised into comparatively harmless channels by the existence of money-making.'[4] The relatively benign form that British social democracy could take in the 1930s is suggested by 'Mass-Observation,' collective observation of such subjects as 'Behaviour of people at war memorials.' 'Mass-Observation,' an organizer wrote, was 'in the tradition of Darwin, Marx, Freud and Breuer.'[5]

Second, the Bloomsbury milieu represented a new conception of interpersonal ethics, one for which society itself was generating a need. Not the generalized other as in Kant and Freud, but the concrete, particularized other was the point of reference. G.E. Moore was the key thinker in this regard. Moore argued that immediate situated relations – for example, to friends, family, and community, took precedence over abstract ideals. To Leonard Woolf, 'we were and always remained primarily and fundamentally a group of friends.'[6] To E.M. Forster, 'if I had to choose between betraying my *country* and betraying my *friend*, I hope I should have the guts to betray my country.'[7] According to Keynes, 'We entirely repudiated a personal liability on us to obey general rules. We claimed the right to judge every individual case on its merits, and the wisdom to do so successfully . . . We were, that is to say, in the strictest sense of the term, immoralists . . . Nothing mattered except states of mind – chiefly our own.'[8]

Third, England had a strong empirical and meliorist tradition. The Tavistock Institute, the major clinic directly influenced by psychoanalysis in Britain in the interwar years and a centre of analytic innovation during the Second World

War, described itself as a mixture of Freud, psychotherapy, eclectic meliorism, managerial innovation and sociology. Its self-proclaimed credo was 'no doctrine, only aims.' Its 'new psychology' stressed 'the whole person' and paralleled the 'mental hygiene' movement in the United States.

One consequence of the integration of analysis into the kind of eclectic and meliorist milieu that Tavistock represented, was the decline of the significance of the Jewish dimension of psychoanalysis in England. The religiosity of Tavistock's clinicians was so pronounced that the clinic was also called the 'parson's clinic.' Ian Suttie's 1935 *The Origins of Love and Hate*, written at Tavistock and organized around the 'innate need for companionship,' is emblematic. It argued that Christianity was a 'system of psychotherapy' in which matriarchal elements were central. Suttie stressed the social over the individual, the external over the internal, the altruistic over the 'selfish,' the mother over the father. The Freudian emphasis on the father, Suttie wrote, with overtones of anti-semitism, 'is itself a disease.'

Another consequence was the focus on child development. Tavistock drew an important part of its income from Rockefeller grants aimed at promoting child study. The interest in early childhood among English analysts antedated Klein's arrival. Susan Isaacs, who later became an analyst, ran a nursery school, the Malting House or Pyke-Isaacs school which encouraged children to 'find out all they can for themselves' and to openly express sexual interests. Ella Sharpe, later Ella Sharpe Freeman (1875–1947), ran a teacher's training centre from 1904 to 1916 when she began to study psychoanalysis.[9]

Finally, Britain had a strong and complex feminist tradition which included but went beyond maternalism. Bronislaw Malinowski, a Polish emigré, had returned from the Trobriand Islands after World War I, insisting he could not locate a single myth of origin in which the father was assigned a role in procreation. John Jakob Bachofen's pervasive influence, James Frazer's twelve-volume compilation of fertility myths, *The Golden Bough*, and the evidence of mother goddesses in the excavations of Minoan–Mycenean civilization in Crete, had all led to serious challenges to Freud's insistence on the Oedipus complex and had already influenced the debates over female sexuality in the late twenties.[10] According to Robert Briffault's 1927 *The Mothers*, 'paternity does not exist.'[11]

The main antagonists in this last important analytic debate were women. This reflected the association of women with the sphere of familial life, as well as the rising importance of professional women inside and outside analysis. Both Anna Freud and Melanie Klein distinguished themselves from Sigmund Freud by their practical experience with children as mothers, teachers and clinicians. Neither were doctors. Both were at the centre of female networks. Otherwise, however, they represented different 'daughterly' relations to their common 'father figure.' Klein was a brilliant, ambitious rebel whose real competitor was Sigmund, not Anna. Anna Freud, by contrast, was a dutiful daughter, sometimes close to being overwhelmed by her sense of responsibility to and for her father. Both women, however, pioneered the shift towards a mother/infant theory.

The beginning investigations of the mother/daughter and mother/son relations were accompanied by great excitement because of their implications for the concepts of ego, gender and society. Concerning the ego, beginning in the late 1920s Klein began to write about the early ego's 'internal objects,' or representations of the mother.[12] This emerging conception culminated in 1935 in Klein's theory of the 'depressive position,' from which most of what was later termed 'object relations' theory descends.

Klein's conception of object relations involved a major shift away from Sigmund Freud. The shift is today often described as one from 'instinct' theory to 'object relations' but this is misleading for several reasons. First, Freud's theory was always object-relational, as his focus on transference makes clear. For Freud, moreover, the term 'object' referred to an *internal* representation and not, as in some later object relations theory, an interpersonal or intersubjective relation. Thus he once criticized Havelock Ellis for describing masturbation as 'auto-erotic,' implying that it was object-relational since it involved mental objects. For Klein, too, an object is an internal representation.[13]

The real difference between Freud and Klein lies in their understandings of authority. For Freud, the ego precedes the superego and has a complex relation, simultaneously dependent, reflective and critical, to it. To Klein, there is no real distinction between the ego and the superego. The ego takes shape in relation to internal representations of the mother and is the centre of 'moral' or, more precisely, 'ethical' relations. Klein argued against Freud that the superego begins in the earliest relation to the mother, not in the context of the Oedipus complex. By the superego she meant feelings of ethical responsibility to concrete others, including particular communities, not the universal morality Freud had in mind. The fact that Klein focused on the first year of life at first made it difficult to grasp this distinction; it also led to the loss of the mediating and reflective role of the ego in her theory.

By situating the superego in relation to the early mother, Klein was suggesting that the impulses with which one struggles are often very primitive, closely tied to biological survival. Freud, in contrast, in situating the superego in relation to the Oedipus complex, was tying it to moral imperatives. This difference emerged in 1930, in a footnote to his *Civilization and Its Discontents*, where Freud criticized Ernest Jones, Susan Isaacs, and Klein, as well as Reik and Alexander, for their 'idea that any kind of frustration, any thwarted instinctual satisfaction, results or may result in a heightening of the sense of guilt.' According to Freud, this was true only of frustrations of the aggressive instincts.[14] Freud, in other words, assumed that the superego could distinguish between impulses, condemning only those determined by the Oedipus complex. For Klein, by contrast, aggression and guilt are components of the earliest dependence; they are associated with conflicts over material needs or primary goods and are not subject to the ego's self-critique.

Klein always described her emphasis on 'internal objects' as an elaboration of the theory of the superego, though she never clarified the differences in her notion of authority from Freud's. In 1942, she asserted that the starting point of her thought was a passage in *The Ego and the Id*, arguing that an ambivalent attitude is present from the first. If Freud had followed up this insight, Klein insisted, he would have wound up moving in her direction: 'the superego is to a large extent due to the sadism projected on to the parents who are thus established in the super-ego as frightening and persecuting figures. That is, however, not just one point, it is *the* point on which my conception of internalized objects has developed.' Arguing against the Viennese ego psychologists, including Anna Freud, she claimed that 'a discovery as great and as fundamental as the superego seemed to be closed soon after its beginning. Who can doubt that the superego was a new beginning towards the understanding of the unc. (*sic.*) And of the internal relationships as they have never been understood before apart from the poets.'[15] Although this passage captures the profound continuities between Klein's work and Sigmund Freud's, it misses the differences. For the latter, the superego is not a representation of the parents, but is rather an imago that results when infants use their identifications to gain control over impulses arising in the id. It does not represent relations but stands above them.

Another way of understanding the shift from Freud to Klein lies in the nature of the inner representational world they describe. For Freud, all objects are shadowed by the paternal imago, whereas Klein describes the psyche as a more three-dimensional world of gratifying and frustrating, rivalrous and supportive, 'part' and 'whole' objects. For Klein, the infant struggles with primary biological and psychological frustration; for Freud, these struggles do not shape the super-ego until the epoch of the Oedipus complex when they are reconfigured as moral imperatives. In both cases the subject struggles to achieve a certain 'goodness' but for Freud the struggle is Kantian and moral, whereas for Klein goodness is concrete and relational. For Freud, the superego is a depersonalized categorical imperative; for Klein, the superego refers to particularized and concrete others. For Freud, the internal world is dominated by the problem of authority; for Klein, it is dominated by responsibility to particular others to whom one has incurred obligations, not in virtue of being generically human, as in Kant, but because one has found oneself in specific relations and circumstances.

The shift initiated by Klein had profound consequences for understanding the ways in which psychoanalysis complicated and radicalized the threefold promise of modernity. The focus on concrete obligations to others could enrich Freud's commitment to self-generated morality. The recognition of the centrality of mothering, and the inescapable psychic residue of a connection between mothering and women, could enrich Freud's emphasis on sexuality. Finally, the object relations paradigm placed intersubjectivity and especially groups at the centre of the conception of society, thus enriching Freud's understanding of the social/sexual or public/private distinction. Just as morality is not necessarily opposed to ethics, and an emphasis on sexuality is not necessarily opposed to an emphasis on reproduction, so respect for the line between public and the private can complement the study of group psychological processes that transgress it.

III Ego autonomy in the epoch of the welfare state

In 1934, at a presentation which has been described as one of the most exciting in the history of psychoanalysis, in a paper apparently provoked by her son's death while mountain climbing, Klein proposed her new conception of the ego.[16] Taking mourning as her starting point, Klein reformulated the theory of the Oedipus complex around the idea that the superego offered the basis for a new conception of the ego, one focused on 'internal relations.' Since, in mourning, we *identify* with lost objects, she used this process to describe how an inner object world could be built up. To conceptualize this inner world, Klein introduced the concept of a 'position,' which she defined as a 'specific grouping of anxieties and defences.' A position can be contrasted to a neurotic conflict. A neurotic conflict is localized, even if its effects are pervasive; a position, in contrast, describes a stance or attitude of the mind as a whole.

Klein described early development – indeed the whole of life – as the story of a shift between two positions: the paranoid-schizoid position and the depressive position. These correspond respectively to the state of not being related to an inter-subjective, ethically meaningful world, on one hand, and the state of being related to such a world on the other hand. In its earliest phase, the psyche is in the 'para-noid-schizoid position': experience is fragmentary and discontinuous; thoughts and feelings happen *to* the subject; persecutory anxiety predominates. The human accomplishment lies in achieving the 'depressive position,' although persecutory anxiety is never fully supplanted. Normally achieved in the first year of life, the depressive position consists in setting up the mother as an internal object. Based on the recognition that the mother is separate, it constitutes the beginning of subjectivity. Since, in Klein's conception, subjectivity involves mourning, sadness, and object loss, she also calls this the 'pining' position. Subjectivity, for Klein, is inseparable from the idea that one has harmed or damaged the internal object on which one depends.

Thus, there is no real distinction for Klein between subjectivity and conscience. The great problem for Klein is building up and maintaining access to an internal object world. Whereas in the paranoid-schizoid position, relations are formed to 'part objects,' the depressive position involves an effort to represent 'whole objects,' in other words, to recognize others as subjects.[17] Since introspection involves an awareness of vulnerability, dependence, and guilt, it gives rise to 'manic' attempts to avoid depression, especially through unreflective action. As one commentator, Donald Meltzer, has noted, the 'heart of the depressive position is the realization that security can only be achieved through responsibility.' The awareness that one can and has hurt an object upon whom one depends spurs the effort at 'reparation,' which is the only goodness we can know. So powerful is the relational paradigm that even love of truth is assimilated to it. In Meltzer's explication of Klein: 'love for the truth becomes very strongly allied to the capacities to appreciate the beauty and the goodness of the object, since manic defences, and through them the danger of regression to the paranoid-schizoid position, have their foundations in an attack on the truth.'[18] For Freud, by contrast, love of truth is not only independent of the love of objects but may well contradict it.

Klein's insistence on the inseparability of the ego from concrete relationships as opposed to universal moral considerations can be seen in her essay on *Citizen Kane*, a film that appeared in 1941. The film's plot is set in motion by young Kane's violent separation from his mother. The sled he uses to defend himself – 'Rosebud' – is the secret to his life. His dying word refers, Klein argued, to 'the breast,' whose sustenance Kane needs but can never allow himself to attain. This sustenance is not mere milk, of course, but refers to the need to heal and reconnect with his painfully aborted relation to his mother. Kane, Klein wrote, was a person whose 'depressive feelings [were] overlaid and kept at bay by manic mechanisms,' i.e., mechanisms of control. What was good in Kane – both in his politics and in his love life – stemmed from his effort to reconnect. Thus he became a reformer not out of a principled sense of right and wrong, but rather through a sense of compassion and concrete obligation to individuals and groups. But, because of his unbearable uprooting, he cannot sustain this effort to connect: 'Long forgotten are the wishes to further the interests of poor people. These . . . soon changed into ways of controlling them.' Similarly, he was attracted by his wife Susan's poverty and helplessness, which reminded him of his own devastated inner state, but after marrying her his feelings 'turned into attempts to control.' 'The more his capacity for love proves a failure,' Klein noted, 'the more the manic mechanisms increase.'[19]

By the late 1930s Klein had created a new language centred less and less on morality and more and more on the problems of building up an internal object world capable of sustaining a complex and deeply felt personal life. This conception involved a different way of conceptualizing modernity than Freud's, one concerned not so much with universal moral issues including those that Marxists had raised, but rather with the effort to maintain small, meaningful interconnected interpersonal communities. This newly emerging ethic of personal life was potentially no less critical than Freud's but it was different. Klein's initiative gave rise to a whole new vocabulary. Winnicott described the modern city as organized around the manic defence: 'the wireless that is left on interminably,' the noise that never ceases. Adrian Stokes explained the reassurance given by arts such as sculpture and architecture as the relief that 'whole objects' provide from persecutory anxiety. The gallery viewer, Donald Meltzer wrote, has 'the aim of carrying out an infantile introjection, with the hope . . . of obtaining something in the nature of a reconstructed object.'[20]

Finally, Klein's work also implied a reformulation of analytic practice, especially its heart, the problem of resistance. A 1936 essay by Joan Rivière exemplified the revision. Whereas, for Freud, the primary source of resistance is unconscious guilt, for Rivière it is the impaired transition to the depressive position. For Freud, accordingly, the analyst should maintain distance or 'neutrality' to allow the person to work through their relation to themself. For Rivière, however, the analyst should be available as an object so the person can work out their relation to objects. Both Freud and Rivière locate the root of resistance in narcissism, but their accounts of narcissism diverge subtly. Freud assumes that narcissism prevents analysis since there is no transference. For Rivière, narcissism is underlaid by a depression based on a denial of dependence or on 'contempt and depreciation' for objects. For Freud, the goal of the analysis is autonomy; all that really matters is for the person to gain the truth about themself. For Rivière, in contrast, what matters is the restoration of an early object relation. 'The love for the internal object must be found behind the guilt,' she advised.[21]

IV   Gender justice and reconciliation: the significance of women's mothering

The discovery of the mother's role in early childhood had enormous consequences for analytic thinking concerning gender, just as it had earlier in the debates over female sexuality. Whereas Freud at first emphasized sexuality and minimized gender difference, the shift to the mother returned the woman's role in reproduction to the center of the analytic conception. As a result, gender, in the sense of identification, as opposed to sexuality as in Freud, became central. Alongside the early analytic writings on male/male – i.e., father/son or brother/brother – relations, a new discourse centered on mother/daughter and sister/sister relations began to develop, one which at first enriched Freud's focus on the father.

As in Freud's circle earlier, these relations were lived as well as studied. As Klein aged, she became a mother figure for a group of younger female analysts. A letter from Joan Rivière to Melanie Klein, written in June 1940, while the Battle of Britain unfolded, helps recreate the way in which Klein had supplanted Sigmund Freud for some analysts, while also suggesting the changes in the view of gender that occurred with the shift to a mother-centred theory. 'When the first official mention of invasion began,' Rivière wrote to her mentor, 'the possibility of our work all coming to an end seemed so near, I felt we should all have to keep it in our hearts . . . as the only way to save it for the future . . . Of course, I was constantly thinking of the psychological causes of such terrible loss and destruction as may happen to mankind. So, I had the idea of your telling me (and then a group of us) everything you think about these causes . . . First what you think about the causes of the German psychological situation, and secondly, of that of the rest of Europe and mainly the Allies, since the last war. To me the apathy and denial of the Allies, especially England, is not clear. (I never shared it). How is it connected with what I call the 'Munich' complex, the son's incapacity to fight for mother and country? . . . One great question is why it is so important to be brave and to be able to bear whatever happens? Everything in *reality* depends on this.'

Rivière's letter is to be found among Klein's papers. Klein filed it with a paper of her own, entitled, 'What does death represent to the individual?' In it, Klein describes Hitler's weapon as a 'destructive and dangerous penis.' In men, Klein wrote, 'hidden, passive homosexual phantasies, plotting and scheming with the destructive father, come to the fore.' 'The guilt about the sadistic alliance with the dangerous father is one important reason for denial.' When the unconscious relation to a sadistic internal father-figure was not understood, it was likely to dominate. For example, the insistence on remaining on the offensive 'expressed the drive towards active and dangerous homosexuality as reaction against the desire and fear of being buggered.'[22] Rivière, too, in her letter had described the British male apathy as the expression of 'homosexual leanings.'

Of course, these formulations are repugnant in light, for example, of today's understanding of how homosexuals were persecuted in pre-war England. Nonetheless, once the documents are interpreted we can see the shift in the understanding of gender that has occurred. The familial imagery is matricentric. The most striking fact is Rivière's wish that Klein explain and protect her children in the face of the emergency. The mother's role has been expanded to the realm of education, protection, guidance. Correspondingly, the father has disappeared: the only significant male role is that of the son. But the son inherits the father's old role as protector. The key question is whether he has the capacity to fight for mother and country, which is to say for children. The man learned from his own vulnerability in childhood – his depressive position – to care for others. The absent sons are involved in sadomasochistic and phallic relations with one another – manic efforts at 'control.' The 'homosexual leanings' to which Rivière refers are men's passive relations to other men. Hitler is a 'phallic,' i.e., 'hard,' threatening figure. The same weakness that leads to British men's unconscious complicity with him prevents them from recognizing their responsibilities to women and children.

The homophobia of the statements cannot be denied, but neither for Rivière, nor for Klein, is a homosexual object choice the issue. Rather the issue is the attempt to redefine the notion of manliness as the ability to protect. Character, for Klein and Rivière, involved an understanding of sexual difference not because Klein and Rivière were enthralled by heterosexuality – on the contrary, their whole imaginary is largely desexualized – but because, within their worldview, a recognition of the role of the mother, for both sexes, was linked to a recognition of vulnerability and dependence for both sexes. The relation to the mother is the key for both sexes, because it is the key to ethical responsibility. Only in that sense is gender important.

The Kleinian worldview was prefeminist (pre-1960s feminist), of course. One might rightly ask, why do Klein and Rivière take for granted that protecting the 'motherland' from the Nazis is predominantly men's responsibility? In fact, of course, the significance of sexual difference faded dramatically in the hurly burly of wartime England. Nonetheless, Kleinian values were not aimed at the suppression of either women or homosexuals. Rather Klein and her followers valued the feeling of obligation between the sexes because it was linked to a recognition of the importance of the mother and the vulnerability of children.

Their outlook can be well contrasted to that of post-World War II American analysis, for which 'castrating mothers' were to be blamed for homosexuality. Meanwhile, Rivière's foreboding sense of the transformative power of world politics proved accurate.

The Kleinian transformation of the promises of autonomy and gender justice were accompanied by a transformation in the notion of democracy. Democracy was redefined to include interpersonal relations, along with the emphasis on the mother and on men's protective role. The new emphasis on 'group-feeling,' as it was called, was precipitated by the experience of World War II.

V World War II, the trauma of English psychoanalysis and the 'group'

The British and central European analysts in London during the Second World War experienced a series of broken connections: the rise of the Nazis and of mass anti-semitism, the destruction of central European analysis, the death of Freud, emigration and now the war. With it, analysts entered into the inner world of bombed civilians, shell shocked soldiers and bereaved children. In England, three quarters of a million men died out of a population of 38 million. About a third of the dead were married. Public grief was common. Often there was no site for a funeral. Analysis in England during World War II was reshaped as part of a process by which the entire British people were assaulted, regrouped and fought back.

This process precipitated the long-developing reorientation of psychoanalysis around the mother/infant relationship. In the words of Peter Homans: 'The metapsychology collapsed in interwar London. Under the impress of . . . social structural change and augmented by national mourning over the losses inflicted by a terrible war, it virtually withered away, to be replaced by clinical and theoretical concerns with attachment, loss and the social world of patients, many of whom were soldiers and children.'[23] We have seen how Klein's early writings began to reconstruct the modern promises of autonomy and gender justice. The experience of the war also changed the earlier assumption of the public/private divide, bringing to the fore a new approach to the social, that of 'group feeling.' The key preoccupations of analysis now became the mother/infant relation, concrete relations with others and group psychology rather than autonomy, sexual difference, and the private/public divide.

This transformation took place in a context of enormous integrative energies. Whereas the Great War encouraged Westerners to confront the internal contradictions of their societies, World War II generated a sense of unity, shared purpose and national confidence. Hostility was externalized, not only during but also after the war. Analysts were caught up in a centripetal process. Destroyed on the continent of Europe, analysis was reborn as part of the vast expansion of post-industrial society fuelled by American capitalism. The result was two-fold. On one hand, analysis grew exponentially and developed a newfound sense of social acceptance. On the other hand, it was absorbed into the disciplinary institutions that were replacing traditional authority.

The new outlook was born during the Blitz in London in 1939–40, where the largest number of continental European analysts had fled. An external emergency drew an entire nation together. Stephen Spender, writing an introduction to a government-sponsored collection of 'War Pictures' noted that in the last war the pictures would have been of the Western Front, but that now they were of the 'bombed city.' The difference was that in the 'Great War' soldiers and civilians experienced passive, distant, helpless suffering whereas in World War II, they had the opportunity for an active, direct response. In part, this was the result of leadership. Winston Churchill, the refugee social theorist Franz Neumann later observed, transformed an unknown into a known danger and therefore 'fulfilled those functions of leadership . . . fulfilled in the life of the individual by the organization of the ego.'[24]

The effect of the German bombing of London was that the war was experienced as 'almost a natural disaster which fosters a single spirit of unity binding the whole people together.' In October 1940, the film-maker Humphrey Jennings wrote to his wife: 'Some of the damage in London is pretty heart-breaking but what an effect it has on people! What warmth – what courage! what determination.'[25] This is a typical letter from the period. Old ties were broken but new loyalties sprang up in an atmosphere of heightened emotion and quasi-politicization. The liberating effects on young people and on women were particularly striking. Class barriers seemed to decline in importance, especially after the East End was bombed and 3.5 million children, many poor, evacuated to the countryside.[26] Perhaps the most dramatic images of the Blitz, memorialized in Henry Moore's drawings, were the individuals and families who occupied the London tubes, against official orders, during the bombing. These drawings symbolized the mingling of public and private that occurs in a city under siege, as well as the attempt to raise children in a semi-communal environment.

Behind the resistance was an almost mythic sense of identification with core Western values. Whereas during the Great War, German music had been frowned upon and even banned, during World War II the allied symbol for victory was the opening bars of Beethoven's Fifth Symphony ('V' in Morse code). Lunchtime concerts were held at the National Gallery (emptied of paintings). In one of the most famous, immortalized in a film by Jennings, the pianist Myra Hess played Beethoven's *Appassionata* sonata followed by Bach's 'Jesu, Joy of Man's Desiring.' In Kenneth Clark's reminiscence, 'in common with half the audience, I was in tears. This is what we had all been waiting for – an assertion of eternal values.'[27]

Behind this imaginary unity was the image of the English people as a family, an image that transcended the distinction between left and right. George Orwell's essay, 'Socialism and the English Genius,' written in London at the height of the bombardment, used this image to argue for the welfare state. What was needed, Orwell argued, was a democratic revolution that would 'break the grip of the monied class.' Otherwise, he continued, Britain would remain a family with the wrong members in control: . . . A rather stuffy Victorian family . . . its cupboards bursting with skeletons. It has rich relations who have to be kowtowed to and poor relations who are horribly sat upon, and there is a deep conspiracy of silence about the source of the family income [the British Empire]. It is a family in which the young are generally thwarted and most of the power is in the hands of irresponsible uncles and bedridden aunts. Still, it is a family. It has its private language and its common memories, and at the approach of an enemy it closes ranks.[28]

In the creation of this imaginary 'family,' the image of the mother played a key role. The most celebrated work of art produced during the war, Henry Moore's *Madonna and Child*, was unveiled in 1943. The sculpture resulted from the initiative of Reverend Walter Hussey who wanted to see the Church of England retake a leading role in the arts. At the dedication of the sculpture, Hussey told the Congregation: 'The Holy Child is the centre of the work, and yet the subject speaks of the Incarnation – the fact that the Christ was born of a human mother – and so the Blessed Virgin is conceived as any small child would in essence think of his mother, not as small and frail, but as the one large, secure, solid background to life.'[29] The image of the mother was also at the centre of the welfare state. After the bombing of the West End of London, the Queen announced her support for socialized medicine, remarking 'the people have suffered so much.'[30] In 1943, Churchill too called for 'a National Health Service [and] national compulsory insurance for all classes for all purposes from the cradle to the grave.'[31] When the National Health Service was finally created in 1948 it was the first health system in any Western society to offer free health care to the entire population, the first based not on the insurance principle, in which entitlement follows contribution, but on universalist principles. This shift was more than a form of material help. It universalized the principle of entitlement and helped sustain a working class, family-centred way of life.

VI   'Group feeling' and the democratization of authority

In the shift towards the emphasis on 'group feeling,' the key idea was, first, that 'the group' or society, like the mother, offered a kind of primal protection to the individual. The infant's relation to the mother foretold the adult's relation to the group. Adults used groups – including such complex social institutions as religion and the economy – as 'objects,' just as infants 'used' their mothers. The preoccupation with infant needs was the analogue to the preceding war's 'shell shock' episode which had spread analytic ideas to so many people. In 1938 a report by psychiatrists predicted that air raids would be devastating and that psychiatric casualties would exceed physical casualties by three to one. In fact, the air raids led to a decrease in attendances at mental hospitals and clinics. Suicides and drunkenness also declined. Edward Glover disbanded the Psychoanalytic Clinic which had been set up for war casualties a month after it opened.[32] These were taken as examples of the significance of morale or 'group feeling.'

Instead of shell shock, the focus of psychiatric attention was on evacuated, orphaned and homeless children. The sense of ruptured connection served as a unifying image for the entire society. Psychoanalysis was at the centre of this image. Rather than helping expose the irrational forces that had caused the war, as it had in the Great War, it now became part of a society-wide healing process. In December 1939, in response to the bombing of London, three British psycho-analysts, D.W. Winnicott, John Bowlby and Emmanuel Miller, wrote a letter to the *British Medical Journal* stating that 'the evacuation of small children between the ages of two and five introduces major psychological problems.'[33] This letter was widely distributed. An important strand of English and American philan-thropy had long focused on the child. The analytic turn towards infant study and advocacy, in the context of a national emergency, brought it much favourable attention. Once the United States entered the war, a transatlantic network formed around such figures as Walter Langer, William Bullitt, Bettina Warburg and Joseph Kennedy, the US Ambassador to England. They helped analysts, such as the Bibrings and the Kris's, emigrate to the US, while also supporting child welfare and development research, especially through the American Foster Parents' Plan for War Children. Anna Freud, the director of Hampstead Nurseries, a complex of residential homes for homeless children, was at the centre of this network.

The contribution of analysts to promoting an understanding of the depth of human dependence and to democratizing psychological knowledge during and after World War II was an historic contribution. Childrearing advice, like education, social work or the juvenile justice system, had been a middle-class activity that looked down on and criticized working-class practices. Analysts promoted a shift towards intuition and emotion, rather than regime, and sought to inculcate trust for the everyday, untutored practices of the working-class mother. Winnicott, who developed his theory of the 'good enough mother', one who provides the frustration optimal for development, rather than one who follows a 'perfect' regime, was affirming what he called the 'ordinary devoted mother.' She was a working-class woman who 'feels,' rather than a middle-class woman who reads child-care manuals and directs servants.

Yet this very contribution was contradictory. The entrenchment of the 'family wage' as the basis of the coming welfare state was accompanied by the entry of women into professions that depended upon the expansion of the welfare state itself, as well as by the increased entry of working-class women into wage labour. Women were thus being interpellated as mothers just as economic conditions were eliminating the single-earner family. The analytic turn towards the mother, rather than building on the earlier rejection of an essentialist notion of gender, now subtly began to reinscribe it.

Along with the reorientation to the mother and infant, British psychoanalysts participated in an important series of experiments in group psychology centred on such matters as 'morale-building,' personality assessment, leadership and rehabilitation, undertaken at the Tavistock Institute and at the Army's psychiatric hospital, at Northfield, near Birmingham.[34] With the outbreak of the war, the liberal and left intelligentsia, who had been staunchly anti-fascist, gained control of the media. They used it to promote the emphasis on the group. In 1940, Edward Glover wrote: 'for the first time . . . the Ministry of Information has established that group feeling is a medico-psychological concern and that it calls for instruments of precision in diagnosis.'[35] In contrast to the earlier conflict between 'true psychoanalysis' and eclecticism, Bowlby, Rickman and other analysts now saw in the 'Tavi' 'a ready made centre for implementing the new dynamic social psychiatry.'[36] The goal was not 'parade-ground efficiency and obedience to officers, but a quasi-democratic "group spirit" . . . The rallying cry is "Team-work": "millions of us, all sticking together . . . There's nothing to stop us, only ourselves."'[37] The analytic input at Tavistock shaped its theories of 'psycho-logical warfare,' national character, and 'culture and personality;' pioneered the introduction of psychotherapy under the National Health Service beginning in 1948; and anticipated, for example in R.D. Laing's work during the 1950s, the 'human potential' movement and anti-psychiatries of the 1960s.

The idea that group feeling was 'a medico-psychological concern,' as well as the emphasis on object relations, was also promoted at Northfield. There, Wilfred Bion – the analyst who was to develop and radicalize Klein's work – argued that Freud failed 'to realize . . . the nature of the revolution he himself produced when he looked for an explanation of neurotic symptoms, not in the individual, but in the individual's relationship to objects,' presumably referring to Freud's solution to the problem of hysteria. Beginning in 1942, at Northfield, Bion and John Rickman tried to get patients to use the group as a personal solution. For example, they allowed a ward of shell shocked soldiers to devolve into chaos, and then to rebuild their relations to one another. As Jacques Lacan later wrote, 'Bion deliberately constructed a group without a leader . . . so as to force the group to take account of the difficulties of its own existence, and to render it more and more transparent to itself.'[38] At Northfield, the use of group psychotherapy expanded and Moreno's 'psychodrama' techniques, by which traumatic experiences were reenacted, were introduced to England. With these investigations, British analysts had the sense of breaking out of an artificially imposed restriction to an 'inner' world. As one participant wrote: 'the Russians are mistaken to think that social is something external and not an internal part of the individual . . . The social and cultural element is deeply ingrained in the individual and is to a large extent unconscious.'[39]

When Lacan visited England in 1947, he was especially struck by these experiments. The war, he wrote, had left him 'with a vigorous sense of the atmosphere of unreality within which the collectivity of the French had lived it' but the English victory 'has a moral source . . . a truthful relation to the real.' He found himself especially impressed by the influence of British analysts among psychiatists, their close relations with society and by the 'Child Guidance' movement. With Bion and Rickman's experiments, he stated, he 'rediscovered the feeling of the miracle that accompanied the first of Freud's steps.'

Just as the focus on interpersonal relations extended the promise of autonomy, and the focus on reproduction extended the promise of gender justice, so the focus on the group extended the promise of democratization. Whereas for Freud, democratization meant the protection of the individual within the private sphere, under the influence of Klein, British object relations emphasized the potentially democratic character of collective activity. It thus began to provide a middle ground between Reich's holism, and Freud's anti-political biases, while also continuing and deepening the social-democratic rejection of 'solitary horseman' notions of the subject. Along with the changed understanding of autonomy and gender justice, group psychology potentially continued the process of radicalizing the enlightenment promise of emancipation in the epoch of the welfare state.

Notes

1 This article is adapted from an overall history of psychoanalysis, *Psychoanalysis, Modernity and Personal Life*, forthcoming from Alfred J. Knopf.
2 Claude Lévi-Strauss, 'The Effectiveness of Symbols,' *Structural Anthropology* (Chicago: Chicago University Press, 1983) pp. 186–205.
3 Sigmund Freud, *The Standard Edition of the Complete Psychological Works of Sigmund Freud*, ed. and trans. James Strachey (London: Hogarth, 24 vols, 1953–74), vol. XVII, pp. 161, 164–5. I follow Philip Rieff's *Freud: The Mind of the Moralist* (Chicago: Chicago University Press, 1979) and *The Triumph of the Therapeutic: Uses of Faith after Freud* (Chicago: Chicago University Press, 1987) on this point.
4 Quoted in Ted Winslow, 'Bloomsbury, Freud and the Vulgar Passions,' *Social Research*, vol. 57, no. 4, Winter 1990, pp. 815–6.
5 Peter Stansky and William Abrahams, *London's Burning: Life, Death and Art in the Second World War* (London: Constable, 1984) p. 84.
6 Raymond Williams, 'The Bloomsbury Fraction,' *Problems in Materialism and Culture: Selected Essays* (London: Verso, 1997) p. 149.
7 Paul Johnson, *Modern Times: The World from the Twenties to the Nineties* (New York: HarperCollins, 1991) p. 167.
8 John Maynard Keynes, 'My Early Beliefs,' (1938) quoted in Robert Sidelsky, *Keynes* (New York: Oxford University Press, 1996) p. 141.
9 Perry Meisel and Walter Kendrick, eds, *Bloomsbury/Freud: The Letters of James and Alix Strachey 1924–1925* (New York: Basic Books, 1985), p. 45.
10 Elizabeth Abel, *Virginia Woolf and the Fictions of Psychoanalysis* (Chicago: Chicago University Press, 1989) p. 26.
11 Robert Briffault, *The Mothers: A Study of the Origins of Sentiments and Institutions* (London: Macmillan, 1927).
12 Joan Rivière wrote that the Kleinian circle considered Freud's 'narcissistic or auto-erotic phase' to co-exist with object relations, 'largely owing to the important [oral] introjective processes' then operating, she explained. Joan Rivière, 'General Introduction,' in Melanie Klein et al., *Developments in Psychoanalysis* (London: Hogarth Press, 1952) p. 13.
13 Joan Rivière: 'the concept of *objects* within the ego, as distinct from identifications, is hardly discussed in Freud's work.' Joan Rivière, 'A Contribution to the Analysis

of the Negative Therapeutic Reaction,' *International Journal of Psycho-Analysis*, vol. 17, 1936, pp. 304–20, reprinted in Martin Bergmann and Frank Hartman, eds, *The Evolution of Psychoanalytic Technique* (New York: Basic Books, 1976), pp. 417–29.

14 Freud, *SE*, XXI, p. 138.

15 Melanie Klein, 'Draft Statement,' 1 January 1942, CKB/FO1/32, British Psycho-Analytical Society.

16 Melanie Klein, 'The Psychogenesis of Manic-Depressive States,' *Contributions to Psycho-Analysis* (London: Hogarth, 1948).

17 Thus, Klein wrote, 'not until the object is loved as a whole can its loss be felt as a whole.' *Contributions*, p. 284.

18 Donald Meltzer (1963) in Adrian Stokes 'Painting and the Inner World,' *The Critical Writings of Adrian Stokes*, vol. III (London: Thames and Hudson, 1978) p. 221.

19 Melanie Klein, 'Notes on Citizen Kane,' [this volume, ch. 13].

20 Klein, *Contributions*, p. 290. Winnicott, 'The Manic Defence,' *From Pediatrics to Psychoanalysis* (New York: Basic Books, 1948) p. 131. Adrian Stokes, *The Image in Form: Selected Writings of Adrian Stokes*, ed. Richard Wollheim (New York: Harper and Row, 1972) p. 68.

21 'It is the love for his internal objects, which lies behind and produces the unbearable guilt and pain, the need to sacrifice his life for theirs, and so the prospect of death, that makes this resistance so stubborn.' 'The love for the internal object must be found behind the guilt.' Joan Rivière, 'A Contribution to the Analysis of the Negative Therapeutic Reaction,' *International Journal of Psycho-Analysis*, vol. 17, 1936, pp. 304–20, reprinted in Bergmann, pp. 417–29.

22 Joan Rivière to Melanie Klein, 3 June 1940, PP/KLE/C95. British Psycho-Analytical Society.

23 Peter Homans, *The Ability to Mourn: Disillusionment and the Origins of Psychoanalysis* (Chicago: Chicago Univeristy Press, 1989), pp. 114, 226f; Ian Suttie, *The Origins of Love and Hate* (London: Kegan Paul, 1945).

24 Franz Neumann, *The Democratic and Authoritarian State* (New York: Free Press of Glencoe, 1957) pp. 406–7.

25 Stansky and Abrahams, p. 101.

26 Harold Perkin, *The Rise of Professional Society* (New York: Routledge, 1988) p. 411.

27 Stansky and Abrahams, p. 98.

28 Peter Hennessy, *Never Again* (New York: Pantheon, 1993) p. 37.

29 Stansky and Abrahams, pp. 50, 60f, 98–9, 101. My description of London during the Blitz is indebted to Stansky and Abrahams.

30 Perkin, *The Rise of Professional Society* p. 413.

31 Hennessy, *Never Again*, p. 123.

32 Philip Ziegler, *London at War* (New York: Knopf, 1995) p. 170.

33 Adam Phillips, *Winnicott* (Cambridge, MA: Harvard University Press, 1988) p. 62.

34 H.V. Dicks, *Fifty Years of the Tavistock Clinic* (London: Routledge, 1970) p. 5. The National Hospital for Nervous Diseases and the Maudsley Hospital were the official psychiatric hospitals, but Northfield and Tavistock were the centres of innovation.

35 Edward Glover, 'The Birth of Social Psychiatry,' 24 August 1940, p. 239, quoted in Nikolas Rose, *Governing the Soul* (London: Routledge, 1990) p. 22.

36 H.V. Dicks, *Fifty Years of the Tavistock*, p. 115.

37 Ben Shepherd, 'A Bunch of Loony-bin Doctors,' *Times Literary Supplement*, 7 June 1996.

38 Jacques Lacan, 'La psychiatrie anglaise et la guerre,' (1947) in *Travaux et Interventions*, quoted in John Forrester, *The Seductions of Psychoanalysis: Freud, Lacan and Derrida* (New York: Cambridge University Press, 1989) pp. 186–7.

39 S. H. Foulkes, 'Discussion of the Soviet View on the Basis of Group and Psychoanalysis,' PP/SHF/F.3/15, British Psycho-Analytical Society.

Chapter 3

Melanie Mell by herself

Translated by Ian Patterson

Editor's note:

This collaborative work, first published in *Cahiers Confrontation* (February 1986), and translated for this collection, follows from Maria Torok's earlier work with Nicolas Abraham. Abraham and Torok challenge the universalizing abstractions of psychoanalysis (the Oedipus complex and the death drive, for example), by insisting on the historical uniqueness of each analytic situation. Instead of subsuming psychic experience under theory, they advocate a form of poetics which is attuned to the gaps in the unconscious that unsettle not only the practice of psychoanalysis, but the coherence of its theoretical claims. These gaps point to a nescience, a piece of un-acknowledged traumatic history that has not, in Abraham and Torok's special sense of the term, been 'introjected' or absorbed, and which is 'encrypted' in the words, signs and associations that make, or un-make, psychic meaning. Abraham and Torok's formulation of this thesis can be traced through the collection *The Shell and the Kernel: Renewals of Psychoanalysis*, ed. and trans. Nicholas T. Rand (1994), and their classic account of cryptonymy can be found in *The Wolf Man's Magic Word: A Cryptonymy*, trans. Nicholas T. Rand (1986). The original title of the present essay, 'Melanie-Mell par elle-même,' also harbours a cryptonym. 'Elle-même' is a partial anagram of 'Melanie Mell.' It is this name or, more precisely, the multiple names of Melanie Klein that

provide Torok, Sylwan and Covello with a key with which to unlock
the secret histories that lie hidden in Klein's work and life. Melanie
Klein's name, once decrypted, reveals a lineage of familial traumas that
restore a historical dimension to the apparent ahistoricism of Klein's
theory. Klein's phantoms are those of her Jewish heritage and in them
lie buried the traumas of persecution. Compared to the vast amount
of scholarly and theoretical work on Freud in relation to Jewish
identity, this crucial aspect of Klein's life has been notably absent in
Klein studies. For Torok, Sylwan and Covello the reason for this
absence or silence lies in Klein's work itself. Her foundational theories
of persecutory phantasy and of the depressive position, they argue,
were set up as a bulwark against the traumatic history of the persecution of the Jews – a history which, at the precise moment when Klein
both modified and consolidated her theories in the 1930s and 1940s,
staged a grotesque and catastrophic return in the Nazi persecution
of the Jews. 'Melanie Mell by herself,' then, is no straightforward
historicization or re-theorization of Klein. In her opening remarks
to the session at Brunel University at which this paper was first
presented in 1981 (see 'Theoretra: An Alternative to Theory' in The
Shell and the Kernel, pp. 253–6), Torok argued that recognizing the
unsaid and unspeakable in psychoanalytic theory requires a poetics of
reading that is like an exchange of gifts between the patient and the
analyst. The collaborative nature of 'Melanie Mell' is, thus, by no
means incidental: by exchanging the names of Melanie Klein, Torok,
Sylwan and Covello also enact a collective recognition of the history
that simultaneously shapes and is obscured by Kleinian theory. (LS)

Introduction

Let's say Melanie Mell is a fairy-tale. If we agree on that we shan't need to feel
bound by considerations about the existence or non-existence of facts. And if we
proceed on that basis, we can begin to think of the fairy-tale as something purely
illustrative, and we can listen to it as offering a means of approach rather than as
telling us something true or false. What we shall really be doing is analysing a
phantom.

But I ought perhaps to remind you what a phantom is. Nicolas Abraham
described this new way of his of looking at metapsychology in 1975.[1] It goes
without saying that 'phantom' is not being used in the normal sense of the word.
I quote:

> The phantoms of folklore merely objectify a metaphor active in the
> unconscious: the burial of an unspeakable fact *within the love-object*. [. . .]

The phantom is a formation of the unconscious that has never been conscious – for good reason. It passes – in a way yet to be determined – from the parent's unconsciousness into the child's. Clearly the phantom has a function different from dynamic repression. The phantom's periodic and compulsive return lies beyond the scope of symptom-formation in the sense of a return of the repressed; it works like a ventriloquist, like a stranger within the subject's own mental topography. The imaginings issuing from the presence of a stranger have nothing to do with fantasy strictly speaking. They neither preserve a topographical status quo nor announce a shift in it. Instead, by their gratuitousness in relation to the subject, they create the impression of surrealistic flights of fancy or of *OuLiPo*-like verbal feats.[2]

Thus the phantom cannot even be recognized by the subject as evident in an 'aha' experience and, during analysis, can only give rise to constructions with all their attendant uncertainties. The phantom may nevertheless be deconstructed by analytic construction, though this occurs without the patients' having the impression that they were in fact the subject of the analysis. It is clear that, in contrast to other types of cases, this work requires a genuine partnership between patient and analyst, the more so since the construction arrived at in this way bears no direct relation to the patient's own topography but concerns someone else's. The special difficulty of these analyses lies in the patient's horror at violating a parent's or a family's guarded secret, even though the secret's text and content are inscribed within the patient's own unconscious. The horror of transgression, in the strict sense of the term, is compounded by the risk of undermining the fictitious yet necessary integrity of the parental figure in question.

Let me offer, among others, one idea to explain the birth of a phantom. The phantom counteracts libidinal introjection; that is, it obstructs our perception of words as implicitly referring to their unconscious portion. In point of fact, the words used by the phantom to carry out its return (and which the child sensed in the parent) do not refer to a source of speech in the parent. Instead they point to a gap, they refer to the unspeakable. In the parent's topography, these words play the crucial role of having to some extent stripped speech of its libidinal grounding. The phantom is summoned, therefore, at the opportune moment, when it is recognized that a gap was transmitted to the subject with the result of barring him or her from the specific introjections he or she would seek at present. The presence of the phantom indicates the effects, on the descendants, of something that had inflicted narcissistic injury or even catastrophe on the parents.

The difference between *the stranger incorporated* through suggestion and *the dead returning to haunt* does not necessarily come to the fore at first, precisely because both act as foreign bodies lodged within the subject. In classical analysis, an attempt is made to uncover the roots in a parental wish. While incorporation, which behaves like a post-hypnotic suggestion, may recede before appropriate forms of classical analysis, the phantom remains

P. Pam's experience of self & the world

beyond the reach of the tools of classical analysis. The phantom will vanish only when its radically heterogeneous nature with respect to the subject is recognized, a subject to whom it at no time has any direct reference. In no way can the subject relate to the phantom as his or her own repressed experience, not even as an experience within incorporation. *The phantom which returns to haunt bears witness to the existence of the dead buried within the other.*

A surprising fact gradually emerges: the work of the phantom coincides in every respect with Freud's description of the death instinct. First of all, it has no energy of its own; it cannot be 'abreacted,' merely designated. Second, it pursues its work of disarray in silence. Let us note that the phantom is sustained by secreted words, invisible gnomes whose aim is to wreak havoc, from within the unconscious, in the coherence of logical progression. Finally, it gives rise to endless repetition and, more often than not, eludes rationalization.

At best, phantom words of this kind can be invested with libido and determine the choice of hobbies, leisure activities, or professional pursuits.

After that preamble, you won't be surprised if my contribution begins with the idea of a dream-angel. There is a good reason for linking angels and phantoms in the sense that one can reveal or disclose the other, speak its name and pronounce its word, announce it in a dream for someone, so that as a result of that annunciation the phantom starts to waver, then gradually to evaporate. Parallel with this the harmful effects of the inexpressible secret begin to emerge: a haunting through the lies of the phantom which transforms its bearer into a puppet by means of its phantasmagorias.

But what has all this got to do with Melanie Mell? Our investigation of her case is part of a current of research which aims to uncover the idiosyncratic particularities that haunt theoretical texts and technical procedures, in the hope of freeing analysis and making it easier to assess. It is not an easy task, and we are only at the very beginning of it. In terms of analysis, creator and work are clearly inseparable, so intimately intertwined that it is sometimes necessary to take the investigation to extreme lengths in order to get to the root of a peculiarity. I'm thinking, for example, of how an 'understanding' of Freud's (very peculiar) theory of femininity required the naming of the hidden wound of a whole family in order to locate the origin of his peculiar assertions.[3]

We are only now beginning to listen to the peculiarities of Kleinian theory from the vantage point of the phantom, and it is the beginning of this listening process that we want to offer you now in three stages.

1. Melanie's secret name.
2. The break with the past and its phantomogenic effect; Melanie's father and her brother Emmanuel.
3. The phantom effect within the system. The central axis or the religion of the Breast: the meaning of its operation in the global picture.

It is this conjunction of issues that we want to bring together here under the title of 'Melanie Mell.'

Part I   Melanie Mell

The signature does not suffer from being in this respect unreadable, or not, at least, if reading means deciphering a meaning or referring to something [. . .] The proper name only resonates, and at the same time is instantly lost, at the moment it becomes its own remains, when it is broken, scrambled, or jammed by its contact with the signature.

(Jacques Derrida, *Glas*)[4]

The dream is an angel, a messenger who, in the nick of time, brings news of a word. For a long time he has been trying to take wing in order to alight on a confused and nameless situation which it is the purpose of his advent to articulate. That is how it comes about that we wake up with the word in our head, and suddenly see everything in a new light.

I realized one morning that a silver dish held out to me in a dream, then struck and violently twisted – all this is taking place in Hungary – was telling me that the dream was to be 'opened' with a Hungarian key, and that the word 'silver' spoken in Hungarian but heard in French would render it intelligible. That was the gospel (*l'évangile*; eu-angelion) or the annunciation of that night. The angel that explained Melanie also came from a Hungarian landscape, and brought the same kind of key.

I only met Melanie Klein – or Little, as that's what *Klein* means in German (little Melanie?) – once in my life and then completely one-sidedly, at the International Congress in 1957. As she made her way through the crowd of people selling Freud medallions and distributing programmes there was something about her that reminded me of the pleasure-boats that ploughed up and down the Danube at Budapest. Her dress was like a black muslin sail, and at her breast she wore a brooch big enough for everyone to notice it and to wonder, discreetly but distinctly, whether she was wearing it on her *good* breast or her *bad* breast. Her appearance as she entered seemed designed to emphasize both *breast* and *blackness*. As with the black sails of her dress, there was something as dark and serious about her look, like the waters of the Danube between the Black Forest and the Black Mother (Melanie-*melanos*-black ship?). She did not know me: I was reading her work, but I did not have the courage to speak to her. If I had done it would certainly have been in Hungarian, as I knew she had spent a number of years in Hungary.[5] I would have felt awkward at embarrassing her with what might have been inappropriate memories there at the Congress, when she was about to explain, in Viennese-inflected English, that . . . under the influence of the death drive, in phantasy, and by all the means sadism could devise, babies attacked the breast.

It did not occur to me that death would claim Melanie so soon, three years after that Congress, in 1960 – and right under her brooch, in her heart – without my having had a chance to talk to her. I was thirty-two, she was seventy-five. Yet I must have had some presentiment of it, because as I listened to her I kept thinking the same thing. If some Herculean arm would only brush aside the medallion merchants and the showmen of holy writ, I would go up to the boat and rock it with the words I so much wanted to say: 'What was the Danube like when you crossed it to visit Ferenczi? Melanie of the Danube, Melanie of the Stomach, Melanie of the Penis, Melanie of the Breast – what is your real name?'

But she died in 1960, as silent on the subject of her origins as the gulls of Budapest are about where they come from. Thus it was that when some years later Nicolas Abraham and I came to write an introduction to the French edition of Melanie Klein's essays we realized that we knew nothing, or very little, about her 'former' life. As far as her name was concerned, Melanie appeared fixed in the recent past.

And of course it was her husband, from whom she had separated long before, who gave his name to her systems, phantasies, anxieties, myths and dogmas. When we talk about the Kleinian breast, the Kleinian system or Kleinian phantasy, we are evoking the name of Klein, the abandoned engineer. But if not Melanie Klein, then Melanie who? It seemed there was no way of knowing. We received no reply to our letters requesting information. Some years later, looking through the *Jewish Encyclopaedia*, we did come across her name, followed by her maiden name. It struck me then in a flash that Melanie had been ashamed of her name. I put away the *Encyclopaedia* without saying anything.

If it had not been for the Latin-American Congress, in connection with which I remembered Melanie Klein, at a distance, and if it were not that I had also been thinking for some years about the phantom return of suppressed names and, finally, if it were not for the fact that I happened to have been reading about the grant, sale and allocation of names to Jewish nationals under the Austro-Hungarian monarchy, the angel might perhaps never have come. (A good example of the return of repressed names is the fact that the name of the photographer Max Halberstadt, Freud's son-in-law, husband of his dead daughter Sophie, father of Ernst, the 'cotton-reel' child, was not used by his son in adulthood. Nonetheless he exerts a kind of haunting of the analytic family through the vowels that designated his profession, OOA (photographer; *Photograph* in German), both from beyond the grave and from *Beyond the Pleasure Principle* in which those vowels occupy a central position, while the photographer's son, having himself become an analyst, buried his father's name and took instead the name of his grandfather. Thus Ernst Halbstadt, Ernst of the cotton-reel, practised psychoanalysis under the name of Freud.[6] We might also instance Klein's son, who anglicized his name to Clyne).

I might just note in passing that a number of scattered issues were clarified by my curiosity about names. Freud and women is one good example of the way in which a traumatic political situation can thoroughly influence a theory, in this case a very odd theory and one which in the last analysis boils down to one name and one word. *Fraïd* would be the pronunciation of 'woman' (*Frau*) in Yiddish, Freud's mother tongue. For Freud (*Fraïd*) this could make woman (*Fraïd*) a container into which, into whom, he could put all the disembodied horror and fright aroused in him not by her, by woman, but by certain monarchical decisions, by their traps, their prisons, their wish to reduce the number of Jews in their territory, and so forth.

The extreme harshness of the prisons established by the monarchy in the region where the Freuds lived (irons and chains were still in use when Freud was a child) was something which the young Freud was very much aware of. The whole family underwent a serious encounter with the police and the judiciary (some aspects of which Barbro Sylwan and I have described), such that the names of certain prisons could not but have left some mark. *Grauhaus* is the name of one of the two prisons that played a part in the Freud family's life from the time Sigmund was eight or nine years old.[7] If we keep that name constantly in mind, we will no longer be surprised at the theoretical peculiarity, so often repeated and faithfully transmitted, of seeing *Grauen* (horror) as the central point in the child's development. For whole generations of analysts, the woman-wife-mother had to bear within her a horror from which one could only turn away with horror. For good reason, since she is the chosen site of the cryptogram which the discoverer of psychoanalysis placed within her. The drama and the horror of the *Freuds' Grauhaus* became the peculiar theory of *horror* in the face of *woman* (*grau-Frau-Fraïd*).

Over time, as the ear becomes more and more accustomed to reading by decrypting, it becomes progressively more open to listening for and maybe even understanding the roots of Melanie's religion of the Breast, established in the wake of Freud's religion of the Phallus. The advent of the angel has always been more propitious than not as far as the constructors of myths and religions are concerned – I believe that phantasies like myths and religions exist solely to form a screen against a reality that is bitterly unpleasant and therefore unintrojectable. Phantasies use all their power of adornment to cover up the drama and to dull its noise. Lulled by religion, the eyes fail to take in the tension of a situation that is actual, painful and threatening. What, then, is the real drama of shame, threat and persecution that has been occluded by the religion of the Breast? Or, again, which moment of that drama is inscribed within it? It might be possible to respond to this question, of course, by saying that Melanie Klein never suffered any threats or any persecution (except perhaps those she underwent at the hands of Edward Glover and the British Society), and that she never experienced persecution in the flesh. Maybe. But only if suffering in her name, because of her name, feeling pain in all the flesh of her lineage, is granted no significance either. Because her name was Reizes.

Melanie Reizes, daughter of Moritz Reizes; that was the name we had no access to, the name that remained silent in respect of the public signature of her work. Reizes. To understand the implications of the name, we need to consult two sorts of reference book: a dictionary, and a work dealing with the renaming of Jews under the Austrian monarchy. The dictionary gives us 'stimulus'; *Reiz* means 'irritation,' 'excitation,' or 'stimulus,' as for example in *Reizschutz*, a term familiar to analysts [in English a 'protective shield against stimuli' – Tr.]. Imagine being called 'Mr Stimulus' or 'Mr Irritation.' The name probably corresponds to a shortened form of *Reizeskind*, 'child of my stimulus (or excitation),' as *Reizes* is not a nominative, but a genitive, *of* excitation. It is not hard to imagine the taunts the young Melanie would have had to put up with from other schoolchildren. Exciting, excited little girl, daughter of excitation. Etymologically the word is cognate with *reissen*, to snatch or to pull. We may recall Freud's analysis of the word in 'The Rat-Man,' where *sich etwas ausreissen* means to masturbate. In slang, *Reisser* means thief, impostor, etc. By allocating them this name, the authorities clearly dealt a painful blow to the orthodox Jewish family Reizes, who lived in Poland before Moritz, Melanie's father, moved to Vienna.

The Jewish Encyclopaedia, which I consulted, and other specialized works, describes the process of renaming the Jews. In France in the eighteenth century, and in other western countries, this process normally happened in accordance with the general rules governing the adoption of names, deriving them from place-names, town or country of origin, skills, occupations, and so forth. This was not the pattern under the Habsburg Empire – far from it. There a market in names enabled the richest to adopt respectable names, while other less noble or elegant names – and some that were unpleasant or demeaning – were sold to the poor. In addition, those who refused to give up their own system of family names were forced to take on names that were positively injurious or shameful. The *Encyclopaedia* contains a list of these. It needs to be read in order to comprehend the full violence of the process, but I shall spare you the details here. There was one other method, too, which consisted of turning a pet name (such as a mother might give her daughter) into a surname, as for example 'My little flower' (*Blümlein*) might produce *Blume* (flower), as in the names Blum or Bloom.

What can you do with the shadow cast over a name that circumstantial sadism has forced on you? You can run away from it, which may be why Melanie Reizes became engaged at seventeen and married a few years later. After that Melanie gave birth to Melitta, Hans and Eric Klein. She got divorced in the 1920s, but kept her married name for the rest of her life (her son, as already noted, changed its spelling to Clyne).

But even though she was now clothed in her husband's name, the cruelty suffered by her family, and engraved in her maiden name, could not be forgotten. It merely underwent some major modifications in respect of its origin and its status. Instead of deriving from the pain and persecution experienced by the Reizes family in Galicia, it stems from the baby's attack on the breast. It no longer has a status in external reality, but shifts from the experience of reality to the production of phantasy. In the Kleinian system, in fact, everything is phantasy, and the multiple dreams to do with the breast as it is both fondled and attacked constitute our mythic history. One of the most important articulations of the system concerns the way the Good Breast is rooted in the subject at the end of the analytical process. 'The good object has taken root': Melanie lays ponderous emphasis on this aspect of her hopes and her results. In the long run, the Breast, the good, triumphs. With the Breast in his pocket, the 'cured' – not to say sane or healthy – person can set off towards new horizons.

In view of the importance and frequency of occurrence of the word Breast in Melanie's theory, I have hypothesized that the real name of the theory is, in fact, breast, and that its authenticating signature is Breast. But I had never previously imagined that Breast could be a cryptonym, a hidden word, *symbolizing the drama of the allocation of names* that took place over a century ago, and repeated as a phantom in the compulsive gift of the Breast in the course of analysis. Nor would I have known anything about it if the angel had not provided me with that revelation. Let me now tell you just what it was that I heard from him.

I was crossing the Danube in a dream, on my way to Ferenczi-Fraenkel's (Fraenkel was his surname before its magyarization), where Melanie's final session was to take place. I was more than half-an-hour early and I was about to set off for a walk down the street when whom should I see but Melanie leaving the house looking distraught. I realized that Ferenczi had not given her her final session, or else had radically shortened it, and I criticized him vehemently. He defended himself by saying that, contrary to his normal practice, he had been obliged to ask her to leave. Because of the professor. The professor had arrived unexpectedly in Budapest from Vienna and Ferenczi had to go and meet him at the station. Seeing me increasingly gloomy and accusatory, Ferenczi said to me, 'But she doesn't need me any more, she understands everything, look how well she understands children.' 'Maybe she does understand children, but does she understand her name? She is down in your book as Melanie Klein, and her daughter, at the lycée, is written down as Melitta Klein.' At that moment, in the dream, I realized the doubling of *mel* in *Melanie* and *Melitta*. And I saw Ferenczi strike his forehead, dash into the street, and run through the avenues and over the bridges of Budapest. Alas Melanie, little Melanie, was already in the train on the way to meet Karl Abraham, the father of cannibalistic incorporation.

When the alarm-clock went off, *mel-mel* was still ringing in my ears. And I understood the effects of persecution: the anguish of shame. Hurt and ashamed, without knowing it, of a name that had been in her family for generations, Melanie proceeded thus: she divided her forename into syllables and gave a fraction of it (the first syllable) to her daughter. Then she hears this syllable in Hungarian so that – translated into all other languages – it becomes the universal symbol of a solid, establishable and good religion, a religion that no monarch would ever want to abolish or persecute. Because *mell*, the syllable *mel* pronounced in Hungarian, means breast.

26 December 1980

MT

I finished writing this on Boxing Day 1980. On 5 January I received a telephone call from Barbro Sylwan in Vienna.

Part 2 Story of a journey to the land of Melanie Mell

On Monday 4 January this year, a day that in Vienna, Austria, is a pale oasis of everyday life in a desert of holidays, I was in the Vienna University Library, as the National Library was of course closed. Time was precious, and even though my curiosity had been aroused by the 'Melanie Mell' that had been ringing in my ears since I had heard it, as you have just heard it now, I was drawn first of all to Freud's 'phantom.'

I wanted to find documentary evidence about the conditions of detention in certain Austrian prisons at the period when Freud was a child and his father's brother was incarcerated, and consequently of the real and traumatic foundations of a whole area of the conceptualization and mise-en-scène of psychoanalysis. To mention just some of the most obvious concepts and metaphors: silence, frustration, isolation, renunciation, work, dream-work, work of mourning, keys, or better, master-keys, trial or process (*Prozess*), admissions, verdicts, judgements, chains, associative chains, chains of thought, links, energy, bound and free, and the pierced and bound feet of baby Oedipus. Nor should we overlook the meaning of the mother-word of psychoanalysis in Greek: *analusis* from *luein*, to free from chains, the chains that in 1867 shackled the legs of those people in Austria who were condemned to 'severe imprisonment.'

In the chapter of *The Interpretation of Dreams* dealing with 'typical' dreams, which Freud interprets as the child's wish that either his brothers and sisters or the parent of the opposite sex should die, he writes that 'Children know nothing of the horrors of corruption, of freezing in the ice-cold grave, of the terrors of eternal nothingness.'[8] The grave that the child is meant to know nothing about might well be very like a gaol. One prison director gave evidence that certain forms of scurvy were caused not only by malnutrition but also by the irons the prisoners wore on their ankles. On a less tragic note there is the anecdote, cited by Freud, about the Jewish marriage-broker who assures the suitor that the girl's father is no longer living. After the betrothal, he admits that the bride's father is serving a prison sentence. Accused of lying, the marriage-broker defends himself. 'Well, what did I tell you? You surely don't call that living?'[9] This description of the grave provokes a question: which of the adults in Sigmund's childhood environment is expressing, through Freud's voice, the idea that children are unaware of the death represented by imprisonment which we, as Freud's readers, immediately interpret as death itself and attitudes to it?

I was relying on finding the information I wanted about prisons in an old exhibition catalogue, not obtainable elsewhere, entitled 'The Grey House' (*das graue Haus*). Earlier that morning I had ventured inside the pale grey edifice of the *Landesgericht*, the Vienna County Court and prison, and exchanged a few words with one of the attendants on duty in the hall. I asked him in passing if this was the building that used to be called 'The Grey House.' The man, who was about thirty-five, strong, large and well-built, as he needed to be in his job, shuddered from head to toe, leaned back in his chair, tilting it back, then recovered himself and smilingly assured me that the modern institution had nothing in common with the name I'd just uttered, and that really it was quite wrong of me to say such inappropriate things.

'The world is so full of phantoms' (to paraphrase a paraphrase) that I ended up giving in to the call of Reizes, despite my worries about time and the bother involved in finding the material.

I looked up Reizes in the author catalogue, vaguely thinking that Melanie's father, the Vienna doctor Moritz Reizes, might have written or inspired something, or left some trace or other that might lead me to his family origins, his background, his career, or the pattern of his life. We know from the chapter on Melanie Klein in Uwe Peters' book on Anna Freud that Moritz Reizes broke with orthodox Judaism when he left a community in Poland (where in Poland?) to study medicine in Vienna at the advanced age of thirty-seven. He specialized in surgery of the jaw.[10] What could have been the circumstances underlying that break, and what might have led him to the jaw in particular?

We know something about the effects of ruptures of this sort, where there is an attempt to suppress the wounds and sores associated with their causes through the silence of the person who is both their agent and their victim. We understand them more fully since Freud's treatment of Sophocles' version of the Oedipus myth. It is silent about the father's rejection of the child, and about the reasons for it, silent about the mother who completes the action of exposing the child by handing him over to the shepherd, silent about Jocasta's silences, silent about the pain inflicted on the child's body and feet, silent about the time spent with each of the shepherds, silent about the silence of Oedipus's adoptive parents at Corinth, a silence that is first of all omission and then a lie. The lie comes in response to Oedipus's question as to whether his parents really were his parents, when he is told not to believe the words of a drunkard. All that remains of Sophocles' play in Freud's version is what we all know: the murder of the father and the incest with the mother as the effect of universal, instinctual, unconscious desires, with blindness, that is 'castration,' as punishment. This is a drama, in short, that is solely concerned with the child.

Under 'Reizes' I found an index card lettered in Gothic script, which read: 'Reizes, Emmanuel, *Aus einem Leben*, Wien, 1906'. Glimpses of a life. While I was waiting for the book to arrive, I opened the *Jewish Encyclopaedia* at the name 'Reizes,' just on the offchance, and came upon an article recounting the martyrdom of two brothers of that name in Poland at the beginning of the eighteenth century, which I reproduce here. Humanity does not change, the stake always finds new enthusiasts.

REIZES (also Reizeles: in Hebrew [. . .]): Hayyim ben Isaac Ha-Levy (1687–1728), and his brother Joshua (1697–1728), rabbis and Jewish martyrs in Poland. Hayyim was a wealthy and learned man. He held the positions of *av bet din* at Lvov (Lemberg) and Rabbi at Kamenka-Bugskaya. Also a member of the Provincial Committee. Director of a yeshiva (talmudic school) in Lvov. In the spring of 1728 the Bishop of Lvov accused the two brothers and other prominent members of the city's Jewish community of attempts to influence Jan Filipowicz, a Jewish apostate, to return to Judaism, and of profaning the Christian symbols he wore. The Reizes brothers were arrested, interrogated, tortured by the Tribunal of the Inquisition, and condemned to the stake. Information about the tragedy of the brothers derives from both Jewish and Catholic sources. According to the Jesuit source, Joshua committed suicide in prison, and his body was broken and then burned at the stake. It also tells how, on the day that Hayyim was to be burned at the stake, a priest made an attempt to convert him in exchange for a pardon 'but was unable to extract anything from his obstinate breast' ('*Sed nihil evicit in obstinato pectore*'). The brothers' property was confiscated and used to finance reinforcement work on the city walls. On the eve of Shavuot, the anniversary of the death of the martyred brothers, a commemorative religious service was regularly held in the Nahmanovich synagogue in Lvov for the repose of their souls.

Despite the familiarity that modernity has given stories like this, I was feeling disturbed by the torture and martyrdom of the Reizes brothers of Lemberg over two hundred and fifty years ago as I returned to my table and found Emmanuel Reizes's book. On the title page I read 'Posthumous works, published by Melanie Klein-Reizes and Irma Schneider-Schönfeld'. Posthumous works – *Aus dem Nachlass*. Here, I said to myself, Melanie is not hiding the name Reizes behind that of Klein. In the absence of any other example of the same signature, we can think of it as a gift from sister to brother, and an inscription of their family bond.

I was also fascinated by the announcement on the same page of a preface by Georg Brandes. In everyone's life there are some names that are familiar, as if they were part of one's family, but whose content is either lost or insufficiently filled in. For me, the name of Georg Brandes is one of them. He was a major figure in literary criticism in Denmark, and throughout educated Europe in the late nineteenth and early twentieth century. Years ago I had read his correspondence and the narrative of his love affair with a Swedish woman writer. I also knew that Freud had read his book on Shakespeare and had met him in Vienna. But how did his name come to be sharing this title page with Melanie Klein-Reizes? I have subsequently tried to find the answer to this question, but so far without success. Meanwhile the preface told me about Emmanuel Reizes and the history of the book I was holding in my hands. I quote Brandes: 'The author of this book died in December 1902 at the age of twenty-five, after long years of suffering. His sisters' love for him meant that they wanted to save his name from oblivion; they could not rest until they had laid before the public the unfinished manuscript, full of life and intellectual vitality, left by their brother as the only souvenir of his short life. The book which we now have is, at all events, the result of their affectionate respect. [. . .] Emmanuel Reizes, son of a doctor, developed twofold heart disease when he was thirteen. As he grew older, he became fully aware of its implications, and calculated that he would not live beyond the age of twenty-five or thirty. [. . .] His condition worsened, slowly but surely, with intermittent and extremely painful crises lasting throughout the period of his illness, and constituting nothing less than a protracted *martyrdom* which he bore with heroism.' Against the advice of his parents and his doctor, Emmanuel studied medicine for three years. He then felt, Brandes tells us, that he needed to travel. 'His over-stimulated (*überreizten*) nerves could no longer put up with the monotony of his existence.' His parents, who were not well-off, found enough money for him to spend six months in Italy. We are now in January 1900. He returned to Vienna, very ill, in June, and learned that his father had died, a fact that had been kept from him. One can imagine good reasons for that silence, but one can also imagine that this exclusion of the son from his father's interment, and the very fact of keeping his death a secret, is nothing but a repetition, an effect of the phantom's characteristic requirement of nescience. One might also imagine that there were elements of tragedy surrounding the father's death which needed to be kept from a young man suffering from a weak heart.

So there I was with this book, leafing through it with no clear idea about where to begin reading. I couldn't borrow it, I wanted to photocopy it but I couldn't because the photocopier was in constant use. Then I noticed, on their own, printed in bold at the top of a page, the two words, *Die Melone*, The Melon. The MEL of MELanie and MELOn came together like the two complementary pieces of a *symbolon*. 'The Melon' turned out to be a Platonic dialogue between two philosophers, master and pupil, Kainokephalikos, the Head, and Gasterokainos, the Stomach (I'm ignoring the implications of 'kainos,' meaning 'new'). The two philosophers, Head and Stomach, contemplate and discuss different aspects of the melon: form, colour, the way its appearance changes in sun and in shadow, its surface and its interior, even the possibility of its non-existence. In the end the melon turns into the breasts of a beautiful girl. I quote. 'her breasts are shining, and as round as the snow-covered hills of the mountains of Boeotia.' A girl with breasts who maybe has the name of one of the author's loving sisters, Melanie-Melonie, Mel. There is a letter from Emmanuel to his sister which could be a possible mark of this love. Emmanuel, thinking he was about to fulfil his long-held desire of going to Spain, wrote to her four days before his death: 'If only it could go on like this for long enough, if only things could be even deeper, richer and fiercer, for You, for me and for everything we love!'

And so the story continues – Melanie Mell, Melanie Breast, melonie. Nor should we forget Sidonie, the sister who died at the age of nine, when Melanie was five and Emmanuel ten tears old. The Reizes family resembles the martyrs of the same name, even coming originally from the same city, Lemberg (Melberg?). Emmanuel, the martyred brother, the little martyr. Little = *klein*; martyr = Martyr. Arthur Klein, fiancé and later husband of Melanie. Arthur Klein: *kleiner Martyr*: little martyr. And there's the stake, the fire that runs throughout the pages beneath her brother's signature that I've read, and the passages quoted by Brandes. Then there's also *Reiz*, excitation, *reissen*, to pull, *Reissen*, pain in the joints, *reisen*, to travel, *zerreissen*, to tear, *hetzen*, to excite or agitate, *heiss*, hot, ardent, feverish, but also, as *heissen*, to name or be called. Listen to Emmanuel: 'I am an immense wound of pain, it burns me like flame, like the fires of hell.' Emmanuel Reizes, in short, comes across as a young *martyr*, *obstinately* struggling against the pain that *tears* at his *chest – obstinato pectore –* a picture very reminiscent of the martyrs of Lemberg.

These fragmentary words, traces, and vestiges of inexpressible events, filtered unaware through a parent's silence, will return to assail mother and psychoanalyst Melanie Klein in the mouths of her sons 'Felix' and 'Fritz.' But Melanie's ear, deaf to their appeal, translates them and betrays them into symbolic equations, true phantom-concealers.

In parenthesis, or apparent parenthesis, let me say something else about Georg Brandes in his capacity as author of the preface to Emmanuel Reizes' book. Flames are present even here: looked at in the same light as 'Reizes,' his name reveals them, for *Brand* means fire, conflagration and *Brandes* is the genitive 'of fire.' Brandes, born in Copenhagen in 1842, was Jewish, and his paternal grand-father was called Cohen. His grandmother's second husband was called Brandes, and the Cohen children took his name. Brandes was neither a believing nor a practising Jew. He had had his Bar-Mitzvah, but never went to a synagogue after that; his mother, otherwise a highly cultivated woman, had not even read the Bible. He was on familiar terms with the cultural aristocracy of all the capitals of Europe, and corresponded with everybody. He intervened ceaselessly against the persecution of minorities, against nationalism, and against racism of every sort and description. 'Every human being alive today has tens of thousands of ancestors. One would have to be very naïve to believe they could all be part of the same tribe.'

Brandes made several extended visits to Poland between 1885 and 1895, and devoted a very interesting book to the country, which he described as suffocating beneath the foreign domination of Russia. Yet although he claimed to 'love Poland as much as liberty' he took up his pen again on behalf of the Polish Jews who were suffering persecution after the defeat of Tannenberg in August 1914. The article he wrote, 'published in Copenhagen and extensively reprinted in the European and American press, expressed vigorous condemnation both of Tsarist power and Polish russophiles. He was particularly critical of Polish intellectuals for, at best, their silence and at worst their participation in the campaign of anti-Semitism.'[11]

It may be objected that this is a digression, but in fact it is leading up to my basic point, which is that psychoanalysis, as thought, written down and bequeathed to us by Sigmund Freud, and as continued by Melanie Klein who greatly extended the universalizing reductions inherent in Freud's work, is a kind of defence, a rampart built both out of the stones of inexpressible suffering and as a wall against that suffering, and against the evocation of martyrs, both distant and near at hand. Both theory and practice seem to conform to the phantoms from which they arise and whose pain and shame they cover up. It had to be the case that whereas Sigmund Freud, Melanie Klein and Georg Brandes each in their place and time had reason to be concerned about the threats that weighed on them and brooded over their lives, it was the one who did not found a religion, the one who was not a psychoanalyst, who was the only one to raise his voice to say that he was aware of both martyrs and torturers.

Even if you trace only one slender thread of these events, it is impossible to escape from fire festivals. At the *Totenfeierfest*, the annual celebration of those who died on 9 November 1923, the annual anniversary of the failed putsch, at which the names of those who died in it were remembered, Hitler would deliver a violently racist, anti-semitic speech to the veterans. This verbal violence increasingly aroused violent action, culminating – before the war – in the *Kristallnacht* of 9–10 November 1938. Every synagogue in Germany was sacked and set on fire, individuals were humiliated, dispossessed and massacred, transported to Dachau, Buchenwald and Sachsenhausen. The fifteen years between 1923 and 1938 was a period during which German-speaking Jews had daily experience of the violence of their persecutors' hatred.

BS

Part 3   Transition

Armed with this new documentation – the preface, the book, the story of the Melon, the case of the martyrs, and Uwe Peters's 1979 biographical information – the three of us, Barbro Sylwan, Adèle Covello and myself, decided to re-read Melanie Klein's essays in the hope of casting further light on the phantom, and then to compare notes. The following is a brief summary of our findings.

*

In 1923, after the first operation on Freud's jaw, Karl Abraham wrote him a letter. Not out of compassion, or a wish to console him, but in order to tell him various items of good news. One of the 'pleasant' things that he reports has to do with Dr Melanie Klein. The Doctor (both the French and the English translations omit the designation) had successfully treated a case of infantile melancholia, by applying Karl Abraham's theory of 'cannibalistic' incorporation.

This letter from Freud's friend in Berlin suggests a number of lines of enquiry that cannot be followed up here. But we can glimpse a few of them in relation to the information we have only fairly recently acquired about the name and profession of the father, Dr Moritz Reizes, the break with his orthodox past, and the fact that during this period (that is, during her stay in Berlin in 1923) when Melanie was commenting on the cases of the children she was analysing, she was commenting primarily on the case of her own children. Not that there is any reason to criticize a mother's desire to help her children overcome their intellectual obstacles by using the analysis she practised, but there is something strange and disturbing in reading the step-by-step description of their symptoms and the apparent reasons for them, both because of the minutely scrupulous description of details and, more centrally, because of the framework set up by the narrative, as Adèle Covello points out.

There seem to be two Melanies here: Melanie, and her neighbour Melanie. Who is describing what? Karl Abraham, who encouraged Melanie (*die Frau Doktor Melanie*) in her work, seems to imply that there was a doctor *within* Melanie, and in fact he may have been right. There is a Doktor, who specializes in maladies of incorporation, maladies of the mouth, the teeth and the jaw muscles: Doktor Reizes. He could have operated on Freud if he was still alive. (And if he could understand Freud's incorporation malady. For let us not forget the famous *C.C. Coraggio Casimiro* that circulated between Freud and Abraham in their correspondence.)[12] It is thus Dr Moritz Reizes who provides the scrupulous descriptions of the two children Felix and Fritz from the viewpoints of a doubled Melanie, doubled both as mother and analyst, and as Melanie and Dr Reizes (her father's phantom). These are her positions as she undertakes the interpretation of her sons Hans and Eric. How does she set about it?

She does so precisely in the manner of a former orthodox Talmudist turned atheist: very scrupulously and very scientifically. Additionally, she wants to bear witness, to make public her intention to use all her authority and expertise to extend the jurisdiction of the laws of unbridled rationalism to encompass the child. There is nothing in the sky except air and clouds; no angels, no God, no Father Christmas. If only Arthur, Arthur Klein, could be somewhere else. Because when he is present, he tells a different story as he believes in God. So the child being analysed, and trying in vain through secret words and unmasked words to reach his mother's hidden (Reizes) identity – she with her 'little-martyr' Emmanuel (as Barbro Sylwan puts it) beside her – feels torn apart and cries out for her to tell him whether or not locksmiths and trains really exist.

The desire on the part of an internal Reizes to bear witness to the break with traditional beliefs can be seen clearly in the series of articles Melanie wrote over the next few years, with 'A Contribution to the Psychogenesis of Tics' providing final and decisive evidence of their abandonment. Melanie's son Felix (Hans), who was to die at the age of twenty-seven (her brother Emmanuel died at twenty-six), suffered from a very serious tic, as a consequence of so-called inhibitions about masturbation in the wake of a phimosis.[13] Note: a phimosis and two operations, one when he was three-and-a-half, the other when he was about ten. 'I, Doctor Moritz Reizes, of Wien, Tiefer Graben 8 ('Tiefer Graben' means 'deep grave') – I, Doctor Moritz Reizes of the Deep Grave, hereby inform the world that my son does not bear the marks of membership of the Jewish family on his body, and never has done. If he is suffering from a tic, that is bound up with the primitive sadististic scene, Oedipus, bad mother, bad breast, stomach pains, etc., and not, let it be understood, because I, Moritz Reizes, am suffering from not being able to say what I am suffering from, as concerns my ancestors, their suffering, and their rage, as well as from not wanting, from *no longer* wanting, to share their martyrs with them. I do not want any more pogroms, any more stakes, any more deaths.'

The best way to summarize all this is to go back, briefly, to Melanie's childhood, where we can see the characteristics that mark the children of parents with a secret. In a family ruled by the law of nescience, the brother–sister relation goes beyond the normal attraction of a libidinal exchange of mingled love and hate. Alliances are created in order simultaneously to read and to stifle the things that neither can nor should be thought about. Emmanuel's essay on 'The Melon' seems to spring from a comparable alliance: one word has escaped from the past that bears the tension of the problem of martyrdom *or* conversion. In his own way he enacts his life by incarnating himself first in the one, then in the other. Is it conceivable that Emmanuel did not wonder about the *black* ('melanos') inscribed in Melanie's name? Must he not, as a young scholar, have believed, deep down, that his sister incarnated, bore a *message*? The text of 'The Melon' shows that he did, and that it was a message traced in her by an invisible hand so that she was never in a position to read it, and yet was the guarantee of its survival and its secrecy. Because that is the effect of the nescience required by the parents' secret.

Through the Melon-mel of Melanie, Emmanuel carries the inscription of the *blackness* of Melanie into his hiding-place: the snowy (white) hill-breasts (*mell*). Similarly the cold of Boeotia, we could say, refers to the burning stake in Galicia. And there, at that stake, burns an *obstinatus pectus*, the same obstinate survival of the *mel* in the brother's Platonic dialogue as in the sister's theoretical system.

Melanie Mell – a fairy-tale. A fiction, but not without foundation. 1934 was not just any year. In 1933 the stake was lit once again in Germany, this time for the burning of books, including the works of Freud, condemned by impious words. Under Melanie's pen, what will become *the* system begins to take shape with the publication of 'A Contribution to the Psychogenesis of Manic-Depressive States', a case we believe to be that of Eric Clyne (cylinder).[14] In this text she describes him as talking obsessively about execution, burning bodies, flaming limbs, boiling oil, frizzling human skin, and Melanie who is in danger of turning a man into a fire. Meanwhile, contemporary history was en route to *Kristallnacht*, when the Nazis set fire to the synagogues, and to six million Reizes gassed and burned.

And Melanie? She sets up a scenario which she reads in terms of the sadism of babies and, as its counterpart, the struggle of the *pectus obstinatus*. But this time it is a different sort of *pectus*. Here is a breast from which *everything* can be extracted. A breast that does convert. In the place of the historical *nihil* we now have *omnia*. And *omnia vicit amor*. The love of the breast triumphs. At a stroke the torturer ceases to be an object of fear. It is a child. Just a child, confronting a play-martyr who is its analyst. Once established, the system of the Good Breast (Good Mel) becomes an ideal barrier against the fear of sadism. By which we mean both the sadism of the stake suffered by the Reizes and the contemporary flames of Nazi Germany. Given its origins in this historical violence, there was only one choice her system could make.

MT

Part 4   Melanie Mell at work

In 1919, at the request of her analyst, Melanie Klein presented her observations of Fritz in a lecture entitled 'The Development of a Child'.[15] What followed is well known: Melanie Klein, working in the Freudian tradition, substantiated the Master's theory of the infantile origin of neuroses, demonstrated that the analysis of very young children was possible and practicable and that such early analysis was beneficial to the child's development and capable of preventing future disturbances and, finally, was an inexhaustible source of unexpected revelations about the origins of the good and bad functioning of the human psychic apparatus.

This fundamental discovery, which has so often been verified and re-verified during sixty years of the psychoanalysis of children, cannot be undermined by Uwe Peters' observation that the children whose analysis Melanie Klein recounts from 1919 to 1925 were Eric and Hans Klein. In retrospect, this observation is obvious; it does not constitute a revelation, but it does relieve a sense of uneasiness in the reader's mind; an unsettling strangeness and an impression of ponderousness, even of confusion, can be created by the minutely scrupulous description of details, by the temporal unfolding of the scenes, by the succession of replies, and by the organization of the narrative framework, in which a veritable avalanche of perennial questions elicits responses from one or other of the two Melanies, Melanie-mother and Melanie her pleasant neighbour. Melanie Klein's scheme for producing blindness and disavowal seems to me to be exemplary of a phantom-effect, as does the persistence of this hypnotic effect on generations of analysts.

Ernest Jones underlines the hypnotic effect of Melanie Klein's writings (an attitude already demonstrated in relation to Freud)[16] by recalling 'the stupendous difficulties'[17] she had to surmount in order to overcome the prejudices of parents and their anxieties about the unknown effects of psychoanalysis on children's development. In the literary fiction employed by Melanie Klein, the other mother (Mrs Reizes?) is extremely docile and manageable. 'As his mother follows all my recommendations I am able to exercise a far-reaching effect on the child's upbringing.'[18]

This misapprehension is not far removed from child psychoanalysis's almost conventional distrust of the bad mother, who is always suspected of wanting to hinder, hamper or even put a stop to her child's psychotherapy. It is all the more strange therefore that, according to her daughter, Melitta Schmideberg, when Melanie Klein came to London at Ernest Jones's invitation, in 1926, she began to analyse the children of several eminent analysts, among others the children of Jones (and, of course, of Mrs Jones). 'Jones regarded the first [*sic*] Kleinian child-analysis as of such historic significance that he set up a glass case containing the toys used in it, as a permanent exhibition at the clinic.'[19] According to Ernest Jones, Melanie Klein did not allow any obstacle to stand in her way, because of 'her amazing moral courage.'[20]

Let's take the 'moral' part first. If the child's repression generates 'shame' and pointless suffering, and if getting rid of it lays the foundations for sanity, mental equilibrium, and harmonious character development, as well as having a decisive effect on the growth of the child's intellectual powers, all of which Melanie Klein appears firmly to have believed in 1919, why wouldn't she have applied the psychoanalytic method to her own children?

And as far as courage is concerned, it must be admitted that a married woman of the Viennese bourgeoisie, with three children aged five, thirteen and fifteen, would have needed plenty of it to ignore her own family and spend all day in the house of her immediate neighbour, deeply involved with her children of five, thirteen and fifteen. She was there every day from dawn till nightfall, while the children were eating, getting dressed, going to bed, even when little Fritz was doing his 'kaki' on the pot. She takes advantage of that situation to provide us (and him) with the first authoritative course of sex education. Fritz 'is sitting early in the morning on the chamber,'[21] where this 'unaggressive and gentle'[22] child poses a series of questions, usually to his mother or to Mrs Klein. And if, having started on an explanation, his mother had to go and do something else, that did not matter, as Mrs Klein could take up the thread and complete the explanation from the precise point at which the mother had had to leave off, without any interruption, either real or symbolic. Everybody accepted this eagerly, from Fritz onwards.

At times the literary presentation creates the illusion that the two mothers were both present simultaneously, one the other's shadow, her phantom, her double, 'risen from the grave.' One example amid several will illustrate this. 'Another time he referred to the processes in the bowel that his mother had explained to him in connection with the enema, and asked about the hole where the 'kakis' came from. While doing so he told *me* that he had looked, or wanted to look, at this hole. He asked whether the toilet paper was for the others too? Then . . . '*Mama, you* make kakis too, don't you?' When she agreed he remarked, 'Because if you didn't make kakis nobody in the world would make them, would they?'[23]

In the course of the discussion that followed her lecture to the Hungarian Psycho-Analytic Society, Dr Anton Freund made two comments to Melanie Klein: one on the conscious and/or unconscious content of the patient's words, and the other on the place and time of the analysis.[24] Dr Freund pointed out that her 'observations and classifications were certainly analytical, but not [her] interpretations,' and further that she should not 'make the analysis the business of life.' What was happening was that 'at night when he should go to sleep [the child] will state that an idea that must be discussed at once has occurred to him. Or he tries to draw attention to himself throughout the day with the same plea and comes along at unsuitable times with his phantasies.' It was therefore necessary to 'set a certain time – even if this had occasionally to be changed – aside for the analysis', and adhere to it steadfastly, even though, 'owing to [their] close daily association', the analyst/mother and the child were often together.[25]

This was well-considered intervention by Freund: a continuous session between a mother and her children smacks of torture, and speaking of nothing except psychoanalysis might easily seem like persecution.[26] Once we know its origins, we can understand the absolute obligation on Kleinians to observe and maintain strict neutrality towards the child, and the proscription of any interference in the child's 'milieu' and of any educative purpose. Until 1932 this strict technical orthodoxy had the dual function of drawing attention away from the first psycho-analyses of Melanie/mother, and of reaffirming, by denying, the strict orthodoxy of the grandparents (the Talmudist-atheist father and the mother who was the daughter of a rabbi).[27] In fact, there are several doublings: the literary fiction produces the analyst and her double, the co-operative neighbouring mother; the child and its parents; and Melanie Klein (the mother) with her children Hans and Eric. Each of these couples echoes the metapsychological couple of Melanie Klein and her phantom father, Dr Moritz Reizes.

Melanie Klein's theory is thus constantly written and effaced, denied and affirmed, translated into unconscious phantasy or into manifest content, in relation to a couple. As Nicolas Abraham puts it, the person 'haunted' by the phantom is caught between two movements: they have to 'at all costs maintain their ignorance of a loved one's secret; hence the semblance of unawareness (nescience) concerning it. At the same time they must eliminate the state of secrecy; hence the reconstruction of the secret in the form of unconscious knowledge.'[28]

From 1919 to 1933 the orthodox-Talmudist-atheist father continued to bear witness to the break with his traditions through the words of his daughter and his grandchildren. The pages devoted to demonstrating the serious harm done to children by a religious education deserve a full re-reading. They are premonitory of what would some years later become the fanatical religion of the Breast: 'The idea of an invisible, omnipotent and omniscient deity is overwhelming for the child [. . .] it overwhelms thought by the authoritative introduction of a powerful insuperable authority, and the decline of the omnipotence-feeling [. . .] is also interfered with. [. . .] This idea of God can so shatter the reality-sense that it [the child] dare not reject the incredible, the apparently unreal, and can so affect it that the recognition of the tangible, the near-at-hand, the so-called 'obvious' things in intellectual matters, is repressed [. . .] The injury done can vary in kind and degree; it may affect the mind as a whole or in one or other dimension to a greater or lesser extent; it is certainly not obviated by a subsequent enlightened upbringing. [. . .] It does not therefore suffice merely to omit dogma and the methods of the confessional from the child's training, although their inhibiting effects on thought are more generally recognized. To introduce the idea of God into education and then leave it to individual development to deal with [means that the child] is so much influenced that he can never again, or only at the cost of great struggles and expense of energy, free himself from it.'[29]

The son-grandson believes in the devil, the Easter hare, Father Christmas, angels and in a God who makes rain and lives in the sky. There is no longer any possibility of evasion, despite the father-husband-son-in-law and his pantheistic conception of the deity. A decision has to be made. 'There is no god [. . .] only air and clouds in the sky.' Eric/Fritz replies, 'I think too that there is no God. [. . .] But electric cars are real, and there are trains too – I was once in one, once when I went to Grandmamma's and once when I went to E.'[30]

The aftermath of these journeys is well-known.[31] Fritz went on to develop a phobia about journeys, drives and walks, and an obsessional and compulsive interest in vehicles and games about vehicles;[32] his mother relates in detail in 1923 all the material in the second stage of the analysis that has to do with journeys, expeditions, trains and electric cars.[33]

The first theoretical hypothesis and the first words of the theory and of the phantom come from the mouth of the child. It is to Fritz that we owe the split between the good and bad mother. In order to please his mother, Fritz had resigned himself two years earlier to saying that God did not exist while on the other hand for ever trying to persuade his mother that there were such things as witches. 'The child said he was afraid of witches because, all the same, it might be that it wasn't true what he had been told about there not being any witches really. There are queens also who are beautiful and yet who are witches too.' He readily admitted to his analyst/mother that 'when he was angry he had wished that she as well as his papa might die.'[34] 'The witch,' Melanie Klein continues (why not the queen?), 'only introduces a figure [. . .] that he had, it seems to me, obtained by division of the mother-imago. [. . .] This second female imago that he has split off from his beloved mother, in order to maintain her as she is, is the woman with the penis.'[35] Two years later (when Fritz is nine) he will complete the theory of dismemberment by introducing a touch of cannibalism (this is in 1923 and Karl Abraham is present).

'Fritz had a marked inhibition in doing long division sums, all explanations proving unavailing, for he understood them quite well, but always did these sums wrong. He told me once that in doing long division he had first of all to bring down the figure that was required and he climbed up, seized it by the arm and pulled it down. To my enquiry as to what it said to that, he replied that quite certainly it was not pleasant for the number – it was as if his mother stood on a stone 13 yards high and someone came and caught her by the arm and tore it out and divided her. Shortly beforehand, however, he has phantasized about a woman in the circus who was sawn in pieces, and then nevertheless comes to life again, and now he asked me whether this were possible. He then related (also in connection with a previously elaborated phantasy) that actually every child wants to have a bit of his mother, who is to be cut into four pieces; he depicted quite exactly how she screamed and had paper stuffed in her mouth so that she could not scream, and what kind of faces she made, etc. A child took a very sharp knife, and he described how she was cut up;[36] first across the width of the breast, and then of the belly, then lengthwise so that the *pipi* (penis), the face and the head were cut exactly through the middle, whereby the 'sense'[37] was taken out of her head. The head was then again cut through obliquely just as the '*pipi*' was cut across its breadth. Betweenwhiles he constantly bit at his hand and said that he bit his sister too for fun, but certainly for love. He continued that every child then took the piece of the mother that it wanted, and agreed that the cut-up mother was then also eaten. It now appeared also that he always confused the remainder with the quotient in division, and always wrote it in the wrong place, because in his mind it was bleeding pieces of flesh with which he was unconsciously dealing. These interpretations completely removed his inhibition with regard to division.'[38]

Melanie Klein describes Fritz's verbalization as 'interpretation.' From then on, all good Kleinians have used Fritz's words to 'interpret' every child's 'inhibition with regard to division.' The child calls up the phantom: tear–cut–journey, Reizes, Reizes, Reizes; the psychoanalyst/mother/Reizes replies, 'He's not saying anything important, he's just playing with toy cars.'

It is she herself, the psychoanalyst/mother/Reizes, who has to translate everything into the universal and terrifying unconscious phantasy, into oral, sadistic and cannibalistic tendencies. If the child speaks spontaneously about cutting, tearing, burning, biting and eating, what universal language could she translate it into?

The problem of the place and duration of the analytic session, and the extra-analytic relations between child and analyst, have continued to haunt Melanie Klein and her pupils ever since. When she came to recount the analysis of Hans/Felix in 1925, she tried to deal with it by loading the reader with inaccurate details: Felix 'came to analysis only three times a week, and as his treatment was repeatedly interrupted, the analysis of 370 hours was drawn out over three and a quarter years.'[39]

Herr Reizes was thirty-seven when he broke with his orthodox past and began to study medicine. At the age of three, Felix was obliged to bear on his body the marks of belonging to a Jewish family. The sequence of threes recurs constantly and remarkably in Felix's 'symptom'. 'At the age of three a stretching of the foreskin was performed on him, and the connection between this stretching and masturbation was specially impressed on him. His father, too, had repeatedly given warnings and even threatened the boy; and as a result of these threats Felix was determined to give up masturbation.'[40]

When this intervention was repeated – when he was ten – he gave up masturbation entirely, but started to suffer an anxiety about contact (an excellent testimony to the surgeon's break with the Judaic tradition!). When he was eleven, he had to have a nasal examination,[41] 'and this reactivated his trauma connected with the surgical manipulation when he was three and led to a renewal of the struggle against masturbation, this time with complete success.'[42]

'Up to his sixth year he had shared his parents' bedroom and his observations of parental intercourse had left a lasting impression on him. [. . .] As a very young child he had enjoyed singing, but at about the age of three he had given it up.'[43] 'The tic comprised three phases. At the beginning Felix had a feeling as though the depression in his neck, under the back of his head, were being *torn* (*reissen*). In consequence of this feeling he felt constrained first to throw his head back and then to rotate it from right to left. The second movement was accompanied by a feeling that something was *cracking* loudly. The concluding phase consisted of a third movement in which the chin was pressed as deeply as possible downward. This gave Felix a feeling of drilling into something. For a time he performed these three movements three times over consecutively. One meaning of the 'three' was that in the tic [says the mother/analyst] Felix played three rôles: the passive rôle of his mother, the passive rôle of his own ego, and the active rôle of his father.'[44]

To her children's words as they seek the phantom, whether these take the form of questions or of symptoms, the phantom replies with the law of nescience. To begin with, it uses the keywords of Freud's theory, but the theory of an other does not provide sufficient guarantees. 'A ghost [*fantôme*] returns to haunt with the intent of lying: its would-be "revelations" are false by nature.'[45] The first pieces of the theoretical edifice are thus put in place in order to bury the inadmissible secret with the universality of symbolic equations and unconscious phantasy.

The Reizes phantom will talk theory, and will speak in order to counter and deny whatever the child says by translating it into unconscious phantasy. Unconscious phantasy has to be universal, with an identical content for each subject in so far as it is the mental expression of libidinal and destructive drives; it must therefore influence and alter the perception and interpretation of reality. The unconscious phantasy thus permanently prohibits any route towards the secret buried in Melanie and her family. Thanks to the 'machinery' called phantasy, Doctor Reizes can hide her story and silence her identity.

But the dramatic external events that were about to unfold in Europe prevented Fritz/Eric and Felix/Hans from continuing to operate the phantasy 'machinery': the 'I don't want to share their martyrdom, I don't want any more pogroms, or burnings at the stake, or death' becomes 'It's got nothing to do with all that because there's no external persecutor to put such an insane project into practice.'

So it is not a question of 'mak[ing] the phantom appear in the light of day, so that, once known, understood and exorcised, the phantom should go from our unconscious, vanish into the reality whence it had come, disappear into a bygone and vanquished world.'[46] The dead man's words buried within Melanie get increasingly involved with external events as Hitler's persecution comes to resonate more and more with what the dead man had found inadmissible. She left Eastern Europe in 1926 in the hope of forgetting her origins, her creed, and the dead. But from 1933 the funeral pyres were set burning again: books (including Freud's) were burned, and on *Kristallnacht* all the synagogues were set ablaze. In Nazi Germany, bitter and implacable persecution affected all Jews, child or adult, orthodox or atheist. Melanie Klein Reizes wanted more and more to shut herself off from a reality that should not concern her.

People began to arrive in England, having escaped from Germany, and to describe the onset of the horror and the appalling madness that was to lead to the deaths of six million Jews. These first Jewish refugees from the continent obliged her to hear the unspeakable. As the tension increased, she began to think of them as adversaries, and tightened her theory a bit further by writing 'A Contribution to the Psychogenesis of Manic-Depressive States' (1934), in which her whole system was sketched out for the first time. In order to bar the way to these avalanches of catastrophe, she attempted to exclude all external reality. Torturers and implacable persecutors were merely unconscious phantasies that used 'all the means which sadism can devise', and derived their energy from the hatred and limitless aggression which existed from the beginning, from birth, in the baby.

The more terrible the surrounding reality became, the tighter Melanie Klein felt obliged to turn the screw of her theory; the institutional consequence was that the theory aroused criticism and disbelief in some quarters, and blind, unconditional fidelity in others. This developed into an argument between two groups of analysts, the Good and the Bad. From its centre in London Klein's theory unleashed systematic proselytism on the part of some analysts who had been captivated, one might almost say hypnotized, by the strength of her certainty about the fundamental value of her discoveries.

Her daughter Melitta, though, seems to have resisted her. 'I was criticized for paying too much attention to the concrete circumstances and the actual situation of the patient [. . .] But I have always thought that the principal complaint against me was that I no longer aligned myself with the Kleinian orthodoxy (Freud being thought at that stage to have been somewhat superseded). Mrs Klein had postulated that the first months of life consisted of psychotic stages and mechanisms, and maintained that the analysis of these stages constituted the essence of psychoanalytic theory and therapy. Her claims grew exorbitantly: she demanded blind fidelity and refused to tolerate any disagreement.'[47]

In 1941 Klein started her analysis of Richard, writing up a full account of it, and publishing six sessions of it in 1945 (although the complete narrative was not published until after her death in 1961). Why, in the middle of the war, did Melanie Klein consider it a matter of urgency to undertake, and write up in such detail, an analysis that could only continue for four months? Many aspects of Richard's case must have evoked her early analytic experiences with Eric and Hans: the symptoms (including the problem of phimosis), the possibility of following things through with him for a while, journeys and displacement, both hers and the child's, the difficulty of limiting the times of the sessions and the time spent talking, the opportunity of distancing the father . . . Twenty years later, she was able to rewrite and recreate the same literary fiction, and stage the same drama.

But this time it was a genuine psychoanalysis, and a faithful illustration of her technique. Above all she was able to listen to and transcribe, over the ninety-three sessions, the panic fear of a child in the face of Hitler and the war he had unleashed, and 'the terrible things he did to the Poles' (First Session).[48] Overwhelmed by the phantom, though, she turns a deaf ear to that aspect of things; she interprets his fear in relation to her system and demonstrates that Hitler is just a way of representing his precocious anxieties: bad father Hitler, bad mother Hitler, Melanie Klein Hitler, father's penis Hitler, faeces Hitler, and so on. The fundamental thing is the urgency of denying the existence of persecution and persecutor. The earliest aggressive impulses play a fundamental rôle, through projection, in the 'construction' of the figure of the persecutor. When she formulates for Richard, for us and for herself, that what indicates improvement is the child's desire to sort out Hitler, to look after him and make him better, she oversteps the mark. One evening Richard's mother telephoned Mrs Klein to tell her about a noticeable improvement in her child's condition; Richard 'had asked whether Hitler could not be psycho-analysed and made better.'[49] The following day, Mrs Klein could not open the door of the playroom where she normally received Richard, and took him to her lodgings instead (where she normally received her adult patients). Richard asked to see Mrs Klein's bedroom, and she took him upstairs and showed him it. She explains in a note to that session the need to take into account the 'much more impetuous' curiosity of children, saying that it is helpful to let them see the rest of the rooms at least once. Here we can see an exact and predictable return of Felix/Fritz.

It was in 1943, while war was raging through the world and at the height of the bombing of London, that the critical discussions of analytical methodology between the Kleinians and anti-Kleinians took place in plenary sessions of the British Psycho-Analytical Society. Melanie, as the accused, ran the risk of being excluded. But in yet another battle between Melanie and her children, she emerged victorious. The good object Mell/Breast (Melanie plus Moritz) was established forever in psychoanalysis. In 1948, in one of the very few (perhaps the only) commentaries she wrote on the events that unfolded during her lifetime, Melanie Klein said that '[I]n the analyses carried out in wartime [i]t appeared that even with normal adults anxiety stirred up by air-raids, bombs, fire, etc. – i.e. by an 'objective' danger-situation – could only be reduced by analysing, over and above the impact of the actual situation, the various early anxieties which were aroused by it.'[50] The 'etc.' here covers the enforced exodus, the deportation and the extermination of the Jews, some of whom she knew, some of whom she had never known, and some of whom she no longer wanted to recognize. She continues: 'In many people excessive anxiety from these sources led to a powerful denial (manic defence) of the objective danger-situation, which showed itself in an apparent lack of fear.'[51] The horrors of the war and persecution, which reawoke in her – now deeply identified with her phantom – something that had to remain buried and inadmissible, made a desperate theorization of Saint-Mell inevitable. Her denial expressed itself as a theory that deprives external reality of any importance; the depressive anxiety that once related to a whole object is thus related to a part-object, namely the Breast, an object with no external reference and, above all, one that can never be criticized.

Here – with Melanie's words – we see the last modifications she made to her theory in the wake of the rise of Nazism and the long experience of the Second World War. The detail of the picture needed completing, some modifications of chronology and changes of emphasis were needed, she said, but it was the concept of the depressive position that necessitated them: 'the modification of my views regarding the earlier onset of depressive anxiety and guilt have not in any essentials altered my concept of the depressive position'.[52] Her claim is that depressive anxiety and guilt are present at a much earlier stage than she had thought in her previous theorization.[53] She now finds depressive anxiety everywhere, and 'closely bound up with guilt and with the tendency to make reparation. [She had previously] suggested that depressive anxiety and guilt arise with the introjection of the object as a whole. [But] further work [. . .] has led [her] to the conclusion that [. . .] depressive anxiety and guilt already play some part in the infant's earliest object-relation, i.e. in his relation to his mother's breast.'[54]

To sum up, then. 'In the first few months of life infants pass through states of persecutory anxiety which are bound up with the phase of maximal sadism [. . .] the young infant also experiences feelings of guilt about his destructive impulses and phantasies which are directed against his primary object – his mother, first of all her breast. These feelings of guilt give rise to the tendency to make reparation to the injured object.'[55] '[D]uring the first three or four months of life, a stage at which (according to my present views) depressive anxiety and guilt arise, splitting processes and persecutory anxiety are at their height [. . .] As a result, the loved injured object may very swiftly change into a persecutor, and the urge to repair or revive the loved object may turn into the need to pacify and propitiate a persecutor.'[56] External events once again open up the dead man's inadmissible wound and he demands compensation; in order to appease him, a new modification of the theory is urgently required.

This modification of her theory enables Klein to push the moment of persecution, of maximal sadism and its terrifying, apocalyptic projections (which of course have no connection with any conceivable external reality) even further back in time, and to bring forward (in time, technique and theory) the depressive moment, in order to save, protect, make reparation for, renew and reinstall in the place it had (apparently) lost, the Good Breast, harmed by our relentless sadism. Only apparently though: 'I now (London, May 1948) correlate the early stages of the Oedipus complex with the depressive position.'[57] The concern (torment/care) for the object must take precedence over the interest of the subject and over every other interest. Here we have a slippage from psychoanalysis to ethics – salvation is only to be found in the love of the object – and from ethics to religion: 'I am the Breast thy God which have brought thee out of the land of Egypt, out of the house of bondage. Thou shalt have no other gods before me.'

In 1957, three years before her death, she wrote *Envy and Gratitude*, in which she fixes the dogma of her religion: the outcome of combat and of psychoanalysis is the restoration and reinstatement in perpetuity of the good object to which one will never again be held to account. This is unconditional capitulation. The Breast has demonstrated its immeasurable goodness by accepting envious attacks without responding to them. It will be able to reign from that point on, as uncontested Tyrant, until the end of time. The Breast-Mel-Tyrant-martyr, venerated and terrible, adulated and hated, will occupy the whole space; thanks to its power and its gifts it will sustain every totalitarian regime. So the circle is closed, the machine can turn perpetually on its own axis, ready to reproduce itself anywhere in the world where an unbearable reality requires nescience.

AC

Translator's note

I have used the published English texts of all quotations from Klein's work, and of other psychoanalytic citations or references. Freud references are to the *Standard Edition*.

Notes

1 Nicolas Abraham, 'Notes on the Phantom: A Complement to Freud's Meta-psychology', in Nicolas Abraham and Maria Torok, *The Shell and the Kernel: Renewals of Psychoanalysis*, vol. 1, ed. and trans. and with an introduction by Nicholas T. Rand (Chicago and London: Chicago University Press, 1994) pp. 171–6.

2 *OuLiPo (Ouvroir de Littérature Potential or Potential Literature Workshop)*: a group of writers established in 1960 by Raymond Queneau, Georges Perec, Jacques Roubaud, Italo Calvino, Harry Matthews and others for the purpose of discovering and exploring new literary structures. Tr./Ed.

3 *See below*, pp. 56–7 Ed.

4 Jacques Derrida, *Glas*, trans. John P. Leavey, Jr and Richard Rand (Lincoln: University of Nebraska Press, 1986), pp. 32b–33b (translation modified) Tr.

5 Hungarian is Maria Torok's mother-tongue. Ed.

6 On this, see the *Sigmund Freud House Catalogue* (Vienna, 1980), p. 45.

7 See Barbro Sylwan, 'Fert-Iki', *Etudes freudiennes*, 13–14 (Paris: Denoël, 1978); Maria Torok, 'L'os de la fin', *Cahiers Confrontation*, 1 (Paris: Aubier, 1979).

8 Sigmund Freud, *The Interpretation of Dreams*, SE, IV, p. 254. Tr.

9 Sigmund Freud, *Jokes and their Relationship to the Unconscious*, SE, VIII, p. 55. Tr.

10 Uwe Henrik Peters, *Anna Freud: A Life Dedicated to Children* (New York: Schocken Books, 1985) p. 85. Ed.

11 Pawel Korzec, *Juifs en Pologne: la question juive pendant l'entre-deux-guerres* (Paris: Presses de la Fondation Nationale des Sciences Politiques, 1980), p. 51.

12 See *A Psycho-Analytic Dialogue: The Letters of Sigmund Freud and Karl Abraham 1907–1926*, eds Hilda C. Abraham and Ernst L. Freud, trans. Bernard Marsh and Hilda C. Abraham (New York: Basic Books, 1965). The editors of the Freud–Abraham correspondence note: 'This refers to the following event: Two guides with whom Abraham had climbed a mountain took some raw meat with them to eat. By the time they reached the hut and set about cooking it, it had gone bad, and one of them encouraged the other to eat it with the words: "*Coraggio Casimiro*"' (p. 146). Karl Abraham is the first to use the phrase in a postcard he wrote to Freud from Rome in 1913. He signs the card 'The Jew survives it! Cordial greetings and *Coraggio Casimiro!*' (p. 146). Ed.

13 Phimosis: a condition in which the orifice of the prepuce is contracted, preventing normal retraction. Tr./Ed.

14 The (anagrammatical) reference is to a dream analysed in 'The Psychogenesis of Manic-Depressive States': see Melanie Klein, *Love, Guilt and Reparation, and Other Works 1921–1945* (London: Hogarth, 1975) p. 279. Tr.

15 In *Love, Guilt and Reparation, and Other Works 1921–1945*, op. cit. pp. 1–53. Tr.

16 See Adèle Covello and Benoît Dalle, 'Une inanalyse didactique', *Cahiers Confrontation*, 3 (Paris: Aubier, 1980).

17 Ernest Jones, 'Introduction' to Melanie Klein, *Contributions to Psycho-Analysis* (London: Hogarth, 1950), p. 10.

18 Melanie Klein, 'Development of a Child', op. cit., p. 2.
19 Melitta Schmideberg, 'Contribution à l'histoire du mouvement psychanalytique en Angleterre', *Cahiers Confrontation*, 3 (Paris: Aubier, 1980). But this raises another curious issue: if we are to believe Melanie Klein, there ought not to be much left of these toys. 'Play-analyses show that when the child's aggressive instincts are at their height it never tires of tearing and cutting up, breaking, wetting and burning all sorts of things like paper, matches, boxes, small toys, all of which represent its parents and brothers and sisters, and its mother's body and breasts.' ('The Early Development of Conscience in the Child', *Love, Guilt and Reparation, and Other Works*, op. cit., p. 255).
20 Ernest Jones, 'Introduction', op. cit., p. 10. The terms used endlessly by Jones and others to typify Melanie Klein's character and approach – courage, moral strength, intellectual openness – recall Mrs Reizes, the Rabbi's daughter. When her husband broke with his orthodox past and set about gaining his medical qualifications, she had no hesitation in opening a shop to help him and to pay for her children's education, while always demonstrating (according to her daughter) great courage, moral strength, and remarkable intellectual openness.
21 Melanie Klein, 'Development of a Child', op. cit., p. 33.
22 ibid, p. 17.
23 ibid, p. 10.
24 These comments must have been received like hypnotic orders. They play a role in the two laws of Kleinism: the strict observance of the time and place of the session, and the obligation to listen solely and exclusively to the 'unconscious content'.
25 Melanie Klein, 'Development of a Child', op. cit., p. 30, p. 50.
26 On this, see the comments of Melanie's daughter Melitta on that period of her life. 'I was brought up with psycho-analysis. My mother, Melanie Klein, believed implicitly in all its premises. From the age of fifteen I regularly attended meetings of the Hungarian Psycho-Analytical Society, at the invitation of its founder and president, Dr. S. Ferenczi, and I was completely familiar with all the psychoanalytic writings of that period' (Melitta Schmideberg, op. cit.).
27 One might be tempted to think, in relation to the long-running conflict between Melanie Klein and Anna Freud, that strict orthodoxy is more of an obligation for a mother who has analysed her own children than for a daughter who has been analysed by her father. It is the daughter who inherits the mission of disseminating into the world the analysis of resistances (including of course those of her analyst-father).
28 Nicolas Abraham, 'The Phantom of Hamlet *or* The Sixth Act *preceded by* The Intermission of 'Truth'', *The Shell and the Kernel*, pp. 187–205 (p. 188). 'The Intermission of 'Truth'', op. cit., p. 188.
29 ibid, pp. 23–5.
30 Melanie Klein, op.cit., p. 7.
31 Melanie adds two trains to her box of toys, and she plays trains with little Dick in 1930, and adds another building block to her phantasy edifice with 'The Importance of Symbol-Formation in the Development of the Ego'. See *Love, Guilt and Reparation, and Other Works*, op. cit., pp. 219–32.
32 Melanie Klein writes that Fritz 'had from his early days had a careful up-bringing by persons who had been influenced by analytic views, but this did not prevent inhibitions and neurotic character traits from arising'. 'Early Analysis', in *Love, Guilt and Reparation, and Other Works*, op. cit., pp. 77–105 (p. 105).
33 'A keen interest in vehicles took the form of watching carts go by for hours at a time from a window or the entrance-hall of the house and also a passion for motoring. His chief occupation was pretending to be a coachman or a chauffeur, chairs being pushed

together to form the vehicle. To this game, which really only consisted in his sitting there quite quietly, he devoted himself so exclusively that it seemed like a compulsion, especially as he had a total disinclination for any other kind of game.' Later on, he also 'played that he was going for a journey under the bedclothes; sometimes he came out on one side and sometimes on the other, and he said when he got to the top that he was now "overground", which he meant to be the opposite of an underground railway' ('Early Analysis', op. cit., pp. 92–3).

34 Melanie Klein, 'Development of a Child', op. cit., p. 41.

35 ibid, p. 42.

36 Fritz is telling the story of the word 'operation': in German, the verb meaning 'to cut up' is 'sezieren', the root of which, 'sezier', is an inversion of the word 'Reizes'.

37 Klein explains in a footnote that the 'sense' was the 'penis'. But then the penis cut through?? . . .

38 'The next day in school, to his and his mistress's astonishment, it turned out that he could now do all his sums correctly. (The child had not become aware of the connection between the interpretation and the removal of the inhibition.)' 'The Rôle of the School in the Libidinal Development of the Child', *Love, Guilt and Reparation, and Other Writings*, op. cit., pp. 59–76 (pp. 69–70, 70n).

39 'A Contribution to the Psychogenesis of Tics', *Love, Guilt and Reparation, and Other Works*, op. cit., pp. 106–27 (p. 106).

40 ibid, p. 106.

41 An interesting return of the Fliess-phantom: *Doctor* Melanie Klein had been made known to Freud by Abraham in 1923, as an item of good news to counterbalance the recent operation on his jaw. Two months before he died in 1925, Abraham wrote to Freud: ' I shall in any case have to undergo some treatment for my nose and throat from Fliess. If this letter were not already unduly long, I would tell you how my illness has most strikingly confirmed all Fliess's views on periodicity' (*A Psycho-Analytic Dialogue: The Letters of Sigmund Freud and Karl Abraham 1907–1926*, eds. Hilda C. Abraham and Ernst L. Freud, trans. Bernard Marsh and Hilda C. Abraham (London: Hogarth, 1965), p. 395.

42 'A Contribution to the Psychogenesis of Tics', op. cit., p. 107.

43 ibid, p. 107.

44 ibid, p. 109 [Covello's italics. Tr.]

45 Nicolas Abraham, 'The Intermission of "Truth"', op. cit., p. 188.

46 ibid, p. 190.

47 Melitta Schmideberg, op. cit.

48 Melanie Klein, *Narrative of a Child Analysis: The Conduct of the Psycho-Analysis of Children as Seen in the Treatment of a Ten-year-old Boy* (London: Hogarth, 1961), p. 19. 'The outbreak of the war had greatly increased Richard's difficulties [. . . and] stirred up his anxieties, and he was particularly frightened of air-raids and bombs. He followed the news closely and took a great interest in the changes in the war-situation, and this preoccupation came up again and again during the course of his analysis.' (p. 16).

49 ibid, p. 184n.

50 Melanie Klein, 'The Theory of Anxiety and Guilt' [1948], in Melanie Klein, Paula Heimann, Susan Isaacs and Joan Rivière, *Developments in Psycho-Analysis*, ed. Joan Rivière, with a preface by Ernest Jones (London: Hogarth, 1952), p. 289.

51 ibid, p. 289.

52 ibid, p. 284.

53 Following the postulate that she applies throughout her work, that the earlier it is, the more important it is.

54 ibid, p. 282.
55 Melanie Klein, *The Psycho-Analysis of Children*, preface to the third edition (London: Hogarth, 1949), p. 11.
56 Melanie Klein, 'The Theory of Anxiety and Guilt', op. cit., p. 285.
57 ibid, p. 13.

Chapter 4

The question child

J.-B. Pontalis

Translated by Catherine and Phillip Cullen

Editor's note:

J.-B. Pontalis focuses on Klein's very earliest writings in this brief section ('Part I') of the essay 'Between Knowledge and Phantasy,' which first appeared in English in *Frontiers of Psychoanalysis* (1981), a translation of *Entre la rêve et la douleur* (1977). The suggestion, which comes through very strongly here, that the early writings are of key importance for an understanding of what is at stake in Melanie Klein's work, is supported by other contributions to *Reading Melanie Klein* (see Bersani, Mitchell and Phillips).

In 'Between Knowledge and Phantasy,' Pontalis is concerned to show that a knowledge adequate to the unconscious is one that would be informed by whatever contradicts it from a place that cannot be fixed or assigned by it. It would be a knowledge that is shaped by what it cannot know. So Klein is exemplary insofar as the early writings show her willing to put psychoanalysis to 'the test of the child's speech.' That is, the knowledge of the child and, later, the psychotic, are what psychoanalytic knowledge 'stumbles over.' The fact that the child in this case has more to say than he actually says indicates a difficulty that shapes psychoanalytic knowledge 'to the present day.' Klein is seen here as willing to engage with what causes her knowledge to stumble. Pontalis reads Klein's first essay (originally written in two parts) as constituting a reversal or change of tack. She begins with an enlightenment question – 'What holds the child back?' – and assumes at first an enlightenment answer (not uncommon in psychoanalysis): repression is the result of social pressure. But the desire for *Aufklärung*, the wish to 'enlighten' the child with sexual knowledge (or psychoanalytic knowledge), as a way of freeing him from the inhibiting power of myth, has to give way to the fact that the child has an internal resistance to enlightenment. It is at this point that Klein's own intensification of Freud's shattering of the myth of the innocent child begins, and it is this, according to Pontalis, that makes her descriptions of the child's interior world so difficult to take. The child possesses a kind of knowledge, an unbound sexuality, that is strictly speaking (in Freud's term) 'ineducable.' The truth that one wants one's child to know cannot replace the unconscious.

One of the most telling features of Klein's first essay is, for Pontalis, the fact that the analyst is also the mother. If sexual knowledge reaches its limit, as Freud suggested it did, with the incest taboo, then what happens when it is the mother, both 'natural object of desire' and 'agent of the prohibition,' who transmits the enlightened sexual knowledge? What is revealed is that infantile sexual theory, rather than being a function of the Oedipus complex, is its very mode of expression. More powerful than either fables or enlightened knowledge, it is a resistance to knowledge that 'says more' than knowledge itself can grasp.

Pontalis's subtle yet persistent reading shows Klein at this early stage stumbling over intractable difficulties and, by being attentive to their implications, taking Freud's most radical discoveries about infantile sexuality even further than he did. Pontalis also argues that Klein's theory, the more it becomes a system, manifests her desire to 'know' the unconscious in its deepest and earliest form – to be there, as it were, at its birth and to mother it. But this earliest stumbling block reveals the fantastic adult desire for knowledge in terms of its obverse – the desire to kill the child off. It is this, for Pontalis, that psychoanalysis must perpetually try to resist. (JP)

Even today, i.e. more than fifty years after its publication, the first of the essays of Melanie Klein's *Contributions to Psycho-Analysis* (1921–45) remains surprisingly alive and forceful. The author's guiding question, which can be considered as the starting-point for all her subsequent research is: what holds the child back? One should note that this question, whether implicit or explicit, is at the very heart of an educator's desire – from Rousseau, in *Emile*, to Maria Montessori – and may well be the cause of pedagogues' aberrations: in such cases the temptations of pedagogics may find their fulfilment in the pupil's murder, as illustrated by Ionesco's *The Lesson*.

At this initial stage, Melanie Klein's (1921) explicit intention was no different to her vocational wish for *Aufklärung*, based on 'psychoanalytical knowledge': 'We shall let the child acquire as much sexual information as the growth of its desire for knowledge requires, thus depriving sexuality at once of its mystery and of a great part of its danger.' Repression was defined in a very exterior way as the product of social pressure, and the most favourable results were expected from lifting the 'burden of superfluous suffering': 'We are laying down the foundations for health, mental balance and the favourable development of character.' The immediate results were to affect the individual, particularly his intellectual power and his creativity; the long-term results were to influence the evolution of humanity.

This, then, was the starting point for Melanie Klein, of whom it was later said that her suggestion that envy and guilt were at the heart of the infant was no more than a psychoanalytical transcription of the myth of original sin. Admittedly, the desire to intervene precociously was not original at the time: many psycho-analysts shared this prophylactic illusion, dreaming of kindergartens where the crystallization of neurosis would be avoided. But in her case it was upheld by a very specific preoccupation. If in her first text Melanie Klein's attention was held above all by the child's inhibitions, it was because they assumed an exemplary value for her: the child had more to say for himself than what he actually said. This was why she refused to see this or that 'characteristic' of the child as a deficiency that, as Anna Freud asserted, one should relate to his nature, to his actually dependent situation or to a stage in his evolution. She therefore chose not to define the conditions which should be fulfilled by child analysis, but to submit psychoanalytical theory and methods to the disconcerting test of the child's speech. With her, psychoanalysis was not properly speaking *applied* to the child or, later, to the psychotic: both held it in check and this difficulty could not be dodged or 'adjusted,' which both caused analysis to stumble and is what shaped it, and continues to shape it to the present day. The technical debate opposing Melanie Klein to Anna Freud reflects the confrontation of two ethics: for Anna Freud, in the end, it was a question of making the child find the adult's alleged autonomy; for Melanie Klein it was a matter of coming to meet the child's psychic reality and measuring adult knowledge against it 'in the spirit of free and unprejudiced research.'

Melanie Klein's case study is not an analysis in the proper sense of the term, but a case of education, with an analytical approach. Melanie Klein observed that she had the possibility of seeing the child and talking with him every day. A relatively vague clinical description indicated that this five-year-old boy was behind in the acquisition of language and, on a more general level, he found it difficult to master elementary symbolism (the notions of time and exchange). Melanie Klein also noted a 'feeling of impotence' ('despite proof to the contrary, he was convinced that he could cook, read, write and speak perfect French'). On the whole, however, he seemed to be a lively and intelligent child endowed with an excellent memory. At about four-and-a-half years he started asking questions (on birth, and later on the existence of god and on life in general) and Melanie Klein retraced the history of this case by following these questions' evolution almost exclusively in terms of their content and their mode.

What did Melanie Klein encounter in her dialogue with little Fritz? Apparently, enough material to prove the well-foundedness of her convictions.

Indeed, Fritz was full of questions and the adult, by not eluding them, by not letting herself be overcome by any uneasiness they might create in her, had the possibility of seeing the child acquire the skill to master the symbolic function and to grasp reality. But at the same time, the limits of the act of enlightening, of educational intervention, became manifest, even when carried out with as much subtlety, constancy and understanding of the child's anxiety as Melanie Klein had. If we limit ourselves to education, we cannot but be aware of the device inherent to inculcating what is called objective knowledge in children. First of all, notice that the expression 'sexual education' conceals a condensation already present in the term 'to inform' (to give indications and explanations, but also to give form to), which is considerably intensified here: is not the aim to *educate* rather than to instruct? To let sexuality run 'loose' – in the same sense as thoughts do – to let it become *educable*, to use Freud's term to contrast *ineducable* sexual instincts with instincts of self-preservation, which are easy to educate. One then understands that the resistance to sexual education should be relatively easy to overcome in the adult, who espouses cultural aims of this type, and that it should be resistant in children, in whom it rocks the very organization of the desires.

Freud (1937) had unhesitating opinions about this matter: 'After such enlightenment children know something they did not know before, but they make no use of the new knowledge that has been presented to them . . . They behave like primitive races who have had Christianity thrust upon them and who continue to worship their idols in secret.' An observation which deserves the attention of those who expect sexual education at school – and by school they do not mean the playground or toilets but the schoolmasters – to provide the most fitting preparation for future matrimonial harmony? For the benefit of those who denounce today's sexual education as excessively normative, it should be added that to avoid this kind of criticism, it is not enough for the teacher simply to change coats. Certain praises of the child's 'polymorphous perversion' smack of adult monomorphous perversion . . . What is at stake here is the right adults assume to *confiscate*, 'for the child's own good' of course, a certain sexuality that knows neither where it is bound nor what it wants. Any discourse *on* the child purporting to speak the child's language *for* him is questionable. Of course, Freud was not always so reserved as to the effects of 'Enlightenment' on the question of sexuality. But it should be noted that the article (for external use only), in which he declared himself strongly in favour of it ('The Sexual Enlightenment of Children,' 1907) was immediately followed by another article, a truly psychoanalytic one this time, on infantile sexual theories (1908), 'theories' of so 'typical' a character that this alone was enough to prove they were based on the truth. There is in fact no contradiction between these two equally Freudian assertions: one must indeed encourage parents and educators not to lie to children, not to answer with 'childish sayings,' in other words with myths concocted by adults for children, but one must not expect such knowledge to replace the unconscious.

Yet Freud's warning was misunderstood by a great number of people, even among psychoanalysts, as if they were convinced that 'infantile sexual theories' were imaginary formations which could not but give way when confronted with positive knowledge. At the most, they could be considered anachronistic relics in that they would only be based on outmoded stages of instinctual organization. That Freud himself may have envisaged things in this restrictive way, I do not deny. But the article's title itself – 'On the Sexual Theories of Children' (1908) – echoing his *Three Essays on the Theory of Sexuality* (1905), the frequency throughout the text of terms such as 'instinct for research,' 'desire for knowledge,' 'sexual desire for knowledge', etc. which indissolubly linked the strength of the wish to the activity of thinking, and finally the implicit oedipal reference, all clearly demonstrate that Freud saw these sexual theories as active organizers which could not be reduced to partial instincts supplying them with their 'language' or to chance perceptions provided by the outside world.

Very soon – and anyone can check this by considering a child's questions even if they are trivial – one is compelled to arrive at a point where knowledge cannot come up with an answer: the incest taboo. The failings of knowledge on sexuality get worse, at the same time as its original function is revealed, when it is transmitted by the one – the mother – who is both the *natural object of desire* and the *agent of prohibition*. Now this was exactly the case here for Melanie Klein was in fact *the child's mother*. The proof of this can be found in another article published in the same period: 'Der Familienroman in Statu Nascendi' (1920). Part of the same observation figures in it, but this time Melanie Klein clearly states: 'My son Eric,' etc. The parent's answer is necessarily faulty: it cannot justify itself in the same terms as those in which the adult asks the child to get his bearings. Hence the reversal that Melanie Klein had the merit to grasp on the spot: the child's fantasies turned out to be a lot closer to what was actually at stake than the knowledge meted out by the adult.

The case-history comprises two stages and two headings. The first heading: *The influence of sexual enlightenment and relaxation of authority on the intellectual development of children* (1919). The second part, written two years later (1921), is headed: *The child's resistance to enlightenment*. These two statements indicate the reversal I have just mentioned. At first, it was a matter of convincing parents and educators of the necessity of not keeping the child in ignorance, of answering his questions without anticipating them, since repression seemed to be triggered off by exterior imperatives, by the adult's refusal or silence; children were considered to possess a natural, spontaneous curiosity: it was the adult who resisted. But it so happened that during the second stage, the child was seen to resist, whether massively through a refusal to know, or, indirectly, through recourse to this or that compulsive activity. Confronted by certain changes in Fritz's behaviour, Melanie Klein wrote: 'I became convinced that the child's very powerful impulse for investigation had come into conflict with his equally powerful tendency to repression . . . after he had asked many and different questions . . . he had . . . come to the point where he avoided questioning altogether and listening as well, *as the latter might, unasked, provide him with what he refused to have.'*

What, in fact, was happening? After Fritz's 'false' beliefs had been vigorously ousted (there was no shilly-shallying in *that* home: the maid was dismissed for having told the child the story of the stork); he had been duly taught the reality of the sexual processes (fecundation, pregnancy), and even after this knowledge had apparently been integrated properly, as was evidenced by the disappearance of the most apparent inhibitions and the end of stereotyped questions, there remained a residue: Fritz continued to be 'attached' (although he knew what to believe and despite repeated correction) to the idea that children grew in their mother's stomach. The stomach become, so to speak, an all-purpose signifier . . . To a child saying: 'Come to the garden,' Fritz replied: 'Go to your stomach'; to people asking him where some object was, he would answer: 'In your stomach.' If he wanted to see his mother naked, it was so as to 'see her stomach and the picture inside it!'

In other words, little Fritz found it difficult to stomach the explanations given him! To interpret this 'residue' as a survival of a sexual theory which he could not renounce – children are made of food and are identical to faeces – would be to mistake the part for the whole; indeed, one should stress that even if it is true that oral and anal body functions and the pleasure attached to them supply the 'theory' with elements of representation, they still do not account for the former, in that its presence remains necessary in the face of and despite positive knowledge. One certainly moves a step forward, as Melanie Klein invited us to, in seeing in little Fritz's belief an aversion to assimilating an awareness of the role played by his father: the sexual theory is then inserted in the oedipal structure. But this does not go far enough: sexual theory, or more generally the construction of the fantasy, is not just a part of the Oedipus complex, but its mode of expression.

The fact that in Fritz's case fantasy should come to oppose the injection of adult knowledge, in so far as it harbours a truth that reality is incapable of providing, is clearly indicated by a kind of slip of the tongue he made at a time when games and fantasies with an oedipal content abounded. Fritz was playing with lead figures, two soldiers and a nurse. 'He said that these were himself and his brother and his mamma . . . "The one that has something prickly down there is me." I [M. K.] ask what is there down there that pricks? He, "A wiwi." "And does that prick?" He, *"Not in the game, but really* – no, I am wrong, not really but in the game."' Here, the mistake stemmed from the truth. For in these circumstances, one cannot invoke the child's difficulty in differentiating the real from the imaginary, a differentiation which would take place progressively and would include moments of failure. He could differentiate perfectly well otherwise, outside the field of human reality involving sexuality – a field which cannot be ascribed any limits: for the child, more than for the adult whose sexual function is truly 'in working order,' nothing is sexual, everything is sexual. For

arrow – the thimble

example: if little Fritz asked how a human being was made, he would be said to have shown sexual curiosity. If he asked 'how much time does tomorrow take to come?' he would be said to be at the metaphysical age. Yet both questions, both 'conceptions' go together.

Infantile sexual theory, which is 'grotesquely misled' (Freud), turns out to be more effective not only than the fables invented by adults for children, but also than the knowledge meted out to them. This is precisely confirmed by the language our little questioner once used ('it is called an oven because it is an oven,' etc.). Melanie Klein saw this, rather too hastily, as a sign of progress in the acquisition of a sense of reality, which was supposed to have followed the true answers supplied to the anxious questions about the difference between the sexes. Fritz was thought to have put a stop to his incessant 'whys' on his own. However, his renunciation revealed a split between a rigorously tautological order of reality – without any differentiation and referring exclusively to himself – and a place of the fantasy where the castration anxiety could expand alone and find an answer.

Earlier on, we mentioned that the enigma concerning the incest taboo was on the horizon of the child's desire for sexual knowledge – or of his sexual desire for knowledge. Little Fritz knew how to lead Melanie Klein to this point, where she could not but stumble. One only has to refer to the answer she gave: she was more than embarrassed, and manifestly caught off her guard. As much in the evocation – if one may call it that – of the sexual act ('Papa can make something with his wiwi that really looks rather like milk . . . he makes it like doing wiwi only not so much') as in the explanation, again if one can call it that, of the mother's prohibition (Every man has only one wife. When you are big your mamma will be old,' etc.). Indeed, what else could one say?

The answer could not but 'ring false' especially as it was proffered at that stage of childhood in which the articulation of desire and prohibition – of desire as a prohibition – was at a prolific period of its development. Only the fantasy's answer can 'ring true,' can offer a space suited to this articulation. Infantile sexual theories, in which one can observe the secondary forms of original fantasies (see Laplanche and Pontalis 1964) constitute a reality homologous to the 'theoretical' character of the oedipal law – a law which 'reality,' that of nature as well as that of social institutions, is incapable of founding.

Was it really, as Ernest Jones (1948) indicated, the shattering of the myth of the innocent child – a myth which is coming back in force nowadays – carried further than by Freud, which ulteriorly rendered Melanie Klein's descriptions of the child's interior world so difficult to admit? In fact, was precocious sadism, which she brought to the fore as early as 1927, i.e., a few years after her observation of Fritz, in an article straightforwardly titled 'Criminal Tendencies in Normal Children,' a fundamental fact for her? In comparison with her starting-point, so obvious in the initial presupposition of *Aufklärung* and of the 'relaxation of authoritarian relations,' the roles have been reversed: everything seems to emanate from the child given over to his interior demons: his 'development' depends solely on the result of a completely interior fight, between good and bad objects, between Eros and Thanatos. But the recognition of this reversal of roles gets us no further; the practice of child analysis seems to be always in danger of filling with guilt either the adult or the child.

Ferenczi (1933), who also recognized the 'confusion of tongues' only to denounce it, considered the child as interiorizing adult desires marked by hate, guilt and prohibition. Invoking his thesis at this point may seem paradoxical as it is already so surprising in itself, inasmuch as it aimed to bring back to life a Freudian conception previous to the discovery of infantile sexuality, by basing itself on seduction: are we not poles apart from Melanie Klein? However, one should not be too hasty to assert that Ferenczi's thesis is no more than a new incarnation of the 'old' Freudian theory of seduction. In the first place, whatever the justified importance he accorded seduction, its value was exclusively illustrative. Other data were taken into account: 'punishments due to passion' and particularly 'the terrorism of suffering,' which makes the child bear the full brunt of the open or secret conflict between family members, thereby assigning him the sole function of bearer and messenger of the parental unconscious. But in Ferenczi's view, seduction raised to its highest pitch the confusion of tongues, the 'premature grafting' of a form of passionate love filled with guilt. Premature grafting: let us bear the image and its body resonance in mind. What Ferenczi further discovered in the privileged example of seduction was a process with far-reaching consequences: identification with the aggressor or, rather, with his introjection. By this he noted a modality of psychism far more fundamental than what, after Anna Freud, was to be described as the defence mechanism (the aggressed becoming the aggressor, the dominated the dominator). Ferenczi spoke of total submission to the aggressor's will induced by fright. The adult's ascendancy, his power to captivate are unlimited. 'A child is being killed,' Ferenczi seemed to be saying, and his entire therapeutic aim was to make him come to life again.

On the contrary, as it seems, Melanie Klein saw the child with sexual and aggressive desires from the outset. But let us note that what allows us to qualify them as such are the *objects* they aim at, not a goal which would be imminent to them. *Envy*, for example, which Melanie Klein finally considered the most primitive perceptible form of the death instinct (to empty the object), is not a 'purely' instinctual force, it cannot be perceived outside its relationship to the object giving rise to it. Whereas even a 'natural' object such as the breast is more than the instinct's correlative – what would satisfy it or not: it is caught in an opposition which defines it (good/bad) and, however fantasied it has the autonomy of a 'person.' Finally, the instinctual field itself is split into life instincts and death instincts and if the primary and permanent cause of anxiety is the danger stemming from the internal work of the shattering, death-carrying instinct, primary objects – breast, penis – are those invested by the libido: their power as objects, the symbolic equivalences between them do not derive from the instinct, but from their own, transindividual nature.

When one objects that Melanie Klein introduced complex object relations practically from the start, one is presupposing the existence of a time when the child's life is purely and simply governed by the search for satisfaction, itself defined as the appeasement of internal tension. In short, the child would exist primarily as an individual bio-physical unit which his permutation would render decidedly dependent, but dependent upon a being of the same nature. Melanie Klein stated something quite different: for her too, the child undergoes a 'premature grafting' of the adult. But whereas Ferenczi, in what one might term his original myth of the meeting between child and adult, envisaged a subject already in possession of his own world, an established language – that of tenderness – upon which the adult's language – that of 'passion' – comes to graft itself by violent intrusion, Melanie Klein claimed to perceive this junction at the very start of the ego's constitution. And where Ferenczi metaphorically invoked the introjection of language, she spoke, in almost literal terms, of the incorporation of objects. The unconscious is no longer a system but a body. The unconscious no longer fastens itself upon 'representations' but upon objects or qualities treated as objects: an unceasing repetition of introjections and projections which comes to a temporary halt – for it is not so much a development as an oscillation – only through the victory of the strongest: the good object.

By not being evasive with the question-child, by reaching his fantasy life, Melanie Klein thought she could go back to a time previous to what is traditionally referred to as the Unconscious/Conscious division brought about by repression. Her assumption was that by going further back in time, she would go deeper and at best would arrive at a primary unconscious. What is more, by attempting to analyse very young children, she thought she would be able to participate in the 'birth' of an unconscious and, as it were, to mother it. It is noteworthy that the more Kleinian language becomes singular, to the point of appearing to be a system, the more monotonous it becomes: a sign of Melanie Klein's conviction that she had acceded to the fundamental terms, the manipulation of which was to ensure her grasp on the psyche's elementary structures.

The circle is closed: from knowledge to fantasy, from fantasy to knowledge. For a moment, the child of psychoanalysis caused his mother's knowledge to waver, but in the end, mother-psychoanalysis regained her balance and thought she had the last word. But any knowledge of the unconscious can only be effectively established if it stands the test of what contradicts it from another place without an appointed, fixed position: the place, or non-place, of the unconscious.

References

Ferenczi, Sandor (1933) 'Confusion of Tongues between Adults and the Child', *Final Contributions to Psychoanalysis*, London: Hogarth, 1955.

Freud, Sigmund *The Standard Edition of the Complete Psychological Works of Sigmund Freud*, ed. and trans. James Strachey, London: Hogarth, 24 vols, 1953–74.

—— (1905) 'Three Essays on the Theory of Sexuality', *SE*, XX.

—— (1907) 'The Sexual Enlightenment of Children', *SE*, IX.

—— (1908) 'On the Sexual Theories of Children', *SE*, IX.

—— (1937) 'Alysis Terminable and Interminable', *SE*, XXIII.

Jones, Ernest (1948) Introduction to Melanie Klein's *Contributions to Psycho-Analysis 1921–1945*, London: Hogarth.

Klein, Melanie (1920) 'Der Familienroman in Statu Nascendi', *Internationale Zeitschrift für Psychanalyse*.

—— (1921) 'The Development of a Child', *Contributions to Psychoanalysis 1921–1945*, London: Hogarth, 1950.

Laplanche, Jean and Jean-Bertrand Pontalis, (1964) *The Language of Psycho-Analysis*, New York: Norton, 1973.

Pontalis, Jean-Bertrand (1977) *Entre la rêve et la douleur*, Paris: Gallimard.

—— (1981) *Frontiers of Psychoanalysis*, London: Hogarth.

Chapter 5

'Tea daddy': Poor Mrs Klein and the pencil shavings

Mary Jacobus

Editor's note:

Mary Jacobus's work on literature, feminism and psychoanalysis is distinguished by its meticulous and sophisticated attention to processes of reading and textuality. The present essay is no exception. Originally published in a special issue of *Women: A Cultural Review* (vol. 1, no. 2, Summer 1990) dedicated to Klein's work, this essay was one of the first to return to Klein with contemporary psychoanalytic and feminist theoretical hindsight. The orthodoxies of that hindsight itself, however, are also put into question here as Jacobus offers a post-Lacanian account of Klein with a twist in its tail. She argues that to return to Klein today is not, as is often assumed, to 'regress' to the pre-verbal or pre-Oedipal of psychoanalytic theory (to a Klein too literal to be of any use to theories of language and signification, and too instinctual – too 'essentialist' – to cause anything but trouble for feminism). Taking Klein at her word does not mean that her words get stuck in the throat of pre-structuralism. Through a detailed reading of Klein's famous essay 'The Importance of Symbol Formation in the Development of the Ego' (1930) ('Little Dick'), Lacan's two 1952 seminars on Klein ('Discourse Analysis and Ego Analysis' and 'The Topic of the Imaginary'), and Kristeva's 'Freud and Love: Treatment and its Discontents,' Jacobus grafts an account of language onto Kleinian theory. Rather than attempt to make Klein palatable for post-structuralist taste, Jacobus's strategy is to ask what it is in Lacan's seminar that both incorporates and 'disgorges' Klein. Thus at the moment Lacan claims to go beyond Klein – beyond her too brutal symbolization of 'Little Dick' and towards his own linguistic inscription of the unconscious – Klein proves to be a little too close to the letter of Lacanian theory for comfort. The brutality that Lacan imputes to Klein's heavy-handed interpretation turns out to match only Lacan's own 'brutal' reading of Klein. This, according to Jacobus, is a case of projective identification – to a T. With an ingenious sleight of hand, she demonstrates that just as identification in its negating form (projective identification) fuels the Lacanian return to Klein, so too identification – this time in its affirmative, empathetic mode – also characterizes Klein's analysis of little Dick. To this extent, Jacobus argues, Klein anticipates the premature empathy that is for Kristeva the hallmark of the early, pre-narcissistic and fragile metaphorization that marks the subject's coming into being. By this reading Klein emerges as the original reader of those first things (to borrow the title of Jacobus's latest book, *First Things: The Maternal Imaginary in Literature, Art and Psychoanalysis* (1995), in which she develops her reading of Klein and object relations), those first significations and identifications that make meaning and being possible. If feminism is to understand not only how sex signifies, but what it is in phantasy and psychic life that makes that signification possible, it could do worse, this essay suggests, than to begin at the beginning and take Klein at her word. (LS)

> . . . *on one occasion, Dick lifted a little toy man to his mouth, gnashed his teeth and said 'Tea daddy,' by which he meant 'Eat daddy.'*

> Melanie Klein, 'The Importance of Symbol Formation
> in the Development of the Ego' (1930)[1]

> *T (ti), the twentieth letter of the English and other modern alphabets, the nineteenth of the ancient Roman alphabet, corresponding in form to the Greek T. . . . in Phoenician, and originally also in Greek, the last letter of the alphabet. It represents the point-breath-stop of Bell's 'visible speech,' or surd dental mute, so called, but in English is gingival or alveolar rather than dental.*

> *Oxford English Dictionary*

One response to the current return to Klein: it feels like eating one's words. Psychoanalytic feminism has been so thoroughly immersed in Lacanian theory for the past decade that taking Klein at her word – reading her literally, as she asks to be read – seems to risk a kind of theoretical regression. Can one renege on Lacan's 'return to Freud,' not to mention the entire freight of post-Saussurean linguistics that it brings in its train? Klein, it goes without saying, lacks any adequate account of the relation between language and the unconscious ('incapable of even so much as suspecting the existence of the category of the signifier' – Lacan's verdict on the Kleinian school).[2] Moving with untroubled literalness between phantasy and its objects, her writing resists the very aspect of Lacanian theory that has made it so inviting to literary theorists and to feminists in quest of a language based account of the relations between sexuality and subjectivity. Hence, for Lacan himself, Klein's interest lies primarily in the account she gives of what he would call 'the domain of the imaginary' (i.e., 'the interplay of projections, introjections, expulsions, reintrojections of bad objects' which underpins object-relations theory), rather than in any account of what she, in his terms, miscalls the 'symbolic' – the realm that Lacan himself identifies with language.[3]

But Klein holds special interest to feminists for her emphasis on the early relations of mother and infant, especially for reconceptualizing the shadowy, so-called preoedipal domain surmised (but tantalizingly unexplored) by Freud, and more recently theorized in the work of Kristeva. This is the domain that psychoanalytic feminism in search of an alternative to the Freudian Oedipus complex or the Lacanian Law of the Father has often nostalgically invoked. Klein's focus on the mother and her theories of 'prematurity' – her insistence on infant phantasies coterminous with the earliest instinctual experience – offers psychoanalytic feminism a way to rethink both the Oedipus complex and the pre-oedipal domain (no longer properly 'pre' in Klein, to the extent that the oedipal itself is characterized by its prematurity).[4] Lacan describes Klein as 'working on the child at the very limit of the appearance of language.'[5] I want to explore this limit in the case history of little Dick recounted by Klein's 1930 essay, 'The Importance of Symbol Formation in the Development of the Ego,' along with Lacan's later rereading of it in his two seminars of 1954, 'Discourse Analysis and Ego Analysis' and 'The Topic of the Imaginary.' At the same time I will try to triangulate the relation between Klein and Lacan by introducing Kristeva's essay, 'Freud and Love: Treatment and its Discontents.'[6] The Kristevan account of abjection and its relation to transference-love – both processes which she views as intimately connected with the early relations of mother and child and with the beginnings of signification – allows for the grafting of language onto Kleinian theory at the very limit of its appearance.

Psychoanalytic feminists tend to come to Klein today by way of Lacan and Kristeva, with a hindsight or *après coup* that has more to do with working back than nostalgia; and so the turn (the spin) I will be giving to 'return' in this essay is necessarily retrospective. I would like to suggest that the alliance of Klein and Kristeva may allow psychoanalytic feminists, so to speak, to eat their words and have them too, refocusing on the question of the 'literal' that teasingly plays in the misplaced T of 'Tea Daddy' as (misplaced) metaphor. Perhaps, then, there is a sense in which the theoretical regression I invoked at the outset mimes its theoretical object. We may be confronting the difficult crossover between, on the one hand, a Kristevan account of signification that is necessarily post-Lacanian, even in its divergence from Lacan, in its insistence on the missing, unsuspected category of the signifier as a necessary condition of the emergence of the subject; and, on the other hand, what Lacan himself views as regressive, a Kleinian account of eating (cannibalism, even), incorporation, and primary identification, or what Klein herself (in the elaborated sense peculiar to her) calls 'projective identification,' which is ambiguously poised on the borderline of instinct and ego.[7] A borderline case – the border between the regressive and the 'premature,' the literal and the metaphorical, or instinct and signification – aptly prompts a return to the scene of symbolic arrest that Klein presents in her case history of little Dick, a four-year-old psychotic characterized by his simultaneous failure to develop in the area of object relations and language. I began this essay intending to explore the possibility of grafting language onto Kleinian theory. As I wrote, however, a different question began to emerge: what role does Klein play for both Lacan and Kristeva? How does theory swallow up or disgorge its others (its 'objects')? Finally, in what ways might a Kristevan 'return to Klein' permit us to hear the 'literal' of the Kleinian text with an ear attuned to metaphor?

I 'Dick is inside dark mummy'

In Lacan's reading, Klein offers little Dick words, simultaneously locating him in language and in a system of symbolic relations. As Klein herself presents it, the case history of little Dick traces the confused beginnings of symbol formation in a child who would now be regarded as autistic, but whom Klein thought of as schizophrenic.[8] Little Dick exemplifies for her the aggressivity of the early oral-sadistic phase, with its focus on biting and devouring the mother's body; a phase which also introduces the Oedipus conflict. The child's phantasized attacks on the maternal body – imagined as a container for the father's penis, for excrement, and for children – has as its object both mother and father, and gives rise to intense anxiety. As Klein writes, 'The object of the attack becomes a source of danger because the subject fears similar, retaliatory attacks from it.' Anxiety sets going the mechanism of identification (with the persecutory penis, vagina and breast), and at the same time fuels the symbolic process – the ever mobile symbolic equations or displaced identifications which Klein views in the light of defences: 'This anxiety contributes to make [the child] equate the organs in question with other things; owing to this equation those in their turn become objects of anxiety, and so he is impelled constantly to make other and new equations ...' (p. 97). Providing the basis for phantasy, Klein's symbolic equations also provide the basis for subsequent relations to, and mastery of, reality.[9] By contrast, a failure in symbol formation – too much anxiety too soon, or the inability to tolerate it – brings to a standstill the child's relation to objects (mother and father), and hence, in Klein's terms, to both language and reality. This is the case with little Dick.

Klein begins by observing that little Dick is indifferent to the presence or absence of his mother or nurse, doesn't play, and has no contact with his environment; he strings sounds together in a meaningless way, constantly repeats certain noises, and uses his small vocabulary incorrectly. Whether obedient or disobedient, he seems to lack affect. On his first visit to Klein he runs about aimlessly in her room and treats her like a piece of furniture, as well as betraying a striking absence of anxiety. Klein concludes that little Dick's arrest is a consequence, among other things, of a difficulty in tolerating anxiety which she attributes to the premature awakening in him of genitality. This prematurity has caused 'a premature and exaggerated identification with the object attacked'; hence his too-early, too-successful defences against that identification, and the arrest of symbol formation. She relates his early difficulties in nursing, like his later refusal to bite up food, to the cessation of phantasy life defensively mobilized against his own sadistic relation to the mother's body. Anxiety has backfired. The very defence that should have opened the doors has closed them, leaving him in a void, without either 'objects' or symbolic representations. But although little Dick is indifferent to his surroundings in general, Klein tells us that there is nonetheless some significant symbolic traffic: 'he was interested in trains and stations and also in door-handles, doors and the opening and shutting of them' (p. 101). With characteristic literalness, she interprets these interests as having to do with penetration into the maternal body (doors and locks are the ways in and out) and dread of what would be done to him after he had succeeded, especially by the father's penis (door-handles stand for the father's penis and his own). Little Dick's literalness – what Hanna Segal calls 'concrete thinking' characteristic of psychosis – colludes with Klein's to give her an opening.[10]

The difficulty in analysing little Dick, for Klein, lies in the absence of symbolic representations. When she plays trains with him, Klein gives him not toys, but representations, names, signs in exchange for toys. Although Klein herself doesn't put it like this, inserting a difference between symbol and thing gives rise to a traffic in what is non-identical; the same sameness-and-difference that distinguishes big and little trains can be thought of as characterizing the relations – the play – of signs:

> I took a big train and put it beside a smaller one and called them 'Daddy-train and Dick-train'. Thereupon he picked up the train I called 'Dick' and made it roll to the window and said 'station'. I explained: 'The station is mummy; Dick is going into mummy.' He left the train, ran into the space between the outer and inner doors of the room, shut himself in, saying 'Dark' and ran out again directly. He went through this performance several times. I explained to him: 'It is dark inside mummy. Dick is inside dark mummy.' Meantime he picked up the train again, but soon ran back into the space between the doors. While I was saying that he was going into dark mummy, he said twice in a questioning way: 'Nurse?' I answered: 'Nurse is soon coming', and this he repeated and used the words later quite correctly, retaining them in his mind.

> (p. 102)

On later visits little Dick again puts the train in the hall, calls for his nurse, and finally, seized with acute anxiety, calls for Melanie Klein herself. In Klein's account, we see that the non-identity of symbols and the thing symbolized leads him simultaneously to anxiety, to object-relations, and to language.[11] It also leads to the surfacing of his sadism against the mother's body; he tries to cut the toy coal out of the toy coal-cart ('Cut'), throws the damaged cart in a drawer ('Gone'), and scratches with his nails on the door of the entrance hall, 'showing that he identified the space with the cart and both with the mother's body, which he was attacking' (p. 103). Little Dick's 'cut' and 'gone' recapitulate both his sadism and his defence against it. The dark space which little Dick inhabits between the two doors is the blank space within the maternal body, emptied of its threatening contents.

Dick, writes Klein, 'cut himself off from reality and brought his phantasy life to a standstill by taking refuge in the phantasies of a dark, empty, vague womb' (p. 105). In terms more Kristevan than Kleinian, one could say that his aggressivity turns to dread of the unnameable. Klein initiates the process of symbolization, not so much by restoring the womb's injurious contents (faeces, urine, penis) as by answering his call with her name-calling. When he attacks a cupboard with spoon and knife, he also 'asked what the different parts were called.' His interest in 'the things themselves' is transformed into an interest in the naming of parts: 'The words which before he had heard and disregarded he now remembered and applied correctly' (pp. 105–6). One intriguing form taken by little Dick's systematic misspeech can be glimpsed in the earlier moment in Klein's account when a linguistic inversion – a slip, a misplaced letter or 'literal' – has him literally eating his words, or rather, the toy man that stands for his all-devouring, Saturn-like father (see Figure 5.1):

> We came to recognize the father's penis and a growing feeling of aggression against it in many forms, the desire to eat and destroy it being specially prominent. For example, on one occasion, Dick lifted a little toy man to his mouth, gnashed his teeth and said 'Tea daddy,' by which he meant 'Eat daddy.' He then asked for a drink of water. The introjection of the father's penis proved to be associated with the dread both of it, as of a primitive, harm-inflicting super-ego, and of being punished by the mother thus robbed: dread, that is, of the external and the introjected objects.
>
> (p. 104)

Here little Dick, in Lacanian terms, acts out his foreclosure of 'the Name of the Father,' the big Dick of language. For little Dick, the paternal phallus is a penile body part – a part that he wants to eat whole. Making a meal of the phallus, instead of naming the father, little Dick seems to say, in this primitive psychic gesture: I am both little Dick and daddy Dick, Saturn's child and Saturn himself. The undifferentiated little Dick and daddy Dick constitute a primitive, devouring identity.

Psychosis could be defined as a letter that has mistaken its place. The first (most literal) sense of 'literal' listed in the *Oxford English Dictionary* (hereafter OED)

Figure 5.1 Saturn devouring his infants, Francisco Goya (1821–3). Madrid, Prado

is 'of or pertaining to the letters of the alphabet.' Little Dick has grasped the principle of linguistic difference (to a T), without being able to apply it to his own condition. The slippage from 'Eat' to 'Tea' sketches this failure to differentiate at the level of the letter; taken literally, taken internally (*à la lettre*), words lapse regressively into the nonsense of psychosis. The world of little Dick is a world equally without difference and affect. As Lacan will write, 'Everything is equally real for him, equally indifferent' (p. 81). His use of language as repetition-without-difference tells the same story (as Klein recounts, 'sometimes he would repeat the words correctly, but would go on repeating them in an incessant, mechanical way' (p. 99). We could call this failure to differentiate 'literalness,' a fixation at the level of the letter; or, alternatively, mistaken identification with the mechanical aspect of language. But mistaken identification also characterizes the vestigial depressive position – associated with the ability to see wholes instead of empty holes (or body parts) – that coexists with little Dick's schizophrenia. Along with his sadism, little Dick shows moments of 'remorse, pity, and a feeling that he must make restitution':

> Thus he would proceed to place the little toy men on my lap or in my hand, put everything back in the drawer and so on. . . . This early identification with the object could not as yet be brought into relation with reality. For instance, when Dick saw some pencil shavings on my lap he said, 'poor Mrs Klein.' But on a similar occasion he said in just the same way, 'poor curtain.' Side by side with his incapacity for tolerating anxiety, this premature *empathy* became a decisive factor in his warding-off of all destructive impulses.
>
> (pp. 104–5)

Mrs Klein and the furnishings are all one to little Dick; from treating her like the furniture, he moves to treating the curtains like her and wanting to repair them. For little Dick, there is no difference between objects and 'objects.' Psychosis, then, could also be defined as empathy that has mistaken its place. To which one might add that the characteristic of Kleinian psychoanalysis is its empathy with – its feeling for – psychosis, its willingness to accompany the regress of the subject's phantasies and projective identifications to the very limit of their appearance.

II 'A very elementary key'

What did Klein do for little Dick? Lacan would reply: she gave him an Oedipus complex. His 'return to Klein' uses her work as the occasion to develop his own ideas about the relations of imaginary and symbolic registers. He first broaches Klein's essay in 'Discourse Analysis and Ego Analysis,' where Anna Freud stands in for 'discourse analysis,' while Melanie Klein represents the analysis of contents ('ego analysis'). Intrigued as he is by her technique – 'as a result of this interpretation something happens' – Lacan repeatedly, strikingly, characterizes Klein's literal-minded application of the Oedipus complex as 'brutal':

> She slams the symbolism on him with complete brutality, does Melanie Klein, on little Dick! Straight away she starts off hitting him large-scale interpretations. She hits him a brutal verbalization of the Oedipal myth, almost as revolting for us as for any reader – '*you are the little train, you want to fuck your mother.*'
>
> (p. 68)

Little Dick is 'eyeball to eyeball with reality,' as Lacan puts it ('The space between the two doors is the body of his mother,' p. 69). Or, a child for whom 'the real and the imaginary are equivalent' (p. 84) is eyeball to eyeball with Mrs Klein, for whom, similarly 'everything takes place on a plane of equal reality – of unreal reality, as she puts it' (p. 82). The two meet in the empty space between the two doors, the space of the maternal body, where Melanie Klein, 'with her animal instinct . . . dares to speak to him' (p. 69). In doing so, Lacan observes, she provokes a response; little Dick's anxiety is translated into a call: 'Nurse!', 'Mrs Klein!'

Properly speaking, for Lacan, little Dick hasn't attained speech: 'Speech has not come to him. Language did not stick to his imaginary system' (p. 84). Thus he remains 'at the level of the call.' Klein's analytic intervention 'literally gives names' to what was before 'neither nameable nor named,' but 'just a reality pure and simple' (p. 69); in Lacan's ventriloquization, 'I won't beat about the bush, I just tell him – *Dick little train, big train daddy-train*' (p. 85). This all-too literal naming is what makes language 'stick' to the trains, door-handles, and '*dark*' of little Dick's imaginary. Klein's words 'graft' the Oedipus complex onto little Dick's symbol-making capacity: 'Melanie Klein's discourse . . . brutally grafts the primary symbolizations of the Oedipal situation onto the initial ego-related [*moïque*] inertia of the child' (p. 85). Lacan locates as the 'Crucial moment, when the sticking of language to the subject's imaginary begins to sketch itself,' Little Dick's one word: 'Station' (p. 85). Only connect. Klein's brutality, a kind of arbitrariness that takes for granted both the unconscious and the Oedipus complex, 'out of habit', allows her to 'bring in verbalization'; in so doing, she symbolizes 'an effective relationship, that of one named being with another' (p. 85). 'The brutal verbalization of the Oedipus myth' is for Lacan the enabling fiction – the brutal graft – which makes it possible for little Dick to enter into a symbolic network of relations and signifiers.[12] Now he can name the father instead of eating him.

When Lacan calls the Oedipus complex 'this nucleus, this little palpitating cell of symbolism' and 'the key – a very elementary key' (pp. 85, 86), he insists that little Dick's access to 'genuine speech' is nevertheless 'not any old speech.' The key fits; Klein's Oedipal story sticks. But not, in Lacan's book, 'literally.' The nucleus or metaphor for all complex structures, the Oedipus complex, according to Lacan, surfaces through a kind of internal force (p. 65); it is too brutal. What is 'brutal' in Klein (i.e. arbitrary, informed by sheer habit) becomes Lacan's own brutal (i.e. highly theorized, deliberate) insistence on the necessity for the subject's integration into a symbolic system, 'not any old' system, but one that is always encoded ahead of time, for which the Oedipus complex is a kind of shorthand or synechdoche (part for whole). At once arbitrary and inevitable, the Oedipus complex is less an explanation than a (linguistic) structure, one that Lacan describes as 'already established, typical and significant.' Or, as he puts it, 'when we get on the trail of the unconscious, what we encounter are structured, organized, complex situations. Freud gave us the first model of it, its standard, in the Oedipus complex' (p. 65). Lacan, then, seems to say that Klein's brutal band-aid, her 'plastering on of the Oedipus complex' ('She plastered on the symbolization of the Oedipus myth,' p. 85) is therapeutic *because* both arbitrary and pre-ordained ('already established'); like metaphor, the Oedipal graft initiates a transfer or carry-over of meaning – in this case from the (literal) object to the 'object,' from the little train that is the little Dick to the daddy-train that is the big Dick.

Lacan sees Klein as getting access to little Dick's unconscious by means of forcible entry with a crudely Oedipal key (Lacan translates it as *'avoir ouvert les portes de son inconscient,'* p. 85n). Klein's own account of Little Dick, however, suggests that something else may also be at stake. Her unthinking attribution of an unconscious to Little Dick resembles the 'premature *empathy'* that Dick himself uses to ward off or repair destructiveness ('Brutality'): 'Poor Mrs Klein,' 'Poor curtains' (and poor little Dick). I want to backtrack in order to pursue the idea of prematurity for a moment – the prematurity that for Klein is the very hallmark of the Oedipus complex. Klein suggests that little Dick's backward-ness in symbol-formation is paradoxically associated with what she sees as his premature genitality, and, consequently, his 'premature and exaggerated identification with the object attacked' (p. 101) – the mother, 'Poor Mrs Klein,' the furnishings in her room. Lacan ventriloquizes this prematurity as Klein's own 'brutal verbalization,' an assault on Little Dick and on her readers that he glosses in words 'almost as revolting for us as for any reader,' namely *'you want to fuck your mother'* (p. 68) – alternatively, in his parodying of Klein's nursery-talk, *'Dick little train, big train daddy-train,'* or, later in his glossing of 'dangerous objects' as 'poo-poo' (p. 82). Here the prematurity or sexual precocity is Lacan's own, like the nursery talk; the child attacked by an adult's revoltingly adult language (or the adult attacked by the revolting nursery language?) is actually ('any reader') assaulted by the notorious mother-fucker in Lacan himself who pooh-poohs (for instance) the ego-psychologists. The scapegoat for Lacanian brutality, not surprisingly, is Melanie Klein.

For Klein, little Dick's 'Poor Mrs Klein' indicates his too-early identification with the object (the mother whom he fears to destroy and whom he fears will destroy him). Klein, we might note, also empathizes, finding in little Dick's empathy not only a defence against his aggressive impulses, but the basis for reparative symbol formation. The 'premature' genitality that Lacan turns into a pre-mature, back-dated version of his own genital sexuality becomes, for Klein, a pre-mature version of psychoanalytic empathy, read back onto the child by what amounts to an act of too-great imaginative projection, a mis-identification. Lacan puts brutally literal words into Klein's mouth (and into little Dick's too, as when he insists that 'There is a subject here who *quite literally* does not reply' (p. 84, my italics): Klein puts meaning into Dick's words (the meaning that Lacan finds all too literal), thereby creating – loosely speaking, projecting – a subject who can reply to her where none is (yet). This form of projection at once resembles and differs from an allied process, projection in its full, psychoanalytic sense – the sense in which 'projective identification' precedes the 'empathy' which in Klein's scheme it enables. Here is the neat anecdote by which Laplanche and Pontalis, in *The Language of Psycho-Analysis*, illustrate the difference between projection in 'the ordinary sense' and 'projection in the Freudian sense' (i.e. as they would wish the term to be understood): 'Surely we have the same position?' says one philosopher to another; 'I hope not,' he replies, in 'a radical rejection of his opponent's ideas – ideas which he is afraid to discover in himself.'[13] What is brutal in Lacan's attribution to Klein of these 'revoltingly' literal words corresponds not only to what is unthinking in Klein, and not only to what is instinctual in little Dick, but to the primary and negative nature of projection itself as a form of rejection – to processes fleetingly glimpsed in these moments of projection and negation in Lacan's own text. As Lacan remarks apropos of projection, 'Here, we are in the mirror relation' (p. 83) – a remark that opens, dizzyingly, onto the imaginary of psychoanalytic theory, where Klein, a theoretical 'mother,' constitutes Lacan's 'object' of enquiry.

III A Brutal Verbalization

Lacan is a master of the 'I hope not' gesture of brutal theoretical self-differentiation that involves radical rejection of his opponents' ideas ('ideas which he is afraid to discover in himself'). 'Brutal,' the OED tells us, brings with it connotations of animality rather than humanity; want of intelligence or reasoning power; animal or sensual nature; rudeness, coarseness, or lack of refinement; and inhumanity in the sense of cruelty, savagery, or ferocity. If Klein is for Lacan deficient on a theoretical level – 'Melanie Klein has neither a theory of the imaginary nor a theory of the *ego*' (p. 82) – Lacan's own writing is often marked, as we have seen, by the polemical deployment of unrefined coarseness ('*you want to fuck your mother*'). And if Klein is the theorist of the instincts and their manifestation in the sadism – the cruelty, savagery and ferocity – of the small child's phantasies about the maternal body, Lacan is the rigorous theorist of the linguistic unconscious whose classic formula, '*the unconscious is the discourse of the other*' receives its most spectacular demonstration in the case of little Dick. 'Brutal,' then, suggests the ways in which Lacan (an analyst not known for pulling his punches) uses Klein's theoretical deficiency – her arrested development – to fuel his own theoretical engine. But Lacan's insistence on Klein's brutality might make us ask: what Kleinian ideas – what aspect of Kleinian theory – may Lacan be afraid to discover in himself? The Klein who becomes Lacan's little Dick ('incapable of even so much as suspecting the existence of the category of the signifier') also strikingly exemplifies the problematic 'place of the imaginary in the symbolic structure' (p. 73) that provides the starting-point for 'the topic of the imaginary.'[14] Lacan's sustained meditation on what, in Klein's case history, 'cannot be understood' reminds us that the door to psychoanalytic understanding is opened on 'the basis of a kind of refusal of understanding' (p. 73). A difficulty in understanding (in Klein's understanding) provides the key.

Melanie Klein's brutality – her brutal application of the Oedipus complex, her failure to suspect 'the existence of the category of the signifier' – is central to the problem that Lacan poses in 'The topic of the imaginary.' I have already indicated how, for Lacan, Klein's sense of 'reality' scarcely differs from little Dick's. As Klein 'grafts' what she calls the symbolic onto little Dick, so Lacan in turn grafts what *he* calls the symbolic onto Klein – not only to reveal her collusion with the non-sense of little Dick's psychosis ('what, in this text, cannot be understood'), but also to effect a forcible cure of her defective, psychotic theory by way of his language. But the graft takes because there is something to get a handle on in Klein, just as there is something in little Dick's psychosis for Klein herself to get a handle on. A residual theory of the imaginary is already present in Klein, just as (Lacan points out) 'the child already has his own system of language' (p. 83). What is it, then, that Lacan may fear to discover in his own ideas? Surely nothing other than the crucial role of the imaginary, the domain which Lacan associates loosely with Klein's account of projective identification and its allied processes, but which in his system is subordinated to the symbolic and to language. To put it another way, if little Dick, lost in the chaos of an unorganized imaginary, stands in Lacan's account for Klein's projective identifications and her inability to distinguish between real and unreal (or literal and metaphoric), we could also speculate that it is the troubling presence of Kleinian object-relations that Lacanian theory is reluctant to acknowledge ('I hope not,' we overhear him say).

We have already seen how both Lacan and Klein, in opening the doors of the unconscious, blur the boundaries between one unconscious and another – using psychosis (what Lacan calls 'too real a relation to reality', p. 87) and empathy (too great an identification with the object) as a means to posit the existence of another subjectivity in their own theoretical writing. And we have seen too that a degree of negation or rejection ('projection' proper) attends the elaboration of Lacanian theory; perhaps any theory. It is just this difficulty in distinguishing what is inside from what is outside that Laplanche and Pontalis, in their dictionary entry for 'Projective Identification,' point to as a theoretical difficulty for the Kleinian concept itself: 'This approach [i.e. Klein's] fails to tackle the problem of whether there is a valid distinction to be made, within the category of identification, between those modes of the process where the subject makes himself one with the other person and those where he makes the other person one with himself.'[15] 'Here we are in the mirror relation' indeed – faced with a confused category of identification which problematizes the process of differentiation in very much the way in which it is problematic for little Dick (and, one might add, in a way which points to the Kristevan category of preoedipal, pre-objectival identification, to which I'll return). In this connection, it's worth mentioning Lacan's own deployment, elsewhere, of a topos that has neither an inside nor an outside (and a hole in the middle): the Klein bottle.[16] Kleinian theory has everything to do with containers and what they contain (the mother's body and its *contenu*). What may well be disturbing to Lacan is the possibility of slippage – the possibility, for instance, of not being able to tell the difference between his theory and hers. Swallowing too much Klein may be what is making Lacan gag.

Lacan claims that the 'elementary key' provided by Klein unlocks not just the less complex structure – the less complex 'complex' – but also the more complex 'complexes,' or what Lacan calls 'a set of relations between subjects of a wealth and complexity besides which the Oedipus complex seems only to be so abridged an edition that in the end it cannot always be used' (p. 86). An abridged edition (shrink-lit, so to speak), the Oedipus complex provides an elementary handbook for analytic technique. For Lacan, the unabridged (unshrunk) edition is language itself. But in this essay, Lacan famously makes his point by appealing not to language but to optics. Calling Klein's case history 'the write-up of an experiment' (p. 80), he invokes 'the experiment of the inverted bouquet' as a stand-in for the mirror phase (see Figure 5.2). Lacan's point is that in order to see the bouquet reflected in the pot you have to have a subject-position (a position that only language – the symbolic – provides). Without it, he says, all you have is 'a sad, empty pot, or some lonesome flowers, depending on the case' (p. 80). Poor curtain . . . with this comical flicker of mis-placed empathy, Lacan returns us to little Dick, for whom the pot is always sad, and the flowers lonesome, since 'in his case, the bouquet and the vase cannot both be there at the same time. That is the key' (p. 82). Without the Kleinian 'symbolic formations' that Lacan redefines as 'imaginative interplay,' all Dick has is the naked reality of objects. In 'the experiment of the inverted bouquet,' the vase is visible, while the hidden bouquet takes its place in the vase by way

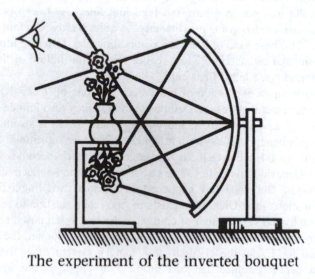

The experiment of the inverted bouquet

Figure 5.2 'A sad, empty pot, or some lonesome flowers', *The Seminar of Jacques Lacan: Book I* (1954)

of an optical illusion, as a reflection of something actually hidden from view (or *vice versa*; in a bit of play on his own account, Lacan suggests that inverting the pot would work just as well): 'let us say that the image of the body . . . is like the imaginary vase which contains the bouquet of real flowers' (p. 79). These are the topsy-turvy, always unstable relations of real and imaginary that only the symbolic can put in their proper place.

For Lacan, the reason little Dick can't put the flowers in the vase is that, while he can *project*, he can't *introject*. Here Lacan pauses to insist on a crucial (linguistic) difference. For him – as opposed to Klein – 'introjection is always the introjection of the speech of the other, which introduces an entirely different dimension from that of projection' (p. 83). But at this point, Lacan takes an unexpected tack. He points out that little Dick can play after all, and not only with 'the container and the contained' (p. 82); he plays with language ('He even makes use of it to play a game of opposition against the adults' attempts to intrude,' (p. 83). 'It isn't language that I am covertly slipping in,' says Lacan – taking by surprise an audience all set to say *'Of course, being Doctor Lacan, he uses this to go on about language again'* (to which he replies a bit too emphatically: 'I hope not'). It is not even, he asserts, 'a higher level of language. It is in fact beneath language, if we're talking of levels' (p. 84), wherever that level might be. Lack ('it lacks') is what even 'a being deprived of language' – a pet, Lacan suggests, but it could be a baby, for that matter – communicates when it calls its owner. The brute wants to be fed. The call implies a possibility of refusal, a demand beyond need. But it is also, deep down ('beneath language'), an instinctual call: 'Feed me, feed me,' the theme song of the all-devouring plant in *Little Shop of Horrors*. When little Dick says 'station' and 'everything starts firing,' we find that what Melanie Klein really did was not feed him, but feed him *lines*. As Lacan puts it, *'The station is mummy. Dick is going into mummy. . . .* She'll only feed him these kind of lines' (p. 85). These kind of lines are a starvation diet. Offering him words in place of instinctual satisfaction, Klein recodes the initial failure of little Dick's nursing as normative. Klein's lines cure.

By transforming an expression of brute need into one of 'lack,' Klein's lines not only fire the machinery of the Oedipus complex; they also initiate a series of substitutions. Or, as Lacan puts it, startlingly, '[Little Dick] is swallowed up in a series of equivalencies, in a system in which objects are substituted one for the other' (p. 86). In the great Oedipal timetable, little Dick becomes Saussure's famous 8:45 Geneva–Paris train.[17] The key is not the line so much as the series of equivalencies. But what has happened in Lacan's own linguistic train of thought? Voracious little Dick, who exists in 'too real a relation to reality,' gets swallowed up by the very system of equivalencies that is supposed to feed him. 'It lacks': by an inversion like that of the vase and the bouquet, the call of the pet becomes, for Lacan the clamour of a hungry system of equivalencies in search of a derailed subject. In this moment of slippage, the insistence of Lacanian theory – *'Of course, being Doctor Lacan, he uses this to go on about language again'* – surfaces as the 'core of this observation' concerning optics, fuelled by its own linguistic drive. What we glimpse, *pace* Lacan himself, is not so much 'the possibility of defining the contained [*contenu*] and the non-contained [*non-contenu*]' (p. 86) which the symbolic gives little Dick, but rather the Klein bottle (the up-ended vase), which has neither inside nor outside – the difficulty of separating imaginary and symbolic in the very machinery of language itself. We might say, then, that where Melanie Klein brutally verbalizes, little Dick gets chewed up in Lacan's pet theory. The corollary of this process is that Kleinian affect and Kleinian instinct ('with her animal instinct') get spat up on the mat. We could call the spit-up 'brutality,' the animal instinct which is the underside of Kleinian empathy. This is the brute that Lacan is afraid to find driving the machine of language.

IV 'Poor Melanie Klein'

Lacan construes little Dick's greater-than-normal potential for empathy as fear of fragmentation: 'When he sees little pencil shavings on Melanie Klein's blouse, the result of a fragmentation, he says – *Poor Melanie Klein*' (p. 70). Or, as Hanna Segal glosses this moment of pathos, 'To him the shavings were Mrs Klein cut into bits.'[18] But this *corps morcelé* also suggests the detritus of a cast-out mother. For Kristeva, abjecting the mother is the condition for self-differentiation on the part of a not-yet subject or 'abject' – the 'abject' being at once little Dick himself and the body of a maternal stand-in, the Kleinian not-yet-object (see Figure 5.3). Kristeva's 'Freud and Love: Treatment and its Discontents' invokes '*Einfühlung* (the assimilation of other people's feelings)' as a means of exploring both analytical transference-love and the pre-objectal, primary identification which (Kristeva argues) is correlative to the abjection of the mother.[19] Probing beyond Lacan's question ('how does the imaginary give rise to the symbolic?'), Kristeva asks instead: 'what are the conditions for the emergence of the imaginary?' She insists on the preexistence of a symbolic function and on '*various dispositions* giving access to that function' (p. 44). Klein writes that little Dick had cut himself off from reality 'by taking refuge in the phantasies of a dark, empty, vague womb' (p. 105). Lacan reformulates this 'reality which knows no development' as 'a single and unique primary identification, with the following names – the *void*, the *dark*.' He goes on: 'This gap is precisely what is human in the structure peculiar to the subject' (pp. 69–70). Kristeva glosses Lacan's gap – a '*gaping hole*' that can also be equated with the arbitrariness of the Saussurean sign – as 'this notion of emptiness, which is at the root of the human psyche' (p. 23).[20] She speculates that 'the *emptiness* that is intrinsic to the beginnings of the symbolic function appears as the first separation between what is not yet an *Ego* and what is not yet an *object*' (i.e., an 'abject'). Primary narcissism, she suggests, may be the defence designed to protect this 'emptiness ... intrinsic to the symbolic function,' introducing the minimal difference without which 'chaos would sweep away any possibility of distinction, trace and symbolization' (p. 24). Identifying with the gap makes signification possible.

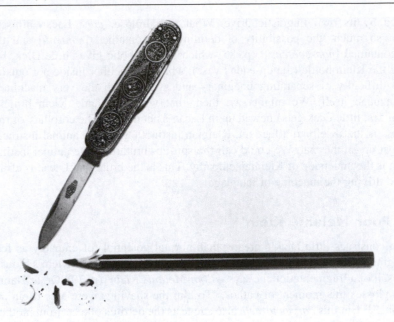

Figure 5.3 'It was very painful when I was sharpened for the first time', Marcello Minale, *The Black Pencil* (1968)

The child, writes Kristeva,

> with all due respect to Lacan, not only *needs* the real and the symbolic – it signifies itself as child, in other words as the subject that is, and neither as a psychotic nor as an adult, precisely in that zone where *emptiness* and *narcissism*, the one upholding the other, constitute the zero degree of imagination.
>
> (p. 24)

Revising 'The Mirror-Phase,' Kristeva posits narcissism as an already ternary, 'complex' structure prior even to the complex structure of oedipalization, and then asks: what preserves or structures narcissistic emptiness? Her answer is 'identification,' which – following Freud's discussion of identification in *Group Psychology and the Analysis of the Ego* (1921) – she refers to as <u>*Einfühlung*</u>, or <u>empathy</u>. Reflecting on the ambivalence of identification, Freud derives it from the oral phase 'in which the object that we long for and prize is assimilated by eating and in that way is annihilated as such' (*SE*, XVIII, p. 105). Shades of 'Tea daddy,' as well as his Kristevan alter ego in the case history appended to 'Freud and Love,' 'Matthew or the Walkman against Saturn' (Matthew wields his ubiquitous headset as a defence against 'the image of the devouring father . . . eating, voracious, insatiable,' p. 54). Properly speaking, this archaic, oral identification, 'where what I incorporate is what I become, where *having* amounts to *being*' (p. 25), precedes identification with an object. Contrasting pre-objectival (preoedipal) identification with the metonymic structure of Lacanian (oedipal) desire, Kristeva equates it with metaphor, especially as it appears in analytical transference and in 'the internal, recursive, redundant logic of discourse, which is accessible within "afterspeech"' (p. 25); that is, in what I have called 'the brute in the machine' – the drive and affect that, for Kristeva, as for André Green, Lacan's vision of language occludes.[21]

References to Klein – 'a theoretician of gratitude seen as "an important off-shoot of the capacity for love"' (p. 27) – surface insistently in 'Freud and Love.' In 'The Origins of Transference' (1952), Klein herself had argued that analytic transference recapitulates the earliest processes of object relations. Anticipating the trajectory of 'Freud and Love,' Klein broaches the matter of transference by way of autoerotic and narcissistic 'states' (as opposed to Freud's 'stages'), and points to an equivocation in Freud's own thinking; might object relations – a more than merely physical relation to the mother's breast – even precede narcissism? Klein goes on to remind her readers of Freud's remarks in *The Ego and the Id* about the first and most important identification with the father of personal prehistory. In a footnote she draws attention to Freud's suggestion 'that these first identifications . . . are a direct and immediate identification which takes place earlier than any object cathexis. This suggestion seems to imply that introjection even precedes object relations.'[22] Klein's tactic here is to suggest that Freud had not yet made up his mind on the question. Kristeva, in turn, builds on Freud's equivocation when she calls 'incorporating and introjecting orality's function . . . the essential substratum of what constitutes man's being, namely *language*' (p. 26). She equates introjection of the speech of the other with identification: 'In being able to receive the other's words, to assimilate, repeat and reproduce them, I become like him: One. A subject of enunciation. Through psychic osmosis/identification. Through love' (p. 26). This loving, preoedipal, nonobjectal identification, a psychic 'osmosis/identification' that 'lets one hold onto the joys of chewing, swallowing, nourishing oneself . . . with words,' reappears in transference-love. In Kristeva's account, as in Klein's, the third term that structures metaphoric identification is Freud's 'father in individual pre-history.'

Is this third term the father, or the mother's desire for the father (or perhaps, 'a coagulation of the mother and her desire', p. 41)? For Klein, the preoedipal relation is by definition a 'relation between *two* people into which no other object enters,'[23] even if a phantasized penis or part-object is included in the maternal relation. Or, as Kristeva puts it, 'Melanie Klein's gratitude is nevertheless and at the same time directed towards the maternal object in its entirety' (p. 28). Kristeva acknowledges that '*empirically*, the first affectations, the first imitations and the first vocalizations as well are directed towards the mother.' Thus, for her, the assumption of any primary identification with Freud's 'father in individual prehistory' on the part of the child 'is tenable only if one conceives of *identification* as being always already within the symbolic orbit, under the sway of language' (p. 27). Here Kristeva goes out of her way to point to a contradiction in Klein. For Klein, love is apparently innate (an instinctual response to the satisfaction at the breast); yet it also functions as a defence, and must therefore belong to the realm of ego-related activities (as an idealization of the 'good' breast that stems from persecution by the 'bad' breast). How are we to explain the contradictory origin of love in both instinct and idealization? In Kristeva's words, 'By what miracle is that possible, in a Kleinian life where two live without a third party other than a persecuting or fascinating penis?' (p. 28). Klein notices an equivocation in Freud: Kristeva opens the fault line in Klein's equivocation over 'good breast' versus 'idealized' object (what is innate as opposed to ego-related, hence involving some form of object relations). Kristeva's lever is the symbolic third term provided by Freud's 'father of individual prehistory.'

By a double movement, Kristeva at once distances herself from what she calls 'Lacanian notions of an always-already-there of language' and inserts a diacritical mark of difference into the space occupied by the preoedipal mother. What Kristeva calls 'the archaic inscription of the father' becomes the sign of the mother's lack of plenitude – a 'Third Party' that prevents her from 'playing at the phallus game all by herself,' as Kristeva puts it, in the back room of Kleinian theory (the space between Klein's two doors):

> In contrast with Melanie Klein's 'projective identification,' the proposition I am offering here has the advantage of pointing to, even before the Oedipal triangle and within a specific disposition, the place of the Third Party; without the latter, the phase Melanie Klein calls 'schizo-paranoid' could not become a 'depressive' phase and thus could not carry the 'symbolic equivalencies' to the level of linguistic 'signs.' The archaic inscription of the father seems to me a way of modifying the fantasy of a phallic mother playing at the phallus game all by herself, alone and complete, in the back-room of Kleinism and post-Kleinism.
>
> (p. 44)

The problem that troubles some feminist readers of Kristeva's more recent work – how does this appeal to the 'father of individual pre-history' differ from Lacan's Name of the Father? – is a nonissue for Kristeva herself; as she poses it, the problem is rather how to avoid the regressive fantasy (or rather, the Kleinian 'phantasy') of a phallic mother. Accordingly she can dismiss as unimportant the question 'Who might be the object of primary identification, daddy or mummy?' (in any case, the answer is: 'both'). Instead, Kristeva asks, apropos of the analytic situation, 'of what value would the question be when it actually bears on states existing on the border between the psychic and the somatic, idealization and eroticism . . . ?' (p. 28). This is the borderline where transference-love appears, and where 'one hears the discourse that is performed there starting with that limit of advent-and-loss of the subject – which is *Einfühlung*.' The 'archaic inscription of the father' enters the picture as a question. What in the mother exceeds her desire for the child, creating the gap (the 'Not I') with which the *infans* can identify?

The 'limit of advent-and-loss of the subject' is played out in the analytic discourse as empathy, the (mistaken) identification which allows metaphor – rather than the mother – to emerge from the vestibule of the unreal-real. For Kristeva, as for Klein, the analyst is also an empathizer, accompanying the patient in a regress 'as far as the limits and accidents of his object relations,' and deciphering a discourse that exists (to rephrase Lacan) at the very limits and accidents of the appearance of language:

> The *Einfühlung* gives the language signifier exchanged during treatment a heterogeneous, drive-affected dimension. It loads it with something preverbal, or even nonrepresentable that needs to be deciphered while taking into account the more precise articulations of discourse (style, grammar, phonetics), and at the same time while cutting through language, in the direction of the unspeakable, indicated by fantasies and 'insight' narratives as well as by symptomatic misspeech (slips of the tongue, illogical statements, etc.).
>
> (p. 29)

Commenting elsewhere on the heterogeneity of the semiotic, Kristeva corrects any misunderstanding that her aim is 'to integrate some alleged concreteness, brute corporality, or energy-in-itself into a language suspected of being too abstract.'[24] For her it is not, and never can be, a matter of turning back to the mother-as-origin, as a literal reading of Klein might tempt us to turn back or regress (the semiotic, Kristeva reminds us, 'is without primacy and has no place as origin').[25] Rather, we should attend to this work of deciphering the unspeakable within speech – attend, that is, to little Dick's 'literal' ('Dick . . . gnashed his teeth and said "Tea daddy," by which he meant "Eat daddy"'). Little Dick's 'symptomatic misspeech,' his slip of the tongue (which is also, as the OED illustrates at length, a slip implicating the teeth), is an illogical statement that partakes of 'the internal, recursive, redundant logic of discourse.' Lacan would see it in little Dick's foreclosure of the Name of the Father. Kristeva, by contrast, suggests that we should view Little Dick's oral incorporation as primary identification. We could redefine this identification as the 'heterogeneity' of metaphor.

'Tea daddy' – the A to T (as the OED has it, 'originally . . . the last letter of the [Greek] alphabet') or Alpha and Omega of all identifications – conjoins the oral drive (biting) to its fathering metaphor (the Saturnine devourer) on the borderline between 'incorporating and introjecting orality's function' that Kristeva defines as the essential substratum of language. In 'Freud and Love,' Kristeva dissociates metaphor from 'the classical rhetorical trope (*figurative v. plain*).' Instead she allies it with 'the modern theories of metaphor that decipher within it an indefinite jamming of semantic features one into the other, a meaning being acted out,' and with 'the drifting of heterogeneity within a heterogeneous psychic apparatus, going from drives and sensations to signifier and conversely' (p. 37). This semantic jamming, with its acting out of meaning and its oscillation between drives and signifiers, serves as a reminder that nothing can ever really be 'literal,' even for little Dick (even for Melanie Klein). The Lacanian insistence of the letter in the unconscious becomes for Kristeva, by way of a Kleinian back-formation, the heterogeneous drift that links drives and signs in the metaphoric structures of transferential discourse. Klein's 'Premature empathy' (Einfühlung) – what might be called 'pathetic fallacy' – represents the first positing of the subject in language, or a founding figural moment, by means of a misplaced identification; it is less a matter of naming (as Lacan had argued) than of misnaming. When little Dick spots the pencil shavings on Melanie Klein's lap, and says 'Poor Mrs Klein' (or even 'Poor curtain'), a Kristevan gloss might run something like this: 'in abjecting the mother, I (mis)identify or metaphorize myself.'

*

Little Dick reminds us that where we have our words, we (once and still) imagine eating them too; but he also reminds us that 'having' and 'eating' – like 'having' and 'being' – delineate the borderline or point of slippage between incorporation and introjection that is constitutive not only of language but of the capacity for linguistic play ('the joys of chewing, swallowing, nourishing oneself . . . with words'). Klein's oedipal lines feed brutal joys, the oral play which accompanies little Dick's symbolic eating (for tea) of Freud's 'father of individual prehistory.' If little Dick bit off more than he could chew, so – at least according to Lacan and Kristeva – did Klein herself. The Lacanian reading brutalizes Klein: the Kristevan reading has an empathetic feel. Rereading Klein's lines with Kristevan hindsight allows us at least to credit them with their prematurity or 'anticipation' – their prior understanding – of the ways in which we might now wish to digest them rather than losing them altogether. I want to end with Klein's brief early note on 'The Importance of Words in Early-Analysis' (1927), in which she relates a game with a child involving a Mr Cookey-Caker (the name represented, she says, 'the making of children in an oral and anal way'): 'The word 'Cookey-Caker' is the bridge to reality which the child avoids as long as he brings forth his phantasies only by playing.' She concludes: 'It always means progress when the child has to acknowledge the reality of the objects through his own words.'[26] Lacan's unsuspected 'category of the signifier' turns out to have been a guest at little Dick's tea party all along. I started by associating the risk of regression in reading Klein with taking her literally. I will end by suggesting that rather than eating Klein's words, we might chew on the play of metaphor that little Dick's unspeakable slip (the meeting point of teeth, tongue, and T) inscribes in the 'literal' of Klein's lines.

Notes

1 *The Selected Melanie Klein*, ed. Juliet Mitchell (Harmondsworth: Penguin, 1986), 104. Subsequent page references in the text are to this edition.

2 Jacques Lacan, *Ecrits: A Selection*, trans. Alan Sheridan (London: Tavistock, 1977), 272.

3 See *The Seminar of Jacques Lacan: Book I*, ed. Jacques-Alain Miller, trans. John Forrester (Cambridge: Cambridge University Press, 1988), 74; subsequent page references in the text are to this edition. Compare Hanna Segal's definition of symbol formation as 'an activity of the ego attempting to deal with the anxieties stirred by its relation to the object'; see 'Notes on Symbol Formation,' in *Melanie Klein Today: Developments in Theory and Practice* (2 vols), ed. Elizabeth Bott Spillius (London: Routledge, 1988), 1:163.

4 See 'Early Stages of the Oedipus Complex,' (1928): 'I have repeatedly alluded to the conclusion that the Oedipus complex comes into operation earlier than is supposed'; *The Selected Melanie Klein*, 89.

5 Lacan, *Ecrits*, 20.

6 Originally published in a shorter version as 'L'abjet d'amour,' in *Tel Quel* 91 (1982), 'Freud and Love' forms Chapter 1 of *Tales of Love*, trans. Leon S. Roudiez (New York: Columbia University Press, 1987). Subsequent page references in the text are to this edition.

7 'In projective identification the subject projects large parts of himself into the object, and the object becomes identified with the parts of the self that it is felt to contain. Similarly, internal objects are projected outside and identified with parts of the external world which come to represent them. These first projections and identifications are the beginnings of the process of symbol formation' (Segal, 'Notes on Symbol Formation,' *Melanie Klein Today*, 1: 164).

8 See *The Selected Melanie Klein*, 95; see also Phyllis Grosskurth, *Melanie Klein: Her World and Her Work* (Cambridge, Mass.: Harvard University Press, 1987), 185–8.

9 See Jacqueline Rose, *Sexuality in the Field of Vision* (London: Verso, 1986), 54–5, for a succinct summary of the difference between Klein's account of symbolization as both an effect of anxiety and a means of transcending it in the interests of mastering reality, and Lacan's emphasis on 'the structure of metaphor (or substitution) which lies at the root of, and is endlessly repeated within, subjectivity in its relation to the unconscious' – displacing the subject and making 'the real' an endlessly returning 'moment of impossibility' onto which symbolic and imaginary are grafted.

10 See Segal, 'Notes on Symbol Formation,' 163.

11 I am indebted to Shoshana Felman's reading of the Lacanian reading of the case history of little Dick. Felman writes: 'Anxiety is linked to the Symbolic. . . . The rising anxiety in Dick embodies his nascent intuition that, in a symbolic system, any element or change has repercussions in the whole. Dick thus develops anxiety, as he passes from *indifference* (everything is equally real) to *difference* (everything is not equally real) . . . '; see *Jacques Lacan and the Adventure of Insight* (Cambridge, Mass.: Harvard University Press, 1987), 116. Despite not pursuing the 'adventure of insight' beyond Lacan's own, Felman's is the most persuasive reading of Lacan's two seminars on Klein currently available.

12 See Felman, *Jacques Lacan and the Adventure of Insight*, especially 117–28 for an extended Lacanian reading of the narrative dimensions of the Oedipus myth.

13 Laplanche, J and J.-B. Pontalis, *The Language of Psycho-Analysis* (New York: Norton, 1973), 355.

14 For an extended discussion of the Lacanian Imaginary, see Rose, 'The Imaginary,' *Sexuality in the Field of Vision*, 167–97.

15 Laplanche and Pontalis, *The Language of Psycho-Analysis*, 357.

16 For Lacan's use of mathematical and geometrical models, see Catherine Clément, *The Lives and Legends of Jacques Lacan* (New York: Columbia University Press, 1983), 160, 161: 'Then there were odd looking bottles with no inside or outside, what mathematicians call Klein bottles . . . Lacan's mathematical objects gave him the means to represent forms without insides or outsides, forms without boundaries or simple separations, forms of which a hole is a constitutive part.' See also Victor Burgin, 'Geometry and Abjection,' in *Abjection, Melancholia and Love: The Work of Julia Kristeva*, eds John Fletcher and Andrew Benjamin (London: Routledge, 1990), 104–23.

17 'The example drawn on here is de Saussure's 8:45 Geneva–Paris express, which, although it can manifestly be a different train from that of the previous day, is yet identifiable as the same since it is different in function from the rest' (Rose, *Sexuality in the Field of Vision*, 184).

18 Segal, 'Notes on Symbol Formation,' 165.

19 For related readings of 'Freud and Love,' see also Cynthia Chase, 'Desire and Identification in Lacan and Kristeva,' in *Feminism and Psychoanalysis*, eds Richard Feldstein and Judith Roof (Ithaca: Cornell University Press, 1989), 65–83, and 'Primary Narcissism and the Giving of Figure: Kristeva with Hertz and deMan,' in *Abjection, Melancholia and Love*, 124–36. Neil Hertz has also developed a reading of 'L'abjet d'amour' ('Freud and Love') that tallies with his invention of a structure that he calls, appropriately for my purposes, 'a sort of capital T lying on its side'; see *The End of the Line* (New York: Columbia University Press, 1985), 217–39, especially 231–2.

20 Kristeva acknowledges her indebtedness for the notion of 'emptiness' to André Green's *Narcissisme de vie, narcissisme de mort* (Paris: Minuit, 1983).

21 See Rose, *Sexuality in the Field of Vision*, 152.

22 *The Selected Melanie Klein*, 205, 240n. See also Jean Laplanche, *New Foundations for Psychoanalysis*, trans. David Macey (Oxford: Blackwell, 1989), 80–1 and 166n, for a pithy discussion of 'the Kleinians' and a reference to this 1952 paper.

23 *The Selected Melanie Klein*, 49n.

24 Rose, *Sexuality in the Field of Vision*, 152, quoted from 'Il n'y a pas de maître à langage,' in *Nouvelle Revue de Psychanalyse* 20 (Autumn 1979): 130–1.

25 See Rose, *Sexuality in the Field of Vision*, 152.

26 Melanie Klein, *Envy and Gratitude* (London: Virago Press, 1988), 314.

Chapter 6

Tolerating nothing

Harold N. Boris

Editor's note:

This article by Harold Boris, taken from his book *Envy* (1994), is an effective demonstration of how psychoanalysts make use of Kleinian ways of thinking, although the pervading influence of Wilfred Bion is also evident throughout his writing. In the Kleinian account, the road to mental health depends on the capacity of an ego to tolerate anxiety produced by the negativity of the death drive. Boris here presents examples of the type of patient who specifically cannot tolerate that negativity, the type of patient for whom 'nothing' – or 'the no-thing' – is intolerable. This type of patient, he begins by pointing out, must be distinguished from others, whose projective identifications fill absence or emptiness with malicious or trouble-some parts of the self. This type of patient, rather, is really oppressed by nothing. For these patients there is no such thing as nothing in the ordinary sense. In the same way that 'nature abhors a vacuum,' these patients abhor any kind of emptiness, which for them literally means death. So there is never nothing as such but a malignant 'thing' wherever emptiness is found.

Boris addresses a problem that is fundamental to Kleinian concerns, that of communicating a knowledge that can only exist outside the logic of the consciously intentional statement, beyond (or before) verbal logic per se. The inability to tolerate nothing is the inability either to acknowledge or to communicate the terror that nothing causes. Thus the problem for these patients is that they must give the analyst knowledge of something that they themselves cannot bear to know. He draws several illustrative strands together to give a picture of the situation faced by both the patient and the analyst. In doing so he uses interpretive 'tools' which in the field of critical theory may well call for sceptical questioning – but as Boris states, he is not working in the realm of provable formulation, he is working in the realm of the unformulable. So his 'use' of diverse examples serves to allow his readers to 'get the idea.' He suggests, for instance, that early mental life is determined in part by a genetic Darwinian 'scheme of things,' according to which some infants feel that they deserve to and thus should die. This feeling surfaces as an intolerable dread of that which cannot be known or thought, a dread that extends throughout life and results in a constant demand for reassurance that cannot be voiced in words. The patient must unconsciously find a way of providing the analyst with the means to 'know' and receive unspeakable thoughts, in a 'projective identificatory relationship' that involves the analyst in 'getting the idea.' Boris's elegant style and evocative exposition provide a stimulating account of how the inexpressible can be expressed. (JP)

A poem Carson McCullers read to (wrote for?) her psychiatrist upon her hospitalization in Payne Whitney, New York:

What the No-thing Isn't

When we are lost what image tells?
Nothing resembles nothing. Yet nothing
Is not blank. It is configured Hell:
Of noticed clocks on winter afternoons, malignant stars,
Demanding furniture. All unrelated
And with air between.
The terror. Is it of Space, of Time?
Or the joined trickery of both conceptions?
To the lost, transfixed among the self-inflicted ruins,
All that is non-air (if this indeed is not deception)
Is agony immobilized. While Time
The endless idiot, runs screaming round the world.

There are some people for whom there is no such thing as nothing. In their psychic calculus, zero does not exist. Inside the zero, where there might otherwise be an absence, there is instead a presence of an absence. One patient, later, when he could afford to be whimsical, described the no-thing inside the zero as a breast sticking its tongue out. What follows are some of the ways I have come to think about this intolerance of nothing.

One way of thinking about it and the way it has mostly been thought about is that what is discovered in the nothing is what has been put or projected there: the self's sadism or beneficence is evacuated into the object and 'discovered' there. I have no difficulty with this formulation. I think there are circumstances in which the aggression induced by frustration or explosions of desire is simply too much, and some form of decompression needs to take place. But this is a temporary affair.

Then there are circumstances in which this frustration induced by the absent or otherwise unsatisfactory object is evacuated not into it, but into an internal representation of it, which also represents the self. This representation precurses the superego and requires of the self that the self locate the remaining affection and disaffections elsewhere. This is the motive for the projection that Freud described when considering the homosexual fundament of paranoia. In Kleinian terms, it is a version of projective identification when the object takes on valued but troublesome aspects of attributes of the self. But this also is not quite what I think is involved.

Rather, I think there is something in some human natures that abhors a vacuum. 'I see what you are saying,' says one patient, 'but as you know it makes no sense to me. When the pain is so steady and so continuous, how can I not believe she is doing it to me. When she was away last weekend, it stopped. I was in peace. I got some work done, for a change; I even cleaned up my apartment. Then around four o'clock on Sunday . . . '

Y: The torment resumed. She might have been back.
P: Yes. Would she call? Should I call?
Y: A steady stream of emissions; an unending current of pain.
P: Well, when she's not there, the agony isn't there. I don't say she causes it, just that she does it.

In this patient, like others of his ilk, the concern is not with motives, as it is with patients who are projecting intentions they do not wish to have associated with themselves. Rather, as he is hoping to make clear, his experience is of a malignant, not a malevolent, emanation. He, at other times, complains bitterly of what he has to do for her (and me) to get the malignance stopped, or at least ameliorated, but he does it all the same. Deeply rooted in his belief system is that there is good in her, if only he can bring it out. He hates any thing in himself that can be understood as implying he overrates his capacity to inflict good or evil. Cause and consequence are blurred, but there is nothing that doesn't contain one or the other.

Nothing as a container

If there is no such thing as nothing, then what may seem like nothing turns out to be a no-thing containing a some-thing as the zero was a breast sticking its tongue out.

Regarding that image, children (and older people sometimes, as well) stick their tongues between their lips when they are concentrating – for example, at 4 or 5 years, forming letters on a page. The body language there seems to be,

'Don't bother me now; I'm trying to express something; I'm not, at the moment, receptive.' This same gesture easily lends itself to defiance and even insult, in the stuck-out tongue: you have nothing to offer me, so there! The breast with the tongue protruding where the nipple might be condenses these images, as if in a dream. The breast says: 'You have nothing to offer me, so there!' This breast is a container that has everything.

However, the reciprocal to that sort of breast, namely the infant, needs the breast in two ways. It needs to take nurture and succour and pleasure out and it needs to put overstimulation in. It is the latter function that the breast with the protruding tongue seems particularly to blockade. The breast may express well enough, but it is unreceptive.

The expressive function of part- and later, perhaps, whole-objects is so obvious and so well known that I shall set it aside and consider the breast that contains so much that it is unreceptive. Is it that unreceptivity that constitutes the malignant thing that is the no-thing in nothing?

The cure for dying

Some infants, more than others, may have an idea that they ought to die, if not now, soon, if not acutely, chronically. I think the idea comes with the genes; it is part of the Darwinian scheme of things, a scheme that I think is more potent in infancy than later, simply because infants have to go on lots of inherited reflexes and such until they can learn things from the family and culture. But as analysis shows, primal programmatic urgencies continue throughout life, showing through like pentimenti when people have setbacks and losses.

In the Darwinian scheme of things, some flourish, some falter. Choosiness is built into the system, such that the fittest display characteristics that assure them (and theirs) advantage in sending their genes into the generational gene pool. Big territory, big tail, big talons and talent are rewarded by being chosen.

But of course this process is not at all fang and claw. Contests for advantage are intense, but brief. The winner shows mercy, the loser deference. This too is programmed in. Some survive, some give way; some dominate, some defer. This process is in effect in territorial disputes, mating contests, and, of course, concerning the pick of the litter.

I think some babies need to ask the breast about their fate. I can't prove this, of course; even the children in my child practice have grown out of infancy by the time I encounter them and their needs are by no means transparent. But I think so all the same, and I tell the children and grown-ups who can tolerate nothing so.

That is, I think the infant who has a dread, a premonition, that it must die puts that sense of impending doom into the breast and awaits the results with bated breath. What I think it wants to hear is: There, there, it's all right, you'll do, not to worry. This is different from a feeding, however munificent, and it has to be personal, not general.

I referred to an idea or premonition. I don't think it an idea in a sophisticated sense or a premonition of a defined fate. Nameless dread or intimation of a terrifying imperative might describe it. When I imagine I encounter it later, in the consulting room, it has a psychosomatic quality – not in the sense of a particular illness, with its acquired symbolic meanings, but in the sense that the dread makes the respiratory and alimentary and vascular systems all awry.

The cure needs to be a personal, not a general, reassurance. By this I mean the baby needs to be sure that it is known; otherwise it will suffer all life long from the idea it is an impostor and in danger of being horribly unmasked. I think there is a way some mothers know their babies and other mothers can't see the baby for the preconception. Preconceived babies have a difficult time getting emotionally conceived, let alone born. As the baby goes about trying to get some idea of who and what he is, he will naturally hope that what he discovers directly about himself enjoys some congruence with what Mother and Father know – even if the knowledge does not reflect well on him. There is a narcissism that is a consolation prize, involving being made much of; but the mirroring that stimulates growth requires fidelity, not flattery.

Memento mori

The imperative to give over and die feels like one were under orders.[1] Of course, if the mother hates the infant, only a very kind fate can rescue it. But we are here concerned with a baby that is trying not to internalize that hate and is therefore looking to a breast to denature it – to rob death of its sting. Must I die? NO: some babies must die, but not you, not yet. For babies, I think this is what being and feeling loved is all about – and, it may be, for others, too.

I am now ready, like the infant itself, to put the two ideas together. The presence of the absence, the malign force, is the conjunction of the breast and the imperative. The breast has refused in its receptive function either to take the threat into it – to take it in as a matter of the utmost seriousness – or to return from its container function as experience of exemption. This, as it were, implicates the breast, which is now experienced as radiating death. The infant leaves a vacuum – hoping, as it were, that the jury is still out – but what it gets back is nothing. It is left to its fate. And given that fate, there can be nothing worse than nothing.

The primary persecution – the unbearable absence of the absent – I have been describing (and attempting to distinguish from projections of motive or intentions) means that the people so plagued grow up with unusual reserves of stubbornness and a feeling that they must continually infuse the other with something the other will accept and use and eventually give back in the form of an exculpation or exemption. At the same time there is at work a vengeful and vindictive spirit, all the more virulent since the blood-price has already been paid. That price is considered paid by virtue – by virtue of the self having been obliged to live under a perpetual sentence of death.

In the consulting room this presents a sometimes puzzling picture of temerity and passivity, of self-sacrifice and vengefulness, of guilt without contrition and of hatred without anger. Perhaps most oddly of all, such people appear to feel of all things 'entitled,' as if they were free to demand anything and to give nothing. But this, of course, is the condemned man's last meal. (I shall return to this point later.)

'Fort–da'

It will not have escaped many readers that we may be back on the road to Thanatos, upon which so many analysts wish Freud had never set foot. But it is with a difference. Freud follows out a particular thread. He is baby-sitting. His grandchild is hurling a wooden spool from its crib. 'Fort–da,' it orders, and its grandfather dutifully returns the spool to its young master, who, of course, hurls it forth once again. Repetition–symbol–ritual–omnipotence. Then: repetition-compulsion, the trauma dream, the exception to the Pleasure Principle. Then Duality, the zest for life and the arcing return, the great parabola, toward nirvana, death, and inorganicity. The cell reproduces itself a limited number of times – period! In its DNA there is a stopping point, beyond which. . . .

I am saying something other than this. I am saying that in what for some people is an absence, a void, an echo, there is for others a presence, a menace, and a pain beyond measure. Nothing doesn't feel like merely nothing, but as a no-thing filled with malign and dreadful implication. These people, despite the evident fact that they were conceived, gestated, and born, have not come fully into possession of their lives.

There is a story regarding Samuel Beckett, the Nobel laureate, for the authenticity of which I cannot vouch. But to my ear it has a ring of truth to it, so I will relay it. Beckett was in therapy with Wilfred Bion. This was in the 1930s, well before Bion had qualified as a psychoanalyst. The therapy was limping along. There were periods of communication and understanding, alternating with periods in which Beckett was ill and mute and hardly there. At these latter times Beckett would begin to muse about going home to Ireland and his mother. Bion would remind him of how disastrous and debilitating those visits always were, and Beckett would nod and leave for Ireland. At length Bion saw that whatever was in this cycle was still inchoate to both himself and his patient, and so he made no efforts to dissuade Beckett from ending the therapy. Instead, he invited Beckett to a farewell dinner, after which they strolled over to the Tavistock, where Jung was lecturing.[2]

Jung's lecture concerned a young girl he had seen, one of whose dreams foretold her early death. But what impressed Beckett was the interpretation of this condition. Jung put it that the girl had been born before she had had a chance of coming fully and securely to life. So that although she had had her nine months in the womb and was presumably of normal health, she was psychically frail and hung to life by a thread.

This, Beckett felt, described himself to a T; this was the interpretation he had been looking for; this is what drove him again and again to his mother and away again feeling deader than ever. Beckett made this the theme of more than one of his novels – *Malloy, Malone Dies*, and particularly *Murphy*, which he wrote not in his mother tongue but in French.[3]

The spool of Freud's grandchild was interpreted by Freud to represent the absent mother and the 'Fort–da' the magical control of the absent object. An alternative view of the spool might have been that it represented not the mother but the child itself, who felt flung away and needed to be regathered and restored. Otherwise why follow the thread to the looming presence of Death when an object relations view would have been the more obvious and parsimonious one?

Coming fully to life

People for whom there is no such thing as nothing cannot, in Gertrude Stein's elegant phrase, believe 'there is no there there.' They have perforce to describe something and what they describe is an experience tantamount to a kind of pure paranoia. In life-historical terms they describe the usual instances of visited pain – bad parents doing bad things. But in these recitations the effect on the analyst they strive for is not sympathy or an alliance of anger or even to have their suffered disappointment made up to them. Rather it is a search for validation: Yes, it did happen; yes, it was terrible. Given any other response, such people feel profoundly misunderstood, even trashed. During particularly long and arduous sieges when the patient simply sees no further use in talking and I am given to feel that my own lack of receptivity is deadening if not veritably deadly, the worse because I am taken to know what is needed and my density is only apparent, not real, I wonder why the patient doesn't leap up from the couch and go to a therapist who can sympathize.

The answer, I think, is that the patient knows something about the doubts that propel these urgent needs for affirmation and validation. That is, the patient senses (later, knows) that the events he or she is narrating are emblematic and factitious.

Now there is something in the practice of psychoanalysis that is different from psychotherapy, and that is the analyst's resolute search for meaning. We, in our way, also say there is no such thing as nothing; everything, we say, has meaning; there is always more there than meets the eye.

> What we call 'seeing the lawn' is only an effect of our coarse and slapdash senses; a collection exists only because it is formed of discrete elements. There is no point in counting them; what matters is grasping in one glance the individual little plants one by one, in their individualities and differences. And not only seeing them: thinking them. Instead of thinking 'lawn,' to think of that stalk with two clover leaves, that lanceolate, slightly humped leaf, that delicate corymb. . . .
>
> (Calvino, 1985, 331)

That is Italo Calvino speaking telescopically through his Mr Palomar. But, closer to home, here is W.R. Bion.

> To the analytic observer, the material must appear as a number of discrete particles, unrelated and incoherent. The coherence that these facts have in the patient's mind is not relevant to the analyst's problem. His problem – I describe it in stages – is to ignore that coherence so that he is confronted by the incoherence and experiences incomprehension of what is presented to him. [. . .] This state must endure until a new comprehension emerges.
>
> (1980, 151)

These qualities of thought provide to the patient the mind he needs in order to come fully alive. He will do so not by verbally pouring his heart out but by introjecting and reprojecting fragments of himself into the analyst.

Splits, fragments, and twinning

The experience that threatens to be recapitulated in the transference reinvokes the dread and the fury the patient must originally have experienced if the patient did not continue to use a particular array of protective maneuvers.

Perhaps foremost among these is the use of pain as an anodyne for pain, or more precisely physical pain as an anodyne for mental pain. This surrogation appears to serve dual purposes. In the first instance, it does offer relief, of a sort, from the more diffuse and nameless pain of persecution without villainy. And in the second it brings into the transference ways the patient when infant and child found to exact a concern, even if falsely extracted and falsely given from the parent. It is to be remembered that it was not the provisioning aspect of the breast that was problematic, but its receptive function.

But there is a third purpose, too. The anxiety the infant experienced was so primary as to be almost as much somatic as psychic. Thus in the consulting room as these crises reemerge, the patient is likely to approach states of somatic shock. Blinding headaches, pallor, trembling, dizziness, palpitations, erratic respiration are all likely to occur. But simultaneous with these states, the patient, emotionally, will feel relatively nothing – for a change!

Needless to say, from the beginning the patient will have felt untaken care of. If he or she survives (I put it this way because I think there are likely to be infants and children who don't) it will have been through the development of a certain kind of precocity, one in which the infant prematurely becomes caretaker to itself. The precocious self is, however, hated. It is a false self jerry-built to save the real self from catastrophe. The false self is so enlarged in this dualization of function and image as to jeopardize the continual existence of the real self. In the analysis the precocious self (I prefer that term, for the term false self has, from Winnicott, a somewhat different and yet precise meaning) – the precocious self, then, is very wary of the analyst. If the analyst allies himself even in the slightest degree with the 'exact replica,' as one of my patients called it, the patient feels his not yet-fully-alive self is being doomed. Here is a dream that puts all of this quite plainly:

> A woman put me in charge of her babies, only they weren't babies, just formless protoplasms, shapeless like amoebas or paramecia, horribly dressed up to look like babies. But they weren't and one was even slipping out of its clothing, bonnets and such, and even out of the carriage or basinet. It was the smaller and more ill-formed of the two, and it was just slipping away, and I was trying to hold onto it. I suppose this is one of those other breast dreams (this is added bitterly) but my mother always said she thought right up till the end that I was twins.

The reference here to the so-called other breast is to an interpretation in which I told this patient that I could imagine an infant held to two entirely ample breasts starving because it could not stand the pain of losing the one upon choosing the other (see Boris, 1994). Soon after this interpretation 'took,' the patient had the first of the twin dreams. In that one the twins were merely heads or headlike things on either end of a rigid tube that made putting both the infants to the breast impossible. The tube was an I.V. tube, also implying a Siamese-twin image. The patient was letting me know that my interpretation was correct, as far as it went, but things were not nearly so simple as that.

The agonizing sense of disparity between the twins is echoed in the following. (The association following the story was to a girlfriend who had a twin sister and how special that must have been.)

> There was a story, the worst and most upsetting story, supposedly a children's story, though how anyone could suppose children would not be horrified by the story, I don't know, can't imagine, about a time when the birds and babies understood one another, talked a common language. Then not only did the babies outgrow the language – but this is the awful part – they forgot they ever could talk to the birds. But the birds remembered and they couldn't understand why the babies weren't as upset as they were. I mean, it's one thing not to be able to talk anymore, but for one to forget he ever talked and so never to know what makes the other so sad is just horrible . . . terrible.

I don't want to suggest that the twinships invoked or implied in these communications are merely self–self realizations. The fury at and envy of the no-thing and what it contains or could contain is such that it is the target of desperate attacks designed to demobilize and demolish its powers of frustration and torment. In his paper on the Imaginary Twin, Bion emphasizes – may I say it – the twin attacks: One splits the breast, the other the self and, indeed, the ego. These splits are then resymbolized along the lines of the Prince and the Pauper, Dr Jekyll and Mr Hyde, true self and false self, good breast and bad. This is the position on matters that Melanie Klein called the paranoid-schizoid position. As Bion (1950) puts it: 'Only when I had been able to demonstrate how bad I was at all levels of his mind did it become possible for him first to recognize his mechanisms of splitting and personification and then to employ them, as it were, in reverse, to establish the contact they had been designed to brook' (p. 19).

Bion's model in this paper and its cohorts (e.g., 'Attacks on Linking,' 1959) is of the perception of a pair who are enjoying and flourishing in an intimacy from which the developing infant feels excluded. Its hatred of the emotions these realizations generate, and 'therefore, by short extenuation, of life itself,' stimulates the 'murderous attack on that which links the pair, on the pair itself and on the object generated by the pair.'

I am plainly placing my emphasis on the 'by a short extension life itself,' which quickly complicates the experience no end.

Surviving

Even a cursory reading of the material from the patient I have cited will reveal the poignancy of the guilt experienced by the survivor. One will live and one will die; one will grow and the other will be forgotten: and it is too unbearable.

In this regard, tolerating nothing takes on a second meaning. The patient now *must* tolerate nothing. Any degree of flourishing, any hedonic pleasures, any development toward well-being, and the fragile connection is severed and the Other dies. Perhaps, needless to say, this means that the patient is not allowed to use analysis to get well in. If development is to take place it has to be on the analyst's head that the implacable blame will fall. This contributes to the patient's need to communicate through projective identification.

A word, therefore, on projective identification. The refusal, as it seems, of the breast to take in the infant's idea that it may have to give way and die seems (if recapitulation in the transference is any guide) like a perverse and deadly mirror that merely refracts and sends back what has been brought to it. Lacan justly uses the mirror motif as an explanation, within his system, of the terrible otherness of the Other. This cool refraction drives the baby toward greater and greater attempts at penetration, mobilizing its native sadism and what it increasingly comes to regard as the sadism of the refraction. When these, as it seems, are then again merely refracted they begin to further endanger the infant, who then can only slow and muffle its attempts to extract what it needs. The precocious self develops and sees to it that the protoplasmic self (to use my patient's image) is not endangered from the emission of refractions.[4] The ruthlessness of the self in respect to the Other – the Other being now the proto self and the breast – is tempered severely by the murderous and envious wishes for the demise of the Other. Then comes a point when the precocious self can no longer ask. It must dawn on the other to give. Of the patients I have been considering in preparing this communication, one was almost totally silent over the two and a half years of therapy, one speaks but is mostly inaudible, and a third speaks as if reporting someone else's experiences. If anything is to be known it is through my getting the idea. A fourth has yet to make any of the usual commitments to analysis. Each session is de novo. These seem to be conditions for survival. Yet, paradoxically perhaps, the very diffidence of such individuals is extraordinarily entitled and taxes one's empathy to the limit. One has daily to experience and cope with a powerful wish for their death; nothing less.

Getting the idea

By far, then, the largest part of what patients of the sort I have been discussing communicate is in the form of projective identification – which is to say they project and the analyst identifies. This is a special sort of relationship.

The transference relationship, it could be said, deals with the expressive function of the object – the breast, penis, and vagina as provisioners, the parents as lovers and rivals, the anus and its productions as coins unto the bargain. Lust and love, envy and jealousy, hatred and rivalry are the states of mind that pertain to this state of affairs.

The people I have been describing bring these interplays into the transference of course, and the tensions and alleviations that characterize the libido and its vicissitudes are dynamic. The projective identificatory relationship, in contrast, is static – fixed.

Since 'projective identificatory relationship' is a piece of jargon of a particularly awkward sort, I shall now abandon it and replace it with the expression: getting the idea. People in this disposition resolutely work at invoking and evoking until the analyst gets the idea. The plan is that the analyst has to get the idea and give it back. The patient experiences great anxiety lest he is the first to get the idea. Verbal communication of the sort I am at the moment doing, in which I have an idea or two that I would like you to consider, is not at all their method of operation. Because they cannot tolerate the experience about which it might be possible to have an idea, the moment they have an inkling of the experience, they project it. If they are lucky, they can project it before the idea dawns or even the experience is experienced as anything more than a premonitory tremor. Such projections have, however, to be received and assimilated. The paranoid personality, especially the psychotic personality, who deals in projecting characteristics and intents, can also distort and disfigure the receiver, who is there perceived as harboring what is projected. But when the projection is meant to be received intact in the hope that the receiver will detoxify, sanitize, moderate, or clarify it, the intent of the projection is not to defile or ravage the receiver.

The problem then is: How can the patient give the analyst to know something the patient cannot stand to know and therefore has no words to tell it in? I am contrasting this with projections in which the patient doesn't want to know, something is true of him but instead wants to believe it is true of the analyst. These disfiguring projections also occur, so it is important clinically and conceptually to know the difference.

This pattern of communication, of course, echoes preverbal communication. It does so because the issue at stake – whether or not one must give way and die – is preverbal, though it is not merely preverbal; for instance, it is reraised with the conception and birth of every successive sibling. But it echoes the preverbal state also because the danger of the question is such as to have successfully caused the question to be refused a conjunction with a verbal idea. The person grows up but the experience stays young – which is why I use part-object terms like breast rather than words like mother.

In the consulting room, then, the analyst must get the idea that these often verbally very sophisticated patients cannot communicate anything of significance in words. Indeed they do not value words except as things by which to evoke the emotional states within the analyst. These patients do not give information; they speak, or as often do not speak, for effect.

From their fruits, so shall ye know them . . . might be the principle these patients follow. The emissions they could not originally put into the breast are now insinuated into the analyst for him to metabolize, detoxify, or gestate as the case may be: and then to return them alive and well. Of course, there is an element belonging to the transference in this, but the essence of the activity is to get the age-old question answered. Its thrust is to achieve a secure birth.

Notes

1 Readers of Iris Murdoch's novels will be particularly familiar with this experience, for she articulates it with precision and moment.
2 Jung was, of course, a great one for inherited archetypes, the racial unconscious and that sort of thing; and Freud was at great pains to put and maintain distance between them. Alix and James Strachey's correspondence during the 1920s on their translation of Freud's writings shows their care in finding words that didn't 'Jungize' Freud's ideas. But in the ongoing questions of Nature vs. Nurture, Freud continued to move to 'Nature', nowhere more so than in *Beyond the Pleasure Principle* of 1920. His critics argue that his choices between the nature of the psyche and the nurture of the child followed what he could believe of his own life history. Thus one could note that in the early 1920s he was analysing Anna, whose life history he may have felt he had reason to know!
3 I am indebted to Margery Sabin of Wellesley College for calling my attention to Bair's (1978) biography of Beckett, from which I recount this story.
4 For the relationship of this dynamic to anorexia nervosa and bulimia, see Boris (1994).

References

Bair, D. (1978) *Samuel Beckett: A Biography*, New York: Harcourt.
Bion, Wilfred (1950) 'The Imaginary Twin', *Second Thoughts*, New York: Jason Aronson, 1967.
—— (1959) 'Attacks on Linking', *Second Thoughts*, New York: Jason Aronson, 1967.

—— (1980) *Bion in New York and São Paulo*. StrathTay: Clunie Press, 1980.

Boris, Harold (1994) *Sleights of Mind: One and Multiples of One*, Northvale, NJ: Jason Aronson.

—— (1994) *Envy*, Northvale, NJ: Jason Aronson.

Calvino, Italo (1985) *Mr Palomar*, trans. W. Weaver, San Diego: Harcourt.

Freud, Sigmund *The Standard Edition of the Complete Psychological Works of Sigmund Freud*, ed. and trans. James Strachey, London: Hogarth, 24 vols, 1953–74.

—— (1920) *Beyond the Pleasure Principle, SE* XVIII.

Murdoch, Iris (1956) *The Flight from the Enchanter*, New York: Viking.

Chapter 7

Negativity in the work of Melanie Klein

Jacqueline Rose

Editor's note:

Jacqueline Rose's essay on the Kleinian concept of psychic negativity is a model of what a 'return to Klein' can achieve. It is one of two remarkable chapters from her book *Why War? – Psychoanalysis, Politics, and the Return to Melanie Klein* (1993), that together offer a sustained and productive reading of Kleinian analysis addressed, in part, to an intellectual constituency familiar with contemporary critical and cultural theory. Rose's writings on psychoanalysis have always empha-sized central yet notoriously unassimilable issues – sexual difference, perversion, fantasy and, here, negativity – that bring psychoanalysis into the political field, thus focusing on the possibility of theorizing the psyche and the social together – or better, of theorizing the psyche as the social (a project developed to some effect in Rose's recent *States of Fantasy* (1996)). In this essay she focuses on the Freud–Klein 'Controversial Discussions' as a key moment in analytic history, from which two issues arise. First is the question about psychic negativity – a question, as Rose demonstrates, that is capable of resisting the various forms of theoretical and clinical institution-alization that psychoanalysis undergoes. The second – which is examined in more detail by Rose in 'War in the Nursery' (*Why War*, pp. 191–230) – concerns the relationship between education and the unconscious, and the crucial question of what is centrally at stake in child analysis. But by reading Klein in the context of this historical moment Rose not only identifies the issues that underlie the row that split the British Psycho-Analytical Society in 1944; she also reveals that the concept of negativity at the heart of the row remains the essentially unassimilable limit of all theory and thus of knowledge in general.

Rose's 'return' to Klein must be thought of as a means of going forward. In a powerful re-reading she shows that it is possible to rethink the epistemological basis for theory itself. Far from being over-empirical or under-theorized, Rose argues, Klein produces a theory that, owing to the nature of what it is attempting to theorize, can neither contain nor delimit itself. In Klein's work 'truth' and 'knowledge' belong not to a scientifically objectifiable order but emerge contingently from the work of psychic negativity, which conditions the infant's relationship to its reality from the beginning. It is this that implies strict limits to the possibility of objective knowledge and, by extension, to the scientific supremacy of the West. Rose reads Klein as 'fleshing out' the Freudian and Lacanian structure of negativity, which is seen as constitutive of the subject. So where Anna Freud argues that an early version of the infant's ego precedes its development, and its acquisition of knowledge is the gradual separation of reality from emotion, Klein insists on negativity as the precondition for the emergence of any ego at all. Negativity in Freud already makes the notion of the infant as pure pleasure-seeker difficult to sustain, but once it is shown that death is central to processes of psychic meaning, the pleasure/reality dichotomy is no longer pertinent. Klein's theory is not an instinctual reductionism but an inflation of the power of phantasy to create or destroy the infant's world. This is a kind of phantasy from which any 'objective' detachment would be impossible – not just for the infant but also for an adult subject and 'an adult science.' The dispute represents not merely the depressing failure that it seemed to be for many participants at the time, but an insight into psychoanalytic theory itself, revealing its creatively unmasterable limits.

In an extraordinary postscript Rose points out a number of analogies between Klein's attempts to theorize psychic negativity and the theoretical difficulties that confront Stephen Hawking's attempt to describe 'black holes' in the realm of cosmology (in his *A Brief History of Time*). What is striking about this section is the revelation of the degree to which elements of phantasy overdetermine Hawking's speculations. (JP)

> Analytic theory has treated the two instincts in an unusual manner: the libido is the first-born and privileged child, the destructive instinct is the latecomer, the stepchild. Libido was recognized as such from the first; the other instinct, its adversary, went under various disguises, and had several names before its true identity was established.
>
> (Paula Heimann, *Freud–Klein Controversies*)

> If we stick to Freud's elaborated categories . . . we are able to conceive the primitive psychical make-up of an infant and the elaborate organization of an adult personality as a lawful continuity.
>
> (Hedwig Hoffer, *Freud–Klein Controversies*)

For anyone attempting to follow the tracks of the psyche across the terrain of contemporary political life, it is hard to avoid Melanie Klein. The new brutalism of Thatcherism in the 1980s and the Gulf War, with its renewed and absolute moral antinomies for the West, are just two instances where some seemingly irreducible negativity, bearer of a violence sanctioned – if only momentarily – by State and subjects, appears to rise up to the surface of political consciousness, setting the parameters of our being-in-the-social, confronting us with something at the limits of psyche and social alike. High priestess of psychic negativity, Melanie Klein pushed the institution of psychoanalysis in Britain – and, some would argue, her child patients – close to the edge. In the tradition of Freud, she saw her task as one of excavation, as the retrieval of something which even Freud, she argued, had barely been able to approach. Thus outmanoeuvring the father of psychoanalysis, while claiming her unswerving loyalty to and continuity with his project, she assigned to him as much the role of repressor as uncoverer of the hidden repressed. And yet, in the recent and continuing turn to psychoanalysis in the humanities, Klein – compared with Freud – has received relatively little attention. Why, then, has there been no rereading of Melanie Klein?[1]

In the context of the humanities, the idea of rereading has become something of a commonplace. Without assuming that a writer has necessarily been read before, it refers instead to a strategy of reading which heads past the most immediate or professionally received meanings of the writer, straight for the points of creative tension in her or his works. This way of reading 'otherwise' is interested in the moments when writing slips its moorings, when it fails – as all writing must fail, it is suggested – its own tests of coherence, revealing – the analogy with analysis is intentional – its 'other' scene. In relation to psychoanalysis, this way of reading, often described as 'deconstructive,' takes on a particular weight. Less interested in a general instability of language, it places itself instead *inside* the psychoanalytic project, aiming to demonstrate the triumph of the unconscious over all attempts at hermeneutic or therapeutic control. In a recent discussion on 'Melanie Klein Today,' organized in London as part of a series aiming to promote dialogue between psychoanalysis in the clinic and psychoanalysis in the academy, Elizabeth Bott Spillius, editor of two volumes of contemporary analytic essays on Klein, argued that Klein was not a theorist in the strict sense of the term.[2] What happens if we read her comment not as a statement *against* theory, but as suggesting that Klein does theory *otherwise*, that Klein produced a theory which, because of what it was trying to theorize, could not, by definition, contain or delimit itself? Another way of putting this would be to ask whether Klein's writing is a monolithic, singular text; or, can she be read as producing in her writing something as intractable, as creatively unmasterable, as what many readers have become accustomed to discovering in Freud?

In the humanities, a post-Lacanian orthodoxy has blocked access to Klein. In a reading of which it should theoretically, according to its own tenets, be more suspicious, this orthodoxy has accused her of taking apart – but only to resolder more rigidly – body, psyche, and speech; it has imputed to her something of a psychic and sexual fix. Klein's ego is too coherent; it eventually takes all conflict and phantasy under its control. Her concept of the instinct is reductive; deriving all mental operations from biological impulses Klein leaves no gaps, no space for the trials and errors of representation, in the mind. Her account of sexuality is coercive; sexual difference, and hence heterosexuality, is given in advance by the knowledge which the bodies of girl- and boy-children are assumed, from the beginning, to have of themselves.[3] And yet, alongside these criticisms we have to place the no less fervent rejection of Klein for proposing something so negative that it is incapable of assimilation by human subjects, by theory. Especially in the United States, Klein's work has been rejected on account of its violence and negativity. It is a critique which, as we will see, was at the centre of the fierce dispute which, in England too, was originally aroused by her work.

Far from offering reassurance, these reactions suggest, Melanie Klein disturbs. That disturbance, largely responsible for the rejection of Klein in analytic circles in the United States, has been mirrored in recent feminist debate. Searching for an alternative femininity free of the dictates of patriarchal, oedipal law, one feminism has turned to the preoedipal relation between mother and girl-child only to find Klein's account of early psychic processes standing in its way.[4] Too negative, this account blocks the new identification, troubles the ideal. Against the idyll of early fusion with the mother, Klein offers proximity as something which devours. Is there a way of linking the two criticisms – Klein as too safe and too dangerous, Klein as taking too much under, letting too much slip out of, control?

It is in the context of these issues that I want to return here to the earliest disagreement over Melanie Klein's work in England, which threatened to divide the psychoanalytic institution and has left its traces on the organization of the Institute of Psycho-Analysis to this day. The focus for this was the 'Controversial Discussions,' relatively unknown outside analytic circles, which took place at the scientific meetings of the British Psychoanalytic Society between 1943 and 1944, centring on the disagreement between Anna Freud and Melanie Klein. In this instance, the theoretical issue reveals itself unmistakably as an issue of the psychoanalytic institution and its continuity. As if in response to the dictates of unconscious time – amnesia as the first stage in allowing something to return – this moment of psychoanalytic history has gradually and recently come back to the fore of debate. In 1991, the full edition of the 'Controversial Discussions' was published as Volume 11 of the New Library of Psychoanalysis, a monumental feat of editing running to over 900 pages and including all the original papers and the ensuing debates (prior to this, only a selection of the papers had been available in a 1952 edition itself reprinted in 1989).[5] Articles have been written on the subject; two books have appeared on the institutional vicissitudes of psycho-analysis in Britain – *Freud in Exile* and an anthology of articles *The British School of Psychoanalysis – The Independent Tradition* (the independents were those who chose to affiliate with neither party to the dispute).[6] Within feminism, a sometimes celebratory (Klein as 'mother' of a new second-generation psycho-analysis), sometimes critical (Klein as sexually normative) attention has produced something, if not quite, in the order of a 'return' to Melanie Klein.[7]

More oddly, this originating moment of local institutional dispute had its highly successful passage across the London stage. Nicholas Wright's play *Mrs Klein* played to packed houses in 1988 at the Cottesloe Theatre, and then transferred to the West End.[8] Vicariously, the play offers the spectacle of three women – Melanie Klein, her daughter Melitta Schmideberg, and Paula Heimann – battling it out over the legacy of Klein's work. Femininity becomes the site on which the vexed question of affiliation and institutional continuity is explored. It is a shocking play, not least of all, as one student commented, because of the terrible way analysts are seen to behave. Now this story of dreadful behaviour on the part of analysts has of course been told over and over again in relation to Freud; for some thinkers, it has become the key to the analytic institution itself (Roazen, Roustang, Derrida, Grosskurth[9]). But this has been seen to date as an affair strictly between men. The affair involved here, by contrast, is strictly between women, between mothers and daughters (literally and metaphorically), which might suggest another reason for looking at it again.

It is a point worth making in relation to a book like François Roustang's *Dire Mastery*, one of the more nuanced, less simply accusatory readings of the historic trials of psychoanalytic affiliation and descent. Roustang traces what he sees as the psychotic fantasies underpinning the institution and its (patri)lineage, and locates these fantasies on more than one occasion in an unconscious image of femininity which, he argues, that same institution refuses and on which it relies. Yet, he never makes the link from there to the work of Melanie Klein, theoretician of the psychotic in all of us and, together with Anna Freud, the first woman inheritor, contester, and transmitter of the legacy of Freud. When Jacques Derrida asks in a final essay in his book on Freud: 'Who will analyse the unanalysed of Freud?' ('*Qui paiera à qui la tranche de Freud?*' more exactly, 'Who pays the price for the unanalysed slice of Freud?'), it is tempting to answer, 'Melanie Klein.'[10] Similarly, Julia Kristeva has argued that Freud's obsessional return to the oedipal narrative was a way of rationalizing his own more psychotic dis-covery of a negativity which he both theorized and effaced. Freud, she suggests, thus repeated in his own intellectual trajectory that process of flight from, disavowal, and semi-recognition of something murderous and unmanageable which, at the end of his life, he read in the story of Moses.[11] What all this points to is a residue – theoretical, institutional, sexual – of the Freudian institution, in which Melanie Klein, or more specifically the controversy over her work, occupies a crucial place.

Two issues arise centrally from this moment of analytic history, both with relevance for how we think about the psyche and the social (the psyche as social) today. First, the concept of psychic negativity in Klein: What is it? Is it an instinctual reductionism, with biology the final court of appeal for what is most troubling in the mind? Or is it something else, perhaps closer to, even if crucially distinct from, the negativity which Lacan places at the heart of subjectivity – not as instinctual deposit, but as the price that all human subjects pay for the cruel passage of the psyche into words? Secondly, what was at stake in the row over child analysis between Anna Freud and Melanie Klein? Central to the psychoanalytic institution is the problem of how to transmit knowledge of – which must mean educating – the unconscious without effacing the force of the unconscious as such. What happens when this problem turns into the question of whether one can, or indeed should, analyse a child? It is the point where the institution comes up against its own subjective origins, or rather the fantasy of its own origins, its own infancy – an infancy which, according to its own theories, it must both relinquish and repeat. It is also one of the points where the issue of power in the analytic scenario reveals itself most starkly, since the analyst's intervention in the mind of the child seems to be disputed according to the alternatives of education or violation, moral control or abuse. Clearly a matter of psycho-politics, because it touches on the limits of the psychoanalytic institution in its dealings with its own outside. But if the issue of psychic negativity can be included under the same heading, it is because it also seems to bring us up against a limit: the limit of what a society, of what a subject, can recognize of itself. It does so, however, in a way which is absolutely unassimilable to that idea of transgressive liberation which has been the most frequent radical political version of Freud (what would a 'liberation' of unconscious negativity mean?).

In the context of Klein's work, the dialogue between psychoanalysis and politics therefore shifts. As it does, we can see just how tightly the institutional and disciplinary boundaries and points of affiliation have recently and restrictively been drawn. Instead of the dialogue between psychoanalysis and literature or film, for example, we find psychoanalysis in confrontation with pedagogy and the law. Instead of the unconscious as the site of emancipatory pleasures, we find something negative, unavailable for celebration or release. One could argue that it has been too easy to politicize psychoanalysis as long as the structuring opposition has been situated between an over-controlling, self-deluded ego and the disruptive force of desire; that this opposition has veiled the more difficult antagonism between superego and unconscious, where what is hidden is aggression as much as sexuality, and the agent of repression is as ferocious as what it is trying to control. Much of the psycho-political colouring of the past decade suggests that the political import of psychoanalysis may reside in what it has to say about the passage across the social of thanatos as much as eros (not the unconscious which the social denies, but the unconscious which it sanctions and pursues). By seeing the unconscious as the site of sexual or verbal free fall, the humanities have aestheticized psychoanalysis, bypassing other points of (greater) friction, both internal to psychoanalytic thinking and in the historically attested confrontations between psychoanalysis and its outer bounds. Could it be that the humanities, inadvertently repeating a legacy of which they have been unaware, have, like psychoanalysis itself, preferred the 'legitimate heir' over the 'stepchild'?

The 'Controversial Discussions' were originally published in 1952 in a collection edited by Joan Rivière under the title *Developments in Psycho-Analysis* (Volume 43 of the Hogarth International Psycho-Analytical Library). The book included three of the original papers; 'The Nature and Function of Phantasy' by Susan Isaacs, 'Certain Functions of Introjection and Projection in Earliest Infancy' by Paula Heimann, and 'Regression' by Paula Heimann and Susan Isaacs. It also included an introduction by Rivière, additional papers by Heimann and Rivière, as well as four papers by Klein, including a revised version of the paper which she herself delivered to the scientific meetings in March 1944.[12] In what follows, I concentrate on the papers by Isaacs, Rivière, and Heimann. Apologias for, and defences of, Klein's work, they speak for Klein, although not in her voice, hovering in that hybrid space of identification where bodies and psyches at once recognize each other as separate and get too close (whether identification as incorporation necessarily destroys its object will be one of the issues of theoretical dispute). Less well known than Klein's own writings, these papers offer perhaps the clearest account in Kleinian writing of negativity in the process of emergence of the subject, as the passage through which subjects come to be. What is also remarkable about them is their degree of theoretical self-elaboration, or self-consciousness about theory, which means that they read very differently from that extraordinary direct lifting of theory out of the act of interpretation which more than one commentator has remarked on in relation to Klein.[13] Taken in conjunction with the responses now made available with the 1991 publication of the full text of the debates, these documents provide a unique opportunity to examine *in statu nascendi* the founding, theoretically, of a school. It should be stressed, then, that this is an analysis of one key moment of self-representation in a body of evolving thought, not an account of what Kleinianism has become, in theory and practice, today.

One reason for the self-elaboration of these papers is that they are presented, had to be presented, in terms of an argument for their own legitimacy, their right to contest areas of Freudian orthodoxy even as they claim to be developing from the true letter of his text. In Britain, Melanie Klein was to find herself at once the heiress and usurper of Freud – brought to England by Ernest Jones in 1926, twelve years before Freud himself arrived in 1938 accompanied by Anna Freud. Recently published correspondence shows Freud, long before his arrival, troubled by a number of Klein's theoretical innovations (on the superego, on the sexual development of the girl), but even more concerned about the critiques of his daughter by Klein and her supporters, which he took as a personal affront.[14] When Anna Freud arrived, therefore, she took up a position which was at once laid down – she was the daughter of the founding father of psychoanalysis – and occupied or contested in advance. Who, we might ask in this context, is the legitimate child?

It follows that Klein and her followers could only partially base their claims for authority on their fidelity to Freud. In his Preface to the 1952 collection, Ernest Jones writes: 'What is certainly illegitimate is the Procrustean principle of assessing all conclusions with those reached by Freud, however great our respect for the latter can and should be.'[15] Joan Rivière opens her General Introduction with this quotation from Freud: 'I have made many beginnings and thrown out many suggestions . . . I can hope that they have opened up a path to an important advance in our knowledge. Something will come of them in the future.'[16] Given what we know of Freud's vexed relation to filiation and legacy, we already have to view this with caution, as something of a rhetorical strategy, a calling up of Freud against Freud. Freud is being invoked here as permitting – demanding even – a future for his discipline which goes beyond his own name (something of a self-cancelling proposition in itself). But it allows Rivière to argue that, while Freud's central discovery was the world of unconscious phantasy, 'there are many problems to which he did not apply it,' which have subsequently been brought nearer to a 'solution' by Klein ('her consistent awareness of its significance').[17] And she continues: 'The circumstances under which his work began and was carried through, i.e. its origin in medicine, no doubt affected his outlook,' leading him to concentrate on the differences between 'normal' and 'morbid' mentality at the expense of general laws and to an overestimation of the 'force of the reality principle.'[18]

The case for Melanie Klein rests, therefore, on this image of her as inheritor of the Freudian 'truth' (Rivière's word), one which the limits of Freud's own scientific training made him unable fully to pursue. What is already clear is that this truth, in the name of which Rivière speaks for Klein, does not belong to an order of scientifically verifiable knowledge. In the heat of the discussions, Susan Isaacs replies to her critics: 'Dr Friedlander refers to the fact that Mrs Klein's views as to mental life is 'inferred knowledge' as of course it is.'[19] Critiquing the Kleinian concept of phantasy, Marjorie Brierley states: 'if we persist in equating mental functions with our subjective interpretations of them, we forfeit our claim to be scientists and revert to the primitive [sic] state of the Chinese peasant who interprets an eclipse as the sun being swallowed by a dragon.'[20] To which Paula Heimann replies: 'The science of psychology is not to be equated with the science of astronomy. What we are studying is not the solar system, but the mind of the Chinese peasant, not the eclipse but the belief of the peasant concerning the eclipse. How do such beliefs arise? . . . And further, how does the knowledge that the sun is not swallowed by a dragon develop in the mind of peasants and philosophers?'[21] For Heimann, psychoanalysis makes no distinction between peasants and philosophers. The unconscious conditions of all knowledge and belief systems are what need to be explained. As Rivière later puts it, citing Bacon: 'There is a superstition in avoiding superstition.'[22] The dispute about the transmission of the Freudian legacy thus appears as a dispute about the possibility of objective knowledge and (thinly veiled behind the first) the scientific supremacy of the West.[23]

These, then, are the grounds of the first opposition to Klein; the second Rivière attributes to Klein's idea of a destructive instinct and a psychotic part in all human subjects: 'The concept of a destructive force within every individual, tending towards the annihilation of life, is naturally one which arouses extreme emotional resistance; and this, together with the inherent obscurity of its operation, has led to a marked neglect of it by many of Freud's followers, as compared with any other aspect of his work'; '[in] the very early phases of mental life . . . she finds in operation mental mechanisms (splitting, projection, etc.) closely similar to those of the psychotic disorders, another aspect of her work which arouses strong emotional resistance.'[24] Thus the argument about fidelity to, and divergence from, Freud carries the weight of psychosis and death – precisely the discoveries which Kristeva argued were rationalized by Freud. (Note too the link between destruction and obscurity as if destruction were conceivable only if it can be fully – scientifically – mastered or grasped.) It is, however, another classic rhetorical move, where opposition or resistance to a theory is seen to belong inside, or be tributary of, what it is that the theory itself invokes. But we should perhaps ask what a legacy can be in this context, how an institution can perpetuate itself, when what it offers as the true content of that legacy is death? Death, after all, as Paula Heimann puts it in her paper on introjection and projection, is the one thing which the mind cannot expel.[25] It is in this context with all its institutional ramifications, that the 'Controversial Discussions' offer their account of what is meant by the destructive impulse or the death instinct in the work of Melanie Klein.

The first thing that becomes clear is that the concept of the death instinct or impulse is in no sense a biologistic concept in the work of Klein.[26] It was the Anna Freudians who insisted on the biological status of the concept (the principle of conservation and the return to the inanimate state) in order precisely to keep it outside the range of analytic work. The objections to the centrality accorded to the concept by Klein rested, therefore, not on her biologizing of the concept (instinctual reductionism) but on the opposite, on the way she assigned to it psychic significance, made it part of the phantasy life of the child. Whether the child could inhabit a world of meanings would be another central issue in the dispute over Klein's work. To cite Isaacs: 'The word "phantasy" serves to remind us always of this distinctive character of meaning in mental life'; Michael Balint: '"Phantasy" suggests "meaning"'; Barbara Lantos: 'This pleasure we call auto-erotic . . . organ pleasure . . . and intellectual pleasure – they all are the same in so far as they are pleasures in themselves, that is to say: pleasures without meaning'; Edward Glover: 'And so we come back once more to the dispute over "meaning" and "implicit meaning."'[27]

Death for Klein was *meaning*, which also meant that death had meaning for the infant. When Freud argues that the infant could have no knowledge of death, this does not preclude the possibility, Rivière argues, that the child 'can experience feelings of the kind, just as any adult can feel "like death," and in a state of great anxiety often does.'[28] What seems to be going on here, if we look closely at the passage, is not an undiluted appeal to feeling, but rather the suggestion that feeling itself is simile ('feel "like death"'), that the most severe anxiety the child can feel opens up the path of indirect representation by putting it at a fundamental, at *the* most fundamental, remove from itself. Thus the child's anxiety becomes the foundation for the first experience of 'as if': 'We surmise that the *child feels as if*'; '"He behaves as if," to my mind, is the same thing as saying "He has phantasies . . ."'[29] It is this fundamental negativity which these papers put at the basis of subjectivity. This is a moment of infancy when, if an ego can be postulated, its powers to integrate mental processes are weak. The problem for Klein's critics was that conflict was seen to arise before there was an ego there to manage it: 'According to the theory of the English school of analysis, intro-jection and projection, which in our view should be assigned to the period after the ego has been differentiated from the outside world, are the very processes by which the structure of the ego is developed.'[30] Edward Glover, in his long critique of Klein published in the first volume of *The Psychoanalytic Study of the Child* in 1945 argued that, unlike the customary teaching which overestimates the primitive ego, there is an underestimation of the primitive ego in Klein.[31] Two common recent theoretical assumptions about Klein therefore fall to the ground: her biologism and the pre-given category of the ego. If Klein was objected to, it was precisely because she was seen as bringing the death drive under the sway of a subject, as making the death drive constitutive of a subject, who is not yet enough of a subject for death to be mastered or controlled.

The third point of dispute was the early relation to the object (these are the three basic points of disagreement which Rivière lists in her Introduction). For the Anna Freudians, the infant – again posited in essentially biological terms – is narcissistic and auto-erotic, pure pleasure-seeker under the sway of the erotogenic zones. One way of describing the Freudian position, then, would be as a plea to keep pleasure out of the reach of meaning, to leave pleasure *alone*: 'Does Isaacs think – as we do – that there are activities just carried out for the sake of auto-erotic pleasure without any phantasies being attached to them . . . just for the sake of the organ-pleasure which is gained?'[32] For the Kleinians, the child relates to the object from the start, meaning not that the child has some inherent capacity for relatedness, the version of object-relations which has become best known, but that even in the state of auto-eroticism there are bits and pieces of objects – fragments of introjects, objects that are not quite objects – inside the mind. Objects without propriety, neither fully appropriated nor whole: 'Miss Freud speaks of object relationship "in the proper sense." I do not think there is a "proper" sense.'[33]

No ownership, therefore, and no agent of control. At each stage, the infant and its world seem to emerge in *absentia*, or *at a loss*. It is by withholding that the external world comes to be. Rivière writes: 'painful experience does much to bring about the recognition of an external object.'[34] The infant oscillates between 'seeking, finding, obtaining, possessing with satisfaction' and 'losing, lacking, missing, with fear and distress.'[35] In this scenario, and despite references to satisfaction obtained, the emphasis is far more frequently on the negative pole. For the loss of the object forces a breach in the primitive narcissism of the subject, a breach which, in a twist, then produces the object as its effect: 'the ego's need to dissociate itself from the unpleasure is so great that it *requires an object* upon which it can expel it . . . For such an experience of unpleasure is too intense to be merely "killed," hallucinated as non-existent. Narcissistic phantasy would thus in itself lead to object-relations and these object-relations will at first be of a negative order.'[36] Note again that reference to death in the instigation of the object, an experience of unpleasure so intense that it cannot be 'killed,' cannot be negatively hallucinated. And note too how different this is from the more familiar idea of hallucination ('narcissistic phenomenon *par excellence*'[37]) – not in this case something desired, but something instead which fails to be effaced. The lost object is not, therefore, only the hallucinated object of satisfaction; it is also and simultaneously an object which, because of this failure of negative hallucination, is required – is actively sought after – *in order to be bad*. In these papers from the 'Controversial Discussions,' the genesis of the famous Kleinian bad object is nothing less than the genesis of the object itself.

Rivière will qualify her account in her 1950 footnotes to her essay: 'The view that the earliest relation was negative and hostile was expressed by Freud. Later work leads to a correction of this hypothesis,' referring to two later papers by Klein included in the 1952 collection; and in her Introduction to the book: 'it will be seen from Chapters VI and VII that this is not Melanie Klein's view.'[38] Likewise she will answer those who objected to the weakness of the Kleinian ego by insisting on its integrative powers. But in the overall context and feel of the papers, these qualifications sit oddly – symptomatic presence of something which it became too difficult to sustain? Another way of putting this would be to ask how an unconscious identification with death *could* – theoretically, institutionally – be sustained. This would be just one way of reading the editing, the start of a theoretical shift between the original discussions and the 1952 publication of the book.

In these earlier papers, it is stated over and over that the subject first comes to experience itself negatively. Self-alienation gives the colour of the subject's coming to-be: 'nothing good within *lasts* . . . the first conscious idea of "me" is largely coloured by painful associations'; 'It would seem with every infant that we have to give far more experimental weight to the felt hostility of the external world over a considerable period in early development than we had thought'; 'the relation of hate to objects is older than that of love.'[39] The persecutory object relation rises up as the first defence against something without 'definite name and shape' (like the patient Klein describes in *Narrative of a Child Analysis* who dreamt of an 'indefinite object' stuck to a car, something which 'she both wished to see and not to see'[40]). Object-relations are 'improvements on' and 'protections against' primordial narcissistic anxiety; distrust of the object is better than despair.[41]

More than primitive instinct, therefore, the Kleinian concept of negativity appears as a psychic activation of the *fort–da* game as famously described by Freud, an answer of a sort to this question which, as Klein and Heimann both point out, was left in suspense by Freud: 'When does separation from an object produce anxiety, when does it produce mourning and when does it produce pain? Let me say at once that there is no prospect in sight of answering these questions.'[42] Freud did not believe that absence of the mother could be connoted as loss of love or anger, whereas for Klein the mother rapidly comes to be experienced as bad. 'This fundamental fear of loss of the loved object,' Klein states, 'seems to me psychologically well-founded' – 'predetermined, one may say, in the infant from the experience of birth.'[43]

It is at this point that the account offered here of psychic beginnings starts to sound uncannily like that of Jacques Lacan; so it is perhaps not surprising to discover Klein and Lacan converging on Freud's paper on 'Negation' (the link is not wholly coincidental, since this was the time when Lacan was working on his never to be completed translation of Klein).[44] 'Negation' was the key text for Rivière, Isaacs, and Heimann, who took it as the model for their theory of the subject's relation to its object-world.[45] Given the awkwardness as we have seen it of their relation to Freud's legacy, the terms with which Rivière declares this affiliation are at least worthy of note: 'one of the richest and most highly condensed productions that he ever composed . . . Melanie Klein's theories dovetail with exquisite precision into its tight and rigorous propositions.'[46] Easy or forced entry? What more fitting image for an intimacy uncertain of the legitimacy of its own claims. As if it were being acknowledged that the only passage for these doubtful inheritors was to come up on Freud from behind (sphincter theory, we might say).

The problem of beginnings, it would seem, is at least partly tributary to the problem of descent. What 'Negation' offers is a way of theorizing a subject who comes into being on the back of a repudiation, who exists in direct proportion to what it cannot *let be*. If there is no presupposed category of the subject in Kleinian theory, then the subject can emerge only in a moment of self differentiation, as a difference from itself: 'when exactly does the ego, the differentiation from the amorphous id, begin?'[47] It is through the category of negation, the category in which Lacan locates the fundamental negativity of the symbolic function, that Klein and her followers find the reply. Let's consider first what Lacan reads in this famous – and famously cryptic – text by Freud.

Lacan's discussion of Freud's article takes up three chapters of the full version of his 1966 *Ecrits* – an analysis by the Hegelian scholar Jean Hyppolite with an introduction and commentary by Lacan.[48] All three were originally part of Lacan's first seminar of 1954 on the technical writings of Freud[49] – the only works by Freud, interestingly, not included in the Pelican Freud, a comment in itself on the severance between psychoanalysis as clinical and as wider cultural discourse in Great Britain today. Hyppolite focuses on this sentence from the end of Freud's paper: 'Affirmation – as a substitute (*Ersatz*) for uniting – belongs to Eros; negation – the successor (*Nachfolge*) to expulsion – belongs to the instinct of destruction (*Destruktionstrieb*).'[50] He reads in Freud's distinction between 'substitute' (or 'equivalent') and 'successor' a crucial difference in the way affirmation and negation relate to the instincts from which they are said to derive. For Hyppolite that 'successor' (as opposed to 'equivalent') opens up a gap between negation and destruction; they are precisely not equivalents, not the same thing. Hence, he argues, we can read in Freud two concepts of negation: on the one hand, a pleasure of denying which results simply from the suppression of the libidinal components under the domination of the instincts – this already suggests, in a way that troubles some cherished boundaries, that the instinct of destruction is attached to the pleasure principle (Rivière: 'many psychic manifestations show that a threat from the death instinct produces a strong uprush of Eros'[51]) – and, on the other, negation as the basis of the symbolic function: 'a fundamental attitude of symbolicity (symbol-making capacity) made explicit.'[52] What Freud's article shows is that this capacity emerges in a 'space of suspension,' from a 'margin of thinking' where thinking – and being – can only emerge through what they relegate to non-being, to the not-thought: 'what one is in the mode of not being it.'[53]

It is this second emphasis which is picked up by Lacan: 'negativity of discourse, insofar as it brings what is not into being, sends us back to the question of what nonbeing, manifested in the symbolic order, owes to the reality of death.'[54] Negation, for Lacan, is death in the structure, or what he also calls the 'real,' which, for symbolization to be possible, has to subsist outside its domain. Negation shows the subject, and its world, arising in an act of demolition. For the subject to enter into the possibilities of language and judgement, something has to be discarded, something falls away. For Lacan therefore, negativity resides on the edge of speech. In an account which is strikingly resonant of this vision, Ella Sharpe reinterprets Melanie Klein: '[the breasts] become the symbol of that undecomposed world which was once the baby's before knowledge entered to start him on the path of detachment.'[55] Knowledge, as much as – inseparably from? – aggression, breaks up the unity of the world. We could say that Lacan goes furthest in detaching negation from the destructive impulse – 'successor' precisely, but not 'equivalent' – because the moment of negation posits the end of equivalence, the end of unity, as such. As Hyppolite puts it: 'primordial affirmation is nothing other than to affirm, but to deny is more than to want to destroy.'[56] For those accustomed to reading Freud in terms of the concept of 'after-effect' (*Nachträglichkeit*), it is easy to read in that *Nachfolge* or 'following after' the idea that what precedes has not necessarily come before.

In this commentary by Lacan, the reference to Melanie Klein, moreover, is explicit. A discussion of Klein's 1930 paper on symbol formation ('The Importance of Symbol-Formation in the Development of the Ego') follows immediately after Hyppolite's commentary when it was originally presented to

Lacan's seminar in 1954, and the discussion ends with a link between Hyppolite and Klein for what they each demonstrate regarding 'the function of destructionism in the constitution of human reality.'[57] In his reply to Hyppolite, Lacan makes a passing reference to a paper by Melitta Schmideberg, identifying her as the first analyst of a patient of Ernest Kris whose acting out of a prematurely cut short orality might explain, he suggests, the relative failure of that earlier analysis with Schmideberg.[58] Thus Lacan's commentary on Freud's 'Negation' leads, in a beautiful circularity, back to Melanie Klein.

In fact, the reference to Schmideberg could be seen as the vanishing-point of Lacan's commentary, as well as of the history and theory being discussed here – a part of analytic literature which, as Lacan says, has 'unfortunately become very difficult of access,'[59] and an orality embedded somewhere in a paper by an analyst, the daughter of Melanie Klein, who, one could argue, as an effect of its unbearable intensity, its acting out inside the analytic institution, will finally reject all such concepts and sever her links with the psychoanalytic world. Ella Sharpe: 'I assume hopefully a possibility of discussing Mrs Klein's theory, of being critical in the constructive meaning of that word, of accepting some things without its being interpreted that one has swallowed Mrs Klein and her work whole.'[60]

It is through orality that Isaacs and Heimann read Freud's paper on 'Negation.' For them, this is the key passage:

> Expressed in the language of the oldest – the oral instinctual impulses (*Triebregungen* – impulses of the drives), the judgement is: 'I should like to eat this,' or 'I should like to spit it out'; and, put more generally: 'I should like to take this into myself and keep that out.' That is to say: 'It shall be inside me' or 'it shall be outside me.' As I have shown elsewhere, the original pleasure-ego wants to introject into itself everything that is good and to eject from itself everything that is bad. What is bad, what is alien to the ego and what is external are, to begin with, identical.[61]

For Isaacs what this passage reveals is that the function of judgement is derived from the primary instinctual impulses. This is the famous 'instinctual reductionism' for which Klein is often criticized.[62] Indeed, Isaacs stresses the concept of derivation, and dismisses Freud's phrase 'expressed in the language of the oral impulses' as 'picturesque.'[63] But, as her commentary on this passage makes clear, it is the mechanisms of introjection and projection which are crucial, and the role of phantasy as the operational link between the two, 'the means by which the one is transmuted into the other': '"I want to eat that and therefore I have eaten it" is the phantasy which represents the id impulse in the psychic life; it is at the same time the subjective *experience* of the mechanism or process of introjection,' an interpretation in turn, therefore, of the symbolic process of taking in.[64] Judgement devours and expels its objects: it derives from an orality which in turn becomes a metaphor for judgement itself. This, as

it, is less derivation than circularity: 'one of the "results of the phantasy
ijection" is the process of introjection.'[65] No less than Lacan's commentary, which turns on the concept of foreclosure, the ability of the psyche under
pressure of denial to wipe something out, this is a process which can have as its
logical outcome the effacement, or scotomization, of the world:

> the mechanism of denial is expressed in the mind of the subject in some such
> way as 'If I don't admit it [i.e. a painful fact] it isn't true.' Or: 'If I don't
> admit it, no one else will know that it is true.' And in the last resort this
> argument can be traced to bodily impulses and phantasies, such as: 'If
> it doesn't come out of my mouth, that shows it isn't inside me'; or 'I can
> prevent anyone else *knowing* it is inside me.' Or: 'It is all right if it comes
> out of my anus as flatus or faeces, but it mustn't come out of my mouth as
> words.' The mechanism of *scotomization* is experienced in such terms as:
> 'What I don't see I need not believe'; or 'What I don't see, other people
> don't, and indeed doesn't exist.'[66]

What is striking about this passage is the way it seems to undermine the very
causal sequence from which it claims to derive. For, if the body can become a
mechanism of disavowal for language ('it is all right if it comes out of my body
as flatus or faeces, but it mustn't come out of my mouth as words'), then the body
is already being inscribed in a linguistic process, is being called up as metaphor
even as it is metaphor – the passage of bodily process into language – that the
subject resists. So the more Isaacs carries out her derivation of phantasy from
impulse, the more the impulse becomes after the fact ('successor' we might say)
the metaphoric correlate of the phantasy it supports. Thus the Kleinians flesh out
the structure of negation. At one level it is without doubt a more literally –
vulgarly – corporeal reading than that of Lacan; but no more than his can it
guarantee the reality of the world which it constitutes but can equally efface.
Orality appears here as the transcription or metaphor of itself. What primacy is
being given here to the concept of the impulse – 'mythological beings superb in
their indefiniteness' as Heimann and Isaacs put it, citing a famous remark of
Freud's?[67]

It is, I think, worth stressing this question of transcription because, in relation
to Klein, it is most often misread. Thus Nicolas Abraham and Maria Torok
criticize what they call Klein's 'panfantastic instinctualism'; while Jean
Laplanche and J.-B. Pontalis take Isaacs's definition of phantasy as the 'mental
expression' of the impulse as evidence of a potential reductionism in Klein, one
which Klein herself resisted but which has been exacerbated by other interpreters
and followers of her work.[68] In her Introduction to the 1952 collection, Rivière
cites Isaacs's definition together with the lines from Freud on which it is
based: 'Freud said: "We suppose that it [the id] is somewhere in direct contact
with somatic processes and takes over from them instinctual needs and gives
them mental expression." Now in the view of the present writers, this *mental*

expression is unconscious phantasy.' But, Rivière continues, the passage goes on: 'There is no impulse, no instinctual urge or response which is not experienced as unconscious phantasy.'[69] The two propositions are clearly not symmetrical: to say that one thing is the *expression of* another is not the same thing as to say that one thing *has to find another* in terms of which it can be expressed. As Isaacs summarized in her original paper, 'instinctual urges . . . cannot operate in the mind without phantasy.'[70] The second implies translation, mediation, or, as Isaacs puts it, 'operative link'; that is, it implies interpretation, or rather mis-interpretation, the word used explicitly by Rivière: 'on Freud's own hypothesis, the psyche responds to the reality of its experiences by interpreting them – or rather misinterpreting them – in a subjective manner.'[71] Subjective experi-ence involves the child in perpetual misreadings of the world: '[the child's] misunderstanding of the situation is precisely that subjective interpretation of his perception.'[72]

Phantasies, Isaacs writes, are the 'expression of wishes and passions': 'It is primarily because he *wants* his urine to be so very powerful that he comes to believe it is so.'[73] The destructive impulse therefore turns on a tautology – destructive because of the omnipotence with which the child wields and translates it to her or his own ends. This is the impulse 'pressed into the service of need' of phantasy, to use Rivière's expression, far more than phantasy as the 'mental expression of' instinctual need;[74] not a reduction of phantasy to a biological instinct, but a massive inflation of the power of phantasy to make, and break, the world.

What emerges most strongly from these papers is the impossibility of assigning some simple origin to destruction. Hate may be older than love, but Melanie Klein's conclusions 'do not stand or fall on the concept of the death instinct.'[75] What seems to be outrageous – paradoxically harder to manage than death as a pure force, as something which assaults the subject from outside, is this internalization of death into the structure. If death is a pure point of biological origin, then at least it can be scientifically known. But if it enters into the process of psychic meanings, inseparable from the mechanisms through which subjects create and recreate their vision of the world, then from where can we gain the detachment with which to get it under control?

It is clear that for the critics of Klein and her supporters, it was the priority accorded to subjective experience and the implications of this for knowledge which was at stake. (Recently Meltzer has suggested that this is *the* philosophical problem posed by Klein.[76]) Klein, Isaacs, and Heimann were confusing 'the mental corollary to instinct' with 'what we are used to call phantasy,' subjective definition with mental mechanism – 'The mixing-up of conceptions impresses all of us as most undesirable'; 'What happens when the distinction is lost?'[77] Each time, Isaacs and Heimann respond by insisting on the impossibility, within the logic proper to psychoanalysis, of holding the elements apart: '*What I believe is that reality-thinking cannot operate without concurrent and supporting Ucs phantasies*' (emphasis original); 'A rigid separation between "mechanism" and "content" is a danger to psychological understanding . . . it springs from a basic fallacy: a rigid divorce between the id and the ego'; 'perception and image-formation cannot be sharply separated from unconscious phantasy'; 'the suggestion that we should discuss "the nature of the process itself" rather than its content seems to rest on a false assumption. The nature of mental process, as well as of the structure and mechanisms of the mind, is partly determined and characterised by phantasies, that is to say, by the subjective content of the mind.'[78] Compare Anna Freud from her 1945 paper 'Indications for Child Analysis': 'All through childhood a ripening process is at work which, in the service of an increasingly better knowledge of and adaptation to reality, aims at perfecting these functions, at rendering them *more and more independent of the emotions until they become as accurate and reliable as any non-human mechanical apparatus*' (my emphasis).[79]

What seems to be involved, therefore, is something in the nature of a boundary, or category, dispute. How much is subjective experience allowed to *take in* (can the category of cats be a member of itself)? Marjorie Brierley proposes that 'introjection' be kept as the term for the mental process, 'incorporation' for the experience of taking things in: 'When the baby is trying to put everything into its mouth, it comes across many things that won't go in. Image formation as a function of mind will not go in to incorporation.'[80] To which Heimann replies: 'Mentally, anything can go into anything.'[81] But if anything can go into anything – both mentally and theoretically, then what is there to distinguish psychoanalysis, as a form of mental activity, from the all-devouring, all-incorporating child?

Or, to put it another way, what is left of identity and its (self-) definition if these distinctions cannot be sustained? If incorporation cannot be distinguished from introjection, or introjection from identification (as Sharpe points out, Freud often blurred the distinction between the two), then the idea of identity as distinct from, even if created through, its objects becomes unclear. How can incorporation be the foundation of identity when it seems to imply as a concept a dissolution of the separateness on which identity relies?[82] The issue here is not whether these distinctions can, or cannot, be theoretically mounted, but the form of loss that seems to threaten when they fail. What do these uncertainties imply for an adult subject (an adult science)?

Brierley makes it explicit that the distinction between subjectivity and mechanism carries with it the distinction between first and third person, between identification and object-relationship, between knowledge and science.[83] If psychoanalysis cannot distinguish between knowledge and phantasy, it becomes an infant incapable of taking its measure of reality, incapable of stepping out into the world. So when Glover insults his adversaries – accusing, for example, Klein of projecting into children, Heimann of playing with Freud's theories like a 'kitten plays with a ball of wool' – I read this as more than personally symptomatic.[84] He has, like others of Klein's critics, spotted one of the most far-reaching and troubling implications of her theories: not just the point convincingly made by many recent commentators of Freud – that psychoanalysis can be only a speculative form of knowledge, that it must, if it is to remain loyal to its object, undo its claims to authority as it goes[85] – but that, in relation to the project of child analysis, that same undoing propels the analyst *and her theories* back into the realm of the child. Psychoanalysis cannot ignore, cannot separate itself from, the unconscious conditions of knowledge. Could it be the force of this recognition during the 'Controversial Discussions' that led, in reaction, to what today is often seen as the opposite – the rigidity of Kleinian interpretation, the fierceness with which Kleinian thinking now lays claim to its status as science? Walter Schmideberg: 'I listened to [the papers] in silence and some of them made me think that the accusations of our enemies that it is impossible to distinguish between the phantasies of the patients and those of the analyst contained more than a grain of truth'; Karin Stephen: 'Do we really know what we are doing?'[86] What happens if we read this as the insight and not the failure of the dispute?

Clearly, then, it is the status of psychoanalysis as scientific knowledge which is at stake – what might be called its coming of age. Is psychoanalysis an adult science? Do children develop from point A to point B, or do they evolve according to a different sequence, one which throws into crisis our idea of what a sequence should be? Thus the question of development arises logically out of the question of knowledge and science. It is, writes Brierley, 'to put the cart before the horse' if you make introjection, based on bodily behaviour, responsible for image formation.[87] If mental mechanisms are partly determined by phantasy, then 'expressed in theoretical terms this would mean that the end results of mental processes determine the processes themselves which is absurd.'[88] Complicated emotional attitudes are assumed to be in existence before instinctual urges; the infant interprets its experience in terms of a superego not yet in force: 'Coming events cast their shadow before.'[89] What has happened to sequence and causality? What priority – theoretically – is being given to unconscious time?

Once again the theoretical point takes its colour from the psychic processes being described. What Brierley and Glover have identified is that Klein's account of beginnings, of the infant's first being in the world, inaugurates circular rather than sequential time. This is how Rivière describes the 'vicious circle' which is the child's first apprehension of cause and effect: '"You don't come and help, and you hate me, because I am angry and devour you; yet I *must* hate you and devour you in order to make you help."'[90] The child is caught in an impasse, 'the fear of destroying the mother in the very act of expressing love for her' and of 'losing her in the very process designed to secure her possessions.'[91] Incorporation does not only take everything in; it also abolishes its object. If we go back to those moments of primordial absence and negation and put them together, we can watch this scenario emerge. What is lost is a persecutor; the only way of being of the object is as something devoured or expelled; the lost object is bad *because* the only way of being the object is as something devoured or expelled. If this is a vicious circle, it is also, in these early papers, a process without end; inherently contradictory, these mechanisms serve the very impulses against which they defend, and they founder on the 'problem of preservation' as emptiness, aggression, and sadistic impulses all return: 'The omnipotence of phantasy is a weapon which cuts both ways.'[92] Similarly, what is seen to resolve the cycle belongs no less in circular time: 'Here we have a benign circle.'[93]

One of the most interesting things about these papers, therefore, is that they lay out so clearly the problem of generating an account of positive development out of the processes they have described – positive as in psychic, positive as in linear time. Not that Klein does not add, as Rivière insists, a new emphasis on the mother as good object, on the early love relation, on the depressive phase in which the child takes everything back (as opposed to 'in') and subjects it to a meticulous and loving repair. 'Even during the earliest stage,' Klein writes, 'persecutory anxiety is to some extent counteracted by the experience of the good breast.'[94] And yet, even inside this account (and on the same page), the experience of gratification turns into idealization, which then sets up the object as 'perfect, inexhaustible, always available, always gratifying.'[95] As Klein puts it in the discussion following her paper in 1944: 'Even when the feeding situation is satisfactory, hunger and the craving for libidinal gratification stir and reinforce the destructive impulses';[96] and again in an earlier paper: 'some measure of frustration is inevitable . . . what the infant actually *desires* is unlimited gratification.'[97] Gratification therefore sets up the terms of its own demise. Or, where it repairs, it also repeats: 'The experience of gratification at the mother's breast after frustration' develops the infant's confidence that 'bad things go and good things come';[98] it enters into the logic of expulsion and projection that it is also intended to subdue.

Klein's contribution to the debate can be read at least partly as a reaffirmation of love against what has come before. But this love, she insists, is complex; it is not a value or thing in itself. If it is present from the earliest stages, it none the less comes at least partly in reply to the mother's demand ('an infant knows intuitively that his smile and other signs of affection and happiness produce happiness and pleasure in the mother'); turning on her pleasure, it seeks out her desires and her words. Klein provides a graphic image of this early relation in the five-month-old patient who put his fingers in Klein's mouth in 'an attempt to fetch the sounds out' (introjection, as Lacan would put it, as 'always introjection of the speech of the other').[99] These feelings, Klein states in reply to Brierley, are not a 'primary simple affect.'[100]

Likewise, reparation can reinforce omnipotence. (Although Klein herself had insisted on the distinction from 1935, one point of dispute was whether it simply derived from Freud's concept of reaction formation and obsessional undoing.[101]) In these discussions the concept of reparation appears less as part of a naturally evolving development, and more as a *requirement*, something enjoined internally and externally – on the child. It is, in fact, striking in the way it appears as a concept in the imperative mode: 'The objects within, feelings about people *must be* put right'; 'The external objects, real parents, brothers and sisters and so on, *must* be pleased and made happy'; 'the full internalization of real persons as helpful loved figures *necessitates* abandoning this defence-method of splitting feelings and objects into good and bad'; 'good and bad feelings *have to be* tolerated at one and the same time.'[102] Manifestly replying to criticisms from the earlier debate, Rivière states: 'The significance of the phantasies of reparation is perhaps the most essential aspect of Melanie Klein's work; for that reason her contribution to psychoanalysis *should not* be regarded as limited to the exploration of the aggressive impulses and phantasies.'[103]

To what *necessity* we might ask – theoretical and institutional as well as psychic – does the concept of reparation correspond? Two recent Kleinian commentators have described the development of the concept as something of a mystery in Klein's work. For Meltzer, at the point where Klein starts to distinguish between manic reparation 'as defence against persecutory or depressive anxiety' and 'something more genuinely in the service of the objects,' it begins to take on a 'more mysterious meaning'; in the discussion cited at the start of this chapter, Elizabeth Bott Spillius described as 'mysterious' the shift of attention from sadism to love in Klein's later work: 'I don't know where it came from.'[104] It is as if reparation can theorize itself only as absolute necessity and/or absolute unknown. What these papers suggest is that reparation cannot be detached from the issue of knowledge. Indeed, one might say that, as psychic process, reparation requires a suspension of absolute knowledge if it is not to turn into pure omnipotent defence. It is not, therefore, to deny the validity of the experience of reparation to note that it has often come to serve in the Kleinian corpus as a solution to difficulties – of negativity, causality, and knowledge – which, in this earlier debate, seem to be without end. The point is made, although from very different perspectives, by both Glover and Lacan.

For it is central to Kleinian theory that the anxiety which leads to fixation and regression in both sexes also plays its part in precipitating the libido on its forward path: 'each of the fixations and pathological symptoms apt to appear at successive stages of development have both a retrogressive and progressive function, binding anxiety and thus making further development possible.'[105] Which is to say that development is in some sense pathological – Heimann calls this the 'negative aspect of progression.'[106] Klein herself states repeatedly, with reference to the depressive position, that each step in unification leads to a renewed splitting of the imagos – of necessity, since the depressive position genetically derives from the paranoid state that it is meant to surpass. What Heimann and Isaacs refer to as a 'benign circle' follows the same logic: 'These ego achievements . . . are prime factors in the fight against anxiety and guilt. A certain degree and quality of guilt and anxiety stimulate reparation and thus encourage sublimation.'[107]

Thus, when Isaacs writes, '*the established principle of genetic continuity is a concrete instrument of knowledge*' (emphasis original), 'the essence of Freud's theory lies in just this fact of detailed continuity,' this is not a developmental paradigm in any straightforward sense.[108] The movement is constantly in two directions – progression being constantly threatened by the mechanisms which move it on. Hence the well-known paradox that, in Klein's account, homosexuality arises out of the anxieties of heterosexual phantasy; that if heterosexuality is somewhere pre-established for the subject, it is so only as part of an unmanageable set of phantasies which are in fact incapable, in the theory, of ensuring heterosexuality itself.[109] As much as the idea of a developmental sequence, this could be argued to be the logic proper to Kleinian thought: 'Anxiety and guilt at times check and at other times enhance the libidinal development'; 'while in some ways these defences impede the path of integration, they are essential for the whole development of the ego.'[110] Thus, as Lacan points out in his commentary on Klein's paper on symbol formation, the ego appears twice over and in the space of a single sentence, as precocious or overdeveloped and as what, through its weakness, is preventing normal development from taking place: 'The early operation of the reactions originating on the genital level was the result of premature ego development, but further ego development was only inhibited by it' (Lacan: 'She says that the ego was over precociously developed . . . and then in the second part of the sentence that it is the ego which is preventing development from taking place').[111]

Too much and too little of an ego whose role it is to master the anxiety out of which it has itself been produced. Anna Freud objects: 'According to the theory of the English school of analysis, introjection and projection, which in our view should be assigned to the period after the ego has been differentiated from the outside world, are the very processes by which the structure of the ego is developed.'[112] Only if the ego comes first is development assured. Those who criticize Klein for developmental normativity (the idea that subjects progress naturally to their heterosexual goals) would do well to note that, at least as much as regards Freud's own normative moments, it is not in these terms that Klein's writings can theoretically sustain themselves.[113] The value of the stress on negativity would then reside in the trouble it poses to the concept of a sequence, the way that it acts as a bar, one could say, to what might elsewhere (and increasingly) appear as normative and prescriptive in the work and followers of Melanie Klein.

For Glover, in his long critique of Klein, a central problem – if not the central problem – was that 'the author cannot tell a developmental story straight.'[114] (For those in the humanities seeking after the trials of writing, this would be the ultimate accolade.) The 'subversive nature' of Heimann and Isaacs's paper on 'Regression' is precisely that 'if fixation can be regarded as a reaction to (result of) regression and if regression itself works backwards through a developmental aggression series, it follows that progression must be attributed to the same factors.'[115] For Glover, this is to undermine or deviate from – the 'biological progression of an instinct-series' – that is, the whole conception of libidinal development as laid down by Freud: 'It subverts all our concepts of progressive mental development.'[116] Only 'if we stick to Freud's elaborated categories,' writes Hoffer, are we 'able to conceive the primitive psychical make-up of an infant and the elaborate organization of an adult personality as a *lawful continuity*.'[117] Thus Melanie Klein, in the eyes of her critics, theoretically disinherits herself.

The objections to these papers thus make it clear that the emphasis on negativity operates not as a primordial, biological pre-given from which an orderly sequence ('an orderly series and correlations') can be derived, but as the subversion of sequence and biology alike. And Glover is explicit that this subversion is the direct consequence of the emphasis on phantasy in the work of Klein. It is at that moment of primitive hallucination when, he argues, the child misinterprets its experience 'against the whole weight of the biological evidence of survival' that the instinct loses the 'realistic aim' on which such a concept of orderly progression relies. And what, Glover asks, does this make of the infant if not 'fantast' and 'fool'?[118]

It seems to me that this is the problem which then works itself out inside the analytic institution and specifically in relation to the analysis of children. Let's note that the genesis of the persecutory object in Kleinian thinking casts a shadow over interpretation, since, according to the logic of negation, interpretation comes as a stranger from the outside. And let's note too that if Klein makes of the analyst a fool and a fantast, it is from this place that the analyst has to try to speak, bridging the gap, as Rivière puts it at the end of her Introduction, between the baby ignorant of the external world and the scientist aware of nothing else. For the baby derives and imputes meanings which, because they do not relate to external or material reality, the scientific worker cannot appreciate. And the analyst can bridge the gap only in so far as 'she can assume the baby's condition.'[119] What is this, other than to require psychoanalysis to enter into what Kleinians seem to theorize, to the consternation of their critics, as an infinite regress? a place which Rivière assigns to those 'gifted and intuitive mothers and women' who know that the child inhabits a world of psychic significance and who are 'almost as inarticulate as babies themselves.'[120] Leaving aside this extraordinary image of women's relationship to language in an introduction to a book in which only women in fact speak,[121] the question has to be asked: What problems must it pose for an analytic school to situate itself in the place of an infant to whom interpretation is by definition unwelcome and who is fantast and fool?

A point finally about the wider political resonance of this dispute. The discussions, as is well known, were staged at the height of the Second World War. The emphasis on negativity, the ambivalence about reparation (reparation as ambivalent), takes its reference from, even as it casts light on, the conflict going on all around. Ella Sharpe comments: 'For a belief in the actual good object the actual bad one results in world affairs with a Hitler-ridden Germany and pipe-smoking optimists elsewhere who say "God's in His Heaven, all's right with the world."' And again: 'The "status quo" is a frequent phrase heard today. The full phrase is "the status quo ante." How many people still hope that the end of the war may mean a restoration of the pre-war conditions for which they are most homesick, although progressive minds on every hand warn us that restoration of old conditions could only lead to renewed disaster.'[122] What clearer statement of the political provenance of theory? What clearer indication that, for this analyst at least, if psychoanalysis concentrates on the good and the restorative, it heads straight into a theoretical and political blind?

A postscript on black holes

During the course of working on this chapter, I read Stephen Hawking's *A Brief History of Time* (I am one of thousands, as it has been at the top of the best-seller list in Britain and the United States since it was first published in 1988).[123] I could not help but be struck by the remarkable analogies between what Hawking was describing in the realm of cosmology, the theoretical difficulties and points of tension of that description, and what Melanie Klein confronted in her attempt to theorize the negative components of psychic life. Hawking's investigation of black holes and the Big Bang theory of the universe can be read as an investigation of how to think negativity and outer boundaries, the points where what we take to be the recognizable and at least partly knowable universe comes into being, goes off its own edges, collapses into itself, ceases to be – all questions which are central to the psychoanalytic discussion of the boundaries, coming into being, and internally intractable limits of the psyche. As Paula Heimann put it: 'when exactly does the ego, the differentiation from the amorphous id begin?'[124] Compare Hawking: 'What really happens during the very early . . . stages of the universe? . . . Does the universe in fact have a beginning? . . . What were the "boundary conditions" at the beginning of time?' (pp. 115, 122).

In his book, Hawking discusses the famous concept of the black hole – points (or singularities) in the universe where all matter collapses in on itself: stars which have contracted to the point where light cannot escape, and if light cannot escape, since nothing can travel faster than light, 'neither can anything else; everything is dragged back by the gravitational field' (p. 87). All-incorporating, the black hole has, at the very least, extraordinarily metaphoric resonance for anyone thinking about Melanie Klein's work (irresistibly, current attempts at unified theory in physics are called 'grand unified theories' or GUTs).[125] However, it is in the relation between the black hole and its conceptual theorization that I think the most interesting points of connection appear. How can a black hole – how can negativity – be thought? This, as much as resistance to the idea of a destructive force in all of us, is what I consider to have been at the heart of the dispute with Melanie Klein.

It is central to Hawking's account of the black hole that what happens inside it cannot, by definition, be known. Since anyone entering a black hole is destroyed by it, she or he cannot observe it; inversely, those at the distance that allows observation are protected from the breakdown of the laws of science which occurs inside a black hole. If you are inside, you lose the capacity and conditions for knowledge; outside, you retain knowledge, but cannot grasp what it is you need to know. The black hole thus provokes two complementary anxieties: too close, it devours you; safely outside, you don't know what's going on. This is called the 'cosmic censorship hypothesis' (rephrased by Hawking as 'God abhors a naked singularity': p. 88). Like the unconscious, a black hole is censored, and can be known only by its effects. As a concept, the black hole wipes out the possibility of knowledge, of its own total or absolute theoretical grasp. It is therefore the place where not only all light and matter, but our laws of science in relationship to them, as well as the relationship we presume between observation and knowledge, equally disappear.

Lacan, in a passage cited by Shoshana Felman, draws on the Heisenberg uncertainty principle also discussed by Hawking (pp. 53–61) – that it is impossible to locate exactly the speed and place of a particle at the same time (the process of locating one affects the other, and conversely): 'as soon as [the elements] are interrogated somewhere, it is impossible to grasp them in their totality.'[126] Hawking's discussion constantly returns to this question of the possibility of knowledge (although in relation to the uncertainty principle he in fact suggests that some forms of unpredictability might be removed). Thus, for example, the question arises as to why this universe, among the possibility of many different universes or regions of a single universe, developed in such a way that complicated organisms are possible, and why the universe is the way that we see it – to which the reply, according to what is called the strong 'anthropic principle' is: 'If it had been different we would not have been here' (pp. 124–7). Not everyone accepts this principle of course – Hawking himself is committed to a unified theory of physics which would ultimately reveal the mind of God. But what is striking about the principle is that the state of the universe is explained as the consequence of the subjects who, according to a more obvious logic, should appear as its effect. Or to put it another way, in this account, it is only through a fantasy of our being-in-the-world that we can theorize the fact that the world comes to be.[127]

It is, therefore, not just that contemporary science points to the 'irreducibility of ignorance' (Felman's expression for the epistemological principle proposed by Lacan[128]), but that the question of knowledge and the question of origins – the question of the origins of knowledge – appear to be inextricably linked. At the very least, the terms of this discussion should act as a caution to any attempt to legitimate psychoanalysis through a naive appeal to science (since today science itself will not support the idea of definitive knowledge to which such descriptions of psychoanalysis make their appeal). More, and in a way that echoes the insistence by Isaacs and Rivière on the inseparability of knowledge and subjective experience, fantasies are always in on the (scientific) act. 'It is greatly to be hoped,' writes Hawking, 'that some version of the censorship hypothesis holds because close to naked singularities it may be possible to travel into the past. While this would be fine for writers of science fiction, it would mean that no one's life would ever be safe: someone might go into the past and kill your father and mother before you were conceived!' (p. 89). The point of quoting this is not to reduce scientific investigation to the status of oedipal fantasy or 'primal scene' (what exactly did parents get up to before one was born?), but, resisting any reduction of psychoanalysis to cosmology or the reverse, to suggest that if knowledge always borders on fantasy, fantasy is always in part fantasy about (the borders of) knowledge. Where does the possibility of knowledge come from? Can we conceive of a limit point where it ceases to be?[129]

It is the advantage of theories like that of the black hole or the Big Bang that they are so apocalyptic. The drama of their imagining compensates for what scares. The idea of something negative as explosion or pure inexplicable force seems oddly to be more manageable or acceptable than the idea of something negative which is at once less certain and which seems to wipe out the conditions through which it can, or should, be known. This, it seems to me, is what we saw in relation to Klein: leave the death drive in the sphere of biological science; don't mix it with meaning, with the psychic glosses and qualifiers of the inner world. It is not just that this brings the death drive in closer (Rivière's comment on psycho-analytic 'resistance' to the death drive); it is also paradoxically that this same proximity weakens its visionary force. In the Kleinian account, it was exactly in proportion as negativity entered the psychic structure that it slipped from the realm of logic and sequence – for the theory and for the psychic development being charted – and out of any totalizing grasp.

It seems significant, therefore, that Hawking has qualified the concept of the black hole – one chapter is entitled 'Black Holes Ain't So Black' – but this is much less often talked about (pp. 99–113). More difficult than the idea of the black hole as total destruct or all-incorporating negativity is the idea that the black hole emits something positive, radiation, which 'seems to imply that gravitational collapse is not as final and irreversible as we once thought' (p. 112). Hawking says that when he presented this result at a conference, he was greeted with incredulity. The images that Hawking offers here are in themselves graphic for psychoanalysis: negative virtual particles which fall into a black hole leaving their positive partner with nothing to 'annihilate with,' at which point the partners either also fall into the black hole or, having positive energy, escape (p. 106). Perhaps we could substitute this strange image of partnership for the dualism of the life and death principles – 'pairing' as an alternative to the notions of 'balance' or 'triumph of one principle over the other' through which the link between them is most often described.

Again, more difficult than the idea of the Big Bang is the idea of a universe without beginning or end. This might be why Hawking's new proposal about the initial state of the universe – no boundary to space–time: 'The boundary condition of the universe is that it has no boundary' (p. 136) – is so unsettling. A universe without boundary disturbs, not just because it leaves so small a 'role for a creator (the Pope instructed the participants at one conference which Hawking attended not to enquire into the Big Bang itself because it was the work of God), but because, paradoxically, it is the idea of something with*out* a limit that pushes us conceptually off the edge.

The issue then seems to be not how much we can take of negativity, but how much negativity itself can take. If it appears to be the potential black hole of psychoanalytic theory, it is perhaps even more disturbing to think that it might not be such an absolute, that there might be random particles which escape (not a collision between two absolute principles but particles left with no one 'to annihilate with'); that the black hole, like theory, cannot get everything under its sway. It is as if negativity can be taken on board only as Big Bang or black hole (without qualification), either pure origin or end.

It feels to me that, against the grain of this way of thinking, Hawking can be fruitfully read alongside Melanie Klein: negativity as the limit of theory or total knowledge; negativity as caught up in the positive partner as much as antagonist, and not something to which the positive can only be opposed. The concept of negativity will not provide us with a clear account of origins (even if it affects the way that the idea of origins can be thought); nor can we place it at the distance from which it could be conceptually controlled; if it is mixed up with the positive, it ceases to be a pure entity; at the same time the positive, implicated in its process, cannot be appealed to as the counter-principle which will placate and subdue it or get it back under control (the relationships are more shifting than this). In Hawking's universe, as I read it, negativity is unavoidable – on condition that we do not reify it, but recognize its place in the speculations which we cannot but choose to spin about the world and about ourselves.

Notes

1 Leo Bersani gives a largely critical appraisal of Klein in 'Death and Literary Authority: Marcel Proust and Melanie Klein,' in *The Culture of Redemption* (Cambridge, Mass. and London: Harvard University Press, 1990) ch. 1 [this volume, ch. 12– Eds]; *Women: A Cultural Review* devoted a large section of its second issue, *Positioning Klein*, to Melanie Klein (Summer 1990). These appear, however, to be exceptions. There is no full discussion of Klein, e.g., in the influential collection *The Trial(s) of Psychoanalysis*, ed. Francoise Meltzer (Chicago: Chicago University Press, 1988). For discussion of feminism and Klein see n. 3 and 4 below.

2 Elizabeth Bott Spillius (ed.), *Melanie Klein Today: Developments in Theory and Practice*, vol. 1, *Mainly Theory*; vol. 2, *Mainly Practice*, New Library of Psycho-analysis, vols 7 and 8 (London and New York: Routledge in association with the Institute of Psycho-Analysis, 1988).

3 The clearest statement of these criticisms, focusing more directly on Ernest Jones but also addressing Klein, is given in 'The Phallic Phase and the Subjective Import of the Castration Complex,' in *Feminine Sexuality – Jacques Lacan and the école freudienne*, eds Juliet Mitchell and Jacqueline Rose (London: Macmillan; New York: Norton, 1982) 99–122; also Juliet Mitchell, 'Introduction' to *Feminine Sexuality* 1–26; and Jacqueline Rose, 'The Cinematic Apparatus – Problems in Current Theory,' in *Sexuality in the Field of Vision* (London: Verso, 1986) 211n. Bersani, 'Death and Literary Authority'; Noreen O'Connor, 'Is Melanie Klein the One Who Knows Who You Really Are?,' *Women – A Cultural Review*, 1, no. 2, 1990, 180–8. For a suggestive discussion of Lacan and Klein, see Malcolm Bowie, *Lacan* (London: Fontana Modern Masters, Cambridge, Mass.: Harvard University Press, 1991) 144–8.

4 See, e.g., Madeleine Sprengnether, '(M)other Eve: Some Revisions of the Fall in Fiction by Contemporary Women Writers,' in *Feminism and Psychoanalysis*, eds

Richard Feldstein and Judith Roof (Ithaca, NY: Cornell University Press, 1989) 298–322. The absence of Klein, both in this article and in Sprengnether's more recent book, *The Spectral Mother – Freud, Feminism and Psychoanalysis* (Ithaca, NY: Cornell University Press, 1990), which describes the absence of/haunting by the mother in Freud's work and the place of the pre-oedipal mother in subsequent analytic theory, seems striking. In discussion following the original presentation of '(M)other Eve' as a paper at 'Feminism and Psychoanalysis,' a conference held at the University of Illinois, Normal, in 1986, Sprengnether explained the absence of Klein in terms of the negative component of Klein's work. See also *The (M)other Tongue: Essays in Feminist Psychoanalytic Interpretation*, eds Shirley Nelson Garner, Claire Kahane and Madeleine Sprengnether (Ithaca, NY: Cornell University Press, 1985) and Jane Gallop's critique in terms of what she calls 'the dream of the mother without otherness' ('Reading the Mother Tongue: Psychoanalytic Feminist Criticism,' in Meltzer (ed.), *Trial(s) of Psychoanalysis* 136.

5 *The Freud–Klein Controversies 1941–45*, eds Pearl King and Riccardo Steiner, New Library of Psychoanalysis, vol. 11 (London and New York: Routledge in association with the Institute of Psycho-Analysis, 1991); and Melanie Klein, Paula Heimann, Susan Isaacs and Joan Rivière, *Developments in Psycho-Analysis*, ed. Joan Rivière, preface by Ernest Jones, International Psycho-Analytical Library, vol. 43 (London: Hogarth, 1952, and London: Maresfield, 1989).

6 The fullest and most informative account is given by Riccardo Steiner, 'Some Thoughts about Tradition and Change Arising from an Examination of the British Psycho-Analytical Society's Controversial Discussions (1943–44),' *International Review of Psycho-Analysis*, 12, 27 (1985) 27–71; see also Pearl King, 'Early Divergences between the Psycho-Analytical Societies in London and Vienna,' and Teresa Brennan, 'Controversial Discussions and Feminist Debate,' both in *Freud in Exile*, eds Edward Timms and Naomi Segal (New Haven, Conn., and London: Yale University Press, 1988) 124–33, 254–74; and Gregorio Kohon, 'Notes on the History of the Psychoanalytic Movement in Great Britain,' introduction to *The British School of Psychoanalysis: The Independent Tradition*, ed. Gregorio Kohon (London: Free Association Books, 1986) 24–50. For a discussion of the controversy, specifically in relation to the concept of phantasy, see Anne Hayman, 'What Do We Mean by "Phantasy"?,' *International Journal of Psycho-Analysis*, 70 (1989) 105–14.

7 Janet Sayers, *Mothering Psychoanalysis – Helene Deutsch, Karen Homey, Anna Freud, Melanie Klein* (London: Hamish Hamilton, 1991); *Women: A Cultural Review*, 1, no. 2. The first reappraisal of Klein in this context, although not explicitly addressed to feminism, is Juliet Mitchell's introduction to *The Selected Melanie Klein* (Harmondsworth: Penguin, 1986). Nancy Chodorow discusses Klein in *The Reproduction of Mothering* (Berkeley, Calif., and London: University of California Press, 1978), criticizing her for instinctual determinism, but praising her recognition, *contra* Freud, of the girl's early heterosexuality.

8 Nicholas Wright, *Mrs Klein* (London: Nick Hern Books, 1988); and review by Elaine Showalter, 'Mrs Klein: the Mother, the Daughter, the Thief and their Critics,' *Women: A Cultural Review*, 1, no. 2, 144–8. Paul Roazen, *Freud and his Followers* (New York: Knopf, 1974; London: Allen Lane, 1975).

9 François Roustang, *Un destin si funeste* (Paris: Minuit, 1976) trans. Ned Lukacher, *Dire Mastery* (Baltimore, Md and London: Johns Hopkins University Press, 1982); Jacques Derrida, 'Du tout,' in *La carte postale – de Socrate à Freud et au-delà* (Paris: Flammarion, 1980) 525–49, trans. Alan Bass, in *The Post Card – From Socrates to Freud and Beyond* (Chicago: Chicago University Press, 1987) 497–521; Phyllis Grosskurth, *Freud's Secret Ring – Freud's Inner Circle and the Politics of Psychoanalysis* (London: Cape, 1991).

10 Derrida, 'Du tout,' 548; trans. 520.

11 Julia Kristeva, 'The True-Real,' in *The Kristeva Reader*, ed. Toril Moi (Oxford: Blackwell, 1986) 214–37. Kristeva is undoubtedly the French psychoanalytic theorist who draws most consistently on the work of Melanie Klein.

12 None of the papers published in the 1952 *Developments in Psycho-Analysis* correspond exactly to the versions delivered to the scientific meetings of the British Society. I therefore use the different versions where appropriate, always indicating the source in the notes.

13 Donald Meltzer comments: 'Any systematic attempt to teach Melanie Klein's work runs almost immediately into difficulties that are the exact opposite of the problems facing one in teaching Freud. Where the theoretical tail wags the clinical dog with him, hardly any theoretical tail exists to be wagged with her,' *The Kleinian Development*, Part 2, *Richard Week by Week* (Perthshire: Clunie Press for the Roland Harris Educational Trust, 1978) 1.

14 *Complete Freud–Jones Correspondence*, ed. R.A. Paskauskas (Cambridge, Mass.: Harvard University Press, 1993); cf. also Steiner, 'Some Thoughts.'

15 Ernest Jones, preface to *Developments in Psycho-Analysis*, v.

16 Joan Rivière, *Developments in Psycho-Analysis* 1.

17 Rivière, *Developments* 2.

18 Rivière, *Developments* 2.

19 Susan Isaacs, opening statement, 'Fifth Series of Scientific Discussions,' 19 May 1943, in *Freud–Klein Controversies* 444.

20 Marjorie Brierley, opening comments on Paula Heimann's paper 'Some Aspects of the Role of Introjection and Projection in Early Development,' 'Sixth Discussion of Scientific Controversies,' 20 October 1943, in *Freud–Klein Controversies* 538–9.

21 Paula Heimann, 'Seventh Discussion of Scientific Controversies,' 17 November 1943, in *Freud–Klein Controversies* 569–70.

22 Rivière, Introduction to *Developments in Psycho-Analysis* 2, 3–4.

23 Meltzer sees this as *the* central problem of Kleinian thought: 'It requires an immense shift in one's view of the world to think that the outside world is essentially meaningless and unknowable, that one perceives the form but must attribute the meaning. Philosophically, this is the great problem in coming to grips with Kleinian thought and its implications' (*Kleinian Development* 86).

24 Rivière, Introduction to *Developments in Psycho-Analysis* 2–3.

25 Heimann, 'Some Aspects of Introjection and Projection,' 511.

26 For a critique of Klein's 'instinctual reductionism,' see Jacques Lacan, 'Phallic Phase and the Subjective Import of the Castration Complex,' and Chodorow, *Reproduction of Mothering*; Jean Laplanche and Jean-Bertrand Pontalis, 'Fantasme originaire, fantasme des origines, origine du fantasme,' *Les Temps modernes*, 215 (1964); trans. 'Fantasy and the Origins of Sexuality,' in *Formations of Fantasy*, eds Victor Burgin, James Donald and Cora Kaplan (London and New York: Methuen, 1986) 5–34; first published in English in *International Journal of Psycho-Analysis, 49* no. 1, (1969) (their criticisms are directed more at Susan Isaacs than Klein); also Nicolas Abraham and Maria Torok, who refer to Kleinian 'panfantastic instinctualism,' 'Deuil ou mélancolie, introjecter-incorporer,' in *L'écorce et le noyau* (Paris: Flammarion, 1987) 259–74; trans. 'Introjection-Incorporation: Mourning or Melancholia,' *Psychoanalysis in France* (New York: International Universities Press, 1980) eds Serge Lebovici and D. Widlöcher 3–16.

27 Isaacs, Balint, Lantos, in *Freud–Klein Controversies* 272, 347, 349; Edward Glover, 'Examination of the Klein System of Child Psychology,' *Psycho-Analytic Study of the Child*, 1 (1945) 103.

28 Rivière, 'On the Genesis of Psychical Conflict in Earliest Infancy,' in *Developments in Psycho-Analysis* 43; paper originally published in *International Journal of Psycho-Analysis* (1936) 395–422.

29 Isaacs, replying to discussion of her paper 'The Nature and Function of Phantasy,' 'Second Discussion of Scientific Controversies,' 17 February 1943, in *Freud–Klein Controversies* 373.

30 Anna Freud, *The Ego and the Mechanisms of Defence* (London: Hogarth Press and the Institute of Psycho-Analysis, 1937) 57; passage cited by Susan Isaacs, 'The Nature and Function of Phantasy,' in *Freud–Klein Controversies* 295. See also Anna Freud, 'Notes on Aggression,' 1949 (1948): 'The presence of mental conflicts and of the guilt feelings consequent on them presupposes that a specific, comparatively advanced stage in ego development has been reached,' *Indications for Child Analysis and Other Papers 1945–56*, in *The Writings of Anna Freud*, vol. 4 (New York: International Universities Press, 1968) 70.

31 Glover, 'Klein System,' 88n. citing his own paper 'Grades of Ego-Differentiation,' *International Journal of Psycho-Analysis* (1930) 1–11.

32 Barbara Lantos, 'Third Discussion of Scientific Controversies,' continuation of discussion of Isaacs's 'Nature and Function of Phantasy,' 17 March 1943, in *Freud–Klein Controversies* 413.

33 Isaacs, 'Fifth Discussion' concluding discussion on 'Nature and Function of Phantasy,' 460.

34 Rivière, 'Psychical Conflict in Earliest Infancy,' 45.

35 Rivière, Introduction 29.

36 Rivière, 'Psychical Conflict in Earliest Infancy,' 45.

37 Melanie Klein, 'The Emotional Life and Ego-Development of the Infant with Special Reference to the Depressive Position,' in *Freud–Klein Controversies* 781.

38 Rivière, 'Psychical Conflict in Early Infancy,' 45n.; Introduction 15.

39 Rivière, 'Psychical Conflict in Earliest Infancy,' 54–5; Isaacs, 'Nature and Function of Phantasy,' 302; Heimann, 'Some Aspects of Introjection and Projection,' 518.

40 Klein, *Narrative of a Child Analysis: The Conduct of the Psychoanalysis of Children as Seen in the Treatment of a Ten-year-old Boy*, in *The Writings of Melanie Klein*, vol. 4 (London: Hogarth, 1961, 1975 and Virago, 1988) 339.

41 Rivière, 'Psychical Conflict in Earliest Infancy,' 47, 49.

42 Klein, 'On Observing the Behaviour of Young Infants,' also cited by Rivière in Introduction 270n., 30; compare Heimann: 'Freud did not enter into the question of what happens in the infant's mind when he abandons the object' ('Certain Functions of Introjection and Projection,' 145).

43 Klein, 'Emotional Life of the Infant,' 763–4.

44 See Phyllis Grosskurth, *Melanie Klein: Her World and Her Work* (New York: Knopf; London: Maresfield, 1986) 376–7.

45 Isaacs, 'The Nature and Function of Phantasy,' Developments 103–7; Isaacs, 'Fifth Discussion,' 'Sixth Discussion,' 466–7; 554; Heimann, 'Some Aspects of Introjection and Projection,' 505–6.

46 Rivière, Introduction 10.

47 Heimann, 'Certain Functions of Introjection and Projection,' 128.

48 Jacques Lacan, 'Introduction au commentaire de Jean Hyppolite sur la "Verneinung" de Freud'; 'Réponse au commentaire de Jean Hyppolite sur la "Verneinung" de Freud'; Appendice 1: 'Commentaire parlé sur la "Verneinung" de Freud, par Jean Hyppolite,' in *Ecrits* (Paris: Seuil, 1966) 369–80, 381–400, 879–88. Throughout this section, where I cite these articles in English, I am making use of Anthony Wilden's unpublished translations of the texts kindly made available to me by Richard Macksey.

49 Lacan, *Le séminaire I: les écrits techniques de Freud* (Paris: Seuil, 1975) 63–73; trans. John Forrester, *Freud's Papers on Technique* (New York: Norton; Cambridge: Cambridge University Press, 1988) 52–61.

50 Freud, 'Negation,' 1925, in *The Standard Edition of the Complete Psychological Works of Sigmund Freud*, ed. and trans. James Strachey (London: Hogarth, 24 vols, 1953–74) vol. 19, 239; *Pelican Freud*, 11. 441.

51 Rivière, 'Psychical Conflict in Earliest Infancy,' 52.

52 Hyppolite, 'Commentaire parlé sur la "Verneinung" de Freud,' 886.

53 Hyppolite, 880. Hyppolite's reading, and Lacan's through Hyppolite, derives strongly from Hegel: 'The dissimilarity which obtains in consciousness between the ego and the substance constituting its object, is their inner distinction, the factor of negativity in general. We may regard it as the defect of both opposites, but it is their very soul, their moving spirit' (*The Phenomenology of Spirit*, trans. J. B. Baillie, rev. ed. (London: Allen and Unwin; New York: Humanities Press, 1949) 96–7; cf. too Kojève's commentary: 'In contrast to the knowledge that keeps man in a passive quietude, Desire dis-quiets him and moves him to action. Born of Desire, action tends to satisfy it, and can do so only by the "negation," the destruction, or at least the transformation of the desired object: to satisfy hunger, for example, the food must be destroyed or, in any case, transformed. Thus, all action is "negating"' (Alexandre Kojève, *Introduction à la lecture de Hegel* (Paris: Gallimard, 1947) 11; trans. James Nichols, Jr. *Introduction to the Reading of Hegel* (Ithaca, NY and London: Cornell University Press, 1969) 3–4. For a discussion of negativity in relation to Hegel and psychoanalysis, see Kristeva, 'La négativité, le rejet,' in *La révolution du langage poétique* (Paris: Seuil, 1974) 101–50, trans. Margaret Waller, *Revolution in Poetic Language* (New York: Columbia University Press, 1984) 107–64.

54 Lacan, 'Introduction au commentaire de Jean Hyppolite,' 379–80.

55 Ella Sharpe, 'Ninth Discussion of Scientific Differences,' discussion of Melanie Klein's paper 'Emotional Life of the Infant,' 1 March 1944, in *Freud–Klein Controversies* 811.

56 Hyppolite, 'Commentaire,' 883.

57 Klein, 'The Importance of Symbol-Formation in the Development of the Ego,' 1930, in *Love, Guilt and Reparation, and Other Works 1921–1945, The Writings of Melanie Klein*, vol. 1 (London: Hogarth, 1975, and Virago, 1988); Lacan, *Le séminaire* I, 81–3, 95–103, 83, trans. 68–70, 78–80, 70. For a discussion of Lacan's reading of Klein's paper, see Shoshana Felman, 'Beyond Oedipus: The Specimen Story of Psychoanalysis,' in *Jacques Lacan and the Adventure of Insight: Psychoanalysis in Contemporary Culture* (Cambridge, Mass.: Harvard University Press, 1987) 105–28. For a discussion in relation to Lacan and Kristeva, see Mary Jacobus, 'Tea daddy': Poor Mrs Klein and the Pencil Shavings' [this volume, ch. 5–Eds].

58 Melitta Schmideberg, 'Intellektuelle Hemmung und Ess-Störung' ('Intellectual Inhibition and Eating Disorders'), *Zeitschrift für psychoanalytische Pädagogie*, 8 (1934) 110–16; Lacan, 'Réponse au commentaire de Jean Hyppolite,' 396–8. [A translation of Schmideberg's article, 'Intellectual Inhibition and Eating Disorders,' is included as an appendix to *Why War?* and is discussed in chapter 6 of that book, 'War in the Nursery.' Eds.]

59 Lacan, 'Réponse an commentaire de Jean Hyppolite,' 396.

60 Sharpe, 'Ninth Discussion,' 804–5.

61 Freud, 'Negation,' 236–7, *Pelican Freud*, 439; cited by Heimann, 'Some Aspects of Introjection and Projection,' 505–6; by Isaacs, 'Sixth Discussion,' 554–5; by Klein, 'Tenth Discussion of Scientific Differences,' formal reply to discussion of 'Emotional Life of the Infant,' 3 May 1944, in *Freud–Klein Controversies* 838 and 843n. (Klein offers a different translation from the version cited here; see Editor's note 843).

62 See n. 26 above.
63 Isaacs, 'Nature and Function of Phantasy,' *Developments*, 104.
64 Isaacs, *Developments*, 104.
65 Isaacs, 'Sixth Discussion,' 555.
66 Isaacs, 'Nature and Function of Phantasy,' *Developments*, 106.
67 P. Heimann and S. Isaacs, 'Regression,' paper presented 17 December 1943, in *Freud–Klein Controversies* 706. See also Ella Sharpe's 1940 paper on metaphor in which she describes all speech as metaphor – 'an avenue of outer-ance' (in itself a play on words) – through which the child, gradually controlling its bodily orifices, makes speech the outlet for tensions no longer relieved by physical discharge: 'So that we may say that speech in itself is metaphor, that metaphor is as ultimate as speech' ('Psycho-Physical Problems Revealed in Language: An Examination of Metaphor,' in *Collected Papers on Psycho-Analysis*, International Psycho-Analytical Library, vol. 36 (London: Hogarth, 1950) 155–69.
68 See n. 26 above.
69 Rivière, Introduction 16, citing Isaacs, 'Nature and Function of Phantasy,' *Developments* 83. Note that in a footnote to this remark Rivière insists that, contrary to responses to Isaacs's paper at the time, this is central to Klein's conceptualization and not an innovation by Isaacs.
70 Isaacs, 'Nature and Function of Phantasy,' in *Freud–Klein Controversies* 313.
71 Rivière, 'Psychical Conflict in Earliest Infancy,' 40.
72 Isaacs citing Freud, 'Nature and Function of Phantasy,' *Freud–Klein Controversies* 280.
73 *Freud–Klein Controversies* 96, 94.
74 Rivière, 'Psychical Conflict in Earliest Infancy,' 50.
75 Heimann, 'Some Aspects of Introjection and Projection,' 518; Klein, 'Eighth Discussion of Scientific Differences,' discussion of Heimann and Isaacs's paper on 'Regression,' 16 February 1944, in *Freud–Klein Controversies* 747.
76 See n. 23 above. Cf. too Steiner: 'The term phantasy . . . after being bounced back and forth throughout these lengthy discussions, seems to have assumed an enigmatic, evocative power. For one side it came to be synonymous with new discoveries – the more the term was analysed, the more it was enriched with new meanings. For the others it seemed to mean something not unlike belief in a new and hazily-defined mysticism. Some of the latter even saw it as something to be exercised by the expulsion of the entire group led by Klein' (Steiner, 'Some Thoughts about Tradition and Change,' 49–50).
77 Kate Friedlander, Marjorie Brierley, in *Freud–Klein Controversies* 409, 536, 539, 536.
78 Isaacs, *Freud–Klein Controversies* 467, Heimann, *Controversies* 580, 572, 570.
79 Anna Freud, 'Indications for Child Analysis,' in *The Psycho-Analytic Treatment of Children* (London: Imago, 1946) 86. [For a discussion of Anna Freud's dispute with Klein, see Jacqueline Rose, 'War in the Nursery,' in *Why War? – Psychoanalysis, Politics, and the Return to Melanie Klein* (Oxford: Blackwell, 1993) 191–230. Eds]
80 Brierley, 'Sixth Discussion,' 537. For a discussion of the possibility of distinguishing between incorporation and introjection in terms of metaphor, see Abraham and Torok, 'Introjection-Incorporation.'
81 Heimann, 'Seventh Discussion,' 571.
82 Sharpe, 'Seventh Discussion,' 582. For a discussion of these problems in relation to Freud's writing, see Mikkel Borch-Jacobsen, *Le sujet freudien* (Paris: Flammarion, 1982), trans. Catherine Porter, *The Freudian Subject* (London: Macmillan; Stanford: Stanford University Press, 1982); also Abraham and Torok, 'Introjection-Incorporation.'

83 Brierley, 'Sixth Discussion,' 536.

84 Glover, 'Sixth Discussion,' 559, 562.

85 See, e.g., Samuel Weber, *The Legend of Freud* (Minneapolis: University of Minnesota Press, 1982); Derrida, 'Speculer sur Freud,' in *La carte postale* 257–409; Borch-Jacobsen *Le sujet freudien.*

86 Walter Schmideberg, 'The Second Extraordinary Business Meeting'; Karin Stephen, 'Resolutions and the First Extraordinary Business Meeting,' in *Freud–Klein Controversies* 86, 50.

87 Brierley, 'Sixth Discussion,' 536–7.

88 Glover, 'Seventh Discussion,' 586.

89 Friedlander, 'Discussion on "Regression"' (discussion circulated only), December 1943, in *Freud–Klein Controversies* 728; Glover, *Controversies* 715.

90 Rivière, 'Psychical Conflict in Earliest Infancy,' 47.

91 Heimann, 'Certain Functions of Introjection and Projection,' 161.

92 Rivière, 'Psychical Conflict in Earliest Infancy,' 53.

93 Heimann and Isaacs, 'Regression,' 703.

94 Klein, 'Emotional Life of the Infant,' 201.

95 Klein, 'Emotional Life of the Infant,' 201.

96 Klein, 'Tenth Discussion,' 836.

97 Klein, 'The Oedipus Complex in the Light of Early Anxieties,' 1945, in *Love, Guilt and Reparation* 408.

98 Heimann, 'Some Aspects of Introjection and Projection,' 523.

99 Klein, 'Emotional Life of the Infant,' 777–8; Lacan, *Le séminaire I* 97; trans. 83.

100 Klein, 'Tenth Discussion,' 834.

101 Isaacs in reply to Glover, 'Fifth Discussion,' 456–7; Klein, 'A Contribution to the Psychogenesis of Manic-Depressive States,' 1935, in *Love, Guilt and Reparation* 265.

102 Rivière, 'Psychical Conflict in Earliest Infancy,' 60, 62.

103 Rivière, 'Psychical Conflict' 62.

104 Meltzer, *Kleinian Development* 46–7. Meltzer relates this issue to Klein's uncertainty about the conceptual status of the depressive position: 'She had never absolutely crystallised this in her mind, for sometimes she speaks of "penetrating" the depressive position, "overcoming", "surpassing", all of which have different implications regarding the meaning of the "depressive position"' (p. 114).

105 Heimann and Isaacs, 'Regression,' 183; cf. also: '[Klein] has shown too that specific anxieties not only contribute in both sexes to fixations and regressions, but also play an essential part in stimulating the libido to move forward from pre-genital positions to the genital one,' (p. 175); and Meltzer: 'The badness must be sufficiently split off . . . [but] it must not be so widely split off as to diminish the anxiety below the level that is sufficient for development' (*Kleinian Development* 64).

106 Heimann, 'Certain Functions of Introjection and Projection,' 162.

107 Heimann and Isaacs, 'Regression,' 703.

108 Isaacs, 'Nature and Function of Phantasy,' *Developments* 75.

109 See esp. Klein, 'Early Stages of the Oedipus Conflict,' 1928, in *Love, Guilt and Reparation* 186–98.

110 Klein, 'Emotional Life of the Infant,' 223, 209.

111 Klein, 'Importance of Symbol-Formation,' 227; Lacan, *Le séminaire I* 102; trans. 87.

112 A. Freud, *Ego and the Mechanisms of Defence* 57, cited by Isaacs, 'Nature and Function of Phantasy,' in *Freud–Klein Controversies* 295.

113 Despite the stress on development in Anna Freud's writing, one could equally argue that it is a simplification to read her work exclusively in such terms. Her famous paper 'Studies in Passivity' gives an extraordinary account of the possible vicissitudes of

sexual identification and desire in relation to masculinity and of the resurgence in adulthood of the most primary forms of identification, at the same time as recognizing the limits of its own model of explanation: 'These interpretations are not satisfying . . . What is left unexplained,' etc. – i.e. the text can be read aporetically as much as developmentally (A. Freud, 'Studies in Passivity,' 1952 (1949–51), in *Writings of Anna Freud*, vol. 4 245–59.

114 Glover, 'Klein System of Child Psychology,' 112.

115 Glover, 'Klein System,' 110.

116 Glover, 'Klein System,' 116.

117 Hedwig Hoffer, 'Fourth Discussion of Scientific Controversies,' continuation of discussion of Isaacs's paper 'Nature and Function of Phantasy,' 7 April 1943, in *Freud–Klein Controversies* 428 (my emphasis).

118 Glover, 'Klein System of Child Psychology,' 99.

119 Rivière, 'Introduction,' 18–19.

120 Rivière, 'Introduction,' 36.

121 As Grosskurth comments: 'The Discussions were dominated by women – and what women they were!' (*Melanie Klein* 316). This quote from the manuscript of Virginia Woolf's *To the Lighthouse*, however, relates interestingly to Rivière's remark: 'Don't we communicate better silently? Aren't we (women at any rate) more expressive silently gliding high together, side by side, in the curious dumbness which is so much [more] to our taste than speech'; cited by Lyndall Gordon, *Virginia Woolf: A Writer's Life* (Oxford: Oxford University Press, 1984) 195. A whole history of women's relationship to language and of psychoanalysis's relation to modernism is implicit in Rivière's extraordinary comment.

122 Sharpe, 'First Discussion of Scientific Controversies,' 'Some Comments on Mrs. Klein's theory of a "Depressive Position,"' in *Freud–Klein Controversies* 340, 805.

123 Stephen W. Hawking, *A Brief History of Time: From the Big Bang to Black Holes* (London and New York: Bantam, 1988). (Subsequent references are cited in the text.)

124 Heimann, 'Certain Functions of Introjection and Projection,' 128.

125 In his Brazilian lectures of 1974, Bion refers to black holes: 'I am familiar with a psychoanalytic theory of the mind which sounds like the astronomical theory of the "black hole"' (W.R. Bion, *Bion's Brazilian Lectures*, vol. 2, (Rio/São Paulo, 1974; Rio de Janeiro: Imago, 1975) 61. Discussing this passage, David Armstrong suggests that the theory of the mind alluded to is Bion's own ('Bion's Later Writing,' *Free Associations*, 3, 2, no. 26 (1992) 267).

126 Felman, 'Psychoanalysis and Education', in *Jacques Lacan and the Adventure of Insight* 78.

127 In his Inaugural Lecture to the University of Cambridge, Hawking states that a quantum theory of gravity (as central to the not yet attained complete unified theory of physics) is essential if the early universe is to be described and its initial conditions explained without 'merely appealing to the anthropic principle' (Hawking, 'Is the End in Sight for Theoretical Physics?,' Appendix to John Boslough, *Stephen Hawking's Universe* (Glasgow: Collins, 1984) 120. For a critique of Hawking in relation to the anthropic principle, see Felix Pirani, 'The Crisis in Cosmology,' *New Left Review*, 191 (January/February 1992) 69–89.

128 Felman, 'Psychoanalysis and Education,' 78.

129 Cf. Bion on the question of reduction: 'Why should a psychoanalyst invent a theory to explain a mental phenomenon and, independently, the astronomers elaborate a similar theory about what they think is a black hole in astronomical space? Which is causing which? Is this some particularity of the human mind which projects it up

into space, or is this something real in space from which derives this idea of space in the mind itself? . . . I have used this idea of modern cosmology as a model for psychoanalysis, but I would also use psychoanalysis as the starting point of an investigation of the human mind' (Brazilian Lectures 61–2).

Chapter 8

The fissure of authority
Violence and the acquisition of knowledge

John Phillips

Editor's note:

In this essay John Phillips offers a new perspective on a set of questions that Klein's critics and advocates alike have found both enigmatic and troublesome: how does the infant get out of phantasy and into reality? If the premature ego is governed by an early and hyper-judgemental super-ego, how do we ever get into a position where we can make sound judgements about what we know? What does it mean to know? Critics of Klein have often damned her work on the grounds that she seems to provide no answer to these questions. The Kleinian phantasy machine, the argument goes, is as insatiable as the super-ego that dominates it: gobbling up the distinctions between phantasy and reality, internal and external, Kleinian theory leaves no space for a consideration of either real external influences (this was Anna Freud's critique) or a nuanced account of historicity (see Torok et al. in this volume). Worse, Klein's version of an early and violent super-ego and her notorious refusal to consider the real authorities (the parents) that influence psychical development seems to lock the child into an obscene super-amorality. One can certainly counter these objections with the argument that Klein's later work on love both reconciles the phantasy-ravaged subject with reality and offers an ethical vision of our psychic lives, but this may not help matters. Appeals to the reality principle cannot fail to evoke a normative and adaptive view of the psyche which, as Moustafa Safouan demonstrated in relation to Freud in his *Pleasure and Being: Hedonism from a Psychoanalytic Point of View* (1983), is profoundly anti-psychoanalytic. It is precisely the way in which our psychic representations of the world refuse to concur with empirical reality that gives psychoanalysis its radical force and this is as true of Klein, Phillips suggests here, as it is of Freud. Similarly, the kind of ethics one may derive from Klein's account of love may run the risk of appearing as reactionary as they are psychically enabling (see Christopher Lasch [1986] extolling the virtues of what he sees as Klein's pre-enlightenment view of morality). Phillips refuses to make Klein into an amoral dupe of her own solipsistic view of phantasy or to adapt her theories to those theories of adaptation which a more conservative approach to her work might endorse. Rather, in a frankly deconstructive reading of her work he seizes on those moments in Klein's writing when her accounts of phantasy, knowledge and authority are at their most ambiguous. Klein emerges as a kind of phenomenologist of the unconscious for whom the question of how we distinguish, or in Phillips's terms 'judge,' between phantasy and reality, inside and outside, is the condition by which we 'know' anything whatsoever. The issue is less one of insides versus outsides than of the 'outside-in-the-inside.' Likewise, authority in Klein belongs neither to the caprice of the super-ego nor to external legislators, but resides in what Phillips calls the 'fissure' between the shapes that the phantasy gives to the world and those elements which both constrain and incite it – contingency, time, death and negativity. (LS)

The authority principle

Permanent submission to the authority principle, permanent greater or less intellectual dependency and limitation, are based on this first and most significant experience of authority, on the relationship between the parents and the little child. Its effect is strengthened and supported by the mass of ethical and moral ideas that are presented duly complete to the child and which form just so many barriers to the freedom of his thought.
(Melanie Klein, 'The Development of a Child', LGR, pp. 35–6)[1]

In Klein's work authority is not simply an attribute of some external object (a parent or teacher), but is an innate internal mechanism that informs all experiences of authority whatsoever. According to this quotation from Klein's early writing, the influence of authority in the development of the child is harmful from the beginning. As an innate principle authority is already the first barrier to the child's freedom and independence of thought. Any dogmatic or didactic presentation that the child later encounters cannot fail to support and strengthen the force of this barrier. So the aim of child analysis is to reduce it. Then the child will be able to critically engage with authorities it finds in the world.

As an innate principle, however, authority also embodies a condition of possibility for development. It is something that the child cannot do without. The child develops an understanding of reality only when it is able to assess the difference between its phantasies and objects. This difference is manifested in the doubling that occurs when an idealized or persecuting super-ego is represented in the image of a real object (in the earliest stages the mother's body). So the omniscience attributed to a parent can only be questioned when there is a palpable difference between phantasy and reality. In short, development is possible when the infant discovers that authority is based on a false or counter-factual attribution.

Klein's antipathy towards authority is therefore ambivalent. On one hand she exhibits all the characteristics of the enlightened scientist for whom only the facts are relevant when seeking the truth. Powerful representatives of authority (gods or parents) simply act as mystical barriers on the way to such truth. On the other hand, there is no knowledge as such 'outside,' awaiting the balanced judgement of the little child as it sheds the influence of constraining authority. Knowledge is actually constituted in the process of finding out about authority. I acquire knowledge not of the outside world but of the disparity between phantasy and objects. This disparity is brought to light in the difference between the phantastic super-ego and the object it doubles.

If Klein advocates a vigorous resistance to the impeding force of authority, a resistance to the false authority of charlatans and tyrants, then such resistance is gained through the awareness of an original, constitutional force that makes fraud and tyranny possible, as well as powerful and effective. Even parents who consistently abdicate all authority over their child will be attributed with it any-way. In this sense authority for Klein takes the role of an originating violence. Violence is the key motif in her extended accounts of infantile phantasy in which the ego and its exterior are engaged in a series of skirmishes. The ego's experience of its exterior involves an interaction between objects, some of which – 'an indefinite number – are persecutors to it, ready to devour and do violence to it' (LGR, p. 285). All relationships, whether between the ego and its objects or between the objects themselves, are considered in terms of a violence that has its primary manifestation in the child's phantasy. The violence of phantasy transforms the exterior by absorption:

> Every injury inflicted in phantasy by the child upon its parents (primarily from hate and secondarily in self-defence), every act of violence committed by one object upon another (in particular the destructive, sadistic coitus of the parents, which it regards as yet another consequence of its own sadistic wishes) – all this is played out, both in the outside world and, since the ego is absorbing into itself the whole external world, within the ego itself.
>
> (LGR, p. 286)

Projection and introjection involve phantastic offensives whereby the object and the ego can each be entered, occupied, controlled, repulsed or withdrawn in a continuing struggle to define and maintain boundaries. Strictly speaking, violence in its primary and originating state is, for Klein, a way of describing an excess

of force which invades or devours. Violence can thus be defined as a forceful
entry into the field of the other, the extension of one field into that of another, or
the consumption of an object by another.[2] The process as a whole, however, is the
consequence of an original, and originating, experience of anxiety, that is, it is
the consequence of a constitutional death instinct. The child's first offensive is
always a defence against anxiety, which, as Klein argues, is felt as a death-threat,
a kind of original invasion that, rather paradoxically, defines the field that is being
trespassed. The death instinct brings the child to life.[3] In short, the infant comes to
define itself in terms of an authority that is invading its space. All relationships
between inside and outside, between ego and object, are made possible by this
phantasy of hostile invasion.

The role of authority in Klein's account of infantile phantasy life has implications not only for the child's acquisition of knowledge but also for the status
of knowledge in the adult world. During the 1930s and 1940s Klein consolidated
her increasingly radical ideas in terms of the paranoid-schizoid and depressive
positions. Klein's accounts of the infant's capacity to 'acquire knowledge'
provide the key to these works. Here it is the very possibility of knowledge,
the possibility of a relation between the child's ego and its objects, that is in the
frame of enquiry.

The Kleinian notion of knowledge must be considered in terms of her account
of its *possibility*. On the one hand, Klein describes how the child gradually
gets to know its external environment. In her early work she argues that it is
essential to reduce both the power of authority and the influence of phantasy,
so that 'the reality principle will rule in the sphere of thought and established
fact' (LGR, p. 24). On the other hand, however, a deeply objective knowledge
in the Kleinian sense demands a knowledge of phantasy itself, as well as an
understanding of the inhibiting power of authority. Without this the 'reality
principle' is just another tyrannous master, because the phantasy of omniscience
remains undiminished. For Klein, objective knowledge is a step towards an
understanding of phantasy. When regarded in the dimension of phantasy the
knowledge that Klein describes bears little resemblance to the cool rationality of
scientific knowledge.[4]

In Klein's account there is no knowledge without a violent engagement with
an ambiguous authority. So Klein questions not only the correlation between
knowledge and truth, but also any possibility of maintaining a distinction
between knowledge and violent invasion. To know, in the Kleinian sense, is to
exercise force, the force of some authority. From the earliest essays to her last
exhausted apologia for love[5] we find that the ambiguous role of authority, or
rather the role of an ambiguous authority, governs everything.

Authorizing–abdicating

If Klein questions the correlation between authority and truth, she also shows
how they cannot be separated. On the one hand authority, especially in its

Para grows a week (handwritten margin note)

absolute form, persecutes and inhibits, causes anxiety and impedes development. On the other hand, there is little truth as such without authority. But when the truth becomes *the truth about authority* then authority becomes enabling rather than just inhibiting and the truth takes on an authority of its own. The Enlightenment ideal of freedom from authority is seriously compromised here in so far as it is authority that the infant needs to know about. Or rather, the omnipotent authority that inhibits knowledge is revealed as the very object of knowledge itself.

The problem is exemplified by Klein's own uncompromising approach within a somewhat contradictory psychoanalysis that must be both an authoritative discourse and an empirical science.[6] She describes what she sees and acts upon what can be shown to be the case in the context of the playroom itself. But while she affirms the need for development in psychoanalysis on the basis of observation and analysis from irrefutable proofs, it nonetheless remains the case that, for her, Freud's central insights are correct.[7] Freud's innovation embodies rules and possibilities that both limit and enable further development. Klein's development as a brilliant and original practitioner brings to light the contended and disputed status of the rules and possibilities that Freud's texts represent, the restless ambiguity of psychoanalytic authority.[8] Klein responds to these peculiar demands by maintaining both sides of an apparent contradiction. While on the one hand Freud's authority remains paramount, on the other, nothing can be accepted on a rigorously scientific basis unless it has been tested. In this way, the logic seems to go, proof provides both a new authority and a restatement of the old.[9] This proof can then be used as a basis for new discoveries and further development.

In Klein's work 'authority,' manifested as a symbolic form within an unconscious process, is something like the difference between observation and legislation, and it mediates between events and phantasies. Take the three modalities that the psychoanalyst must operate with. First, there is the field of the symptom, indicating an obscure displacement and resulting in significant expressions, spoken or written, dreamed or made in play. Second, there is the analyst's own perspective in the transference, a position supported by professional psychoanalytic authority, case histories and scientific formulations, the body of psychoanalytic teaching, the sometimes instinctive authority of clinical practice, all of which provide the means for interpretations that must be tested in the clinical situation. Here simple facts, small details, empirical certainties provide a third modality, the transient empirical field that can always be used although it does not have the power of generalization. Rather it is constituted by events, contingencies, happenings, comings and goings, which occur in the field of the reality principle and thus allow the child to gradually assess the difference between its phantasy and what actually happens.

These different modalities, as we learn from Klein's earliest published work, are precisely equivalent to those that are encountered by the child, whose symptoms bear on a tension between his experience of empirical reality and stories he has been told. Thus in the 1921 paper 'The Development of a Child' (LGR, pp. 1–53), 'Fritz' can be sure of the existence of his breakfast (which he can eat) and his Granny's house (which he has been to), but the question of God remains obscure (because he has never seen God). In exploring his reality he must be able to move between the reassuring (and satisfying) empirical existence of his breakfast and powerful if obscure stories about God. His own developing knowledge has been impeded by the idea of his parents' omniscience and he is thus unable, according to Klein, to objectively explore the things that remain mysterious. An 'accidental' event solves the problem. His father has said 'yes' there is a God. His mother now, quite independently, says 'no' there is no God. This ambiguity, Klein says, serves to 'diminish the excessive authority of the parents, to weaken the idea of their omnipotence and omniscience' (LGR, p. 7) and thus to solve the developing child's dilemma over the nature of his reality. So authority mediates between reality and phantasy but acts as a stimulus to development only when it becomes ambiguous or fragile.[10]

In this early paper Klein introduces the pattern that some of her most important and consistently held views will take. The pattern involves a violent interplay between phantasy and reality, mediated by authority. Despite the fact that in this early essay she exhibits the attitude of the enlightened scientist, affirming the necessity of 'sexual enlightenment' and the 'relaxation of authority,' the formulation already suggests that authority is something one cannot do without. She already regards three principles as innate. There is an 'impulse to question' (corresponding to the pleasure principle), repression (corresponding to the reality principle) and a third 'authority principle' (LGR, p. 23), which combines an innate need for authority with a developmental need to overcome authority and is described as a 'rule of limits' (LGR, p. 24). Its extreme form embodies the notion of 'the belief in the omnipotence of thought' which, she says, is sustained by the idea of God (the absolute authority). Successful development is dependent upon the moderation of both the phantastic belief in omnipotence and the omnipotent character of authority:

> The complete development of the reality principle as scientific thought, however, is intimately dependent upon the child's venturing betimes upon the settlement he must make for himself between the reality and the pleasure principles. If this settlement is successfully achieved then the omnipotence feeling will be put on a certain basis of compromise as regards thought, as wish and phantasy will be recognized as belonging to the former, while the reality principle will rule in the sphere of thought and established fact.
>
> (LGR, p. 24)

This formulation of 'the omnipotence feeling' prefigures the position that authority emerges out of, its predecessor being an early and violent super-ego in the paranoid-schizoid and depressive positions of Klein's later theory. The authority principle enables the child to construct a relationship between mysteries and simple facts. It mediates between phantasy and reality, between desire and its repression, between omniscience and its compromise, because it somehow belongs to both. The authority that enables the child to construct such a relationship is thus an abdicated authority, that is, not a non-authority but rather an authority given-up, that withdraws as it authorizes. In Klein's work it is this authorizing/abdicating process that mediates the relation between phantasy and external situations.

The process takes its early psychic form in a doubling and folding back of defensive forces, which, when excessive, tend to impede development. For instance, according to her 1946 paper 'Notes on Some Schizoid Mechanisms', the phantasy of entering the object through projective processes in order to control it can result in an introjection which:

> may then be felt as a forceful entry from the outside into the inside, in retribution for a violent projection. This may lead to the fear that not only the body but also the mind is controlled by other people in a hostile way. As a result there may be a severe disturbance in introjecting good objects – a disturbance which would impede all ego functions as well as sexual development and might lead to an excessive withdrawal to the inner world.
>
> (EG, p. 11)

The return of an originating defensive force is in this sense the manifestation of an impedance, in which the attempt to control a dangerous outside results in the outside attacking the inside, taking control and thus impeding further development. The ego, by splitting its objects into good and bad, is attempting to control a hostile outside, but in phantasy the object can duplicate, redouble and return each defensive gesture, compelling further strategies.

The infant's development is constantly threatened by this impedance, yet it is a kind of general impedance over the whole process that enables the infant to develop out of it. The depressive position, which is essentially a critical modification of the paranoid-schizoid position, involves lessening or limiting the schizoid mechanisms:

> During the second half of the first year the infant makes some fundamental steps towards working through the depressive position. However, schizoid mechanisms still remain in force, though in a modified form and to a lesser degree, and early anxiety-situations are again and again experienced in the process of modification.
>
> (EG, p. 15)

The 'process of modification' acts on the force of the schizoid mechanisms as an impedance that organizes and contains them. Impedance is thus both the result of excessive defence, the cause of both neurotic and psychotic states, and the facilitator of favourable development, of mental health (LGR, p. 129). Impedance does not merely hinder development, as an independent force may retard the progress of some other force. Rather development takes the form of impedance itself. Development begins by impeding itself. In mechanical terms, impedance in the paranoid-schizoid position involves a powerful defensive mechanism that feeds back to produce a spiralling pattern of counter-defences. In the depressive position the force of these violent acts is harnessed by an increasingly cohesive ego. This depressive force impedes the antagonistic paranoid-schizoid forces, which already manifest a process of force/counter-force, in a prototypical form of what I have already referred to as authorizing/abdicating.

Favourable development of the ego depends upon its capacity to contain these violent forces, the most primitive of which is, for Klein, anxiety. The ego that Klein describes is more or less cohesive and correspondingly more or less tolerant, depending on the build up of an adequate 'capacity' for tolerating anxiety: 'The greater or lesser cohesiveness of the ego at the beginning of post-natal life should be considered in connection with the greater or lesser capacity of the ego to tolerate anxiety which, as I have previously contended, is a constitutional factor.' So cohesiveness can be considered in terms of capacity and tolerance, on one hand as a defence against anxiety, on the other as the power to tolerate it. This constitutional anxiety thus becomes the enigmatic key to the whole process.[11] This is what governs the tendency in early psychic life for the ego to alternate between cohesion and 'falling into bits'. It is the notion of the death instinct that makes the formulation possible: 'I hold that anxiety arises from the operation of the death instinct within the organism, is felt as fear of annihilation (death) and takes the form of fear of persecution'. The process results in a counter-defensive dispersal of anxiety, manifested in the cutting off of emotions and 'a feeling akin to death' (EG, p. 4). What the infant is actually vulnerable to is excessive anxiety about its own defences against the death instinct, which is the absolute terrifying authority at this early stage. These elements (the death instinct, anxiety, authority) remain enigmatic, but favourable development depends on the infant's capacity to tolerate both the violence of their encroachment and their mystery.

Inner and outer

In connection with the enigma of the death instinct there is an integral ambiguity in Klein's account that rests on the relation between objects and phantasy. It is possible to extend and formalize this ambiguity so that in effect we can read two disparate explanations of development, neither of which functions as an adequate account of the relation between an external and internal reality.[12] What we appear to be engaged with is a disparity in which an attempt to account for the infant's spatial phantasy of inside and outside reveals an ambiguity about the nature of the difference between phantasy and reality itself. Klein's own account becomes fissured in her attempt to account for the way the infant's world is divided into external and internal space.

On one side, development is self-contained; the ego develops on the basis of defences against constitutional anxiety. Here anxiety is consequent on constitutional factors characterized by the death instinct, which creates a feeling of persecution and a fear of (intellectual and emotional) death. In this case, persecution is felt as an attack from the outside but is in fact a result of projective identifications.[13] Now on this basis the early ego has everything it needs for complete development, so that stimuli from the outside will tend to be superfluous. Any that does occur, however, may have excessively harsh consequences. Klein insists on the importance of the carer's response to the infant's needs, a response which must avoid any 'harmful superfluity' (LGR, p. 26). So superfluous interference from 'outside' will unnecessarily – accidentally – impede the infant's development. For optimum results it must be kept to a minimum. What is disturbing about the 'outside' at this stage is its superfluity, its accidental excess, its damaging 'eventness' over and above the child's constitutional needs. Development thus begins to look like an orbit of impulses, or like an electric circuit in which the impulse is produced through the induction of an alternating current, so that development from the paranoid-schizoid position to the depressive position can be regarded as if it was like a turning-down (depressing) of the volume control of an electric amplifier.[14] In Klein's account the power used for depressing the excess force is the excessive power of that force itself.

However, a development that contains itself within itself, confined to the solipsism of subjective anxiety, does not accord with Klein's notion of object-relations; and this is where the other side comes in. Here we must take into consideration a situation which for a child involves the asymmetrical interaction between an internal phantastic super-ego and real objects outside. By this account the doubling of inside and outside coincides with a relation between non-identical elements that nonetheless can be exchanged, or rather, which the infant desires to make the same. This interaction is described by Klein, especially in her work of the 1930s and 1940s, as a form of defence intrinsic to development. In *The Psycho-Analysis of Children* she states that:

> The small child's super-ego and objects are not identical; but it is continually endeavoring to make them interchangeable, partly so as to lessen its fear of the super-ego, partly so as to be better able to comply with the requirements of its real objects, which do not coincide with the phantastic commands of its introjected objects . . . The child has to cope with the difference between the demands of its super-ego and those of its real objects, with the result that it is constantly wavering between its introjected objects and its real ones – between its world of phantasy and its world of reality.
>
> (PC, p. 180)

The significant factor here is the sheer difference between phantasy and the object.[15] The relationship between phantasy and reality cannot be reduced to an internal field of objects in which interference from the outside is the excessive element. Here interference is essential. But what form does it take? The internal object is a 'double' of the external one with characteristics attributed to it by the internal mechanics of phantasy. The child, according to Klein, borrows a 'picture' from the external world for its own internal phantasy (LGR, p. 249). This 'picture' belongs to the external world but its character owes little to 'external' reality. The internalized 'double' is beast-like, monstrous, ghostly, dangerous, mysterious, etc. owing to repressed aggressive impulses that influence the child's unconscious equation of monstrousness with parents (or authority).[16]

In her 1940 paper, 'Mourning and its Relation to Manic-Depressive States,' Klein engages directly with the relationship between the phantastic and monstrous 'double' and its external 'model':

> In the baby's mind, the 'internal' mother is bound up with the 'external' one, of whom she is a 'double,' though one which at once undergoes alterations in his mind through the very process of internalization; that is to say, her image is influenced by his phantasies, and by internal stimuli and internal experiences of all kinds.
>
> (LGR, p. 346)

At this stage the autonomy of psychic life is barely ruptured by anything from outside. The outside is rather a set of imagos, images, configurations, a network of models, a mere surface which the infant can unconsciously use as vehicle or form for phantastic processes, the impulses of destruction, greed and gratification, the defences against anxiety, etc. How then does the child get access to external 'reality'? And how does 'reality-testing' manifest itself beyond the phantasy?

What for Klein is critical in this relationship is not the status of 'reality' but the status of the 'inner world,' the infant's unconscious phantasy life. 'Reality', for Klein is less something to which a child should be adapted; it is rather a kind of tool or measure that the child might learn to use in order to discover the truth about his or her own inner world. External situations provide images, pictures, models and events that can be tested, observed, reasoned about:

> When external situations which he lives through become internalized – and I hold that they do, from the earliest days onwards – they follow the same pattern: they also become 'doubles' of real situations, and are again altered for the same reasons. The fact that by being internalized, people, things, situations and happenings – the whole inner world which is being built up – becomes inaccessible to the child's accurate observation and judgement, and cannot be verified by means of perceptions which are available in connection with the tangible and palpable object-world, has an important

bearing on the phantastic nature of this inner world. The ensuing doubts, uncertainties and anxieties act as a continuous incentive to the young child to observe and make sure about the external object world, from which this inner world springs, and by these means to understand the internal one better.

(LGR, p. 346)

The internalization (the making phantastic) of people, things, situations and happenings renders these things immediately inaccessible to 'accurate observation and judgement.' By internalizing the outside world, so that the outside is now inside and transformed, the child finds itself on the outside, unable to understand the inside. The 'ensuing doubts' arise from the obscurity of phantasy in relation to observable reality. The resulting alteration in 'the phantastic nature' of the inner world allows the anxious child some access to it. The child can now regard it as enigmatic in relation to a residue of the external situation (the field of the observing eye) which has not disappeared from observation and so remains accessible to judgement. In order to understand this internal world, the child continues to test and experiment with the world of objects, which it can do because a residue that has not been transformed by phantasy remains to be observed.

The infant must learn to make judgements rather than phantasize about the object world, and it does this by testing neither the object nor the phantasy but the transformation between them. An objective judgement is thus a judgement about the relation between fleeting empirical forms and the established patterns of phantasy, a judgement about the difference between them. It is the capricious super-ego that embodies the difference. So true judgement, in the Kleinian sense, corresponds neither to the judgement of the philosophical subject whose eye governs a static universe of objects, nor to a normalizing judgement that measures objects against homogenizing criteria. Rather it is a judgement about the super-ego as that which embodies the difference between objects and phantasy.

While the child's experience of its super-ego – the imago of the mother, for instance – is always governed by phantasy, the small influence which the 'actual' mother exerts is nonetheless significant, though this has little to do with parental agency. The mother represents a continuous supply of formal proofs – absence, presence, anger, revenge, etc.: 'The visible mother thus provides continuous proofs of what the 'internal' mother is like, whether she is loving or angry, helpful or revengeful' (LGR, p. 346). The visible representatives of external reality must be fitted into the pattern of psychic life but as they disappear into it their forms remain outside. The child must then learn to make use of these forms as a way of influencing the development of psychic reality. This is the process of 'acquiring knowledge':

In the process of acquiring knowledge, every new piece of experience has to be fitted into the patterns provided by the psychic reality which prevails at the time; whilst the psychic reality of the child is gradually influenced by every step in his progressive knowledge of external reality.

(LGR, p. 347)

The object-world can be understood only within the pattern of whatever psychic reality prevails at the time, although that may undergo a 'gradual influence' when tested against external forms. So even though external forms can influence the pattern of phantasy, they can only ever be understood through that pattern. The infant never inhabits the object world in the way that it inhabits the phantasy. The infant is therefore never free of phantasy as such, for every time it thinks it is outside it is in fact inside again and vice versa. The phantasy encompasses both outside and inside because the spatial relationship (where the boundary is the site of violent encroachments) is itself a function of phantasy. The only aspect not 'imprisoned' in the phantasy is what remains of the object 'outside.' What remains outside the spatial pattern is something like the passing of time. The accidental eventness, the coming and going of forms and images, constitutes an irreducibly temporal dimension that the phantasy dramatizes spatially. What has to be 'fitted into the patterns of the psychic reality which prevails at the time' is 'new experience.' The child must learn to prepare its phantasy for the 'new.' This is the function in Klein's work of the super-ego, the capricious object of knowledge, the embodiment of disparity, the impulse to observation. The child continues to alter the pattern of its phantasy because the object remains essentially unknowable in its temporal dimension. Knowledge can at best only gradually reduce unpredictability.

Already there

There are, then, two irreconcilable aspects to Klein's model of development.

The first is mechanical. Defence impedes and enables development, so that as a direct result of a constitutional death instinct anxiety compels defence, which produces more anxiety, building up to a depressive position in which the phantasy world of the child can integrate the split-off parts of its object to construct a roughly continuous relation between its own psychic reality and the events and conditions of the outside world. This occurs within an essentially fixed orbit and should undergo at most only minor disturbances from the exorbitant and superfluous activities of external agents (the parents). On this model strong emotions of love and hate are always reactivations of internal mechanisms.

The second aspect is symbolic. It is like a reparation for damage caused by the fierce autonomy of psychic life and compensates with a more integrated understanding of 'objective' conditions. In this case the super-ego is the site of continuous transformations. The form–phantasy double (strictly speaking, of course, the symbol[17]) must be pushed to the point of ambiguity so that judgements can be made about the difference between what one sees and the beliefs one has, that is, about the difference between what is visible and what is emotional. This kind of judgment is, for Klein, the very possibility of objective knowledge.

The two aspects cannot be reconciled as they stand but they can be brought together in a way that transforms them both. If the conditions at the beginning of life are considered to be already excessive – anxiety is *always* excessive, *always* superfluous – then interference from the 'outside,' which opens and disturbs the process of development and which causes anxiety to be defended against, is *already* part of psychic life. In this sense, external reality is an a priori condition of infantile development, as the 'outside-in-the-inside' or the enigmatic object in the phantasy.

This ambiguity does not after all distinguish between these two different accounts of development; rather, accidental, superfluous external stimuli repeat conditions that are already there at the beginning of life – the always excessive anxieties that are responses to the threat of absolute emotional impedance. So Klein's imperative that external authority should be kept to an absolute minimum, that authority is superfluous and always excessive, bears on the fact that excessive authority is already there; that the child *must* find it in some form which can be tested and understood, as a way of understanding the mysterious and frightening world in which psychic reality develops. The capricious authority that the child finds in the external world is an anti-factual construction, always supported by 'the mass of ethical and moral ideas.' Its force, taken over from the imagos modelled on the pictures of the parents, is strictly and necessarily accidental, because the child's reality (the outside) is an unpredictable future. The caprice of absolute authority is the child's response to the contingencies of the outside. On this reading the child is born not as a closed circuit of alternating impulses, a fragile entity at the mercy of external influences, but already as the enigmatic opening to the violence of the outside (its encroachment into the space of phantasy). This earliest position supplies the conditions for each occasion where 'external' events provide material for the 'inner' world. A fissure, as a kind of original opening to the outside, makes possible all relations. Out of this fissure comes every experience of authority, including both the death instinct and the super-ego. Each functions in the same way within a pattern of phantasy that must maintain absence, negativity and mystery in the process of acquiring knowledge. In other words, these persecuting authorities represent an intrinsically unknowable element that, whether in phantasy or reality, makes knowledge and its acquisition possible.

Although Klein is rarely critical of scientific knowledge per se – on the contrary, she consistently affirms its necessity – her account of its possibility throws it into a new perspective. At first sight it appears that the child comes to know its external reality by fitting what it finds into the internal pattern of phantasy and gradually modifying the pattern until it adequately corresponds to what is really out there. But the process that Klein describes is, to the contrary, a ceaseless interplay of form and phantasy around an originating experience –

death, violence, negativity – that always intervenes in the child's relation to the outside, as a 'continuous incentive' to observation. The child comes to know its external environment because paradoxically it cannot be known as such. So within the register of knowledge itself Klein refers knowledge back to its possibility (its impossibility). The truth of scientific knowledge would, for Klein, be the specific pattern of the undoubtedly powerful phantasy that gives it its meaning and value.

Within Klein's critique of authority it is therefore possible to read a counter-critique of knowledge. An examination of the ambiguity between inside and outside in Klein reveals that the child never gets out of the phantasy because the child was never strictly speaking inside it, and that goes for the outside as well. The spatial structure is produced by the phantasy of originating violence, an encroachment that produces the space it invades. This is the case for the object too – it exists in a space produced by the infant's own phantasy of encroachment, invasion and repulsion. What Klein's critique of authority fails to account for or explain is the necessity of the superfluous element. What is authority for?

Authority opens a space within which the object may be entertained. It is only when authority is abdicated that this 'entertainment' will cease to feel like war. The neonate finds itself face to face with an outside extending into a future that no single authority governs (a powerful defence against this future – when even delays in feeding become physical encroachments – is to spatialize it in the phantasy of the object's inside). An object that acts in a singular way, addresses me personally, and then absents itself is what makes the future of my objects possible. The alterability of phantasy keeps it open to a correspondingly incal-culable future (the accident of parents who appear or disappear unexpectedly), a violence that has nothing to do with persecution, a necessary violence of events and accidents, that encroaches my space with its unsettling temporality. Acquiring knowledge is learning to make decisions, learning to cut through the inhibitions that phantasy imposes on judgement, learning to use a necessary violence.

Impossible love and violent conclusions

In her final work Klein points out that mental health is not necessarily equivalent to success (EG, p. 270). Mental health, rather, depends upon what she calls 'depth.' 'Depth' would awaken in knowledge an awareness of the phantom of its own authority. It refers to the capacity to 'deeply experience sorrow,' and to gain 'an insight into one's inner life, and therefore a real understanding of others.' An understanding of others outside phantasy must begin with an understanding of what cannot be known of the other. I can know this depth only when I have the power to let go of my defences against the unknowable, when I know that acquiring knowledge is aspiring to the impossible.[18]

In the late papers Klein seems to concede a more determining role in mental health to what she calls 'the capacity for love.' Mental health is 'based on an interplay . . . between the impulses of love and hate – an interplay in which the capacity for love is predominant' (EG, p. 271). What could 'love' be, then, in the Kleinian scheme of things, if not the impossible? Even if we could accept the hypothesis of the impossible – to fill all the gaps in knowledge – then that would close off the possibility of any further knowledge, any further integration, any progress or development. Absolute knowledge is death. Just as infantile development depends on negativity, object relations depend on the impossibility of the fully integrated relation. With full integration the future of my objects or any future object would be impossible. Knowledge must learn to live with the impossible. The defining experience situates the neonatal being at the edge of a temporal abyss, a seemingly endless stretch of unpredictable dangers, in which death is linked to a temporality determined only in the future of a phantom authority. The intolerable experience of time is only the beginning of learning to love what cannot be known – an aporia for 'the mass of ethical and moral ideas.'

Violence in the Kleinian sense, as forceful entry, or extension of one field into another (projection and introjection), cannot be distinguished from knowledge, but plunges it into the ethical sphere. In the sphere of 'practical reason,' which is defined by concepts of law and justice, this sense of violence can be attributed to any number of forces as they clash, whether in situations that approach an absolute absence of law (brute force) or in situations where the law itself is said to embody the most profound violence.[19] The law, even when it wishes to be just, must recur on an originally unjustifiable and excessive force as its own foundation, instituting its authority in the breach. A just law *implies* violence as its very possibility, and it is the promise of this law that makes all relations possible. Klein from beginning to end would rather have done without the violence that she fully explored. Her work shows us that one cannot do without it but must acknowledge its necessity as a basic responsibility to the object itself.

Notes

1 All references to the work of Melanie Klein are to the four volumes published by The Hogarth Press in 1975, abbreviated as follows: LGR refers to *Love, Guilt and Reparation and Other Works, 1921–1945*; EG refers to *Envy and Gratitude and Other Works, 1946–1963*; PC refers to *The Psycho-Analysis of Children*; and NCA refers to *Narrative of a Child Analysis*.

2 Klein uses the term 'violent' to describe these kinds of projections and introjections. She also describes the child's experience of anxiety in terms of 'forces,' which it attributes to objects, though she qualifies her use of 'force' as 'a rather adult word for what the young infant dimly conceives of as objects' (EG, p. 49). What is unmistakable is that the earliest manifestation of the object is felt as a potentially dangerous force and a violent encroachment, which can be good or bad.

3 Despite Klein's insistence, especially at the end of her career, on the importance of love, this cannot be regarded as an originating impulse. At best the introjection of good objects constitutes an aspect of one of the many defensive mechanisms in the early stages, that of idealization, which – like splitting, denial and omnipotence – is always a strategy of protection from 'a dangerous and persecuting object.' See

'The Origins of Transference' (EG, p. 49). Here the feelings of love and hate are the consequences of defensive splitting.

4 Jacqueline Rose describes a moment during the Controversial Discussions when, in response to Marjorie Brierley's attempt to distinguish between the knowledge of the rational scientist and the 'primitive' beliefs of a Chinese peasant, Paula Heimann points out that psychoanalysis should make no such distinction. For the Kleinians 'the unconscious conditions of all knowledge and belief systems are what need to be explained.' By putting the conditions of all knowledge into question any easy correlation between scientific knowledge and 'truth' is suspended. The dispute between the Kleinians and Anna Freudians about Freud's heritage thus 'appears as a dispute about the possibility of objective knowledge and (thinly veiled behind the first) the scientific supremacy of the West' (this volume, ch. 7).

5 Melanie Klein, 'On Mental Health' (1960) EG, pp. 268–74.

6 We have Freud's own authority for describing psychoanalysis in this way. In the last paragraph of his 'Two Encyclopedia Articles' he claims that 'Psychoanalysis as an empirical science . . . keeps close to the facts in the field of its study, seeks to solve the immediate problems of observation, gropes its way forward by the help of experience, is always incomplete and always ready to correct or modify its theories.' This kind of statement is commonplace in Freud's writings.

7 This also goes for Freud's fiducial colleagues, two of whom, Karl Abraham and Sandor Ferenczi, were Klein's training analysts and early teachers.

8 For an example of the way psychoanalytic institutions attempt to legislate see Edward Glover's historical account of the Kleinian deviation in 'The Position of Psycho-Analysis in Great Britain,' *British Medical Bulletin* (1949) VI 1–2, 27–31. Also in *Selected Papers on Psycho-Analysis*, vol. I: *On the Early Development of Mind* (London: Imago Publishing Company, 1956) pp. 352–63. On Freud's own responses to schismatic members of the psychoanalytic movement see 'On the History of the Psychoanalytic Movement'; and see Ernest Jones's account in *Sigmund Freud: Life and Work*, vol. II (London and New York: Hogarth, 1955) pp. 142f. For one of Freud's many statements on the need for independent development and his dislike of *Weltanschaungen* see *Inhibitions, Symptoms and Anxiety*, not by chance one of the crucial texts for Klein's own development.

9 Juliet Mitchell points out that Melanie Klein should be acclaimed not for the failures and successes of orthodoxy, but for her own ideas. Yet Mitchell also stresses that Klein's new departures from Freud must be seen in the context of, and in relation to, his own innovation (see her 'Introduction to Melanie Klein,' this volume, Chap 1, p. 13). For a discussion of the relationship between Klein's psychoanalytical formulations and those of Freud and contemporary Freudians see James S. Grotstein, 'The Significance of Kleinian Contributions to Psychoanalysis: IV. Critiques of Klein,' *International Journal of Psychoanalytic Psychotherapy* 9 (1982–83) pp. 511–35.

10 The relationship between psychoanalytic and parental authority is particularly complex in this case, for the analyst and the mother are the same person; 'little Fritz' is of course Klein's son. It does illustrate how the analyst in Klein's conception can reduce the severity of the phantastic super-ego by occupying its position and somehow demonstrating its weakness in contrast to the child's phantasy.

11 The question of what is constitutional and what acquired in mental life has haunted psychoanalysis throughout its existence. While Freud increasingly stresses the importance of unconscious acquisition he is nonetheless fascinated by the possibility of a constitutional origin, revealed in his intermittent interest in Darwin and Lamarck, the hypothesis of phylogenesis, which reaches fruition in the controversial *Totem and Taboo*. Almost the opposite of Freud's tendency towards biologism is brought out in Jacques Lacan's 'lack' in the signifier, which notoriously grounds unconscious life in

language. See Jean Laplanche, *New Foundations for Psychoanalysis* (Oxford: Basil Blackwell, 1989), for a lucid account of the problem of foundation. Klein is apparently convinced by the notion of the death instinct as a basic and all-purpose beginning, and it embodies for her the best example of anxiety-already-there. But see Lyndsey Stonebridge for a probing account of Klein's inability to find a place for anxiety, 'Anxiety in Klein: The Missing Witch's Letter' (this volume, ch. 10).

12 See J.R. Greenberg and S.A. Mitchell, *Object Relations in Psychoanalytic Theory*, Cambridge, Mass.: Harvard University Press, 1983 for an account of the different and contradictory accounts of object relations in Klein's work.

13 This pattern also constitutes the earliest model for repression so that, as Klein writes, 'in this early phase splitting, denial and omnipotence play a role similar to that of repression at a later stage of ego-development' (EG, p. 7).

14 Klein's technical language sometimes overlaps with the language of classical mechanics and electromagnetics. There are moments when it seems possible to construct an account of infantile development based on impedance in its electrical sense, that is, as the combined effect of resistance and reactance on an alternating current. Thus the overall impedance of an electric circuit is the sum total of its capacity (the resulting current). As a metaphor, however, it is potentially misleading for it suggests an occult, mystical concept of originating force, current or flux. Gilles Deleuze and Félix Guattari's interpretation of Klein in *Anti-Oedipus* (Minneapolis: University of Minnesota Press, 1983) seems to favour this thought, and Julia Kristeva's adoption of Klein for her elaboration of 'the semiotic *chora*' in *Revolution in Poetic Language* (New York: Columbia University Press, 1978) seems to be based on a similar concept of impulse. Kristeva locates the mother's body, as 'the addressee of every demand,' in 'the place of alterity.' In my reading of Klein alterity occupies the place of the impulse (death-drive, anxiety, authority), which does not seem to me to be quite the same thing. Klein is not (certainly not always if ever) a pantheist. The electromagnetic concepts are problematic because in Klein the impedance and the originating current would need to be one and the same thing, which is impossible. For a useful account of what electromagnetic fields are really like see Herbert P. Neff, *Basic Electromagnetic Fields* (New York: Harper and Row, 1981).

15 See Shoshana Felman, *Jacques Lacan and the Adventure of Insight* (Cambridge, Mass.: Harvard University Press, 1987), for a reading that suggests that the 'difference' in this context gives the child access not to reality but to the symbolic in the Lacanian sense (p. 116). Mary Jacobus (this volume, ch. 5) goes some way in developing that reading of Klein.

16 See 'The Early Development of Conscience in the Child' (LGR, pp. 248–57).

17 See 'The Importance of Symbol Formation in the Development of the Child' (LGR). If it was possible to read Klein through a theory of the signifier, as Jacques Lacan does with Freud, one would be tempted to focus on the role of the super-ego. But, strictly speaking again, there is no signifier in Melanie Klein. Nor is there a signified, of course, nor, strictly speaking, is there a referent or object as such (but cf. Mary Jacobus in this volume). The Kleinian unconscious is not structured like a language. Rather the Kleinian scheme reveals the a priori possibility of language as such. See 'Hanna Segal interviewed by Jacqueline Rose,' in *Women: A Cultural Review*, vol. 1, no. 2 (Summer 1990) for a Kleinian response to the question of Lacan and language (pp. 208–9).

18 In this context Hanna Segal's 'A Psychoanalytic Approach to Aesthetics' may suggest how questions of aesthetics can be related to the epistemological and ethical spheres. She argues that 'in a great work of art the degree of denial of the death instinct is less than in any other human activity . . . [rather] the death instinct is acknowledged, as fully as can be borne.' This way of assessing art echoes Klein's

own imperative for mental health, that the death instinct should be acknowledged as fully as can be borne.

19 See Walter Benjamin, 'Critique of Violence,' (1921) for a key essay on violence and justice. *One-Way Street and Other Writings* (London: Verso, 1979) pp. 132–54. For Jacques Derrida's reading of Benjamin's 'Critique of Violence' and the definitive statement on deconstruction and justice, see 'Force of Law: The Mystical Foundations of Authority,' trans. Mary Quaintance, *Deconstruction and the Possibility of Justice*, eds Drucilla Cornell, Michel Rosenfeld and David Gray Carlson (London: Routledge, 1992). My reading of Melanie Klein has been greatly influenced by my understanding of this article.

References

Benjamin, Walter (1979) 'Critique of Violence,' *One-Way Street and Other Writings*, London: Verso, 132–54.

Deleuze, Gilles and Felix Guattari (1983) *Anti-Oedipus: Capitalism and Schizophrenia*, trans. Robert Hurley, Mark Seem and Helen R. Lane, Minneapolis: University of Minnesota Press.

Derrida, Jacques (1992) 'Force of Law: The Mystical Foundations of Authority', trans. Mary Quaintance, in *Deconstruction and the Possibility of Justice*, eds Drucilla Cornell, Michel Rosenfeld and David Gray Carlson, London: Routledge.

Felman, Shoshana (1987) *Jacques Lacan and the Adventure of Insight*, Cambridge, MA: Harvard University Press.

Freud, Sigmund *The Standard Edition of the Complete Psychological Works of Sigmund Freud*, ed. and trans. James Strachey, London: Hogarth, 24 vols, 1954–73.

—— (1913a) 'On the Claims of Psychoanalysis to Scientific Interest', *SE*, XIII.

—— (1913b) *Totem and Taboo*, *SE*, XX.

—— (1914) 'On the History of the Psychoanalytic Movement', *SE*, XIV.

—— (1922–3) 'Two Encyclopaedia Articles', *SE*, XVIII.

—— (1926) *Inhibitions, Symptoms and Anxiety*, *SE*, XX.

Glover, Edward (1949) 'The Position of Psycho-Analysis in Great Britain', *British Medical Bulletin* VI 1–2, 27–31. Also in *Selected Papers on Psycho-Analysis, vol. I: On the Early Development of Mind*, London: Imago Publishing Company, 1956, 352–63.

Greenberg, J.R. and S.A. Mitchell (1983) *Object Relations in Psychoanalytic Theory*, Cambridge, MA: Harvard University Press.

Grotstein, James S. (1982–3) 'The Significance of Kleinian Contributions to Psychoanalysis: IV. Critiques of Klein', *International Journal of Psychoanalytic Psychotherapy*, vol. 9, 511–35.

Jones, Ernest (1955) *Sigmund Freud: Life and Work*, London and New York: Hogarth.

Klein, Melanie (1975) *Love, Guilt and Reparation, and Other Works 1921–1945. The Writings of Melanie Klein*, vol. I. London: Hogarth.

—— (1975) *The Psycho-Analysis of Children, The Writings of Melanie Klein*, vol. II. London: Hogarth.

—— (1975) *Envy and Gratitude and Other Works 1946–1963, The Writings of Melanie Klein*, vol. III. London: Hogarth.

—— (1975) *Narrative of a Child Analysis: The Conduct of the Psychoanalysis of Children as Seen in the Treatment of a Ten-year-old Boy, The Writings of Melanie Klein*, vol. IV. London: Hogarth.

Kristeva, Julia (1978) *Revolution in Poetic Language*, trans. Margaret Waller, New York: Columbia University Press.

Laplanche, Jean (1989) *New Foundations for Psychoanalysis*, trans. David Macey, Oxford: Blackwell.

Lasch, Christopher (1986) 'Reply to Phyllis Grosskurth, "Melanie Klein: Creative Intellectual of Psychoanalysis"', *Salmagundi*, Spring–Summer, 70–1.

Neff, Herbert P. (1981) *Basic Electromagnetic Fields*, New York: Harper and Row.

Rose, Jacqueline (1993) *Why War? – Psychoanalysis, Politics, and the Return to Melanie Klein*, Blackwell: Oxford.

—— (1990) 'Hanna Segal interviewed by Jacqueline Rose', *Women: A Cultural Review*, vol. 1, no. 2, Summer, 208–9.

Safouan, Moustafa (1983) *Pleasure and Being: Hedonism from a Psychoanalytic Point of View*, trans. Martin Thom, London: Macmillan.

Chapter 9

Moral sadism and doubting one's own love

Kleinian reflections on melancholia

Judith Butler

Editor's note:

One of the most perturbing, not to say fascinating, aspects of Klein's writing lies in her graphic descriptions of loss, guilt and love. But the question of how we might relate the 'internal worlds' of the mourner and melancholic, which Klein details with such brilliance, to forms of social love and social guilt has remained relatively unexplored. In her introduction to *The Psychic Life of Power* (1997), Judith Butler queries the assumption that Klein's views on love refer to a psychic economy that seems to have 'no socially significant residue,' and asks 'is the social significance of guilt to be traced in a register other than that of prohibition, in the desire for reparation?' (p.26). This essay answers that question and, in so doing, demonstrates the importance of Klein's work to contemporary theoretical and philosophical debates about the formation of the subject, the nature of power and the status of psychoanalysis as a discourse that not only describes psychic life but also produces the tropes by which we come to categorize it – inside/outside, for example, or interiority/sociality.

Butler's own work has consistently challenged such categories; not by dismissing them, but by carefully drawing attention to the paradoxes inherent in theoretical, psychoanalytic and philosophical thought and by addressing the important question of how these paradoxes are lived in social and political terms. Only by pursuing these paradoxes, for Butler, can we hope to account for and address the psychic and social dynamics of gender and sexuality (see both *Bodies That Matter: On the Discursive Limits of 'Sex'* (1993) and *Gender Trouble: Feminism and the Subversion of Identity* (1990)).

The present essay begins with an account of the 'paradox of melancholia' in Klein's work. This paradox has a close affinity with what Butler describes in *The Psychic Life of Power* as the 'paradox of subjection.' In Butler's words: 'To be dominated by a power external to oneself is a familiar and agonizing form power takes. To find, however, that what "one" is . . . is dependent upon that very power is quite another.' Power not only breaks us, it makes us. By tracing the ways in which Klein's theories of object loss and the formation of conscience supplement Freud's, Butler shows how Klein offers a theory of guilt without prohibition. The introjection of the lost object, for Klein, and the rage, aggression and guilt that are both the effects and causes of loss, force us to think in terms other than the intrusion of an external morality into the psychic life of the subject. In a detailed and supple reading, Butler traces the way that, for Klein, aggression and guilt are turned back on the ego in its effort to save the object, and indeed to save a life understood in terms of our relation to others, from destruction. By Butler's reading, Klein's account of an internal world ravaged by rage and guilt is not, as some of her critics have charged, simply a morbid and solipsistic model of intrapsychic relations: rather, loss, guilt and love in Klein reveal how the ego is always and precariously socially attached. (LS)

Melanie Klein's reflections on loss, melancholia, and mourning are distinguished by their emphasis on the paradox of melancholia as a sustained and internalized aggression.[1] At stake is not only the question of how a rage waged against the one who is lost becomes a rage against oneself, but rather, how loss follows from rage, and how rage threatens an obliteration of the object field. Although her views take their point of departure from Freud and, in particular, his reflections on mourning and melancholia (1917), they also complicate the relation between aggression, guilt and melancholia in ways that alter the Freudian model.[2]

For Klein, the object that is lost is 'introjected' (p. 117), where 'introjection' implies an interiorization of the object as a psychic object, and where the process of introjection is understood, in part, as being in the service of cannibalistic fantasy. Significantly, however, the process of introjection that appears at first to have the preservation of the lost object as its goal comes to put the survivability of that object at risk (thus posing the threat of a second loss). For Freud, the act of 'internalization' by which the lost other (object or ideal) is rendered as a feature of the psyche is that which also 'preserves' the object. Introjection, for Klein, cannot be sustained. The object psychically remaindered is said to be taken inside 'owing to an excess of cannibalistic impulses in the ego, [and] this introjection miscarries.' In effect, the ego,[3] in its cannibalism, consumes the introjected object, and so the object is lost anew, lost *as* the introjected object. At this point the ego has no one to blame for the loss but itself, and this reflexive turn of accountability becomes the condition of heightened guilt. In the place of grief for another emerges the inverted figure of rage, one that is equivocally the cause and result of the loss at issue. Whereas Freud conjectures in 'Mourning and Melancholia' (1917) that the rage may be against the one who is gone *for being gone*, subsequently, he also speculates that all relations of human love may have ambivalence as their condition, and that the rage that follows loss may well be a rage sustained against the living one as well.[4] Indeed, for Klein, the rage that follows loss may well be an extension of the rage that always almost annihilates its object from the start. If Freud identifies ambivalence as what attends to all human relations of love, Klein specifies aggression as one part of that ambivalent structure, with 'preservation' as the other, and identifies the act by which the other is taken in (and potentially preserved) as a psychic object as always almost risking the annihilation of that other.

What takes the place of the object is the consuming aggression of the ego, an aggression that Klein calls cannibalism, but which she also identifies, significantly, as one of the effects of 'moral sadism.' The development of moral sadism presupposes that whatever primary form aggression takes is transformed in a secondary way and, as it were, moralized in and through that transformation. In this act of moralization, the 'critical voice', which Freud identifies in melancholia, is at first the voice of another berating the ego subsequently uncovered as the voice of the ego as it would have spoken to the lost other if it could have spoken; thus, the voice of moral sadism is essentially equivocal, a rendering reflexive of rage that constitutes the surviving subject's self-annihilating soliloquy.

For Klein, introjection remains a tenuous process, and the object rendered psychic through introjection is periodically consumed (negated through incorporation) or expelled (negated through externalization). In 'A Contribution to the Psychogenesis of Manic-Depressive States' (1935), she makes clear the genetic link between paranoia and melancholia (p.119). Melancholia internalizes an object that comes to persecute the object, creating an unsurvivable situation for the ego and, hence, precipitating the expulsion of the internal object, often without regard to whether it is, in Klein's sense, 'good' or 'bad.' Paranoia precipitates the expulsion of all objects, and thus leads to the fear of expelling 'good' objects as well and, hence, emerging objectless and without attachment in the world. If any and all objects carry the persecutory function, then any and all objects threaten the annihilation of the ego, and so must be annihilated. It is not that some objects are consoling, and others threatening, but that object-status as such is a sign of their potential or actual persecutory force.

As mentioned above, Freud traced the super-egoic function in 'Mourning and Melancholia' to the internalization and transformation of the lost other as a recriminating *voice*, a voice that spoke precisely what the ego would have spoken to the other had the other remained alive to hear the admonitions of the one who was left. This transmutation of one's own hypothetical voice into the voice of the one who is gone is a transmuting of the voice against the absent other into the voice of the other against the remaining one. Thus one's own voice becomes alienated in the hypostasized voice of the other, and one comes to suffer the very recriminations that would have been directed against the other and which become, through deflection, directed back against oneself. Recrimination that remains unspeakable against the other becomes finally speakable only against the self, a saving of the other, even in death, from one's own voice; an imperilling of one's own existence by one's own voice, where one's own voice actualizes and returns from an elsewhere with lacerating force.

Klein takes this scenario of the heightened super-ego in melancholia and recasts it as psychic servitude, describing at length 'the slavery to which the ego submits when complying with the extremely cruel demands and admonitions of its loved object which has become installed within the ego.' (p.123). She continues: 'these strict demands serve the purpose of supporting the ego in its fight against its uncontrollable hatred and its bad attacking objects, with whom the ego is partially identified' (p.123). Significantly, the moralization of the voice as 'cruel demands and admonitions' precipitates the formation of the super-ego. The super-ego is not erected primarily as a restraint upon libidinal desire, but rather as the circuitry that appropriates and defers primary aggression and its annihilating consequences. The super-ego thus supports the ego in its fight against its own 'uncontrollable hatred' seeking to control an uncontrollable hatred by marshalling it against itself, a hatred which, unchecked, moves the ego towards a perilous self-sacrifice.

This hatred, aggression, or sadism, rarely receives an aetiological account in Klein; more often than not, it functions as a given of psychic life. Every ego carries the potential to destroy the objects that form the world of its psychic attachments, and so every ego must have its sadism put in check by a super-ego that turns out to be nothing other than the reflexive rerouting against the ego of that primary aggression. The ego is said to be unable to recognize fully the disaster created by its own sadism (p. 124) until it has 'introjected the object as a whole.' With this introjection of the object, the ego is entered into a *moral* relationship to the object, suffering 'an overwhelming feeling of guilt towards it' (p.125).

The libidinal attachment appears constitutively bound up with cannibalism or sadism, and so the ego, starting to fear the effects of its own sadism, develops anxiety about the well-being of the object, and is concerned for signs of its own possible disintegration. The ambivalence of the ego, however, precipitates another reaction as well; in relation to this object it feels anxiety and remorse as well as 'a sense of responsibility,' protecting itself against persecutors who are the psychic figures for the ego's own destructive impulses. Indeed, persecution is distributed in fragments, signifying the break-up of the object (through aggression) and the return of that destruction in dismembered form. Klein thus refers to the psychic scene of fragments of a disintegrated object in which each piece grows again into a persecutor. The ego is not merely frightened of the spectre of fragmentation it has produced: it also feels sadness towards the object, responding to the impending loss of the object, a loss that it can, may, or will institute as a consequence of its own destructiveness (indeed, the 'can, may, or will' of the act forms the syntax of its constitutive anxiety).

We may think we can discern in this kind of explanation a double source of affect in Klein: aggression and protection. But it seems clear that protection is also derived from aggression, for what the ego attempts to protect the object against is its own destructiveness. Anxiety, responsibility, protectiveness, and sadness all appear at least partly derived from the sadistic impulse, and they are, according to Klein, 'among the essential and fundamental elements of the feelings we call love' (p.125).

The ego's hatred for its own hatred, as it were, finally outweighs the reproaches against the object in the case of melancholia. The ego's own feelings of unworthiness proceed from the fact that it hates, and through its hatred imperils the object; its own capacity to imperil the object, or indeed, its own desire to vanquish the object is then transmuted into its own mindfulness of destructiveness, and feelings of unworthiness which, carrying the force of moralization, emerge to stop that destructiveness from becoming act.

Indeed, in the situation of melancholia, the loss that is mourned is the one wrought, as it were, by one's own hand, resituating loss within a double-scene of mastery and morality. Klein writes that,

> it is the ego's unconscious knowledge that the hate is indeed also there, as well as the love, and that it (the hatred) may at any time get the upper hand (the ego's anxiety of being carried away by the id and so destroying the loved object), which brings about the sorrow, feelings of guilt and the despair that underlie grief. This anxiety is also responsible for the doubt of the goodness of the loved object.
>
> (p.125)

From an unconscious knowingness of one's own hatred and its destructive effects, the destruction of the loved object is conjured. In relation to that conjuring, anxiety emerges first about the safety of the object of love. That dissonance within love, that fearing for precisely what one seeks to preserve from one's own destructiveness, becomes the occasion and structure of doubt. Doubt then marks the vacillation between love and hate; it is the epistemic effect of ambivalence, and of the desire to annihilate that which one at once seeks to protect from any such annihilation.

Klein then cites Freud at this moment, remarking that 'doubt is in reality a doubt of one's own love and "a man who doubts his own love may, or rather *must*, doubt every lesser thing"' (p.126).[5] What Klein underlines here is that doubt carries the trace of aggression, and that certainty, in its ideality, involves the acknowledgement of aggression, where acknowledgment does not expunge the aggression in question, but performs the check upon its actualization that quells the anxiety for the object and the doubt about the sustaining power of one's own love.[6] Doubt transmutes aggression into a problem of knowing, but it also constitutes a felt sense of incapacity; it is the unknowingness of aggression as it unmoors the sense of knowing one's capacity for love.

In 'Mourning and Melancholia' Freud gave an account of how mourning institutes the super-ego and, indeed, the split between ego and super-ego which, in 1917, marks the primary psychic division. He argued that the inception of this division follows from the internalization of the lost other, object, or ideal into the ego, an internalization which is, in the case of melancholia, coextensive with the diminution of the ego itself. 'In grief the world becomes poor and empty; in melancholia, it is the ego itself' (p.246).[7]

The ego emerges within this scenario as a candidate for the beratements and accusations of the super-ego, and the super-ego emerges as the trace of the other within the psychic landscape of the survivor, a trace to be found in the figure of the voice of relentless criticism. The internalization of the other in melancholia is not a simple mimetic restitution of an external object into an internal one, for the process by which the distinction between internal and external takes place is one which is itself produced by the interiorization performed by melancholia.

In *The Psychic Life of Power* (Butler, 1997) I argued that melancholia cannot be comprehended by explanatory schemes that rely on unproblematized conceptions of internal and external space. Our ability to refer to psychic space through tropes of internality are themselves effects of a melancholic condition. The withdrawal of the object into the psyche is at once the opening up of the psyche as a space of interiorization. 'Inner worlds' and the like are so many fabricated effects of this process of melancholia. Thus, the inner world in the Kleinian sense could not be said to preexist this process of melancholic self-division. Internality would be one of the very effects of this melancholic diremption of the world into internal and external horizons. Indeed, Freud's account of melancholia unwittingly implies that psychoanalytic topographies of mind are implicated in the very phenomenon of melancholia. Melancholia may be understood as the very process whereby the mind becomes figured as an internal landscape, instituting the distinction between internal and external 'worlds.'

Klein's topography is in some ways brought into crisis through Freud's account of melancholia as responsible for the division between internal and external worlds. And yet, her emphasis on preserving the object, which pre-figures the work of reparation, suggests that incorporation also has its benevolent and ego-sustaining dimension, one that Freud overlooks in the effort to link melancholia with the institution of the super-ego. As the distinction between mourning and melancholia becomes increasingly difficult to sustain for Freud,[8] Klein reinstitutes the distinction by insisting that the incorporative fantasy central to melancholia is precisely the mechanism of melancholia's undoing. The final 'preservation' of the object is obviously imagined as something other than the psychic crypt. And yet, that more affirmative and less costly protection of the other may not quite lead to the conjectured 'peace and harmony' she imagines at the end of 'Mourning and its Relation to Manic-Depressive States' (p.174), for this ideal is unbalanced by the persistence of ambivalence as a structuring modality of all relations.

Although the topographies of internal and external world appear to ground the explanations that Klein provides of melancholia, a thoroughgoing psychoanalytic explanation must offer some account of the way that such distinctions emerge as the very effects of the melancholia under question. Indeed, it is unclear to me that one needs to accept the topographical schemes that Klein offers in order to affirm the specific dynamic of sadism, moralization, and self-doubt that she sketches with such skill. Indeed, it may be that the dynamic relations she describes are not fully-dependent upon the untheorized topographies she provides. Obviously, a fuller treatment of this claim would require a much longer inquiry than I can offer here. But I hope to have suggested how such an insight might work through a brief recapitulation of her supplement to Freud's account of melancholia, and to offer as a coda of sorts a similarly brief account of how guilt is produced not through the internalization of an external prohibition, but through an internal mechanism that seeks to save objects from the ego's own destructive possibilities.

Freud's view of internalization in 'Mourning and Melancholia' emphasizes the way in which the object is preserved or housed within a psychic topos as a way of preserving the object and, accordingly, saving the ego from the recognition of loss. For Freud, internalization tends to be understood as incorporative,[9] where the effect of this incorporation of the lost other (ideal or object) is its transfiguration into a critical voice within the psyche, directed at the ego. The scene in which a voice which is apparently not the ego's becomes directed at the ego precipitates the emergence of the ego as separate from the super-ego; the distinction, as it were, is dependent upon the splitting and alienated return of the critical voice in question. Freud suggests that the judgements that the super-ego is understood to be levelling against the ego are similar to those that the ego levelled or, rather, would have levelled, against the lost other (p.248); hence, the critical voice embodies a transfiguration of (unspoken) aggressive criticism against the lost one into aggressive criticism against oneself. The 'turning' of criticism against oneself that was once reserved for the other not only stifles and refracts that original criticism into a mode of reflexivity or, indeed, makes it a constitutive modality of reflexivity (as Nietzsche would have it), but guards the (now) imagined other against that criticism, understood to be the expression of an aggression against that other. Indeed, this can mean protecting the dead other against criticism which is, after all, a way of refusing to acknowledge the death of the other; protectiveness revives the other in an imaginary present. Klein, of course, emphasizes this protective mechanism, suggesting that what thwarts sadism is not the internalization of a moral interdiction, but the recognition that, unchecked, sadism would lead to the destruction of the object. And this must be stopped not because it is morally wrong, but because it leaves the ego without the possibility of attachment and, hence, destroys the ego as well.

It is the exigencies of life, as it were, and not morality that produce the morality that stops aggression. The ambivalence towards the object requires that aggression or 'sadism', in Klein's view, be stopped before it destroys the object altogether, not because the ego knows such destruction to be wrong (especially the infantile ego), but because the ego seeks to preserve the object if only because its own survivability depends upon the continuing existence of that object. Thus, dependence checks sadism, and facilitates the melancholic process whereby an aggression against the other becomes an aggression against oneself.

The basis of that aggression is understood in various ways, and it might make sense to assume that whatever these multiple sources are, they converge and compound at the site of melancholic internalization. Freud suggests at one point that the aggression is directed against the other precisely because the other is gone, and the ego, suffering abandonment, blames and berates that other for leaving. But towards the end of the essay, he ventures a speculation that will become central to the thinking of melancholia in his later work, in the work of Lagache (1938, 1956),[10] Klein, and Abraham and Torok. The aggression towards the one who is lost or dead indicates a primary ambivalence in relations to others, and it becomes poignant at the moment in which an other is lost precisely because that loss is a fulfilment of a wish to destroy that other. The melancholic might thus be said to be in a constant quandary over whether one's wish has had the efficacy of an act, whether the loss that has been realized was causally induced by the desire to destroy the one who is lost. The fantasies of omnipotence attributed to manic mourning (Lagache) seem linked to this equivocation of wish and act in the sphere of fantasy.

Lagache writes that the conflict in mourning is one in which the dead person (assuming the loss is that of death)

> plays the role of moral authority that is on the side of death and against life
> . . . Identification with the dead is an attempt to appease the guilt of living
> and maintaining the relationship with the dead, in a masochistic form other
> than dying . . . Consciousness is thus torn between an obligation towards the
> dead that stipulates dying and the wish to live. The meaning of the work of
> mourning is not only or essentially detachment from a love object on which
> acts of love can no longer be performed: *it is the destruction of a moral
> authority that does not permit being alive.*
>
> (pp. 181–2, my emphasis)

Klein's contribution to the Freudian account of melancholic is, at least, two-fold: first, in emphasizing the act of internalization by which an aggression against the other becomes an aggression against oneself, she shows that the emergence of moral sadism is motivated by the desire to protect the other against oneself, and the degree of moral condemnation is in direct proportion to the sadism by which it is fuelled. Significantly, it is not the presence of a moral interdiction against sadism that precipitates the reflexive turn, but the reflexive turn that renders the ego vulnerable to cruel admonition and a moralistic alignment with death. Further, the effort to save the other from destruction is motivated by a desire to preserve and sustain that lost other, to reverse or forestall the loss of the object precisely in order not to become an ego without an object of attachment, an ego in an objectless world, an ego who will perish from lack of love. A Nietzschean resonance can be read in Klein, for in the same way that Nietzsche proclaims that one would rather will nothingness than not will at all, so Klein engages the melancholic condition to show how precisely what is lost, absent, or dead nevertheless becomes an object to conjure and sustain.

Secondly, Klein seeks to use this argument to counter the notion of incorporative internalization that receives emphasis in Freud in which the other is internalized only as a persecutory or critical agency. Despite her pervasive and graphic insistence on persecutory objects, she also insists that the early internalization of 'good objects' is both possible and necessary to insure later experiences of mourning that exceed melancholic conclusions.

When Lagache concludes that melancholia issues 'an obligation toward the dead that stipulates dying,' he offers a formulation for loyalty to the dead that might well be traced back to Antigone. The incorporation of the dead other must diminish the ego to such an extent that living in that diminished state amounts to a practice of dying (which is, eerily, how Socrates describes the vocation of the philosopher). Although the notion that this is an obligation or stipulation suggests that it is a prohibition imposed from external sources, a moral law imposed on an ego who then succumbs to its demands, this is only apparently the case. The 'one' who would succumb emerges precisely from a prior split, namely, the melancholic occasion in which the ego forms in distinction from the critical voice of equivocal origin, and where that voice becomes the foundation for the law that then only and always appears tenuously external to the ego in question.

This fidelity to death must nevertheless be sustained, and sustained by an energy that is itself the threat to that enterprise's success. What counters the loyalty to the dead is the willingness to betray them, and to do it in the name of life; indeed, it is nothing less than recommitting the crime or, rather, converting the loss into a crime of one's own doing by abandoning those who are already gone. In other words, the choice of life requires committing the very crime for which one fears being held culpable and in this way not circumscribing the judgement, but braving its force and surviving its condemnation, reversing precisely the order of things dictated by 'morality': allowing the aggression against the one who will never feel it in order to protect oneself against death.

Notes

1   I am grateful to Esther Sanchez-Pardo for introducing me to the importance of the work of Melanie Klein and for her own work on Klein and melancholia, forthcoming in part in *Gender and Psychoanalysis*. I am also indirectly indebted to Jacqueline Rose's essay, 'Negativity in the Work of Melanie Klein', in *Why War? – Psychoanalysis, Politics, and the Return to Melanie Klein* (Oxford: Basil Blackwell, 1993) pp. 137–90 [Chap 7 in this volume.] All references to Melanie Klein's 'A

Contribution to the Psychogenesis of Manic-Depressive States' (1935) and 'Mourning and its Relation to Manic-Depressive States' (1940) are from *The Selected Melanie Klein*, ed. Juliet Mitchell (Harmondsworth: Penguin, 1986).

2 For a more detailed analysis of Freud's account of melancholia, see 'Psychic Inceptions: Melancholy, Ambivalence, Rage', Chapter Five in *The Psychic Life of Power: Theories in Subjection* (Stanford, CA: Stanford University Press, 1997), pp. 167–200.

3 For the moment I am staying within Klein's vocabulary of the 'ego' without offering an account of its formation or genesis. My sense is that although it functions, as do so many other concepts in Klein, as a spatial category, it is the site for a certain metaleptic reversal of love and hate and probably not finally captured through a spatializing trope.

4 'The loss of a love-object is an excellent opportunity for the ambivalence in love-relationships to make itself effective and come into the open', 'Mourning and Melancholia', *SE*, XIV, pp. 250–1.

5 Klein cites Freud, 'Notes Upon a Case of Obsessional Neurosis' (1909), *SE*, X, p. 241.

6 Acknowledgement may well be one of the benefits of a reflexive turn that in its first emergence serves the purposes of self-beratement.

7 Freud, *SE*, XIV.

8 See *The Psychic Life of Power*, pp. 133–5, 192–3.

9 For an excellent consideration of various views of internalization within Freud and for an effort to redescribe internalization as a fantasy that makes no metapsychological presuppositions, see Roy Schafer, *Aspects of Internalization* (New York: International Universities Press, 1968) and *A New Language for Psychoanalysis* (New Haven, CT: Yale University Press, 1976), pp. 155–78.

10 See Daniel Lagache, 'The Work of Mourning: Ethnology and Psychoanalysis', published originally in 1938, and 'Pathological Mourning' (1956), a revision and extension of his earlier argument, *The Works of Daniel Lagache: Selected Papers, 1938–64*, trans. Elisabeth Holder (London: Karnac Books, 1993).

References

Abraham, Nicolas and Maria Torok (1994) *The Shell and the Kernel: Renewals of Psychoanalysis*, ed. and trans. Nicholas T. Rand, Chicago: Chicago University Press.

Butler, Judith (1990) *Gender Trouble: Feminism and the Subversion of Identity*, New York: Routledge.

—— (1993) *Bodies that Matter: On the Discursive Limits of 'Sex'*, New York: Routledge.

—— (1997) *The Psychic Life of Power: Theories in Subjection*, Stanford, CA: Stanford University Press.

Freud, Sigmund *The Standard Edition of the Complete Psychological Works of Sigmund Freud*, ed. and trans. James Strachey, London: Hogarth, 24 vols, 1953–74.

—— (1909) 'Notes Upon a Case of Obsessional Neurosis' *SE*, X.

—— (1917) 'Mourning and Melancholia', *SE*, XIV.

Klein, Melanie (1935) 'A Contribution to the Psychogenesis of Manic-Depressive States', *The Selected Melanie Klein*, ed. Juliet Mitchell, Harmondsworth: Penguin, 1986.

—— (1940) 'Mourning and its Relation to Manic-Depressive States', *The Selected Melanie Klein*, ed. Juliet Mitchell, Harmondsworth: Penguin, 1986.

Lagache, Daniel (1993) *The Works of Daniel Lagache: Selected Papers, 1938–64*, trans. Elisabeth Holder, London: Karnac Books.

Rose, Jacqueline (1993) 'Negativity in the Work of Melanie Klein', *Why War? – Psychoanalysis, Politics and the Return to Melanie Klein*, Oxford: Basil Blackwell (this volume, ch. 7).

Sanchez-Pardo, Esther, (forthcoming) *Gender and Psychoanalysis*.

Schafer, Roy, (1968) *Aspects of Internalization*, New York: International Universities Press.

—— (1976) *A New Language for Psychoanalysis*, New Haven, CT: Yale University Press.

Chapter 10

Anxiety in Klein

The missing witch's letter

Lyndsey Stonebridge

Editor's note:

In this essay Lyndsey Stonebridge shows how Melanie Klein, in working through a troubled, adversarial phase of British psychoanalytic history, assigns anxiety the role of psychic agency. This reading develops out of her study of British psychoanalysis and modernist aesthetics, *The Destructive Element: British Psychoanalysis and Modernism* (1998), in which Stonebridge excavates vital yet neglected contexts for rethinking the relations between politics, aesthetics and psycho-analysis. Stonebridge's essay reveals the extent to which archival work can produce new contexts for thinking through Klein's writings as well as for the role of psychoanalytic theory (the Second World War is shown to be crucial in this respect and relates this essay to Eli Zaretsky's, in this volume).

Klein's clinical and theoretical work begins with anxiety. In the psychoanalytic playroom, the primary task for the analyst is to interpret (or even, as in the famous case of little Dick, to induce) the child's anxiety. For Klein there can be no symbolization and therefore no analytic work without anxiety. Neither, Stonebridge suggests here, can there be anything like an ego. Most commentators agree that part of Klein's singular contribution to psychoanalytic theory rests with the emphasis that she places on anxiety: anxiety, so to speak, is what makes Kleinian analysis and Kleinian theory work. In this, Klein shows her debt to Freud. Freud's first detailed case-history of a child, 'Analysis of a Phobia in a Five-Year-Old-Boy' (1909) brilliantly details the interplay between anxiety and the formation of phobias in the horse-dreading Little Hans (who, in many ways, is the elder psychoanalytic brother of both little Dick and Klein's own child, little 'Fritz'). Freud's writings on anxiety make a decisive contribution to the genealogy of this most enigmatic of affects (a genealogy which includes the work of Nietzsche,

Kierkegaard and Heidegger). Klein departs from Freud by being faithful to the complexities of his final theory of anxiety. In this, Stonebridge suggests, Klein too deserves careful consideration both as a theorist of anxiety and as an anxious theorist.

She begins not with a reading of Klein as such, but with Samuel Weber's exemplary and groundbreaking readings of Freud and Lacan (1982, 1991). Weber teases out the impropriety of anxiety as a psychoanalytic concept, a non-cognitive and non-symbolizable element that shapes Freud's *Inhibitions, Symptoms and Anxiety* while refusing to 'settle into its folds.' What is missing from Weber's reading, Stonebridge suggests, is Klein. When Weber's reading of Freud's *Inhibitions* is set beside Klein's reading of the same text a new angle emerges from which to read anxiety. Rather than move beyond anxiety (as Lacan claims to have done) Klein consistently (repeatedly) fails to go beyond anxiety, and the inconsistencies that these repetitions of failure produce reveal a pattern that mimics the pattern of anxiety itself. By grafting, or superimposing, the destructive instinct onto Freud's account of anxiety, Klein produces something that can be reduced neither to the scandalously bleak and pessimistic solipsism that many of her critics accuse her of, nor to the redemptive power of love and/or reality that Klein herself promotes as a way out of the vicious circle of infantile destruction—envy—guilt. Rather, anxiety *checks* Klein's conclusions at significant points, revealing at each stage of the ego's activity a repetition of its earliest moments, its constitution by its splitting.

Stonebridge concludes with the suggestion that anxiety in Klein may be read as a form of possibility, which she links, in another telling configuration, to Klein's response to the wartime situation. If the ego's story is one of survival in a world that constitutes it in anxiety, as shattered, then anxiety is also its own (and only) form of survival. Anxiety is its mode of possibility. (JP)

> Psychotherapy cannot remove ontological anxiety because it cannot change the structure of finitude. But it can remove compulsory forms of anxiety, and reduce the frequency and intensity of fears. It can put anxiety in its proper place.
>
> Paul Tillich (Tillich, 1954–64: 199)

The time has come to pause and consider. What we clearly want to find is something that will tell us what anxiety really is, some criterion that will enable us to distinguish true statements about it from false ones. But this is not easy to get. Anxiety is not so simple a matter [. . .] I therefore propose to adopt a different procedure. I propose to assemble, quite impartially, all the facts that we know about anxiety without expecting to arrive at a fresh synthesis.

Sigmund Freud, *Inhibitions, Symptoms and Anxiety* (Freud, 1926: 288)

I still cannot answer what made me feel that it was anxiety that I should touch and why I should proceed in the way I did, but experience confirmed that I was right.

Melanie Klein (Klein PP/KLE/A52)[1]

No more than Tillich does Freud think he can change the structure of finitude, but neither, it seems, can he quite put anxiety in its proper place. Two-thirds of the way through *Inhibitions, Symptoms and Anxiety* (1926) Freud pauses. What he wants is something that will indeed assign anxiety a place ('What we clearly want . . . is something that will tell us what anxiety really is'); but for Freud the only way to get to that place is to let anxiety run its own unpredictable course ('I propose to assemble . . . all the facts we know about anxiety without expecting to arrive at a fresh synthesis'). According to Samuel Weber it is precisely this lack of propriety about anxiety that makes *Inhibitions, Symptoms and Anxiety* such an important test case for psychoanalytic theory and, in particular, for meta-psychology. Freud's discussion, he says, 'demonstrates that anxiety *has no proper place*: it marks the impossible attempt of the ego to construct or delimit such a place, but this place is inevitably displaced, dislocated' (Weber, 1991: 58). If anxiety cannot be put in its place then neither can the ego, and as a consequence the authority of the second topography begins to waver. Anxiety puts Freudian metapsychology itself, as it were, beside itself.

Anxiety causes this kind of trouble for psychoanalysis partly because it is not a key psychoanalytic term: Freud neither invented it, rediscovered it nor transformed it (Weber, 1982: 49). Rather anxiety comes to psychoanalysis from the outside, harassing it yet refusing to settle into its folds. As a result, argues Weber, there has 'been little tendency among the followers of Freud to assign anxiety that signal importance that Freud himself never doubted it had' (Weber, 1982: 49). In this essay I want to focus on the work of one of Freud's followers who undoubtedly gave anxiety if not a proper, then at least a central place: Melanie Klein. Distinguishing her work from Fairbairn's in 1946, Klein insists that while his 'approach was largely from the angle of ego-development in relation to objects,' hers 'was predominantly from the angle of anxiety and its vicissitudes' (Klein, 1988b: 3). The narrative that leads the infantile ego from a state of indiscretion to self-possession by a gradual modification of its relation to objects that is so often associated with Klein is not, therefore, as far as she is concerned, the key issue in her work. Not only does Klein take anxiety as seriously as Freud, but she also claims to go further than him. In some unpublished notes she comments 'Freud himself having reached his climax in

Inhibitions, Symptoms and Anxiety not only did not go further, but rather regressed'(Klein PP/KLE/P.33). Only Melanie Klein, perhaps, could describe Freud's tentative discussion of an early super-ego in that text as a form of climax. If Freud is going back it is not difficult for Klein, merely by sticking with anxiety, to appear to go forward. But her claims go deeper than this. Freud wasn't just going back, he was being *held* back. 'I am concerned that Anna's influence was one of the factors that held him back'(Klein KLE/P.33), she concludes. This reference to Anna Freud and so by direct inference to the Controversial Discussions that tore apart psychoanalysis in Britain during World War II, suggests that anxiety is not just a matter for the ego or, indeed, for metapsychology, but also for the legacy and history of psychoanalysis itself. If psychoanalysis cannot assign anxiety a proper place, it might be worth asking instead what place, at a specific historical moment, here the war-torn British home front, anxiety assigns psychoanalysis.

As is well known, Freud began with a concept of anxiety as an effect of the transformation of libido but, with the advent of the second topography and his dismissal of Otto Rank, moved onto a much more complex reading of anxiety in which he sought to understand the way the ego constituted itself, erected its frontiers, via its anxious relations to the outside world. In *Inhibitions, Symptoms and Anxiety* Freud explains how anxiety constructs the ego: how anxiety sets up the dialectic between inside and outside, for example, and how the temporality of anxiety both as the repetition of a past trauma and a signal of a danger to come gives that ego a narrative, a kind of history. At the same time, as Weber argues, the very effort of explanation, the constant repetition in Freud's text that makes his discourse as anxious as the ego he describes, puts that ego into question, displacing it and decentring it. As contemporary psychoanalytic theory has moved, with Lacan, beyond the dream of keeping the ego intact, it has also tended to move beyond anxiety. This, at any rate, was Lacan's aim in the unpublished *Séminaire X: l'angoisse*; a text which, as Weber points out, offers a passage through anxiety to the more familiar Lacanian concern with lack. For Lacan the ego is not, as it is for Freud, 'the actual seat of anxiety' (Freud 1926: 297), rather anxiety relates to the 'desire of the Other.' '*Dès ce premier abord, j'ai indiqué que la fonction angoissante du désir de l'autre, était liée a ceci que je ne sais pas quel* objet (a) *je suis pour ce désir*' ('From the start, I have indicated that the anxiety-provoking function of the desire of the other was tied to the fact that I do not know what *objet a* I am for this desire' (Lacan 3.7.63: 364–5)). For Lacan, anxiety only gives the ego a place in so far as it signals the subject's own lack. Where then does this familiar trajectory from Freud to Lacan leave Klein? Weber himself drops a suggestive clue here. At the close of his remarkable essay on anxiety in Freud and Lacan, he quotes Kierkegaard:

> Anxiety discovers destiny, but just when the individual wants to put his trust in destiny, anxiety turns around and takes destiny away, because destiny is like anxiety, and anxiety, like possibility, is a 'magic picture.'

He adds:

> The Danish word that is here rendered as 'magic picture' is: *Heksebrev*,
> literally: witch's letter. A 'witch's letter' is a 'set of picture segments of
> people and animals that recombine when folded and turned.' If we ever get
> 'beyond the limits of anxiety,' [...] we might well find a witch's letter
> waiting there to greet us.
>
> (Weber 1991: 167)

For Weber, anxiety is like a magic picture because, as for Lacan, it is non-
cognitive and non-symbolizable and yet makes subjectivity a possibility.
Pertinent as this is to Weber's discussion, I suspect that a certain witch's letter
has been mislaid here. Take, just for a start, one of Klein's characteristically
evocative descriptions of the phantasy life of the child. This child is a five year
old whose anxiety provoking imaginary menagerie is populated by 'elephants to
stamp the foe to a pulp, [...] leopards to tear him to bits and [...] hyenas and
wolves to eat him up.' Within the folds and turns of this phantasy, the animals
re-combine into a terrifying anthropomorphic corporeality, 'the elephant
being his muscular sadism; the animals that tore, his teeth and nails, and the
wolves, his excrements' (Klein, 1932: 127). A witch's letter, perhaps, to the
letter, this may be the nearest one can get to an idea of what anxiety *looks like*
for Klein.

This description is from Klein's first published book *The Psycho-Analysis of
Children* (1932). The second section of the book was based on a series of lectures
she gave in London in 1927, that is, one year after Freud's *Inhibitions, Symptoms
and Anxiety* and the same year as the publication of Anna Freud's *Introduction
to the Technique of Child Analysis* and the ensuing symposium on child analysis
in which were heard the first salvoes between Anna Freud and Klein that were
to sound across English psychoanalysis during the war. The symposium was
a public demonstration of the extent to which Klein had began to irritate the
Freuds by this time. Phyllis Grosskurth in her biography of Klein goes so far as
to speculate that *Inhibitions, Symptoms and Anxiety* might be read as Freud's
response to Klein's early work, and points out that Freud wrote it in the summer
of 1925, that is, at the same time that Klein was giving her first London lectures
(at the invitation of Ernest Jones) that make up the first section of *The Psycho-
Analysis of Children*.[2] Freud's repeated repudiations of any Kleinian influence
in his correspondence with Jones would suggest this is unlikely – unless, of
course, the strength of these repudiations belies Freud's sense of an unwelcome
proximity between his work and Klein's.[3] The book's various cross-Channel
excursions also leave an enigmatic trail in the passage from Klein to Lacan. Klein
was totally charmed when she first met Lacan and in November 1949 gladly
gave him the rights to translate *The Psycho-Analysis of Children* (Klein
KLE/C3:22/1/52). Klein was less charmed, in fact she was furious, when nothing
had emerged by 1952 and she promptly terminated Lacan's contract (still, she

writes to her new translators, the Boulangers, 'it is no good crying over spilt milk' (Klein KLE/C3:11/9/52)).

Between Freud and Lacan, then, Klein's *The Psycho-Analysis of Children* is indeed something of a missing witch's letter. In this story of deferred translation, its destiny both opens and closes the possibility of a reading of anxiety that might rest between Freud and Lacan.

Reading this letter with an eye not to Klein's consistency but to her many inconsistencies, is one way to begin both to understand the centrality of anxiety within her own work and to tell another story about the passage of anxiety through psychoanalysis. The theoretical chapters of *The Psycho-Analysis of Children* contain a challenging, complex and detailed reading of Freud's *Inhibitions, Symptoms and Anxiety*. Put simply, what Klein does here is to paste her belief in a primary and innate aggression onto Freud's reading of anxiety. Anxiety thus becomes yoked to the origins of the early super-ego and hence to a precocious and inexorable guilt. This bleak belief in the primacy of the death drive and an original and inevitable culpability is, of course, the scandal of Kleinian theory – both for her detractors, for those at the Controversial Discussions and for many today. With one all-encompassing theoretical swoop, it looks as if Klein deprives anxiety of the ignorance and innocence and hence the ambivalence with which Kierkegaard, for one, once labored to bestow it.[4] As Anna Freud will later suggest, Klein appears to lock the child into a phantasy world of the analyst's own making, fattening it up with interpretations which begin and end with its own anxious aggression. Anna Freud's own concern in *The Ego and the Mechanisms of Defence* was with 'objective anxiety'; for her the task for the analyst was to show the child that there was really nothing to be anxious about.[5] Klein, on the contrary, insisted that there *was* something to be anxious about – oneself, and one's own primary rage. It is not difficult to see why Klein's critics should detect a form of pessimistic solipsism here. Leo Bersani, for example, in his essay in this volume suggests that Klein attempts to legitimize, and so make culturally normative, the violence she claims inheres in the anxious origins of the ego. From here it is not too difficult to re-read Klein's theory of reparation as an attempt to make a moral out of the anxiety-driven aggression upon which her theory rests: the radical child analyst becomes an avatar of a culture that endorses the death drive.[6]

But as with Freud, anxiety has an ambiguous status in Klein's writing; both motivating her theoretical conclusions and checking them at significant points in a manner which is, in fact, very similar to that described by Weber in his reading of *Inhibitions, Symptoms and Anxiety*. Moreover, the question that Weber sees anxiety posing for Freud is one that can equally be applied to Klein: 'Is anxiety a constitutive process by which the psyche maintains its coherence and identity or does it ultimately entail their dissolution?' (Weber, 1991: 152). In other words it is also possible to argue that for Klein, as for Freud, while anxiety ensures that the ego defends itself, guaranteeing its integrity against a world of difference, it also shatters the coherence of the ego and de-possesses it of authority.

So if we go back to Klein's reading of Freud in *The Psycho-Analysis of Children* what initially looks like heavy-handedness turns out to be something more subtle and provocative. Klein, like Weber after her, is fascinated by problems that Freud has in marrying his early economic theory with the second topography. In particular, she seizes on the difficulty he has in reconciling the fact that while anxiety is a threat which emanates from outside of the ego, it is also experienced as an internal and instinctual threat by the psyche. For Freud anxiety arises first from need, a 'situation of helplessness,' provoked by an absence (Freud, 1926: 294). This, then, is a relation of exteriority forcing the premature ego to recognize its own helplessness in relation to the outside world. For Klein, this anxiety is repeated internally in the psyche as a response to the death drive: 'We know that the destructive instinct is directed against the organism itself and must therefore be regarded by the ego as a danger. I believe that it is this danger which is felt by the ego as anxiety' (Klein, 1932: 126). But although this may look like an argument for the innate primacy of the death drive, it is the phenomenology of that drive exemplified in Freud's 'The Economic Problem of Masochism' (1924) that Klein is drawing on here. Hence, while it seems as if Klein is simply claiming a monadic autonomy for the psyche, the apparent interiority she sets up within it is both marked and produced by a crucial dialectic between inside and outside. As such anxiety focuses attention on a kind of primary masochism of the ego as a condition of its very possibility. Discussing the way that the infant masters its anxiety, Klein states:

> It seems to me that the ego has yet another means of mastering those destructive impulses which still remain in the organism. It can mobilize one part of them as a defence against the other part. In this way the id will undergo a split which is, I think, the first step in the formation of instinctual inhibitions and of the super-ego which may be the same thing as primal repression.
>
> (Klein, 1932:127)

Klein is laying the ground here for what will later become the paranoid-schizoid position. The threat that anxiety poses is to the integrity of the ego, the *I*; yet what Klein appears to be saying is that it is only in relation to this threat that the 'I' actually constitutes itself as such, via its splitting (primal repression). Klein's insistence on an early internalization of the super-ego is not, therefore, simply a commanding intrusion wading in from the outside to tame a primary aggression; rather anxiety in Klein sets up a model in which the inner phantasy world is marked by a prior exteriority which then sets up the interiority of the psyche.

Like Freud then, Klein is using anxiety to construct a narrative of the genesis of the ego and, as with Freud, this is a story which continually disrupts the coherence which it at the same time endeavours to secure. At the beginning of anxiety – at the beginning of the ego and at the beginning of Klein's work – anxiety lays bare the precarious formation of the ego. Moreover, anxiety in Klein marks the beginning of a relation to the super-ego which is defined not only by prohibition and guilt (as in the classic Freudian account of the Oedipus complex), but which also continually foregrounds the sadism of the super-ego itself.[7] Denial, splitting, omnipotence and idealization, says Klein, characterize the ego's relation to its objects at this point as, under the exacting commands of the super-ego, the desire to make good emerges as just as tyrannical as that to make bad. Anxiety, hence provokes aggression, and aggression more anxiety in what Klein aptly calls a 'vicious circle.' Now one can certainly, following Bersani, read this as a form of complicity with a culture which sanctifies aggression and the death drive. Or you can turn this argument around and suggest, instead, that what Klein is beginning to tell is a story of the ego's survival in a world which constitutes it, not as whole, but as shattered through the vicissitudes of its own anxious being. The extent to which Klein tries and, as I'm about to suggest, fails to square her own vicious circle, in other words, can also be read as a mark of a refusal to arrest, make normative, or legitimize the anxiety upon which her own theory rests.

But so far I've only told part of this story, and it would be quite wrong to suggest that Klein gives up on the ideal of a fully functioning social ego. Far from it. For both the child and, indeed, for the status of Kleinian psychoanalysis as a theory not only of the psyche, but also of the cultural and social value of the ego, the imperative at this point in Klein's reading is to extricate both child and theory from the potential solipsism of her description of the anxious genesis of the ego. Indeed, just as for Freud, as Weber puts it, the imperative was to prevent his discourse on anxiety becoming itself an 'anxious discourse,' so too for Klein in the remaining chapters of *The Psycho-Analysis of Children*.[8] But as Klein attempts to master anxiety, to put it in its proper place, what emerges is not so much a narrative that synthesizes anxiety, but a series of repetitions by which Klein's own theory comes to mimic the logic of anxiety itself.

There are two main paths, according to Klein, through which the infant can exit from the vicious circle in which anxiety entraps it: first, the ascendancy of the libidinal trends that ensure that Eros eventually triumphs over the death drive and second, what Klein refers to as 'reality testing' through which the child becomes better able to reconcile the difference between inner and outer worlds. Take first, the idea that libidinal trends will win over aggression. Love, it seems, can triumph over anxiety or, as Klein puts it, 'the vicious circle dominated by the death-instinct in which aggression gives rise to anxiety and anxiety reinforces aggression can be broken by the libidinal forces when these have gained in strength' (Klein, 1932: 150). But she then adds that this temporal progression to libidinal binding is predicated upon a prior regression to and repetition of early anxiety. The spectre of the Kleinian super-ego that not only prohibits libidinal tendencies, but *demands* them, returns: 'anxiety and a sense of guilt reinforces libidinal fixation and heightens libidinal desires (Klein, 1932: 115). No progression to libidinal binding then, without a necessary regression to the anxiety provoked by the ever-commanding super-ego. In as much as the strengthening of the libido guarantees Klein's emerging reparative hypothesis, recreating love out of anxiety, by the same logic this seemingly redemptive trajectory perpetuates the vicious circle it is supposed to break.[9]

If the super-ego can appear to both incite and prohibit the libido so perversely, this is because, for Klein, it is experienced by the child through phantasy – hence its overwhelming monstrosity and crude morality. By reality testing, argues Klein, the child outwits the super-ego and gains proof of the essential goodness of its 'real objects'; anxiety is modified and reparation in earnest can begin. By now it should perhaps come as no surprise to find that reality testing for Klein is something of an anxious affair. As for Kierkegaard, anxiety for Klein is synonymous with a certain kind of ignorance. Reality testing, knowing what it is one should *really* be anxious about, in Klein's account, is a form of epistemological crisis. The child's relation to the external world is always mediated through phantasy: 'the child's sadistic phantasies about the interior of the mother's body,' Klein says, 'lay down for him a fundamental relation to the external world and to reality' (Klein, 1932: 174). So originally, anxiety is linked with the failure of knowledge to provide the ego with an adequate account of its object. Moreover, as Klein points out over and over again, knowledge and judgement are inextricable from the drives hence, she stresses, the 'real' mother 'no more satisfies the infant's desire to know than she has satisfied his oral desires' (Klein, 1932: 148). Reality no more measures up to what Klein calls the infant's epistemological drive (*Wisstrieb*) than it satisfies his oral drive. It is the absence of knowledge, the *gap* between drive and object, that characterizes the infant's quest for reality. What Klein will later refer to as 'accurate observations and judgement' (Klein, 1988a: 346), thus only secure the ego's relation to the outside world, to the extent that they also expose the precarious hold the infant has on reality. For Klein, anxiety tells you that you only know to the extent that you do not know.[10]

Each time Klein attempts to go beyond anxiety, then, anxiety returns to check and disrupt the very unity and coherence it is meant to ensure. As much as for Freud, the vicissitudes of anxiety in Klein both unify and entail the dissolution of the ego and the theory which is simultaneously attempting to produce and sustain it. Indeed, it is as if the success of arriving at a stable ego, in the form of integration and unification, is dependent upon a *failure* to square the vicious circle of anxiety and, thereby, to 'make good,' or in Bersani's terms to legitimize, the anxiety which is born with the harsh admonitions of a persecutory super-ego. A prime mover, anxiety is both a cause and an effect of the constitution of the ego, and both the symptom and the cure in the psychoanalytic playroom.

No more than Freud, then, does Klein put anxiety in its proper place. But neither does she, as will Lacan, go beyond anxiety. Rather her work remains in the grip of anxiety's dynamics: Klein will later insist that all she had to say began with *The Psycho-Analysis of Children*. With this reading in mind, the subsequent construction of the great theoretical edifice of the Kleinian theatre of object relations in later years might be read as an effort to check anxiety, to once more attempt to put it in its proper place. In *Developments in Psycho-Analysis* (Klein et al., 1952) the collection which came out of the Controversial Discussions and which in many ways secured the reputation of the Kleinians, Joan Rivière claims that Klein has found an answer to the questions that eluded Freud in *Inhibitions, Symptoms and Anxiety* (a claim which echoes Klein's own 1948 paper 'On the Theory of Anxiety and Guilt'). Persecutory anxiety now belongs to the ego's fear for itself, whilst depressive anxiety is linked to the fear for the loved object in consequence of the damage done to it in phantasy.[11] While this might look like a thoroughgoing systematization of anxiety – an appropriate anxiety for an appropriate object and each in its proper place – note too that each position entails a *repetition*, and not an overcoming, of anxiety. Why then, finally, does Klein hesitate to go beyond anxiety? Or to go back to my original question, what place, between the late 1920s and the 1940s, does anxiety assign Kleinian psychoanalysis?

On June 3 1940, Joan Rivière issues Klein an invitation.

My dear Melanie

When the first official mention of invasion began the possibility of your work all coming to an end seemed so near. I felt we should all have to keep it in our hearts, perhaps, as the only way to save it for the future. Also of course I was constantly thinking of the psychological causes of such terrible loss and destruction as may happen to mankind. So I had the idea of your telling me (and then a small group of us) everything you think about these causes, so that all of us who can understand these things at all should share and know as much as possible, to help prevent it.

(Klein: PP/KLE/C.96)

Rivière then arranges a time and place for the meeting and signs off with the words, 'I am so looking forward to Saturday – psa is a great anodyne in all this anxiety!' The upshot of this request is Klein's unpublished paper 'What Does Death Represent to the Individual?' But in this paper it is less the case that psychoanalysis is the great anodyne in anxiety; rather it is anxiety that is the anodyne in psychoanalysis. And, as with other contemporary theoretical pharmaceuticals, it is the kind of drug, to use an appropriately Kleinian allusion, that poisons as it cures.

Klein, like many analysts at the time, is intrigued by the impact of war-time anxiety on her analysands. In particular she is fascinated by the extent to which the threat of war, in Anna Freud's terms an 'objective anxiety,' fails to remain objective and becomes entangled with early anxiety and guilt. War, for Klein, provokes phantasy and brings in its wake what she memorably terms 'Fifth column phantasies and guilt'(Klein PP/KLE/C.95). Once the internal world of the sadistic super-ego is confirmed by the equal sadism of the outside world (so much for reality testing) what results, unsurprisingly, is an anxiety-ridden paralysis of the ego. As Klein puts it:

If the feeling that external war is really going on inside – that an internal Hitler is fought inside by a Hitler-like subject – predominates, then despair results. It is impossible to fight this war, because in the internal situation catastrophe is bound to be the end of it.

(Klein PP/KLE/C.95: 2)

For Klein the answer to this lack of agency, however, does *not* lie with a straightforward overcoming of anxiety or an attempt to repair one's own violence, and hence neither does Klein directly propose the erection of a functional, integral social ego ready for war on the home front. The way forward, rather, lies with a repetition, as it were, backwards to the origins of anxiety. Klein argues 'an important step in development is the capacity to allow oneself to split the imagos into good and bad ones . . . Only thus it is possible to hate with full strength what is felt to be evil in the external world' (Klein PP/KLE/C.95:1–2). No move forward to action in the world without the repetition of the paranoid-schizoid anxiety that marked the ego's coming into being. It seems to me that this is less some kind of solipsism of the ego, than an attempt on Klein's part to turn anxiety into a form of possibility; a possibility for the kind of action that emerges, maybe, from a political as well as a psychic form of hate. This suggestion is, of course, scandalous to the extent that it relies neither on the supposed health of the depressive position nor on the work of reparation as a more traditional Kleinian approach might insist, but on a form of psychic failure. As such, Klein's refusal to go beyond anxiety here also suggests a kind of internal resistance to the more culturally and socially complicit plots towards which some forms of Kleinism undoubtedly tend. In what Auden called the 'age of anxiety,' Klein refuses to put anxiety in its proper place but insists on leaving the ego shattered and dislocated by the vicissitudes of anxiety. Perhaps it is only in this way that anxiety can continue to do its work: or as Gillian Rose has argued, albeit in a different context, it is only by remaining *within* anxiety that the ego can look both backwards to the guilt that constituted it and forwards towards some kind of freedom.[12]

Notes

1 This article was given as a paper at the 'History of Psychology, Psychiatry and Psychoanalysis Seminar' in Cambridge in November 1995. I am very grateful to John Forrester for the invitation and to all participants for their helpful discussion. All quotations from Melanie Klein's unpublished work are from the Klein archives held in the Contemporary Medical Archives Centre at the Wellcome Institute of the History of Medicine, and are reproduced here by the kind permission of The Melanie Klein Trust. I am indebted to Elizabeth Bott Spillius for her most gracious and rigorous reading of an earlier draft, and for her corrections and comments. An earlier version of the second half of this article appears in *The Destructive Element: British Psychoanalysis and Modernism* (Basingstoke: Macmillan, 1998).

2 Phyllis Grosskurth, *Melanie Klein: Her World and Her Work* (London: Hodder & Stoughton, 1985) 173.

3 See *The Complete Correspondence of Sigmund Freud and Ernest Jones, 1908–1939*, ed. R. Andrew Paskauskas (Cambridge, Mass. and London: Harvard University Press, 1993) and in particular the exchanges over Klein's criticisms of Anna Freud's work in the Autumn of 1927.

4 Cf. Kierkegaard (1894): 'He who becomes guilty in anxiety becomes as ambiguously guilty as it is possible to become' and 'the individual, in anxiety not about becoming guilty but about being regarded as guilty, becomes guilty', *The Concept of Anxiety: A Simple Psychologically Orienting Deliberation on the Dogmatic Issue of Hereditary Sin*, ed. and trans. Reidar Thomte (Princeton, New Jersey: Princeton University Press, 1980) 61, 73.

5 See Anna Freud, *The Ego and the Mechanisms of Defence* (1937), trans. Cecil Baines (London: Hogarth, 1966) 58–70.

6 Leo Bersani, 'Death and Literary Authority: Marcel Proust and Melanie Klein' (this volume, ch. 12), *The Culture of Redemption* (Cambridge, Mass. and London: Harvard University Press, 1990) 7–28.

7 See also Melanie Klein 'The Early Development of Conscience in the Child' (1933) and 'On Criminality' (1934), *Love, Guilt and Reparation and Other Works 1921–1945*, London: Virago, 1988. For a comparative view of the sadism of the super-ego see Jacques Lacan, *Le séminaire livre VII: l'éthique de la psychanalyse, 1959–1960* (Paris: Seuil, 1986).

8 I am primarily concerned here with Klein's earlier work on anxiety. A full account of its vicissitudes through to her concept of depressive anxiety would require a more extended analysis.

9 Here I am indebted to Jacqueline Rose's reading of how Klein's developmental narrative is troubled by the centrality of regression in her work. See Rose, 'Negativity in the Work of Melanie Klein', *Why War? – Psychoanalysis, Politics, and the Return to Melanie Klein* (Oxford: Basil Blackwell, 1993) 168–170 (this volume, ch. 7).

10 Cf. John Phillips, 'The Fissure of Authority: Violence and the Acquisition of Knowledge,' (this volume, ch. 8).

11 Joan Rivière, 'Introduction', *Developments in Psycho-Analysis*, Melanie Klein, Paula Heimann, Susan Isaacs and Joan Rivière (London: Hogarth and Institute of Psycho-Analysis, 1952) 30.

12 Gillian Rose, 'Anxiety of Beginning: Kierkegaard, Freud and Lacan', *The Broken Middle* (Oxford: Basil Blackwell, 1992) 85–112.

References

Bersani, Leo (1990) *The Culture of Redemption*, Cambridge, Mass. and London: Harvard University Press.

Freud, Anna (1937) *The Ego and the Mechanisms of Defence*, London: Hogarth, 1966.

Freud, Sigmund *The Standard Edition of the Complete Psychological Works of Sigmund Freud*, ed. and trans. James Strachey, London: Hogarth, 24 vols, 1953–74.

—— (1924) 'The Economic Problem of Masochism', *SE*, XIX.

—— (1926) *Inhibitions, Symptoms and Anxiety*, *SE*, XX, and *The Pelican Freud Library*, vol. 10, trans. James Strachey, ed. Angela Richards. All references refer to Pelican edition.

Grosskurth, Phyllis (1985) *Melanie Klein: Her World and Her Work*, London: Hodder & Stoughton.

Jones, Ernest (1993) *The Complete Correspondence of Sigmund Freud and Ernest Jones,*

1908–1939, ed. R. Andrew Paskauskas, Cambridge, Mass. and London: Harvard University Press.

Klein, Melanie (1932) *The Psychoanalysis of Children*, London: Virago, 1989.

——, Paula Heimann, Susan Isaacs and Joan Rivière (1952) *Developments in Psycho-Analysis*, London: Hogarth and Institute of Psycho-Analysis.

—— (1988a) *Love, Guilt and Reparation and Other Works 1921–1945*, London: Virago.

—— (1988b) *Envy and Gratitude and Other Works 1946–1963*, London: Virago.

Kierkegaard, Soren (1894) *The Concept of Anxiety: A Simple Psychologically Orienting Deliberation on the Dogmatic Issue of Hereditary Sin*, ed. and trans. Reidar Thomte, Princeton, New Jersey: Princeton University Press, 1980.

Lacan, Jacques (1986) *Le séminaire livre VII: l'éthique de la psychanalyse, 1959–1960*, Paris: Editions du Seuil.

—— *Le séminaire livre X: l'angoisse, 1962–1963*, unpublished.

Rose, Gillian (1992) *The Broken Middle*, Oxford: Basil Blackwell.

Rose, Jacqueline (1993) *Why War – Psychoanalysis, Politics, and the Return to Melanie Klein*, Oxford: Basil Blackwell.

Stonebridge, Lyndsey (1998) *The Destructive Element: British Psychoanalysis and Modernism*, Basingstoke: Macmillan.

Tillich, Paul (1954–64) *Systematic Theology: I–III*, Chicago: Chicago University Press.

Weber, Samuel (1982) *The Legend of Freud*, Minneapolis: University of Minnesota Press.

—— (1991) 'The Witch's Letter', *Return to Freud: Jacques Lacan's Dislocation of Psychoanalysis*, trans. Michael Levine, Cambridge: Cambridge University Press.

Chapter 11

A psychoanalytic approach to aesthetics

Hanna Segal

Editor's note:

Hanna Segal's sustained study of aesthetics from the point of view of Kleinian psychoanalysis combines analytic wisdom, clinical experience, literary criticism and aesthetic philosophy to produce an adventurous yet meticulously supported hypothesis that aims to explain the enigma of art, artists and aesthetic pleasure. First presented in 1947, one can almost hear the echo of Adorno and Horkheimer's acerbic critique of the culture industry from a year earlier. 'Great artists,' they had said (casting scornful eyes over Hollywood), 'were those who used style as a way of hardening themselves against the chaotic expression of suffering.' Segal's vision of the artist, whose neurosis may be incapacitating in life, is of one who nonetheless has two essential components of judgement at his command: a deep know-ledge of and capacity to tolerate the condition of his ruined internal phantasy, and an intimate knowledge of the material properties of his chosen medium, 'be it words, sounds, paints or clay.' The crux is that artists know how to 'use their death drive' to mould lifeless matter magically. Tragedy is the clearest example of the way an artist can style something beautiful, rhythmic and unified out of the destroyed and fragmented world of the early depressive position. This is also what distinguishes good art from merely pleasant art or from just plain bad art, Segal argues, again echoing Adorno and Horkheimer – and in search of an answer to a question that for a long time now has been rather unfashionable in mainstream humanities circles: what constitutes good art? Her answer – that it is the capacity to tolerate and utilize the death instinct as fully as can be borne – suggests that it may well be worth returning to the question of aesthetics today.

Segal takes Proust as an example to show how Kleinian concepts can help in an understanding of the artist's impulse to create, thus

uniting Proust and Klein in a common aesthetic. For Segal, the task of
the artist lies in creating a world rather than simply in imitation.
Rooting the so-called 'wish to create' in the early depressive position,
when the world within is destroyed and fragmented, Segal goes on to
argue that all creation is really the re-creation of a lost and ruined
whole, an internal world and self, whose dead fragments can be
reassembled in new, less fragile forms, from the sustaining magic of
the most helpless despair. Segal concludes by arguing that the
artist's achievement is to give full expression to the tension and union
between the death and the life instincts, between ugliness and beauty.
Tying the aesthetic function to the destructive impulse, Segal thus
implies that the most powerful aspect of aesthetic experience lies
in the degree to which the death instinct can be acknowledged.
Borrowing and doubling Dilthey's concept of *nach-erleben* – identifying
with the other through the work and identifying the work with the
ruined inner world – Segal offers a truly suggestive account of
aesthetic judgement. Her 'Postscript,' thirty-three years on, is significant in that it changes very little, but does add some complexifications
based on work by Adrian Stokes and Elliot Jaques. (JP)

In 1908 Freud wrote: 'We laymen have always wondered greatly – like the
cardinal who put the question to Ariosto – how that strange being, the poet,
comes by his material. What makes him able to carry us with him in such a way
and to arouse emotions in us of which we thought ourselves perhaps not even
capable?' And as the science of psychoanalysis developed, repeated attempts
were made to answer that question. Freud's discovery of unconscious phantasy
life and of symbolism made it possible to attempt a psychological interpretation
of works of art. Many papers have been written since, dealing with the problem
of the individual artist and reconstructing his early history from an analysis of
his work. The foremost of these is Freud's book on Leonardo da Vinci. Other
papers have dealt with general psychological problems expressed in works of art
and show, for instance, how the latent content of universal infantile anxieties is
symbolically expressed in them. Examples are Freud's 'The Theme of the Three
Caskets' (1913), Ernest Jones's 'The Madonna's Conception through the Ear'
(1914), and Melanie Klein's 'Infantile Anxiety-Situations Reflected in a Work of
Art and the Creative Impulse' (1929).

Until recently such papers were not mainly concerned with aesthetics. They
dealt with points of psychological interest but not with the central problem of
aesthetics, which is: What constitutes good art and in what essential respect is it
different from other human works, from bad art in particular? Psychological
writers attempted to answer such questions as: How does the poet work? What
is he like? What does he express? In the paper 'The Relation of the Poet to

Day-Dreaming' (1908) Freud has shown how the work of the artist is a product of phantasy and has its roots, like children's play and dreams, in unconscious phantasy life. But he did not attempt to explain why we should derive such pleasure from listening to the daydreams of a poet. How he achieves his effects is to Freud the poet's 'innermost secret.' Indeed, Freud was not especially interested in aesthetic problems. In 'The Moses of Michelangelo' (1914) he says 'I have often observed that the subject-matter of works of art has a stronger attraction for me than their formal and technical qualities, though to the artist their value lies first and foremost in these latter. I am unable rightly to appreciate many of the methods used and the effects obtained in art' (p. 257). He was also aware of the limitations of analytical theory in approaching aesthetics. In the preface to the book on Leonardo he says that he has no intention of discussing why Leonardo was a great painter, since to do that he would have to know about the ultimate sources of the creative impulse and of sublimation. This was written in 1910. Since that time the work of Melanie Klein has thrown more light on the problem of the creative impulse and sublimation, and has provided a new stimulus to analytical writers on art. In the last fifteen years a number of papers have appeared dealing with problems of creation, beauty, and ugliness. I would mention, in particular, those by Ella Sharpe, Paula Heimann, John Rickman, and W.R.D. Fairbairn in this country, and H. B. Lee in the U.S.A.

Maybe it is possible now, in the light of new analytical discoveries, to ask new questions. Can we isolate in the psychology of the artist the specific factors which enable him to produce a satisfactory work of art? And if we can, will that further our understanding of the aesthetic value of the work of art, and of the aesthetic experience of the audience?

It seems to me that Melanie Klein's concept of the depressive position makes it possible at least to attempt an answer to these questions.

The 'depressive position,' as described by Melanie Klein, is reached by the infant when he recognizes his mother and other people, and among them his father, as real persons. His object relations then undergo a fundamental change.[1] Where earlier he was aware of 'part objects' he now perceives complete persons; instead of 'split' objects – ideally good or overwhelmingly persecuting – he sees a whole object both good and bad. The whole object is loved and introjected and forms the core of an integrated ego. But this new constellation ushers in a new anxiety situation: where earlier the infant feared an attack on the ego by persecutory objects, now the predominant fear is that of the loss of the loved object in the external world and in his own inside. The infant at that stage is still under the sway of uncontrollable greedy and sadistic impulses. In phantasy his loved object is continually attacked in greed and hatred, is destroyed, torn into pieces and fragments; and not only is the external object so attacked but also the internal one, and then the whole internal world feels destroyed and shattered as well. Bits of the destroyed object may turn into persecutors, and there is a fear of internal persecution as well as a pining for the lost loved object and guilt for the attack. The memory of the good situation, where the infant's ego contained the whole loved object and the realization that it has been lost through his own attacks, give rise to an intense feeling of loss and guilt, and to the wish to restore and re-create the lost loved object outside and within the ego. This wish to restore and re-create is the basis of later sublimation and creativity.

It is also at this point that a sense of inner reality is developed. If the object is remembered as a whole object, then the ego is faced with the recognition of its own ambivalence towards the object; it holds itself responsible for its impulses and for the damage done to the external and to the internal object. Where, earlier, impulses and parts of the infant's self were projected into the object with the result that a false picture of it was formed, that his own impulses were denied, and that there was often a lack of differentiation between the self and the external object, in the depressive phase a sense of inner reality is developed and in its wake a sense of outer reality as well.

Depressive phantasies give rise to the wish to repair and restore, and become a stimulus to further development only in so far as the depressive anxiety can be tolerated by the ego and the sense of psychic reality retained. If there is little belief in the capacity to restore, the good object outside and inside is felt to be irretrievably lost and destroyed, the destroyed fragments turn into persecutors, and the internal situation is felt to be hopeless. The infant's ego is at the mercy of intolerable feelings of guilt, loss, and internal persecution. To protect itself from total despair the ego must have recourse to violent defence mechanisms. Those defence mechanisms which protect it from the feelings arising out of the loss of the good object form a system of manic defences. The essential features of manic defences are denial of psychic reality, omnipotent control, and a partial regression to the paranoid position and its defences: splitting, idealization, denial, projective identification, etc. This regression strengthens the fear of persecution and that in turn leads to the strengthening of omnipotent control.

But in successful development the experience of love from the environment slowly reassures the infant about his objects. His growing love, strength, and skill give him increasing confidence in his own capacities to restore. And as his confidence increases he can gradually relinquish the manic defences and experience more and more fully the underlying feelings of loss, guilt and love, and he can make renewed and increasingly successful attempts at reparation.

By repeated experiences of loss and restoration of the internal objects they become more firmly established and more fully assimilated in the ego.

A successful working through of the depressive anxieties has far-reaching consequences: the ego becomes integrated and enriched through the assimilation of loved objects; the dependence on the external objects is lessened; and deprivation can be better dealt with. Aggression and love can be tolerated, and guilt gives rise to the need to restore and re-create.

Feelings of guilt probably play a role before the depressive position is fully established; they already exist in relation to the part object, and they contribute to later sublimation; but they are then simpler impulses acting in a predominantly paranoid setting, isolated and unintegrated. With the establishment of the depressive position the object becomes more personal and unique and the ego more integrated, and an awareness of an integrated internal world is gradually achieved. Only when this happens does the attack on the object lead to real despair at the destruction of all existing complex and organized internal world and, with it, to the wish to recover such a complete world again.

The task of the artist lies in the creation of a world of his own. In his introduction to the second Post-Impressionist Exhibition, Roger Fry writes: 'Now these artists do not seek to give what can, after all, be but a pale reflex of actual appearance, but to arouse a conviction of a new and different reality. They do not seek to imitate life but to find an equivalent for life.' What Roger Fry says of post-impressionists undoubtedly applies to all genuine art. One of the great differences between art and imitation or a superficial 'pretty' achievement is that neither the imitation nor the pretty production ever achieves this creation of an entirely new reality.

Every creative artist produces a world of his own. Even when he believes himself to be a complete realist and sets himself the task of faithfully reproducing the external world, he in fact only uses elements of the existing external world to create with them a reality of his own. When, for instance, two realistic writers like Zola and Flaubert try to portray life in the same country, and at very nearly the same time, the two worlds they show us differ from each other as widely as if they were the most fantastic creations of surrealist poets. If two great painters paint the same landscape we have two different worlds.

> . . . and dream
> Of waves, flowers, clouds, woods,
> Rocks, and all that we
> Read in their smiles
> And call reality

How does this creation come about? Of all artists, the one who gives us the fullest description of the creative process is Marcel Proust – a description based on years of self-observation and the fruit of an amazing insight. According to Proust, an artist is compelled to create by his need to recover his lost past. But a purely intellectual memory of the past, even when it is available, is emotionally valueless and dead. A real remembrance sometimes comes about unexpectedly, by chance association. The flavour of a cake brings back to his mind a fragment of his childhood with full emotional vividness. Stumbling over a stone revives a recollection of a holiday in Venice which, before, he had vainly tried to recapture. For years he tries in vain to remember and re-create in his mind a living picture of his beloved grandmother. But only a chance association revives her picture and at last enables him to remember her, and to experience his loss and mourn her. He calls these fleeting associations *intermittences du coeur*, but he says that such memories come and then disappear again, so that the past remains elusive. To capture them, to give them permanent life, to integrate them with the rest of his life, he must create a work of art. 'Il fallait . . . faire sortir de la pénombre ce que j'avais senti, de le reconvertir en un équivalent spirituel. Or ce moyen qui me paraissait le seul qu'était-ce autre chose que de créer un oeuvre d'art?' ('I had to recapture from the shade that which I had felt, to reconvert it into its psychic equivalent. But the way to do it, the only one I could see, what was it – but to create a work of art?')

Through the many volumes of his work the past is being recaptured; all his lost, destroyed, and loved objects are being brought back to life: his parents, his grandmother, his beloved Albertine. 'Et certes il n'y aurait pas qu'Albertine, que ma grandmère, mais bien d'autres encore dont j'aurais pu assimiler une parole, un regard, mais en tant que créatures individuelles je ne m'en rappellais plus; un livre est un grand cimetière ou sur la plupart des tombes on ne peut plus lire les noms effacés.' ('And indeed it was not only Albertine, not only my grandmother, but many others still from whom I might well have assimilated a gesture or a word, but whom I could not even remember as distinct persons. A book is a vast graveyard where on most of the tombstones one can read no more the faded names.')

And according to Proust, it is only the lost past and the lost or dead object that can be made into a work of art. He makes the painter, Elstir, say: 'On ne peut recréer ce qu'on aime qu'en le renonçant.' ('It is only by renouncing that one can re-create what one loves.') It is only when the loss has been acknowledged and the mourning experienced that re-creation can take place.

In the last volume of his work Proust describes how at last he decided to sacrifice the rest of his life to writing. He came back after a long absence to seek his old friends at a party, and all of them appeared to him as ruins of the real people he knew – useless, ridiculous, ill, on the threshold of death. Others, he found, had died long ago. And on realizing the destruction of a whole world that had been his, he decided to write, to sacrifice himself to the re-creation of the dying and the dead. By virtue of his art he can give his objects an eternal life in his work. And since they represent his internal world too, if he can do that, he himself will no longer be afraid of death.

What Proust describes corresponds to a situation of mourning: he sees that his loved objects are dying or dead. Writing a book is for him like the work of mourning in that gradually the external objects are given up, they are reinstated in the ego, and re-created in the book. In her paper 'Mourning and its Relation to Manic-Depressive States' (1940), Melanie Klein has shown how mourning in grown-up life is a reliving of the early depressive anxieties; not only is the present object in the external world felt to be lost, but also the early objects, the parents; and they are lost as internal objects as well as in the external world. In the process of mourning it is these earliest objects which are lost again, and then re-created. Proust describes how this mourning leads to a wish to re-create the lost world.

I have quoted Proust at length because he reveals such an acute awareness of what I believe is present in the unconscious of all artists: namely, that all creation is really a re-creation of a once loved and once whole, but now lost and ruined object, a ruined internal world and self. It is when the world within us is destroyed, when it is dead and loveless, when our loved ones are in fragments, and we ourselves in helpless despair – it is then that we must re-create our world anew, reassemble the pieces, infuse life into dead fragments, re-create life.

If the wish to create is rooted in the depressive position and the capacity to create depends on a successful working through it, it would follow that the inability to acknowledge and overcome depressive anxiety must lead to inhibitions in artistic expression.

I should now like to give a few clinical examples from artists who have been inhibited in their creative activities by neurosis, and I shall try to show that in them it was the inability to work through their depressive anxieties which led to inhibitions of artistic activity, or to the production of an unsuccessful artistic product.

Case A was a young girl with a definite gift for painting. An acute rivalry with her mother made her give up painting in her early teens. After some analysis she started to paint again and was working as a decorative artist. She did decorative handicraft work in preference to what she sometimes called 'real painting,' and this was because she knew that, though correct, neat, and pretty, her work failed to be moving and aesthetically significant. In her manic way she usually denied that this caused her any concern. At the time when I was trying to interpret her unconscious sadistic attacks on her father, the internalization of her mutilated and destroyed father, and the resulting depression, she told me the following dream: She had seen a picture in a shop which represented a wounded man lying alone and desolate in a dark forest. She felt quite overwhelmed with emotion and admiration for this picture; she thought it represented the actual essence of life; if she could only paint like that she would be a really great painter.

It soon appeared that the meaning of the dream was that if she could only acknowledge her depression about the wounding and destruction of her father, she would then be able to express it in her painting and would achieve real art. In fact, however, it was impossible for her to do this, since the unusual strength of her sadism, her resulting despair, and her small capacity to tolerate depression led to its manic denial and to a constant make-believe that all was well with the world. In her dream she confirmed my interpretation about the attack on her father, but she did more than this. Her dream showed something that had not been in any way interpreted or indicated by me: namely, the effect on her painting of her persistent denial of depression. In relation to her painting the denial of the depth and seriousness of her depressive feelings produced the effect or superficiality and prettiness in whatever she chose to do – the dead father was completely denied and no ugliness or conflict was ever allowed to disturb the neat and correct form of her work.

Case B was that of a journalist aged a little over thirty, whose ambition was to be a writer, and who suffered, among other symptoms, from an ever-increasing inhibition in creative writing. An important feature of his character was a tendency to regress from the depressive to the paranoid position. The following dream illustrates his problem: He found himself in a room with Goebbels, Goering, and some other Nazis. He was aware that these men were completely amoral. He knew that they were going to poison him and therefore he tried to make a bargain with them; he suggested that it would be a good thing for them to let him live, since he was a journalist and could write about them and make them live for a time after their death. But this stratagem failed and he knew that he would finally be poisoned.

An important factor in this patient's psychology was his introjection of an extremely bad father-figure who was then blamed for all that the patient did. And one of the results was an unbearable feeling of being internally persecuted by this bad internal father-figure, which was sometimes expressed in hypochondriacal symptoms. He tried to defend himself against it by placating and serving this bad internal figure. He was often driven to do things that he disapproved of and disliked. In the dream he showed how it interfered with his writing: to avoid death at the hands of internal persecutors he had to write for them to keep them immortal; but there is, of course, no real wish to keep such bad figures alive, and consequently he was inhibited in his capacity for writing. He often complained, too, that he had no style of his own; in his associations to the dream it became clear that he had to write not only for the benefit of the persecutors, and to serve their purposes, but also at their command. Thus the style of his writing belonged to the internal parental figure. The case, I think, resembles one described by Paula Heimann (1942). A patient of hers drew a sketch with which she was very displeased. The style was not her own – it was Victorian. It appeared clearly during the session that it was the result of a quarrel with another woman, who stood for her mother. After the quarrel the painter had introjected her as a bad and vengeful mother, and, through guilt and fear, she had to submit to this bad internal figure; it was really the Victorian mother who had dictated the painting.

Paula Heimann described this example of an acute impairment of an already established sublimation. In my patient his submission to a very bad internal figure was a chronic situation preventing him from achieving any internal freedom to create. He was basically fixed in the paranoid position and returned to it whenever depressive feelings were aroused, so that his love and reparative impulses could not become fully active.

All the patients mentioned suffered from sexual maladjustments as well as creative inhibitions. There is clearly a genital aspect of artistic creation which is of paramount importance. Creating a work of art is a psychic equivalent of pro-creation. It is a genital bisexual activity necessitating a good identification with the father who gives, and the mother who receives and bears, the child. The ability to deal with the depressive position, however, is the precondition of both genital and artistic maturity. If the parents are felt to be so completely destroyed that there is no hope of ever re-creating them, a successful identification is not possible, and neither can the genital position be maintained nor the sublimation in art develop.

This relation between feelings of depression and genital and artistic problems is clearly shown by another patient of mine. C, a man of thirty-five, was a really gifted artist, but at the same time a very ill person. Since the age of eighteen he had suffered from depression, from a variety of conversion symptoms of great intensity, and from what he described as 'a complete lack of freedom and spontaneity.' This lack of spontaneity interfered considerably with his work, and, though he was physically potent, it also deprived him of all the enjoyment of sexual intercourse. A feeling of impending failure, worthlessness, and hopelessness marred all his efforts. He came to analysis at the age of thirty-five because of a conversion symptom: he suffered from a constant pain in the small of his back and the lower abdomen, a pain aggravated by frequent spasms. He described it as 'a constant state of childbirth.' It appeared in his analysis that the pain started soon after he learned that the wife of his twin brother was pregnant, and he actually came to me for treatment a week before her confinement. He felt that if I could only liberate him from the spasm he would do marvellous things. In his case, identification with the pregnant woman, representing the mother, was very obvious, but it was not a happy identification. He felt his mother and the babies inside her had been so completely destroyed by his sadism, and his hope of re-creating them was so slight, that the identification with the pregnant mother meant to him a state of anguish, ruin, and abortive pregnancy. Instead of producing the baby, he, like the mother, was destroyed. Feeling destroyed inside and unable to restore the mother, he felt persecuted by her; the internal attacked mother attacked him in turn and robbed him of his babies. Unlike the other three patients described, this one recognized his depression and his reparative drive was therefore very much stronger. The inhibition both in his sexual and artistic achievements was due mainly to a feeling of the inadequacy of his reparative capacity in comparison with the devastation that he felt he had brought about. This feeling of inadequacy made him regress to a paranoid position whenever his anxiety was aroused.

Patient D, a woman writer, was the most disturbed of the patients here. A severe chronic hypochondriac, she suffered from frequent depersonalization and endless phobias, among them food phobias leading at times to almost complete anorexia. She had been a writer, but had not been able to write for a number of years. I want to describe here how her inability to experience depression led to an inhibition of symbolic expression.

One day she told me the following dream: She was in a nursing home and the matron of this home, dressed in black, was going to kill a man and a woman. She herself was going to a fancy dress ball. She kept running out of the nursing home in various fancy disguises, but somehow something always went wrong, and she had to come back to the nursing home, and to meet the matron. At some point of the dream she was with her friend Joan.

Her friend Joan was for my patient the embodiment of mental health and stability. After telling me the dream she said: 'Joan was not in a fancy dress, she was undisguised, and I felt her to be so much more vulnerable than me.' Then she immediately corrected herself: 'Oh, of course I meant she was so much less vulnerable than me.' This slip of the patient gave us the key to the dream. The mentally healthy person is more vulnerable than my patient, she wears no disguises and is vulnerable to illness and death. My patient herself escapes death, represented by the matron, by using various disguises. Her associations to this dream led us to a review of some of her leading symptoms in terms of her fear of, and attempted escape from, death. The disguises in the dream represented personifications, projective and introjective identifications, all three used by her as means of not living her own life and – in the light of the dream – not dying her own death. She also connected other symptoms of hers with the fear of death. For instance, her spending almost half her life lying in bed, 'half-dead,' was a shamming of death, a way of cheating death. Her phobia of bread, her fear of sex, appeared to her now as ways of escaping full living, which would mean that one day she would have 'spent her life' and would have to face death. So far, she had almost lived on 'borrowed' life. For instance, she felt extremely well and alive when she was pregnant – she felt she lived on the baby's life; but immediately after the baby's birth she felt depersonalized and half-dead.

I mention here only some of her striking symptoms, which all pointed in the same direction – to a constant preoccupation with the fear of death. The analyst, represented by the matron, tears off her disguises one after another and forces her to lead her own life and so, eventually, to die.

After some three sessions completely taken up with the elaboration of this theme, she started the next one with what appeared to be a completely new trend of thought. She started complaining of her inability to write. Her associations led her to remember her early dislike of using words. She felt that her dislike was still present and she did not really want to use words at all. Using words, she said, made her break 'an endless unity into bits.' It was like 'chopping up,' like 'cutting things.' It was obviously felt by her as an aggressive act. Besides, using words was 'making things finite and separate.' To use words meant acknowledging the separateness of the world from herself, and gave her a feeling of loss. She felt that using words made her lose the illusion of possessing and being at one with an endless, undivided world: 'When you name a thing you really lose it.'[2] It became clear to her that using a symbol (language) meant an acceptance of the separateness of her object from herself, the acknowledgment of her own aggressiveness, 'chopping up,' 'cutting,' and finally losing the object.

In this patient the loss of the object was always felt as an imminent threat to her own survival. So we could eventually connect her difficulties in using language with the material of the earlier sessions. Refusing to face this threat of death to her object and to herself, she had to form the various symptoms devised magically to control and avoid death. She also had to give up her creative writing. In order to write again, she would have to be stripped of her disguises, admit reality, and become vulnerable to loss and death.

I shall now briefly describe a session with the same patient two years later.

She had known for some time that she would have to give up her analysis at the end of the term, through external circumstances. She came to this session very sad, for the first time since it became clear that she would end her analysis. In preceding sessions she felt nausea, felt internally persecuted and 'all in bits and pieces.' She said at the beginning of the session that she could hardly wait to see me for fear that her sadness would turn into a 'sickness and badness.' She thought of the end of her analysis, wondered if she would be able to go on liking me and how much she would be able to remember me. She also wondered if she in any way resembled me. There were two things she would wish to resemble me in: the truthfulness, and the capacity to care for people which she attributed to me. She hoped she may have learned these from me. She also felt I was an ordinary kind of person, and she liked that thought. I interpreted her material as a wish to take me in and identify herself with me as a real 'ordinary' feeding breast, in contrast to an earlier situation when an idealized breast was internalized, which subsequently turned into a persecuting one.

She then told me the following dream: A baby has died or grown up – she didn't know which – and as a result her breasts were full of milk. She was feeding a baby of another woman, whose breasts were dry.

The transference meaning of that dream was that I weaned her – my breast was dry – but she acquired a breast and could be a mother herself. The baby who 'died or grew up' is herself. The baby dies and the grown woman takes its place. The losing of the analyst is here an experience involving sadness, guilt (about the rivalry with me in relation to the baby), and anxiety (will she be able to go on remembering me?). But it is also an experience leading to the enrichment of her ego – she now has the breasts full of milk and therefore need no longer depend on me.

Towards the end of the hour, she said: 'Words seem to have a meaning again, they are rich,' and she added that she was quite sure she could now write, 'provided I can go on being sad for a while, without being sick and hating food' – i.e., provided she could mourn me instead of feeling me as an internal persecutor.

Words acquired a meaning and the wish to write returned again where she could give up my breast as an external object and internalize it. This giving up was experienced by her as the death of the breast, which is dried up in the dream, and the death of a part of herself – the baby part – which in growing up also dies. In so far as she could mourn me, words became rich in meaning.[3]

This patient's material confirmed an impression, derived from many other patients, that successful symbol formation is rooted in the depressive position.

One of Freud's greatest contributions to psychology was the discovery that sublimation is the outcome of a successful renunciation of an instinctual aim; I would like to suggest here that such a successful renunciation can happen only through a process of mourning. The giving up of an instinctual aim, or object, is a repetition and at the same time a reliving of the giving up of the breast. It can be successful, like this first situation, if the object to be given up can be assimilated in the ego, by the process of loss and internal restoration. I suggest that such an assimilated object becomes a symbol within the ego. Every aspect of the object, every situation that has to be given up in the process of growing, gives rise to symbol formation.

In this view, symbol formation is the outcome of a loss; it is a creative act involving the pain and the whole work of mourning. If psychic reality is experienced and differentiated from external reality, the symbol is differentiated from the object; it is felt to be created by the self and can be freely used by the self. I cannot deal here extensively with the problem of symbols; I have brought it up only insofar as it is relevant to my main theme. And it is relevant in that the creation of symbols, the symbolic elaboration of a theme, is the very essence of art.

I should now like to attempt to formulate an answer to the question whether there is a specific factor in the psychology of the successful artist which would differentiate him from the unsuccessful one. In Freud's words: 'What distinguishes him, the poet, the artist, from the neurotic daydreamer?' In his paper 'Formulations Regarding the Two Principles of Mental Functioning' (1911), Freud says that the artist 'finds a way of return from this world of phantasy back to reality; with his special gifts he moulds his phantasies into a new kind of reality' (p. 19). Indeed, one could say that the artist has an acute reality sense. He is often neurotic and in many situations may show a complete lack of objectivity, but in at least two respects he shows an extremely high reality sense. One is in relation to his own internal reality, and the other in relation to the material of his art. However neurotic Proust was in his attachment to his mother, his homosexuality, his asthma, etc., he had a real insight into the fantastic world of the people inside him, and he knew it was internal, and he knew it was phantasy. He showed an awareness that does not exist in a neurotic who splits off, represses, denies, or acts out his phantasy. The second, the reality sense of the artist in relation to his material, is a highly specialised reality assessment of the nature, needs, possibilities, and limitations of his material, be it words, sounds, paints, or clay. The neurotic uses his material in a magic way, and so does the bad artist. The real artist, being aware of his internal world, which he must express, and of the external materials with which he works, can in all consciousness use the material to express the phantasy. He shares with the neurotic all the difficulties of unresolved depression, the constant threat of the collapse of his internal world; but he differs from the neurotic in that he has a greater capacity for tolerating anxiety and depression. The patients I described could not tolerate depressive phantasies and anxieties; they all made use of manic defences leading to a denial of psychic reality. Patient A denied both the loss of her father and his importance to her; Patient B projected his impulses onto an internal bad object, with the result that his ego was split and that he was internally persecuted; Patient C did the same, though to a lesser extent; Patient D regressed to the schizoid mechanisms of splitting and projective identification, which led to depersonalization and inhibition in the use of symbols.

In contrast to that, Proust could fully experience depressive mourning. This gave him the possibility of insight into himself, and with it a sense of internal and external reality. Further, this reality sense enabled him to have and to maintain a relationship with other people through the medium of his art. The neurotic's phantasy interferes with his relationships, in which he acts it out. The artist withdraws into a world of phantasy, but he can communicate and share it. In that way he makes reparation, not only to his own internal objects, but to the external world as well.

I have tried, so far, to show how Melanie Klein's work, especially her concept of the depressive position, the reparative drives that are set in motion by it, and her description of the world of inner objects, throws new light on the psychology of the artist, on the conditions necessary for him to be successful, and on those which can inhibit or vitiate his artistic activities. Can this new light on the psychology of the artist help us to understand the aesthetic pleasure experienced by the artist's public? If, for the artist, the work of art is his most complete and satisfactory way of allaying the guilt and despair arising out of the depressive position and of restoring his destroyed objects, it is but one of the many human ways of achieving this end. What is it that makes a work of art such a satisfactory experience for the artist's public? Freud says that he 'bribes us with the formal and aesthetic pleasures.'

To begin with, we should distinguish between the aesthetic pleasure and other, incidental pleasures to be found in works of art. For instance, the satisfaction derived from identification with particular scenes or characters can also arise in other ways, and it can be derived from bad as well as from good art. The same would apply to the sentimental interests originating in memories and associations. The aesthetic pleasure proper, that is, the pleasure derived from a work of art, unique in that it can only be obtained through a work of art, is due to an identification of ourselves with the work of art as a whole and with the whole internal world of the artist as represented by his work. In my view all aesthetic pleasure includes an unconscious reliving of the artist's experience of creation. In his paper 'The Moses of Michelangelo' (1914), Freud says: 'What the artist aims at is to awaken in us the same mental constellation as that which in him produced the impetus to create.'

We find in Dilthey's philosophy (Hodges 1944) the concept *nach-erleben*. This word denotes for him our capacity to understand other people from their behaviour and expression. We intuitively reconstruct their mental and emotional states, we live after them; we re-live them. This process is, he says, often deeper than introspection can discover. His concept is, I think, equivalent to unconscious identification. I assume that this kind of unconscious reliving of the creator's state of mind is the foundation of all aesthetic pleasure.

To illustrate what I mean I will take as an example the case of classical tragedy. In a tragedy the hero commits a crime: the crime is fated, it is an 'innocent' crime, he is driven to it. Whatever the nature of the crime, the result is always complete destruction – parental figures and child figures alike are engulfed by it. That is, at whatever level the conflict starts – *Oedipus Rex*, for instance, states a genital conflict – in the end we arrive at a picture of the phantasies belonging to the earliest depressive position where all the objects are destroyed. What is the psychological mechanism of the listener's *nach-erleben*? As I see it, he makes two identifications. He identifies himself with the author, and the whole tragedy with the author's internal world. He identifies himself with the author while the latter is facing and expressing his depression. In a simplified way one can summarize the listener's reaction as follows: 'The author has, in his hatred, destroyed all his loved objects just as I have done, and like me he felt death and desolation inside him. Yet he can face it and he can make me face it, and despite the ruin and devastation we and the world around us survive. What is more, his objects, which have become evil and were destroyed, have been made alive again and have become immortal by his art. Out of all the chaos and destruction he has created a world which is whole, complete, and unified.'

It would appear, then, that two factors are essential to the excellence of tragedy: the unshrinking expression of the full horror of the depressive phantasy and the achieving of an impression of wholeness and harmony. The external form of classical tragedy is in complete contrast with its content. The formal modes of speech, the unities of time, place, and action, and the strictness and rigidity of the rules are all, I believe, an unconscious demonstration of the fact that order can emerge out of chaos. Without this formal harmony the depression of the audience would be aroused but not resolved. There can be no aesthetic pleasure without perfect form.[4]

In creating a tragedy, I suggest, the success of the artist depends on his being able fully to acknowledge and express his depressive phantasies and anxieties. In expressing them he does work similar to the work of mourning in that he internally re-creates a harmonious world which is projected into his work of art.

The reader identifies with the author through the medium of his work of art. In that way he re-experiences his own early depressive anxieties, and through identifying with the artist he experiences a successful mourning, re-establishes his own internal objects and his own internal world, and feels, therefore, reintegrated and enriched.

But is this experience specific to a work of art that is tragic, or is it an essential part of any aesthetic experience? I think I could generalize my argument. To do so I shall have to introduce the more usual terminology of aesthetics and restate my problems in new terms. The terms I need are *ugly* and *beautiful*. For Rickman, in his paper 'On the Nature of Ugliness and the Creative Impulse' (1940), the ugly is the destroyed, the incomplete object. For Ella Sharpe (1930) ugly means destroyed, arythmic, and connected with painful tension. I think both these views would be included if we say that ugliness is what expresses the state

of the internal world in depression. It includes tension, hatred, and its results –
the destruction of good and whole objects and their change into persecutory
fragments. Rickman, however, when he contrasts ugly and beautiful, seems
to equate the latter with what is aesthetically satisfying. With that I cannot agree.
Ugly and beautiful are two categories of aesthetic experience and, in certain
ways, they can be contrasted; but if beautiful is used as synonymous with
aesthetically satisfying, then its contradictory is not ugly, but unaesthetic, or
indifferent, or dull. Rickman says that we recoil from the ugly; my contention is
that it is a most important and necessary component of a satisfying aesthetic
experience. The concept of ugliness as one element in aesthetic satisfaction is
not uncommon in the tradition of philosophical aesthetics; it has been most
strikingly expressed, however, by the artists themselves. Rodin writes: 'We
call ugly that which is formless, unhealthy, which suggests illness, suffering,
destruction, which is contrary to regularity – the sign of health. We also call ugly
the immoral, the vicious, the criminal and all abnormality which brings evil – the
soul of the parricide, the traitor, the self-seeker. But let a great artist get hold of
this ugliness; immediately he transfigures it – with a touch of his magic wand he
makes it into beauty.'

What is beauty? Taking again the beautiful as but one of the categories of the
aesthetically satisfying, most writers agree that the main elements of the beautiful
– the whole, the complete, and the rhythmical – are in contrast with the ugly.
Among analytical writers, Rickman equates the beautiful with the whole object,
while Ella Sharpe considers beauty essentially as rhythm and equates it with the
experience of goodness in rhythmical sucking, satisfactory defecation, and sexual
intercourse. To this I should add rhythmical breathing and the rhythm of our
heartbeats. An undisturbed rhythm in a composed whole seems to correspond
to the state in which our inner world is at peace. Among nonanalytical writers,
Herbert Read comes to a similar conclusion when he says that what we find
rhythmical are simple arithmetical proportions which correspond to the way we
are built and our bodies work. But these elements of beauty are in themselves
insufficient. If they were enough we would find it most satisfactory to contemplate a circle or listen to a regular tattoo on a drum. I suggest that both beauty,
in the narrow sense of the word, and ugliness must be present for a full aesthetic
experience.

I would reword my attempt at analyzing the tragic in terms of ugliness and
beauty. Broadly speaking, in tragedy ugliness is the content – the complete ruin
and destruction – and beauty is the form. Ugliness is also an essential part of the
comic. The comic here is ugly in that, as in caricature, the overstressing of one or
two characteristics ruins the wholeness – the balance – of the character. Ugly and
tragic is also the defeat of the comic hero by the sane world. How near the comic
hero is to the tragic can be seen from the fact that outstanding comic heroes of past
ages are felt, at a later date, to be mainly tragic figures; few people today take
Shylock or Falstaff as figures of fun only; we are aware of the tragedy implied.
The difference between tragedy and comedy lies, then, in the comic writer's

attempt to disassociate himself from the tragedy of his hero, to feel superior to it in a kind of successful manic defence. But the manic defence is never complete; the original depression is still expressed and it must therefore have been to a large extent acknowledged and lived by the author. The audience relives depression, the fear of it, and the aggression against it which are expressed in a comedy and its final successful outcome.

It is easier to discover this pattern of overcoming depression in literature, with its explicit verbal content, than in other forms of art. The further away from literature the more difficult is the task. In music, for instance, we would have to study the introduction of discords, disharmonies, new disorders which are so invariably considered to be ugly before they are universally accepted. New art is considered difficult; it is resisted, misunderstood, treated with bitter hatred, contempt; or, on the other hand, it may be idealized to such an extent that the apparent admiration defies its aim and makes its object the butt of ridicule. These prevalent reactions of the public are, I think, manifestations of a manic defence against the depressive anxieties stirred by art. The artists find ever new ways of revealing a repressed and denied depression. The public use against it all their powers of defence until they find the courage to follow the new artist into the depths of his depression, and eventually to share his triumphs.

The idea that ugliness is an essential component of a complete experience seems to be true of the tragic, the comic, the realistic – in fact, of all the commonly accepted categories of the aesthetic except one. And this single exception is of great importance.

There is, undoubtedly, a category of art which shows to the greatest extent all the elements of beauty in the narrow sense of the word, and no apparent sign of ugliness; it is often called 'classical' beauty. The beauty of the Parthenon, of the Discobolos, is whole, rhythmical, undisturbed. But soulless imitations of beauty, 'pretty' creations, are also whole and rhythmical; yet they fail to stir and rouse anything but boredom. Thus classical beauty must have some other not immediately obvious element.

Returning to the concept of *nach-erleben*, of experiencing along with another, we may say that in order to move us deeply the artist must have embodied in his work some deep experience of his own. And all our analytical experience as well as the knowledge derived from other forms of art suggests that the deep experience must have been what we call, clinically, a depression, and that the stimulus to create such a perfect whole must have lain in the drive to overcome an unusually strong depression. If we consider what is commonly said about beauty by laymen, we find a confirmation of this conclusion. They say that complete beauty makes one both sad and happy at the same time, and that it is a purge for the soul – that it is awe-inspiring. Great artists themselves have been very much aware of the depression and terror embodied in works of classical beauty which are apparently so peaceful. When Faust goes in search of Helen, the perfect classical beauty, he has to face unnamed terrors, to go where there is no road:

Kein Weg! Ins Unbetretene
Nicht zu Betretende; ein Weg ins Unerbetene,
Nicht zu Erbittende.

He must face endless emptiness:

– Nichts Wirst du sehn in ewig leerer Ferne,
Den Schritt nicht horen den du tust,
Nichts Festes finden, wo du ruhst.[5]

Rilke writes: 'Beauty is nothing but the beginning of terror that we are still just able to bear.'

Thus to the sensitive onlooker, every work of beauty still embodies the terrifying experience of depression and death. Hanns Sachs, in 'Beauty, Life and Death' (1910), pays particular attention to the awesome aspect of beauty; he says the difficulty is not to understand beauty but to bear it, and he connects this terror with the very peacefulness of the perfect work of art. He calls it the static element; it is peaceful because it seems unchangeable, eternal. And it is terrifying because this eternal unchangeability is the expression of the death instinct – the static element opposed to life and change.

Following quite a different trend of thought I come to similar conclusions about the role of the death instinct in a work of art. Thus far my contention has been that a satisfactory work of art is achieved by a realization and sublimation of the depressive position, and that the effect on the audience is that they unconsciously relive the artist's experience and share his triumph of achievement and his final detachment. But to realize and symbolically express depression the artist must acknowledge the death instinct, both in its aggressive and self-destructive aspects, and accept the reality of death for the object and the self. One of the patients I described could not use symbols because of her failure to work through the depressive position; her failure clearly lay in her inability to accept and use her death instinct and to acknowledge death.

Restated in terms of instincts, ugliness – destruction – is the expression of the death instinct; beauty – the desire to unite into rhythms and wholes – is that of the life instinct. The achievement of the artist is in giving the fullest expression to the conflict and the union between the two.

This is a conclusion which Freud has brought out in two of his essays, though he did not generalize it as applicable to all art. One of these essays is that on Michelangelo's Moses (1914), where he clearly shows that the latent meaning of this work is the overcoming of wrath. The other essay is his analysis of the theme of the three caskets (1913). He shows there that in the choice between the three caskets, or three women, the final choice is always symbolic of death. He interprets Cordelia in *King Lear* as a symbol of death, and for him the solution of the play is Lear's final overcoming of the fear of death and his reconciliation to it. Freud writes: 'Thus man overcomes death, which in thought he has acknowledged. No greater triumph of wish fulfilment is conceivable' (p. 254).

All artists aim at immortality; their objects must not only be brought back to life, but that life must also be eternal. And of all human activities art comes nearest to achieving immortality; a great work of art is likely to escape destruction and oblivion.

It is tempting to suggest that this is so because in a great work of art the degree of denial of the death instinct is less than in any other human activity, that the death instinct is acknowledged, as fully as can be borne. It is expressed and curbed to the needs of the life instinct and creation.

Postscript 1980: aesthetics

Looking back on this paper, the first one I presented in the Society in 1947, although it was published much later, I still find myself in agreement with its main thesis, namely, that the essence of the aesthetic creation is a resolution of the central depressive situation and that the main factor in the aesthetic experience is the identification with this process. I should, however, now emphasize more the role of the idealization arising from the paranoid-schizoid position. I am in agreement here with Adrian Stokes (1965), who says that the artist seeks the precise point at which he can maintain simultaneously an ideal object merged with the self, and an object perceived as separate and independent, as in the depressive position.

I would also have liked to link my work with the paper of Elliot Jaques (1965) on the midlife crisis, and to describe in more detail the difference between a pre-midlife and a post-midlife crisis type of creativity. I think that before the midlife crisis the artist seeks more the ideal object, and that past the midlife crisis he is more in search of the re-creation of the object as seen in the depressive position.

Notes

1   For the description of the preceding phase of the development see Klein (1940) and Rosenfeld (1952).
2   This theme was later linked up with the Rumpelstiltskin theme of stealing the baby and the penis, but I cannot follow it up here.
3   I have given here only the transference meaning of the dream in order not to detract from my main theme. The transference situation was linked with past experiences of weaning, birth of the new baby, and the patient's failure in the past to be a 'good' mother to the new baby.
4   Roger Fry says: 'All the essential aesthetic quality has to do with pure form,' and I agree; but he adds later: 'The odd thing is that it is, apparently, dangerous for the artist to know about this.' Roger Fry feels that it is odd, I think, because of an inherent weakness of the formalist school he represents. The formalists discount the importance of emotional factors in art. According to Fry, art must be completely detached from emotions, all emotion is impurity, and the more the form gets freed from the emotional

content the nearer it is to the ideal. What the formalists ignore is that form as much as content is in itself in expression of unconscious emotion. What Fry, following Clive Bell, calls *significant form*, a term he confesses himself incapable of defining, is form expressing and embodying an unconscious emotional experience. The artist is not trying to produce pretty or even beautiful form; he is engaged on the most important task of re-creating his ruined internal world, and the resulting form will depend on how well he succeeds in his task.

5 [The Mephistopheles quotations are both from Goethe's *Faust*, Part Two, Act One, '*Finistere Galerie*' (Gloomy Hallway) – Ed.

> There is no way! Into the unpassable,
> No one has ever entered! A way to what cannot be asked for,
> No one has ever requested!
>
> There will be nothing to see in that empty distance,
> You will not hear the sound of your own steps,
> There will be no ground when you come to rest! *Ed.'s translation*]

References

Ehrenzweig, A. (1918) 'Unconscious Form-Creation in Art', *British Journal of Medical Psychology*, 21: 88–109.

Fairbairn, W.R.D. (1938) 'The Ultimate Basis of Aesthetic Experience', *British Journal of Psychology*, 29: 167–81.

Freud, Sigmund *The Standard Edition of the Complete Psychological Works of Sigmund Freud*, ed. and trans. James Strachey, London: Hogarth, 24 vols, 1953–74.

—— (1908) 'The Relation of the Poet to Day-Dreaming', SE, 9.

—— (1910) 'Leonardo da Vinci and a Memory of His Childhood', *SE*, 11.

—— (1911) 'Formulations Regarding the Two Principles of Mental Functioning', SE, 11.

—— (1913) 'The Theme of the Three Caskets' SE, 12.

—— (1914) 'The Moses of Michelangelo' SE, 12.

Fry, Roger (1920) *Vision and Design*, London: Chatto and Windus.

—— (1926) *Transformations*, London: Chatto and Windus.

Heimann, Paula (1942) 'A Contribution to the Problem of Sublimation and its Relation to Process of Internalization', *International Journal of Psycho-Analysis*, 23: 8–17.

Hodges, Herbert (1944) *Wilhelm Dilthey: An Introduction*, London: Routledge and Kegan Paul, 1969.

Jaques, Elliot (1965) 'Death and the Mid-Life Crisis', *International Journal of Psycho-Analysis*, 46: 502–14.

Jones, Ernest (1914) 'The Madonna's Conception through the Ear', *Papers in Applied Psycho-Analysis*, vol. 2, London: Hogarth, 1951, pp. 266–357.

Klein, Melanie (1929) 'Infantile Anxiety-Situations Reflected in a Work of Art and the Creative Impulse', *International Journal of Psycho-Analysis*, 10: 136–43; in Melanie Klein, *Contributions to Psycho-Analysis, 1921–1945*, London: Hogarth, 1948, pp. 227–35.

—— (1935) 'A Contribution to the Psychogenesis of Manic-Depressive States', *International Journal of Psycho-Analysis*, 16: 145–74; in Melanie Klein, *Contributions to Psycho-Analysis, 1921–1945*, London: Hogarth, 1948, pp. 282–310.

—— (1940) 'Mourning and its Relation to Manic-Depressive States', *International Journal of Psycho-Analysis*, 21: 125–53; in Melanie Klein, *Contributions to Psycho-Analysis, 1921–1945*, London: Hogarth, 1948, pp. 311–38.

Lee, H.B. (1939) 'A Critique of the Theory of Sublimation', *Psychiatry*, 2: 239–70.

—— (1940) 'A Theory Concerning Free Creation in the Inventive Arts', *Psychiatry*, 3: 229–93.

Listowel, Earl of (1933) *A Critical History of Modern Aesthetics*, London: Allen and Unwin.

Read, Herbert (1931) *The Meaning of Art*, London: Heinemann.

—— (1934) *Art and Society*, London: Heinemann.

Rickman, John (1940) 'On the Nature of Ugliness and the Creative Impulse', *International Journal of Psycho-Analysis*, 21: 294–313; in John Rickman, *Selected Contributions to Psychoanalysis*, New York: Basic Books, 1957, pp. 68–89.

Rosenfeld, Herbert (1952) 'Notes on the Psycho-Analysis of the Superego Conflict of an Acute Schizophrenic Patient', *International Journal of Psycho-Analysis*, 33: 111–31.

Sachs, Hanns (1910) 'Beauty, Life and Death', *American Imago*, 1: 81–133.

—— (1942) *The Creative Unconscious: Studies in the Psychoanalysis of Art*, Cambridge, Mass.: Sci-Art Publishers.

Sharpe, Ella (1930) 'Certain Aspects of Sublimation and Delusion', *International Journal of Psycho-Analysis*, 11: 12–23; in Ella Sharpe, *Collected Papers on Psycho-Analysis*, London: Hogarth, 1950, pp. 125–36.

—— (1935) 'Similar and Divergent Unconscious Determinants Underlying the Sublimations of Pure Art and Pure Science', *International Journal of Psycho-Analysis*, 16: 186–202; in Ella Sharpe, *Collected Papers on Psycho-Analysis*, London: Hogarth, 1950, pp. 137–54.

Stokes, Adrian (1965) *The Invitation in Art*, London: Tavistock.

Chapter 12

Death and literary authority
Marcel Proust and Melanie Klein

Leo Bersani

Editor's note:

One way to approach Leo Bersani's essay might be to read it as a bold and irreverent re-writing of Hanna Segal's 'A Psychoanalytic Approach to Aesthetics' (although Bersani does not mention Segal by name). Like Segal, Bersani couples Klein with Proust. But where Segal calls on Proust to both develop and consolidate Klein's theories of art and reparation, Bersani questions the nature of aesthetic authority itself. Bersani is interested in those moments in psychoanalytic theory when it unhouses its own categories. It is when psychoanalysis shifts its hermeneutic gears and begins to mimic the psychic processes that it pertains to describe that Bersani reveals it to be at its most radical (and troublesome). Bersani's virtuosity as a reader of psychoanalysis, particularly of Freud, is brilliantly exemplified in his classic study *The Freudian Body: Psychoanalysis and Art* (1986). What is distinctive about Bersani's reading of psychoanalysis is the way he transforms critique into polemic and questions our assumptions about culture and sexuality. This is exactly what his reading of Klein and Proust sets out to do. The essay was originally published as the first chapter to *The Culture of Redemption* (1990), in which Bersani presents a powerful critique of our belief in art's ability to redeem (or in Kleinian terms, repair) sexuality and history. Cultural forms, by this reading, are less a way of ennobling life (improving it by repeating it and so redeeming it) than an insidious downgrading of experience. Clearly Klein's reparative hypothesis is grist to the mill for this vision of art as a kind of 'annihilating salvation' (Bersani's words): just as Proust's *A la recherche du temps perdu* famously lays out a blueprint for the superior truths of aesthetic recollection. But for Bersani – and of course Proust – these redemptive strategies are only the beginning of the story. Closely following Proust's 'circular hermeneutics' Bersani discloses a more radical Proust – and a more radical Klein. Reading Klein's 1923 essay, 'Early Analysis,' Bersani uncovers a theory of sublimation which runs directly counter to what he sees as the more valorizing tendencies of her later work. In this paper, Bersani argues, Klein sketches out an erotics of identification and repetition in which sublimation is defined not, as in her later work, as a defensive attempt to repair damage done, but as a kind of non-referential (non-symbolizing and non-reparative) drive of sexual energy. One of the reasons why contemporary literary theory has tended to overlook Klein rests with the idea that her theories of art and symbolization are both too heavy-handed and too normative to be of any use to literary study. Attempts to counter that impression could do worse than to begin with Bersani's provocative re-reading. (LS)

What is the redemptive power of art? More fundamentally, what are the assumptions that make it seem natural to think of art as having such a power? In attempting to answer these questions, I will first be turning to Proust, who embodies perhaps more clearly—in a sense, even more crudely—than any other major artist a tendency to think of cultural symbolizations as essentially reparative. This tendency, which had already been sanctified as a more or less explicit dogma of modern high culture by Proust's time, persists in our own time as the enabling morality of a humanistic criticism. I will argue that the notion of art as salvaging somehow damaged experience has, furthermore, been served by psychoanalysis—more specifically, by a certain view of sublimation first proposed rather disconnectedly by Freud and later developed more coherently and forcefully by Melanie Klein. The psychoanalytic theory I refer to makes normative – both for an individual and for a culture – the mortuary aesthetic of *A la recherche du temps perdu*.

As everyone knows, involuntary memories play a crucial role in the Proustian narrator's discovery of his vocation as a writer. Let us begin with a somewhat untypical example of the genre, the passage in *Sodome et Gomorrhe* describing the 'resurrection' of Marcel's grandmother on the first evening of his second visit to Balbec. This passage reformulates the importance of memory for art in terms of another relation about which the theoretical passages concluding *Le temps retrouvé* will be at once prolific and evasive: the dependence of art on death.

This dependence is obliquely defined in two very different ways, and the difference is first pointed to by what the narrator describes as the painful contradiction inherent in his involuntary memory. On the one hand, the possession of others is possible only when they are dead; only then is nothing opposed to our image of them. Biological death accomplishes, or literalizes, the annihilation of others that Proust tirelessly proposes as the aim of our interest in others. 'The living reality' of his grandmother at the moment of involuntary memory is exactly equivalent to her ideal penetrability. At such moments, the narrator writes, nothing remains of past joy and past suffering other than 'the self that originally lived them.'[1] The posthumous possession of others is always an unprecedented self-possession.

And yet there is of course a real loss. It is, however, by no means certain that it is the grandmother herself who has been lost, since her death is seen primarily as having deprived Marcel of himself. When the narrator speaks of 'that contradiction of survival and annihilation so strangely intertwined within me (*cette contradiction si étrange de la survivance et du néant entre-croisés en moi*),' he means, first of all, that his grandmother has suddenly been resurrected in him and, second, that death has erased his image from her tenderness ('*un néant qui avait effacé mon image de cette tendresse*').[2] In a sense, then – and quite bizarrely – it is Marcel's grandmother who has survived her death and Marcel himself who has disappeared. Nothingness, as the narrator strikingly puts it, had made of his grandmother 'at the moment when I had found her again as in a mirror, a mere stranger whom chance had allowed to spend a few years with me . . . but to whom, before and after those years, I was and would be nothing' (2: 785–6; 2: 758–9). In these boxes of survival and nothingness placed one within the other, the living grandson sees an image of his grandmother contained within his own image; but her image – although it can now be nowhere but in him – no longer contains him. Hidden within this strangely specular relation to his grandmother's renewed presence is Marcel's own absence. The unprecedented self-possession I referred to is identical to an irremediable loss of self.

Who, finally, is that 'mere stranger' now seen for the first time? More significant, I think, than the posthumous porousness of the other is the fact that the grandmother is only now authentically *other*. It could perhaps be said that the only way we ever experience death (as distinct from dying) is in a change in the mode of a relation. Marcel's involuntary memory returns his grandmother to him as the *outside of thought*: that is, not as someone who can be desired or appropriated or dialectically related to, but simply as someone who existed beside him, a mere other presence in the world. A relation of desire has, it would seem, been replaced by a juxtaposition. This change is of course noted with despair, and yet it could also be said that Marcel now experiences his grandmother's death as a retroactive – and spectral – rediversification of the world. Desire in Proust works to reduce the world to a reflection of the desiring subject; death, however, would seem to be the condition for an escape from the self-repetitions initiated by desire and a restoring to the world of those differences that promoted anxious desire in the first place. From this perspective, death recreates (in, so to speak, reverse affectivity: pain is substituted for excitement) Marcel's exhilarated shock, frequently recorded in the early volumes, at discovering his own absence from the world.

Death experienced within an involuntary memory thus helps to define involuntary memory as a kind of death. For if such memories revive the past as nothing more than the self that lived it ('*le moi qui le vécut*'), they also effect, belatedly and retroactively, a radical separation of the self from the world. If, for example, the Madeleine resurrects a wholly internalized Combray, it also projects or throws forth from within that internalization a Combray of pure appearance, a Combray that persists phenomenally, from which all Marcel's past interests – from which Marcel himself – have been evacuated and to which a new relation must be invented. I want to approach the consequences for art of this contradiction by way of a long detour. Perhaps the most curious aspect of the passage from *Sodome et Gomorrhe* I have been discussing is the narrator's undecidable relation to it. There are two temporal perspectives in the passage (the moment of the memory at Balbec and the moment of writing) and three central terms (the painful *impression* itself, the *truth* to be extracted from that impression, and the role of *intelligence* in the extracting process). At the end of an extremely dense analysis of 'cette contradiction si étrange de la survivance et du néant entre-croisés en moi,' the narrator writes:

> I did not know whether I should one day distil a grain of truth from this painful and for the moment incomprehensible impression, but I knew that if I ever did . . . it could only be from such an impression and from none other, an impression at once so particular and so spontaneous, which had neither been traced by my intelligence nor attenuated by my pusillanimity, but which death itself, the sudden revelation of death, striking like a thunderbolt, had carved within me, along a supernatural and inhuman graph, in a double and mysterious furrow.
>
> (2: 786–7; 2: 759)

What can this mean? We might reasonably think that the few pages we have just read are the expression of any 'truth' which may have been contained within that past impression. The narrator has been moving easily – as he does throughout the novel – from certain interpretations of his experience (or, as he would say, certain truths) that appear to date from the time of the involuntary memory to reflections on the incident as he now writes about it. He had apparently already understood and suffered from the contradictory nature of his grandmother's 'resurrection,' while certain other thoughts presented as general laws are perhaps disengaged at the moment of writing. Thus the narrator's remark that 'the living reality' of the past 'does not exist for us until it has been recreated by our thought,' and the sentences in which, again using the present, he traces the relation between the 'perturbations of memory (*troubles de la mémoire*)' and 'the heart's intermittences (*les intermittences du coeur*)' bring a kind of interpretative closure *now* to Marcel's memory at Balbec (2: 783–4; 2: 756). But the status of these confidently formulated laws – obviously made with the aid of intelligence – is suddenly thrown into doubt by the claim that if he were one day to disengage some truth from his involuntary memory, it could only be from the 'particular' and 'spontaneous' impression itself, which had not, he adds, been traced by his intelligence. Furthermore, since it was in the past that he realized these preconditions of truth, this insight into that peculiar intersection of survival and nothingness – an insight also belonging to the past – cannot really be part of the desirable truth apparently still to come.

Will it ever come? And what is the relation to that truth of the text we have been reading? It is as if the narrator were making explicit here the ambiguous status of the entire Proustian text. I speak of an ambiguity that has led some of Proust's readers to raise the extremely peculiar question of whether or not the text we have is the one the narrator tells us, at the end of *Le temps retrouvé*, that he finally set out to write. It is the Proustian narrator himself who sows the seeds of that doubt by promoting, throughout the work, precisely the kind of undecidability we have located in the passage from *Sodome et Gomorrhe*. And his hesitation about whether the work he is writing is the work he has chosen to write can be traced to the effects, on the process of writing, of a conception of art as a kind of remedial completion of *life*.

If the narrator encourages the reader's doubt about whether this is the work he speaks of writing at the end of *Le temps retrouvé* he leaves us in even greater doubt about the relation of this work to his life. On the one hand, 'the function and the task of a writer,' as the narrator will conclude in *Le temps retrouvé*, 'are those of a translator' (3: 926; 3: 890). Art would be 'our real life, reality as we have felt or experienced it (*notre vraie vie, la réalité telle que nous l'avons sentie)*' (3: 915; 3: 881). Moved by what would appear to be the extreme purity of this referential aesthetic, the narrator even distrusts the element of work in art. In *A l'ombre des jeunes filles en fleur* he recalls wondering if 'the differences between one man's books and another's were not the result of their respective labours' – and if art would not thereby be mere artifice, or even deception (*'s'il n'y a pas dans tout cela un peu de feinte'*) – 'rather than the expression of a radical and essential difference between diverse personalities' (1: 591; 1: 549). And during the period of his love for Albertine in Paris, Marcel is 'troubled' by Wagner's *'habileté vulcanienne'*: 'if art is no more than that' – that is, superior craftsmanship, 'the result of industrious toil' – then 'it is no more real than life' and there is no reason to regret his lack of literary talent (3: 159; 3: 161–2). Art, then, is 'real' to the degree that it discovers and expresses a pre-existent truth; it is 'factitious' (the *'réel–factice'* opposition is Proust's) to the extent that it produces a 'truth' of its own, a truth derived from the conditions and constraints of literary performance.

But how are we to understand a translation more real than its original? Marcel's literary education culminates in the discovery that the only life worth living is life 'realized within the confines of a book (*réalisée dans un livre)*' (3: 1088; 3: 1032). Outside a book, that same life is both worthless and a source of suffering: hence the narrator's astonishing and relentless condemnation of his nonetheless meticulously recorded experience. If Marcel continuously reproaches himself for having friendships, for going into society, even for falling in love, it is, he suggests, because he should have been at home trying to get to the bottom of his impressions of friendship, society, and love. In the work of art, a certain type of representation of experience will operate both as an escape from the objects of representation and as a justification (retroactive, even posthumous) for having had any experiences at all. In Proust, art simultaneously erases, repeats, and redeems life. Literary repetition is an annihilating salvation.

It would be a simplification of this project to say of it, as Sartre has said of Flaubert, that for Proust art is a strategy of derealization. In *La recherche* the imaginary is considered as the mode in which life is most authentically realized: art is a kind of epistemological and moral surreality, the interpretation of sensations, as the narrator writes in *Le temps retrouvé*, as signs of laws and ideas. If the Proustian novel's relation to the Proustian narrator's experience is, however, necessarily and irremediably ambiguous, this is because Proust is continuously having to decide how to place phenomena within an essentializing version of them. The subject of the Proustian novel is the relation between truth and existence, and the ontological undecidability of all the events recorded in the novel reflects the problematic nature of that relation. In what mode do phenomena persist in the record of their essence? In a sense, *La recherche* moves towards a relatively simple answer to that question: in the later volumes, the phenomenal is more and more absorbed in the universally valid formula, the general law. The adequate formulation of a truth would make the representation of phenomena superfluous. But Proust is clearly reluctant to divorce truth entirely from the experience that it ultimately invalidates. His narrator therefore seeks to 'repeat' his experience in a way that will deprive it of any existential authority. The transcendence of phenomena depends on a certain discrediting of phenomena at the very moment of their representation.

As the major step in this manoeuvre, experience is divorced from a securely locatable subject of experience. Whose life is the narrative recording? The autobiographical 'I' *of La recherche* is not named until we are more than two thousand pages into the novel. Even then, only a first name is given in a dizzyingly hypothetical manner. The narrator is speaking of Albertine waking up in the bedroom of his Paris apartment: 'Then she would find her tongue and say: "My" or "My darling" followed by my Christian name, which, if we give the narrator the same name as the author of this book, would be (*eût fait*) "My Marcel" or "My darling Marcel"' (3: 69; 3: 75). This extraordinary violation of the convention according to which a fictional narrator cannot possibly 'know' the author of the novel in which he himself figures is nonetheless consistent with the destabilization of self initiated by the act of writing. *A la recherche du temps perdu* is a nonattributable autobiographical novel. The experience it records may, it is suggested, belong to Marcel Proust, or it may belong to a fictional character named Marcel, or it may belong to a fictional character not named Marcel. Or, finally, it may belong to no one at all. In *Le temps retrouvé* the narrator praises the modest heroism of the rich Larivière couple during World War I who, after their nephew's death at the front, come out of retirement to work fifteen hours a day, without wages, in his young widow's Parisian café. Theirs, we are told, is the only real name and the only real story in the entire work; everything else is fictive, everything else has been invented 'in accordance with the requirements of my theme (*selon les besoins de ma démonstration*)' (3: 876; 3: 846). If this is the case, and if we are to take the narrator's literary programme seriously, we would have a book of nearly unimaginable originality: a wholly invented translation. The translation of particular experience into general laws is conceivable and is not, properly speaking, an invention; much more difficult to conceive is an entirely fictive life that would nonetheless be the 'real life,' life as he felt or experienced it, of – whom? Is the narrator himself to be included among the 'invented' elements of his work? If the narrator is *not* to be thought of as his own invention, how do we locate, and what is the status of, a figure whose real life is 'remembered' entirely in fictive terms? How can the reality of the subject be distinguished from the wholly invented experience by which, after all, we know that subject?

One could say that the narrator momentarily steps outside the fictive relations he has invented for himself in order to pay tribute to the Larivière couple. One is, of course, even more tempted to appeal to biography in order to say that the tribute represents an unassimilated intrusion into the narrative of Proust himself. The passage is, however, less interesting as a strictly local puzzle or anomaly than as a crystallization of a more pervasive doubt in the novel. In *La recherche*, translation into art means departicularization, and this is the case even when particular people and events are being represented. It is as if the narrator – or Proust – had first of all abstracted his experience into general laws and then deduced another version of the particular from those laws, a kind of second-degree particularity of experience disengaged from existence. The narrator suggests something very much like this when he writes in *A l'ombre des jeunes filles en fleur*: 'Thus it is useless to observe customs, since one can deduce them from psychological laws' (1: 552; 1: 513). In *La recherche* the situation is somewhat more complicated, since it is the already fictive narrator – and not Proust the author – who speaks of having entirely invented a past for the purposes of his '*démonstration*.' Thus a fictive narrator's invented past would ultimately derive from that narrator's 'real' life – which of course means from an equally fictive life. The latter would, however, be a fiction that has not been invented; having been, as it were, bypassed in the move from the more or less verifiable real life of the author Marcel Proust to the narrator's invention of *his* life, it would have the remarkable referential status of a necessary origin that has never been realized, either biographically or novelistically.

Gilles Deleuze has compared Proustian essences to Leibnizian 'monads,' each of which expresses the world from a distinctive point of view. The world thus expressed, Deleuze writes, 'does not exist outside the subject expressing it, but it is expressed as the essence not of the subject but of Being, or of the region of Being which is revealed to the subject'.[3] Thus the '*morceau idéal*' of Bergotte is at once the most individual and the least particular aspect of Bergotte. It is an individuality somehow detached from the point of view of experience, a repetition or translation of Bergotte that is simultaneously wholly different from Bergotte. In art, the particular is resurrected as the individual; or, to put this another way, art in Proust is, at least ideally, *truth liberated from phenomena*.

What is, however, most striking about this programme in *La recherche* is that it is indissociable from the kinds of questions I have been raising – questions about the narrator's identity, about the invented or remembered nature of his recorded past, about whether this is the book the theory of which is given at the end of *Le temps retrouvé* and, to return to the question raised by the 'inter-mittences du coeur' passage from *Sodome et Gomorrhe* – about the degree to which the work we are reading is actually expressing those truths or essences that literature presumably disengages from experience. That is, Proust problematizes the very signs by which we might recognize the success of his narrator's literary enterprises. And in each case the problematization takes the form of an uncertainty, traced within the text itself, about whether experience has been sufficiently departicularized to qualify as truth. It is, moreover, as if this uncertainty were being expressed in relation to the particular itself – which would mean that the move into truth or essences – would not be necessarily, or even primarily, a generalizing move, but would require a *displaced repetition* of the particular.

We are meant to see the narrator in two quite different relations to each of the people and events he records: first, as Marcel knowing these people and living these events (in *La recherche*, this essentially means in relations of desire to them) and, second, as the narrator now writing about the first relation. The second relation is the only justification for the first one. Furthermore, it is a justification that, strictly speaking, requires no content: it is the narrator's present *position* that principally operates the reversal of value. And this position can be defined as the intrinsically superior one of death. 'All those men and women who had revealed some truth to me and who were now no more, appeared again before me, and it seemed as though they had lived a life which had profited only myself, as though they had died for me.' The narrator continues: 'A book is a huge cemetery in which, on the majority of the tombs, the names are erased and can no longer be read' (3: 939–40; 3: 902). The perspective of death permits the resurrection of others as redemptive truths. But, unlike the involuntary memory that resurrects Marcel's grandmother as a wholly other presence in the world – a presence that no longer contains Marcel and that he can no longer appropriate – the death evoked as a condition of art in *Le temps retrouvé* is the retrospective absorption of others into the narrator's 'monadic' point of view. *A la recherche du temps perdu* proposes death as a metaphor for the artist's relation to the world in two contrasting ways. On the one hand, the death of others definitively ejects or expels Marcel from their being and thereby recreates the world as difference. On the other, their death both ends all resistance to Marcel's voracious desire to appropriate them *and* allows him to reconstruct the objects of his desires as invulnerable truths. Experience destroys; art restores.

In what way is experience – or, more precisely, desire – destructive? Rather than attempt to answer my question directly, I will reformulate it in other contexts – thereby evoking the concentric circles of *La recherche* itself, in which each section is a mistaken yet illuminating replication and *approfondissement* of the preceding section. Proust's novel offers us the model for a circular, or non-narrative, criticism. Although *La recherche* proceeds narratively towards a conclusive vindication of Marcel's vocation as an artist in *Le temps retrouvé*, this classical movement towards a resolution and revelation is undermined as it takes place. Because the entire work is written after its own climax, the reader is implicitly invited to find the theoretical formulations of the final pages super-fluous: we should, ideally, be able to infer them from the work they inform from beginning to end. Suspense is promoted as a primary value of reading at the same time that the reader is encouraged *to read without suspense* – or, in other terms, to invent a motive for reading unsustained by a promise of epistemological gain. Everything is present from the start, and this is rendered thematically visible by the schematic treatment of all the major topics of *La recherche* (memory, nature, love, social life, art) in *Combray*. The subsequent sections of the novel, instead of adding anything radically new to what the early pages have already given us, provide a kind of mnemonic hermeneutics on the themes of the first volume. *La recherche* continues to repeat its own beginning with an increasingly bloated intelligibility. The rather simple chronological linearity of the novel is thus complicated by a movement of circular repetition – or, more exactly, by the simultaneously amplifying and replicative movement of concentric circles.

We may see in the tension between these two movements a structural analogue of Proust's conflicting views of the relation between phenomena and truth, or between experience and art. Is life always prior to the essences that art alone disengages? Or is art a certain type of repetition of the phenomenal itself, a repetition that, far from substituting truth for appearances, continuously re-presents appearances in order to test modes of interpretation freed from the constraints of anxious desire? If I now turn away from Proust in order, as it were, to repeat him psychoanalytically, this move can be taken as the procedural expression of my own interest in the possibility of a circular hermeneutics – that is, in the possibility of repetition as the occasion for revising the terms of our interest in the objects of our interpretations.

*

What is the place of sexuality in culture? Or, to put this question in Freudian terms, how are cultural activities 'invested' with sexual interests? In one of her first papers – the 1923 essay entitled 'Early Analysis' – Melanie Klein proposes what her later work compels us to recognize as some very non-Kleinian answers to these questions. The essay I refer to – based on three unpublished papers – is difficult and diffuse. The first half is an extremely dense theoretical discussion; the second half is a considerably more relaxed, and intellectually less interesting, case history. Klein begins with a therapeutically oriented discussion of the role of anxiety in the 'neurotic inhibitions of talent.'[4] The basis of such inhibitions is, as we might expect, 'a strong primary pleasure which had been repressed on account of its sexual character' (EA, p. 77). The analyst reverses the inhibiting mechanism by helping the patient to release, recognize, and work through the anxiety that the mechanism has 'bound' and thus to return to the original, anxiety-provoking pleasure. But now the pleasure can be enjoyed: 'By successful removal of the inhibition, I do not simply mean that the inhibitions as such should be diminished or removed, but that the analysis should succeed in reinstating the primary pleasure of the activity'(EA, p. 78). This local conclusion on the paper's second page is extremely important, for it raises questions that will lead to the most original moments in the discussion. There is apparently a nonproblematic, non-neurotic, sexualizing of ego interests – of those 'talents' referred to in the essay's first sentence. The patient's analysis ends not with a separation of libidinal tendencies from ego activities, but rather with a recognition of their compatibility. In other words, the nonsexual can be sexualized in an analytically irreducible way: therapy ends here, and there is nothing more to be interpreted.

How has this happened? After a couple of pages of following Freud on the question of the repression of affects and their transformation into anxiety, Klein comes back to the mechanism of inhibition as a potentially healthy mode of binding and discharging anxiety. Such apparently nonneurotic inhibitions imply, Klein writes, 'that a certain quantity of anxiety had been taken up by an ego-tendency which already had a previous libidinal cathexis' (EA, p. 81). Thus the argument returns – in different terms – to the 'primary' investment of ego activities with sexual pleasure. The so-called nonneurotic inhibition leans on an already established sexualizing of ego interests. Klein asserts that priority when, several pages later, she writes: 'We may suppose that for a sublimation to be inhibited it must have actually come into existence as a sublimation' (EA, p. 90). The crucial notion of sublimation had entered the argument almost immediately after the sentence about anxiety's having been taken up by ego tendencies with 'previous libidinal cathexis,' and in the first appearance of the concept Klein equates 'the capacity to sublimate' with 'the capacity to employ superfluous libido [before, it is implied, either fixation or repression] in a cathexis of ego-tendencies' (EA, p. 81).[5]

A few pages later, in a paragraph of great originality that somewhat perversely manages to present itself as a summary of the theories of four other analysts (Hans Sperber, Sandor Ferenczi, Ernest Jones and Freud), Klein discusses the origin of those libidinally invested ego tendencies that, by 'taking up' the anxiety connected to sexual pleasures, help to produce inhibitions of 'normal' rather than 'neurotic' intensity. What she describes is a movement from identification to symbolism, and the description is particularly interesting in view of the very different ways in which identification is defined in her later work. Here identifi-cation would appear to be the exact opposite of object relationships; it is the activity of what might be called an appetitive narcissism. The first identifications in this process take place on the child's own body; referring to speculations made by Freud and Ferenczi, Klein speaks of equivalences that the child sees 'in the upper part of its body for each affectively important detail of the lower part'(EA, p. 85). Identification thus works here as an extension of regions of pleasure: both the child's own body and the world of objects are tested for their capacity to repeat certain sensations, to generalize originally local sensations. Furthermore, in both identification and the displacement of libido to new objects and ego activities (a displacement that constitutes symbol formation), it is, for Klein, the identification itself that produces pleasure and not, as Jones argues, a prior 'similitude of pleasurable tone or interest' that would be the precondition for comparisons and identifications (EA, p. 85). 'Objects and activities,' she writes, 'not in themselves sources of pleasure, become so through this identification, a sexual pleasure being displaced onto them' (EA, p. 85).

Now when Klein gives examples of symbol formation, she actually seems to be describing symbolic *symptom* formation: that is, the choice of certain objects and ego activities because of their resemblance to the repressed memories and fantasies. In this view, the symbolizing process would be nothing more than a compulsive substitute for the frightening or forbidden original pleasures. It is here that the originality of Klein's argument risks being dissipated as sublimation once again begins to look like a specialized branch of symptomatology. This blurring of definitions has of course occurred frequently in the history of psychoanalytic theory. Freud himself left us no sustained analysis of sublimation, and his own discussions of literature and the visual arts tend to stress either the compensatory or the symptomatic nature of art. Not only do the mechanisms of sublimation often seem indistinguishable from those of repression and symptom formation in much psychoanalytic writing; the work of art is often 'treated' – interpreted and, one might almost say, cured – as if it were little more than a socialized symptom. It is therefore all the more interesting to see Klein's attempt in 'Early Analysis' to locate the specificity of a sublimating mechanism. Perhaps the most crucial factor in this effort is her assumption of a certain quantity of 'superfluous' or 'suspended' libido. She speaks, for example, of 'the ability to hold libido in a state of suspension' as a 'contributing factor' to the capacity to sublimate (EA, p. 87). It is as if the history of an individual's sexuality included a moment of significant uncertainty about the fate of sexual energy. Or, in other terms, it is as if sexual excitement exceeded the representations attached to it and therefore became greedily, even promiscuously, available to *other* scenes and *other* activities. And the displacement of libido onto other object and ego activities can be called symbol formation only if we specify that these objects and activities *act symbolically without symbolizing anything external to them.*

Only if we see her argument moving in this direction can we understand Klein's surprising remark that when 'pleasurable situations, actually experienced or phantasized' are 'given play in an ego-tendency . . . the fixations are divested of their sexual character' (EA, pp. 87–8). What can this mean except that the ego tendencies in question can no longer be considered 'symbolic' in the sense in which Klein – like most analysts – usually understands that word? We would have a nonallusive or nonreferential symbol. In sublimation, ego activities become 'symbols' in the sense that the most diverse cultural activities 'symbolize' the libidinal energy with which they are invested. We would not have a symbol that merely participates in the nature of an extrinsic symbolized object or activity (as, to use one of Klein's own examples, 'athletic movements of all kinds stand for penetrating into the mother' [EA, p. 86]). Rather, forms of culture would symbolize nothing more than that which is already contained within them: the sexual energy that thereby 'acts as the stimulus and driving force of talent' (EA, p. 88). Thus the most varied ego interests would represent symbolically not specific sexual fantasies but the very process by which human interests and behaviour are *sexually moved*. From this perspective, sublimation can no longer be described (as it usually has been) in terms of a drive whose aim has been changed or displaced, for the drive in question would be, precisely, an aimless one, a kind of floating signifier of sexual energy. Sublimation would describe the fate of sexual energies detached from sexual desires.

*

But the view of sublimation as coextensive with sexuality occupies only a marginal place in the development of Kleinian theory. 'From the beginning of my psychoanalytic work,' Klein wrote in 1948, 'my interest was focused on anxiety and its causation, and this brought me nearer to the understanding of the relation between aggression and anxiety.'[6] In effect, during more than forty years of analytic practice and speculation, Klein elaborated the most radical – at once the most compelling and the most implausible – theory regarding infantile anxiety and aggression in the history of psychoanalysis. I will assume a certain familiarity with the broad outlines of this theory. Klein divides the first year of human life into two periods, or 'positions,' the first dominated by anxiety over external and internal threats to the preservation of the ego (the 'paranoid-schizoid position') and the second characterized principally by anxiety about dangers felt to threaten the loved parent as a result of the infant's fantasized aggressions (the 'depressive position'). Also crucial are the notion of a defensive mechanism preceding repression, a mechanism that would involve the splitting of the introjected object into a good one and a bad one; the contention that Oedipal conflicts and the development of a superego take place much earlier than Freud thought; finally, the fundamental argument – on which everything else depends – about the importance of fantasy from almost the very beginning of life. If we accept the argument about fantasy, then we should also recognize that Klein's scenarios of infantile violence, for all their apparent extravagance, rigorously and brilliantly spell out the consequences for our object relations of those destructive desires that Freud had already associated with infantile sexuality. Klein traces the history of the infant's attempts to deal with the anxieties engendered by a sexuality that is *born as aggression*. This history begins at birth. A complex nonverbal syntax of fantasmatic introjections and projections constitutes the infantile ego's defences against internal and external bad objects, against, perhaps most profoundly, its own impulses to destroy both itself and the objects it loves.

Sublimation becomes, in this view, the infant's most sophisticated defence against its own aggressions. The awesome nature of this defensive enterprise can be understood from the following description in the essay 'The Early Development of Conscience in the Child':

In attacking its mother's inside . . . the child is attacking a great number of objects, and is embarking on a course which is fraught with consequences. The womb first stands for the world; and the child originally approaches this world with desires to attack and destroy it, and is therefore prepared from the outset to view the real, external world as more or less hostile to itself, and peopled with objects ready to make attacks upon it. Its belief that in thus attacking its mother's body it has also attacked its father and its brothers and sisters, and, in a wider sense the whole world, is, in my experience, one of the underlying causes of its sense of guilt, and of the development of its social and moral feelings in general. For when the excessive severity of the super-ego has become somewhat lessened, its visitations upon the ego on account of those imaginary attacks induce feelings of guilt which arouse strong tendencies in the child to make good the imaginary damage it has done to its objects. And now the individual content and details of its destructive phantasies help to determine the development of its sublimations, which indirectly subserve its restitutive tendencies, or to produce even more direct desires to help other people.[7]

Sublimations have now become symbolic reparations, and in the light of the new concept Klein has begun to modify the entire process outlined in 'Early Analysis.' In a 1930 reference to that essay Klein, speaking once again of Ferenczi's and Jones's notions of identification and symbol formation, writes: 'I can now add to what I said then . . . and state that, side by side with the libidinal interest, it is the anxiety arising from the phase that I have described [of 'excessive sadism' towards the mother] which sets going the mechanism of identification.' From this point on, the emphasis is on identification not as an attempted repetition of pleasure but as an attempted flight from anxiety. The child conceives a dread of the organs it wishes to destroy (Klein mentions 'penis, vagina, breasts'), and 'this anxiety contributes to make him equate the organs in question with other things; owing to this equation these in their turn become objects of anxiety, and so he is impelled constantly to make other and new equations, which form the basis of his interest in the new objects and of symbolism.' In this way, Klein concludes, 'not only does symbolism come to be the foundation of all phantasy and sublimation, but, more than that, it is the basis of the subject's relation to the outside world and to reality in general.' Generalized anxiety has more or less replaced generalized libidinal interest. More precisely, symbolism deflects anxiety by bringing 'into phantasy the sadistic relation to the mother's body.'[8] This process will be described in somewhat more positive terms in subsequent formulations (Klein will assert that love for the first objects must be maintained in successful sublimations), but even then symbols remain 'substitute objects.' That is, whatever the distribution of anxiety and love may be in the move from the mother's body and the child's fantasized contacts with her body, to other objects and other activities, the latter have now become, in Kleinian theory, *restored versions* of the former.

In what sense can these new relations properly be called object relations? In the sublimating process outlined in 'Early Analysis,' libidinalized ego interests are not substitutes for some original (but now repressed) pleasure. In that version of sublimation, sexuality provides the energy of sublimating interests without defining their terms. We would have, as I have suggested, a nonallusive or non-referential version of sexualized mental activities; as a result, the sexualization of those activities could be thought of as a heightening rather than as a blurring of their specificity. But from the perspective of Klein's later theory of sublimation, the ego's 'new' object relations are, by definition, new relations to old fantasy objects. Originally the ego is involved in a relation to a real other body (the mother's) but, curiously enough, as the ego develops, its relations become more spectral or fantasmatic. The objects and interests that symbolically represent the subject's early relation to the world of objects are restitutive repetitions of those early relations, which means that they fantasmatically recreate what was already a fantasmatic remodelling of the world. These new sublimations are, as it were, at two removes from any real objects; they are fantasy reparations of fantasy destructions.

We can see the basis for a return to Proust in this psychoanalytic echo of the Proustian notion of art as a redemptive replication of damaged or worthless experience: in both cases, sublimations integrate, unify, and restore. But this restorative activity would make no sense if it were not being performed on earlier or original experience. The very function of art in Proust would be threatened if it introduced us to a world of authentic difference: in an aesthetic of reparation the artist's life – a life at once 'translated' and made 'more real' – is the only legitimate subject of art. Klein herself points to the solipsistic nature of this operation when, in 'A Contribution to the Psychogenesis of Manic-Depressive States,' she traces 'the desire for perfection' to 'the depressive anxiety of dis-integration, which is thus of great importance in all sublimations. She speaks of patients who have 'a beautiful picture of the mother, but one which was felt to be a *picture* of her only, not her real self. The real object was felt to be unattractive – really an injured, incurable and therefore dreaded person.'[9] What is restored therefore never existed; the 'perfect' object is nothing more than a function of the attacked object. And this is by no means true only of disturbed or neurotic patients. Insofar as the process of idealization 'is derived from the need to be protected from persecuting objects, it is a method of defence against anxiety.'[10] Excessive idealization denotes that persecution is the main driving force,[11] but the logic of Kleinian theory would, I think, allow us to rephrase this as: 'Some degree of persecution is always the motivating force of any degree of idealization.' If the sublimated object is by definition an idealized object – both a mental construct and a 'better' (repaired and made whole) version of an originally dangerous, injured, and fragmented object – we can also say that sublimation is disguised as transcendence.[12] Intellectually valuable pursuits and aesthetically pleasing objects are, in this view, disguised repetitions of an infantile defence against infantile aggressions.

My aim is neither to deny nor to defend the validity of this theory of sublimation. It may in fact be the case, as Jean Laplanche has suggested, that sublimation has two quite different modes of operation: one corresponding to what Klein described in 'Early Analysis' as the investment of ego interests with a kind of floating or suspended sexual energy, and the other corresponding to the appropriation of the entire cultural field either as 'substitute objects' for the desired and feared objects or as a repository of more or less socially useful activities in which the aims of sexuality can be symbolically deflected.[13] Significantly, a theoretical shift or hesitation analogous to Klein's can also be located in Freud. It could be shown, for example, that while proposing in the first chapter of his essay on Leonardo da Vinci a view of sublimation very much like the one outlined in 'Early Analysis,' Freud nonetheless goes on to treat Leonardo's work as psychologically compensatory and symptomatic. Indeed, far from pursuing a concept of sublimation as an appropriation and elaboration of sexual impulses, Freud will come to consider sublimation as one of the desexualizing activities of the ego – an activity that, furthermore, makes the ego particularly vulnerable to the death instinct. This shift, I think, must be understood in connection with the development of a theory of the ego as itself constituted by a partially desexualizing process of identification with lost or abandoned love objects. From the point of view of the tripartite systemic view of the mind elaborated in *The Ego and the Id* (1923), sublimation would be a relation to objects that is structurally determined by the already established relations among those internalized and lost objects which make up an ego and a superego.[14]

In Freud, and particularly in Klein, the kinds of spectral repetitions on which art in Proust seems to depend are presented as a goal of normative development. What I have wished to suggest is that such theories of the restitutive or redemptive power of cultural forms and activities are themselves symptomatic versions of the very process they purport to explain. Both this process and its theoretical legitimations give us extraordinarily diminished views of both our sexuality and our cultural imagination. The forms of culture become transparent and – at least from an interpretive point of view – dismissible: they are, ultimately, regressive attempts to make up for failed experience. And the fragmenting and destructive aspects of sexuality gain the ambiguous dignity of haunting the invisible depths of all human activity. Sexuality is consecrated as violence by virtue of the very definition of culture as an unceasing effort to make life whole, to repair a world attacked by desire. A fundamentally meaningless culture thus ennobles gravely damaged experience. Or, to put this in other terms, art redeems the catastrophe of history.[15] To play this role, art must preserve what might be called a moral monumentality – a requirement that explains, I believe, much of the mistrust in the modern period of precisely those modern works that have more or less violently rejected any such edifying and petrifying functions. Claims for the high morality of art may conceal a deep horror of life. And yet nothing perhaps is more frivolous than that horror, since it carries within it the conviction that, because of the achievements of culture, the disasters of history somehow do not matter. Everything can be made up, can be made over again, and the absolute singularity of human experience – the source of both its tragedy and its beauty – is thus dissipated in the trivializing nobility of a redemption through art.

*

What *are* – to draw a final interpretive circle – the dangers of desire in Proust? Let us first of all acknowledge the outlines of a novel of *happy* desire in *La recherche*, of a desire that exuberantly dismembers its objects. There is a Baudelairean mobility of desire in Proust, an extravagant excess of desirous fantasy over a presumed original object of desire. Like Baudelaire, the Proustian narrator shows desire cutting persons into bits and pieces, happily transforming them into partial objects. Perhaps no volume is more abundant than *A l'ombre des jeunes filles en fleur* in what might be called the appetitive metonymies of desire, the simultaneous reduction and enrichment of Albertine and her friends through those extrahuman associations by which, for example, they are metamorphosed into stems of roses profiled against the sea. If Marcel's desires here are, as he claims, never for persons ('The most exclusive love for a person is always a love for something else' [1: 891; 1: 833), it is because those desires are too impatient for any such psychologically constitutive and reflective activity. Indeed, the constitution of persons is linked to the emergence of a novel of *un*happy desire, a novel that depends, we might say, on Marcel's misreading of the otherness inherent in desire. Desire becomes identical to anxiety as soon as Marcel begins to understand the disappearance of the object not as a function of the energy of his desire but rather as the consequence of an evil intention on the part of the other. Thus desire's mobility is interpreted paranoiacally: the other has a secret, and that secret is itself a desire excluding Marcel. Significantly, it is now that the other is reconstituted as a personality – as a psychological individual who can make Marcel suffer. Thus what would appear to be a humanizing of the other – the transformation of Albertine from a 'moment' or unit in the metonymic chain of desires into a young girl with a particular history and particular desires – is actually a tactic of intended mastery over the other. Only as a person can Albertine perhaps be penetrated and made to suffer; the desexualization of desire and the invention of character are, in Proust, the preconditions for a ruthless if futile effort to absorb the other.

The most radical manifestation of this effort is of course Marcel's imprisonment of Albertine in his Paris apartment. The motive for the imprisonment, recorded in the remarkable final pages of *Sodome et Gomorrhe*, is the discovery that Albertine is a friend of Mlle Vinteuil and of her female lover. We return once again to an involuntary memory, this time to the most painful one of all: Albertine's revelation catapults Marcel back to the lesbian scene between those two young women he had witnessed years before through the window of Vinteuil's home at Montjouvain. Once he feels convinced of Albertine's lesbianism, the only truthful way to portray her relation to him would be 'to place Albertine, not at a certain distance from me, but inside me' (2: 1154; 2: 1116). What is this internalized yet impenetrable otherness?

To repeat the psychological law I just quoted: 'The most exclusive love for a person is always the love of something else.' If the narrator occasionally encourages us to understand this as a formulation of desire's mobility (to desire Albertine is to desire a certain type of seascape), it can also be taken to summarize the novel's more frequent demonstrations of desire's fixity. A certain resemblance among the women we love, the narrator writes, can be traced to 'the fixity of our own temperament'; the different loved ones are nothing more than a product of that temperament, 'an image, an inverted projection, a negative of our sensibility' (1: 955; 1: 894). Is it possible, then, to see one's own temperament or sensibility apart from these alien images of desire? The narrator's discovery of repetition in desire (of similarities among the women he pursues) leads him to a question about himself analogous to the one we have seen him ask about others. Jealousy of the other is the paranoid interpretation of desire's mobility. But, towards the end of *La prisonnière*, the narrator writes: 'As there is no knowledge, one might almost say that there is no jealousy, save of oneself' (3: 392–3; 3: 386), which suggests that the withheld secret Marcel anxiously pursues in others may be the projected secret, the fantasy formula, of his own desires.

The most accurate sexual metaphor for a hopeless pursuit of one's own desire is undoubtedly the heterosexual's jealousy of homosexuality *in the other sex*. I spoke of Albertine's sudden displacement from outside Marcel to inside Marcel as the internalization of an impenetrable otherness. I should now refine this formula: first of all, it is her inwardness that Marcel has internalized. The Albertine now making him suffer within himself is not the body that made an excited Marcel move from her to the sea but, instead, the desiring Albertine, the girl who could give Marcel the key to her desires by letting him hear 'the strange sound of her pleasure *(le son inconnu de sa jouissance)*' (2: 1154; 2: 1117). This internalized interiority of otherness is, for Marcel, the experienced otherness of his own interiority. Albertine's lesbianism represents a nearly inconceivable yet inescapable identity of sameness and otherness in Marcel's desires; lesbianism is a relation of sameness that Marcel is condemned to see as an irreducibly unknowable otherness. He shares Albertine's love for women, but not her point of view: from what perspective of anticipated pleasures does she seek out bodies in which she will find reminders of her own? Thus in the final pages of *Sodome et Gomorrhe* the banal thematization of homosexuality in the essay that opens the volume – a thematization at once sentimental and reductive – is brushed aside (as is the secondary and, in a sense, merely anecdotal question of 'sexual preference') by an extraordinary reflection on what might be called the necessity of homosexuality in a universal heterosexual relation of all human subjects to their own desires.

The last pages of *Sodome et Gomorrhe* depict several agitated displacements. Marcel is thrown back to the scene at Montjouvain and to the anguish of the *drame du coucher* at Combray; Albertine moves from somewhere outside Marcel to somewhere within him; and, in an echo of the passage we began by considering, Marcel's mother, as she enters his hotel room at dawn, resembles *her* mother so strongly that Marcel momentarily wonders if his grandmother has been 'resurrected.' These displacements and metamorphoses bring us back to what has always been a central question in *La recherche*: how does one thing evoke another? Or, more fundamentally, what are the modes of mobility in consciousness? The Proustian protagonist is always asking questions about what lies behind phenomena. There is a more or less happy version of this movement at Combray, in Marcel's anticipation that the spectacles of nature will 'open up' and reveal 'the secret of truth and of beauty' behind them. But the final pages of *Sodome et Gomorrhe* introduce us to the anguish of transcendence: 'Behind Albertine,' the narrator writes, 'I no longer saw the blue mountains of the sea, but the room at Montjouvain where she was falling into the arms of Mlle Vinteuil with that laugh in which she gave utterance, as it were, to the strange sound of her pleasure' (2: 1154; 2:1117).

The narrator conceives of both the happy and the unhappy examples of this movement as leading to a kind of truth: to the essences behind natural phenomena, to the presumed reality of Albertine's desires. But *Sodome et Gomorrhe* suggests that the truth behind appearances may be nothing more than a degraded version of appearances, a kind of shadowy simulacrum. The spectralizing effect on reality of this movement into truth – of this essentializing or antiphenomenal movement – is obliquely indicated by the narrator's description, on the last page of *Sodome et Gomorrhe*, of the dawn as a kind of abstract or unreal sunset. Looking out of his window at the end of the sleepless night following Albertine's revelation, Marcel finds, in the new day, reminders of evening: both in the sight of the woods that he and Albertine, after a late afternoon nap, would often leave at sunset, and in the spectacle of boats that Marcel had frequently seen bathed in the oblique light of sunset as they returned to harbour in the evening and that are now illuminated by the slanting rays of the rising sun. Thus dawn evokes dusk, but dusk perceived as 'an imaginary scene, chilling and deserted, a pure evocation of a sunset which did not rest, as at evening, upon the sequence of the hours of the day which I was accustomed to see precede it, detached, interpolated, more insubstantial even than the horrible image of Montjouvain which it did not succeed in cancelling, covering, concealing – a poetical, vain image of memory and dreams' (2:1168; 2:1130). In the sickening inconsistency of this false sameness, we are far from the presumed Proustian ecstasy of metaphorical equivalents. Here that trembling of surfaces – often the sign of a revelatory intrusion of essences and of temporal depths into the world of perceived phenomena – is repeated as a kind of contamination of nature itself by Marcel's wilful and anguished pursuit of the truth of desire, of desire reduced to its essential formula. The perception of a certain type of light common to dawn and dusk is experienced as the nausea of inhabiting the desert of metaphorical essences, and it provokes in Marcel a nostalgia for the 'impurities' of temporal sequences and contexts.

I propose that we consider this scene as an unintended emblem of an aesthetic of art as truth divorced from phenomena, a truth seen here as merely an evocative sameness, an exact yet alien repetition of phenomena. In the myth of art as both a translation of life and as more real or more essential than life, the imaginary adheres to the real not in order to impart an existential authority or legitimacy to art, but instead to reproduce the real without any such authority, to demonstrate the superiority of the image to the model. And yet, precisely because of this adherence, the 'substitute objects' of art continuously remind us of the objects they are meant to annihilate or transcend; what purports to be an essentializing repetition turns out to be the symbolic reminder, the symbolic symptom, of phenomena at once erased and indelible.

And yet, as in Klein, we have seen hints in Proust of a quite different view of the sublimating activity of art. I have spoken of the involuntary memory, that resurrects Marcel's grandmother as possibly, and paradoxically, inaugurating a presence at last freed from Marcel's appropriation of that presence, and I have referred to the appetitive metonymies of desire in *A l'ombre des jeunes filles en fleur*. If consciousness in Proust seeks most frequently to go behind objects, there is also a move – wholly different in its consequences – *to the side of* objects. In the passage we have been considering from *Sodome et Gomorrhe*, the encouragement to make the latter move comes from an unexpected source. In order to distract Marcel from his suffering, and to keep him from losing 'the benefit of a spectacle which [his] grandmother used to regret that [he] never watched,' his mother points to the window (2: 1167; 2: 1129). But while she thus encourages a lateral mobility away from her and from the hotel room and towards the sea, the beach, the sunrise, Marcel sees *behind* the sea, the beach, and the sunrise the spectacle of Albertine at Montjouvain with Mlle Vinteuil. However little Marcel appears to attend to it, we may nonetheless consider the mother's gesture as an instructive reminder of the power of appearances to defeat what may be imagined to lie 'behind' them. Or, to put this in terms I have already used, we could say that Marcel's mother seeks to distract him from his hallucinated transcendence of phenomena and thereby to point, ultimately, to *the possibility of pursuing not an art of truth divorced from experience, but of phenomena liberated from the obsession with truth.*

Still the substance of the very passage in which this possibility is raised appears to preclude it. Not only does Marcel see Montjouvain behind the spectacle of sea and sun; more fundamentally, the rising sun becomes a lurid metaphor for Marcel's future inability *not* to see behind such spectacles, for the reduction of the world to a monotonous and ineluctable reflection of his suffering:

> And thinking of all the indifferent landscapes which were about to be lit up and which, only yesterday, would have filled me simply with the desire to visit them, I could not repress a sob when, with a gesture of oblation mechanically performed and symbolizing, in my eyes, the bloody sacrifice which I was about to have to make of all joy, every morning, until the end of my life, a solemn renewal, celebrated as each day dawned, of my daily

grief and of the blood from my wound, the golden egg of the sun, as though propelled by the rupture of equilibrium brought about at the moment of coagulation by a change of density, barbed with tongues of flame as in a painting, burst through the curtain behind which one had sensed it quivering for a moment, ready to appear on the scene and to spring forward, and whose mysterious frozen purple it annihilated in a flood of light (*creva d'un bond le rideau derrière lequel on le sentait depuis un moment frémissant et prêt à entrer en scène et à s'élancer, et dont il effaça sous des flots de lumière la pourpre mystérieuse et figée*).

(2:1166; 2:1128)

'The bloody sacrifice of all joy' that Marcel sees symbolized in the spectacle of the sunlight bursting into his room is the sacrifice of the spectacle itself. It is the sacrifice of the pleasure he had earlier known of anticipating scenes from which he is absent, landscapes beneficently resistant to his need to find himself in them. These waves of light symbolize their own pathetic availability to the symbolic imagination.

But the narrator's account of that past moment partially defeats its symbolic content: its literary reformulation helps to *desymbolize* it. The sentence I have quoted reinstates lost appearances. Far from being erased in the burst of sunlight, '*la pourpre mystérieuse et figée*' of the curtain is – verbally – highlighted. Placed at the end of this long sentence in which the skeletal structure has itself been nearly buried by all the modifying phrases and clauses, the curtain negates its own disappearance and appears – climactically and triumphantly (if also mistakenly) – as the strongest presence of the remembered scene. Syntactic resources operating independently of the impulse to symbolize 'save' the purple curtain both from being erased by the sun's golden light *and* from having that luminous erasure interpreted as a mere symbol of Marcel's pain. Like the resurrections of involuntary memory, the return to the past in literature means a certain loss of Marcel as an actor in that past and results in an unprecedented visibility of past appearances. The death of the past is also a liberation from the constraints of anxious desire, constraints that threatened to erase the phenomenal diversity of the world from the field of Marcel's troubled vision.

Thus the move to art in *La recherche* is not only an annihilating and redemptive replication of experience; it also makes possible a kind of post-humous responsiveness to surfaces, a redefining enactment of Marcel's interest in the world. From this perspective, art would be our 'real life' not in the sense of an essentializing version of experience, but rather as a first or original (but originally missed) contact with phenomena. *The reappearance of the world* in Marcel's book is perhaps anticipated by his mother's pointing to a spectacle that her son will take in only when he gives it back to the world, this time as literature. In a final, Kleinian version of that maternal lesson – a version faithful to Proust's unsophisticated and salutary insistence (already formulated by the grandmother in *Combray*) that consciousness *profit* from art (that the only just criticism is a moral criticism) – let us say that the occasions of our interest in reality far exceed the range of our symbolic use of the real to rewrite a history of anxious desire. Furthermore, for Marcel – but perhaps not only for Marcel – to desymbolize reality may be the precondition for re-eroticizing reality.

Notes

1 Marcel Proust, *Remembrance of Things Past*, trans. C.K. Scott Moncrieff and Terence Kilmartin; and Andreas Mayor, 3 vols (London: Chatto and Windus, 1981) 2: 783–4. The original French is from Proust, *A la recherche du temps perdu*, eds Pierre Clarac and André Ferré, 3 vols (Paris: Gallimard, 1954) 2: 756–7. All further references to this work (the translation and the original in that order) are included in the text.

2 Moncrieff and Kilmartin translate this phrase as 'an annihilation that had effaced my image of that tenderness.' My own translation – somewhat less probable grammatically – is, as it were, solicited by my interpretation of the entire passage and more specifically by the narrator's remark, quoted next in my text, that he 'was and would be nothing' both 'before and after' the death of that 'mere stranger' his grandmother had now become (2:785; 2:115).

3 Gilles Deleuze, *Proust and Signs*, trans. Richard Howard (New York: Braziller, 1972) pp. 41, 43.

4 Melanie Klein, 'Early Analysis,' *'Love, Guilt and Reparation,' and Other Works 1921–1945* (New York: Dell, 1975) p. 77. All further references to this essay, abbreviated EA, are included in text.

5 In the sharp distinction that Klein makes in this essay between neurotic fixations and sublimations, the crucial point appears to be what happens to suspended libido. 'In hysterical fixation . . . phantasy holds so tenaciously to the pleasure situation that, before sublimation is possible, it succumbs to repression and fixation.' One page later Klein writes: 'In my opinion we find that a fixation that leads to a symptom was already on the way to sublimation but was cut off from it by repression.' And, in her brief account of Freud's essay on Leonardo da Vinci, Klein concludes: 'In Leonardo the pleasurable situation [gratification through fellatio] did not become fixated as such; he transferred it to ego-tendencies.' It is true, however, that Klein sometimes speaks of this process as a transfer of an already defined, even already fixated, pleasurable situation; she will also write that the step from identifications to symbol formation – a developmental step obviously crucial for cultural sublimation – takes place when 'repression begins to operate' (EA, 86–9). The ambiguities here may have to do with Klein's failure (or unwillingness) to recognize how radical her position in 'Early Analysis' is. This suggestion seems all the more probable in the light of her later, and more 'official,' views of sublimation.

6 Klein, *On the Theory of Anxiety and Guilt, Envy and Gratitude and Other Works, 1946–1963* (New York: Dell, 1975), p. 41.

7 Klein, 'The Early Development of Conscience in the Child,' *Love, Guilt and Reparation*, p. 254.

8 Klein, 'The Importance of Symbol-Formation in the Development of the Ego,' ibid., pp. 220–4.

9 Klein, 'A Contribution to the Psychogenesis of Manic-Depressive States,' ibid., p. 270.

10 Klein, 'Some Theoretical Conclusions Regarding the Emotional Life of the Infant' (1952), *Envy and Gratitude* (New York: Dell, 1975) p. 64.

11 Klein, *Envy and Gratitude*, ibid., p. 193.

12 For two quite different views on the relation between sublimation and idealization, see Guy Rosolato, *Essais sur le symbolique* (Paris: Gallimard, 1964), pp. 170–80, and Donald Meltzer, *Sexual States of Mind* (Perthshire: Clunie Press, 1973), pp. 122–31.

13 See Jean Laplanche, *Problématiques III: La sublimation* (Paris: Presses Universitaires de France, 1980).

14 [See Leo Bersani, *The Culture of Redemption* (Cambridge, Mass.: Harvard University Press, 1990), ch. 2, in which Bersani develops these ideas in the context of the ambiguous positioning of narcissism in Freudian thought – Eds.]

15 In an important essay (originally published in German in 1937) on the segregation of culture within bourgeois society, Herbert Marcuse defines the role of culture in a civilization anxious to divert human beings to their real material situation, and to suggest that the private realm of the soul, where high culture is enjoyed, somehow makes up for debased and unjust social conditions: 'Culture should [according to the modern bourgeois view of it] ennoble the given by permeating it, rather than putting something new in its place. It thus exalts the individual without freeing him from his factual debasement. Culture speaks of the dignity of "man" without concerning itself with a concretely more dignified status for men. The beauty of culture is above all an inner beauty and can only reach the external world from within. Its realm is essentially a realm of the *soul*.' This cultural ideal, Marcuse argues, has best been exemplified by art, and for good reason, since 'only in art has bourgeois society tolerated its own ideals and taken them seriously [even while segregating them] as a general demand.' Marcuse, 'The Affirmative Character of Culture,' in *Negations: Essays in Critical Theory* (Boston: Beacon Press, 1968), pp. 103, 114.

Chapter 13

Notes on *Citizen Kane*
Introduction by Laura Mulvey

Melanie Klein

Introduction

One of the most immediately interesting things about Melanie Klein's notes on *Citizen Kane* is her sense that the film can be understood through and with psychoanalysis. She finds it quite easy to use her own terms and her own approach to psychoanalysis in her notes. But there is something tentative about them. It is as though Klein is hesitating; she would have liked to go further with the analysis but held back. Of course, she had only seen the film once and it was, after all, only a film. But her instinct is right. As I have described elsewhere, most writing about this most written-about and debated film conspicuously overlooks its debt to psychoanalytic themes.[1] The discovery of Klein's notes and her professional, if instinctive and tentative, understanding of Kane's character provides a new and fascinating corroboration of the film's psychoanalytic frame of reference.

When *Citizen Kane* was released in 1941, it created a scandal in the United States. The press immediately spotted the correspondence between the fictional Charles Foster Kane and the greatest of the real, live press tycoons of the day: William Randolph Hearst. *Time* magazine of 24 January 1941 describes the pre-release screening for Hearst papers' columnist Louella Parsons:

> Lolly Parsons nearly fell off her chair. On the pre-view screen before her, Orson Welles, the bearded boy, was playing Citizen Kane in a manner that reminded columnist Parsons irresistibly of her boss William Randolph Hearst. She rose like a geyser . . . The result was that no more mention of RKO pictures appeared in Hearst papers.

The Hearst papers could make or break a film. In a desperate, but ineffectual, attempt to neutralize the damage, Welles issued a press release which generalized Kane's narrative trajectory in psychoanalytic terms. Among other points, it said:

> In his subconscious [Rosebud] stood for his mother's love which Kane never lost. In his waking hours, Kane certainly forgot the sled and the name which was painted on it. Case books of psychiatrists are full of these stories.

The press conference that followed was not a success. The newspaper men were not interested in psychoanalysis; they were only interested in the Hearst connection. Finally, Welles said: 'It may be dollar book Freud, but that's the way I understand the film.'

To my mind, Welles's seemingly derogatory 'dollar book' remark accidentally stranded the very significant psychoanalytic aspect of *Citizen Kane* outside the pale of serious attention. The very reputation of the film, widely held to be one of the greatest films of all time, left it suspended in a miasma of enigma. The investigator's last throwaway remark about Rosebud ('Maybe it's just a missing piece in the jig-saw puzzle') seems superficially to imply that the mystery is insoluble and is thus representative of the ultimate unknowability of the human condition. Melanie Klein, however, is not fazed. She recognizes that the film's truth cannot lie in the cacophony of voices that tell its story. She says:

> Interesting and amusing that this reporter, having found that the whole inquiry wasn't worth while because it doesn't mean anything. However, that doesn't seem to be the opinion of the author, because in many ways he seems to know a great lot of the unconscious processes underlying and influencing Kane's development and life.

She has grasped the gap between the (on-screen) narrator's vision and the clues, spread across the story's visual register, that point to a discourse, even if 'dollar book,' of the unconscious. The clues to this discourse are, of course, only available to author and audience; access to them cannot be gained through the characters. And most particularly, they are only available to an audience that will look and then interpret the objects and images on the screen rather than simply listen to the 'manifest' content contained in the dialogue.

Klein's first interpretation of *Citizen Kane* comes as no surprise. When she points out that 'Kane's dying word [Rosebud] refers to the breast,' one's instinctive response is: 'Well, she would, wouldn't she?' But, although her analysis of Kane remains sketchy, her use of certain other key words is illuminating if expanded and related back to the film. Klein sees Kane as out of touch with his depressive feelings, due to the fact that the 'rosebud' inside him is insecure and endangered. As he grows up, he fails to find any compensation for the loss of this love object and becomes more and more prone to manic mechanisms. By the time he meets Susan, he is unable to love, only to control and idealize. 'Nevertheless, the longing for the rosebud, for the good breast – carried always in his pocket – shows what he wished to preserve inside himself.'

Klein pays surprisingly little attention to the most psychoanalytically interesting scene in the film. The first flashback of Kane's life story is the founding moment of his psychic history, the story's primal scene, as it were. In a truly phantasmatic landscape a small boy is traumatically taken from his parents with their acquiescence. The scene cannot be analysed according to any rules of rationality or verisimilitude. The parents' characters, for instance, are strikingly incoherent. However, their very incoherence makes sense within the Kleinian terms of infantile ambivalence and the splitting of objects, including the parents, into good and bad. Charlie, still secure in his mother's love, acts out what, in Klein's terms, would probably amount to aggression towards his mother. The child happily slides down a snowy slope and throws a snowball. In a reverse shot that shows an isolated log-cabin in a snow-covered landscape, the snowball hits the sign saying 'Mrs Kane's Boarding House' squarely between the 'Mrs' and the 'Kane.' Mrs Kane's severe and unmotherly appearance contrasts with her caring, motherly, love for Charles. Mr Kane pleads to keep his son and Charles's attitude to him is affectionate and trusting. But a bad and dangerous burst of anger threatens his son. This exchange between mother and father:

Mr Kane: What that boy needs is a good thrashing.
Mrs Kane: That's what you think, do you Jim? That's why he'll be brought up
    where you can't get at him.

seems to rationalize the separation of mother and son. The scene is riddled with the inconsistency of phantasy.

These kinds of ambivalences and splits are compatible with Klein's vision of the infant's relation to its good and bad objects. (Even as he shouts out 'Union for Ever' Charles seems to be acting out a child's equally normal phantasy of omnipotence.) Literally speaking, Charles should have moved past that phase; but his infantile phantasies are elided along with a moment that freezes and disrupts normal development and moulds the raw material of psychic struggle into the shape that will be Charles Foster Kane. The first moment he meets Mr Thatcher, Charles attacks him with the sled, showing the strong feelings of persecution that will haunt him for the rest of his life. As his beloved mother sends him away from her, the little sled called Rosebud lies abandoned, buried by the snow. Banished from the good object (in Klein's words the breast), Charles has little hope of internalizing it. The sled is invested with all the emotion of loss, the early losses and separations out of which the ego must develop now condensed into one traumatic loss. The sled, the representative of good objects, attacked its persecutor. Abandoned and buried in the snow, it signifies Charles's future psychic state, persecuted by 'bad' objects while pining for the loved 'good' object. This traumatic moment is frozen in the timelessness of the unconscious.

*

As Melanie Klein notes, Kane's subsequent development is controlled by manic mechanisms. She dwells more on his incapacity to love and his failed marriages than his persecutory and manic symptoms. She does, however, comment on the obviously manic aspect of his collection of statues, their significance as inanimate representatives of his desire to keep alive 'loved people inside,' and his grandiose plans for Xanadu. In fact, Kane seems to epitomize the symptoms of 'hypomania.' In her classic essay 'Mourning and its Relation to Manic-Depressive States,' written just one year before the release of *Citizen Kane*, Klein had written:

It is characteristic of the hypomanic person's attitude towards people, principles and events that he is inclined to exaggerate evaluations: over-admiration (idealization) or contempt (devaluation). With this goes his tendency to conceive of everything on a large scale, to think in large numbers, all of this is in accordance with the greatness of his omnipotence by which he defends himself from losing the one irreplaceable object, his mother, which he still mourns at bottom.[2]

Being one of the richest men in the world, it is easy for Kane to indulge his hypomania and the story is, at least on the surface, the story of his hypomanic symptoms. For instance, he moves from journalism into politics to win not so much political power as such, but to secure the love of the American people. According to Klein, phantasies of omnipotence also date back to infancy with the splitting of ego and object, the denial of psychic reality, the conjuring up of 'the ideal object and situation and the equally omnipotent annihilation of the bad persecutory object and the painful situation.'[3]

Kane suffers from intense persecutory and paranoid feelings, once again indicating the stunting of his psychic development and his inability to reach the depressive position. The first half of his story consists of battles for control against persecutory 'bad' father figures and culminates in his paranoid and aggressive political war with the Gettys. It is perhaps at this point that one might take issue with Klein's contention that Kane is 'not ill' because he still functions in the world. A fiction necessarily takes liberties and blurs lines, exaggerating symptoms for dramatic effect. One weakness in Klein's notes is a tendency to try to figure out Kane and his relationships as though they existed in the real world. However, Klein points quite rightly to Kane's idealization and control of Susan which dominate the second part of his story. In keeping with Klein's description of schizoid object relations, Kane's attitude to Susan is narcissistic in his projection of both the good and bad parts of the self into another person. Klein notes:

> Both these types of narcissistic relation to another object often show strong obsessional features. The impulse to control other people is, as we know, an essential element in obsessional neurosis.[4]

But Kane's failure to control the opinion of the world by making Susan into an opera star leads to a retreat that Klein also associates with the schizoid position. She describes 'a shrinking from people in order to prevent both a destructive intrusion into them and the danger of retaliation by them.'[5] Kane's shrinking from people is marked, as usual, by omnipotence and grandiosity and he literally builds a castle to protect himself and Susan, his idealized object, in their retreat.

*

Melanie Klein correctly, if only implicitly, links the opening scene of Kane's story, when his mother sends him away from her love and their log-cabin home, with the last scene of his story, when Susan has left him in Xanadu, a travesty of a home and a metaphor for internal death and emptiness. Klein says: 'Susan leaves Kane. The reaction to her parting is the rosebud. The only object he preserves from her room which he picks up obviously unconsciously . . . ' Kane, now lonely and elderly, reacts to Susan's departure with an ungovernable rage, smashing her bedroom and everything in it rather as Klein describes the child's destructive rage in response to maternal punishment in Ravel's *L'enfant et les sortilèges*.[6] His rage is calmed when he suddenly sees a toy, a glass ball containing a snowstorm and, as he picks it up, the snow swirls around a little log cabin, exactly like his own lost home. He puts it in his pocket and the butler overhears him say to himself 'Rosebud.' The snowstorm toy reactivates memories of his early loss and his earlier happiness, both of which are invested in a memory of the sled. Klein described the process of mourning as follows:

> the person . . . reinstates his internalized good objects (ultimately his loved parents) . . . Thereupon the early depressive position, and with it anxieties, guilt, feelings of loss derived from the breast situation, the Oedipus situation and all other such sources are reactivated.[7]

When Kane loses Susan, he remembers the sled, Rosebud, which not only stands, in his unconscious, for the loss of his mother but also stands for the good objects he once internalized in infancy.

Why it is inevitable that Thompson, the investigator, will be unable to crack the Rosebud enigma is, as Melanie Klein points out, because the answer is locked in Kane's unconscious. And as the unconscious is outside time, the painstaking chronological biography that Thompson reconstructs is doomed to failure. His witnesses' memories are equally stuck on the manifest surface of things, only their inconsistency points to signs or symptoms of Kane's psychic life. Juliet Mitchell comments on Klein's attitude to time. For Klein, she says, past and present are one. Infancy is a perpetual present in which:

> Time for [pre-Oedipal infants] would seem to be nearer to spatial relationships; here, there; come, gone; horizontal, punctuated by duration rather than an historical, vertical temporal perspective.[8]

The narrative structure of *Citizen Kane* does not unfold along a straight line. Although the flashbacks are told in roughly chronological order, with some overlaps, the story plays with time using devices specific to the cinema to merge place across time and time across place. The end of the film returns to its beginning, closing a circle. But more significantly, the film uses the rosebud device to evoke the language of the unconscious, inhabited by objects which act as markers of determinant moments and boundaries between states of memory and forgetfulness.

As I have described elsewhere, the *Citizen Kane* script grafts a recognizable portrait of a well-known, right-wing, public figure onto a childhood that belongs to American myth and not to the origins of William Randolph Hearst. The story gives 'Hearst' a fictional childhood trauma, separation from mother and home, which cloaks his early memories in obscurity and, thus, attributes to him a fictional unconscious. It is arguable, to my mind, that Kane's story has an allegorical function which relates to Welles's politics and political fears at the time. The script was developed during the 'phoney war' period, in February 1940, and went into production in June, after the fall of France. The United States was locked in battle between isolationists (for whom the Hearst press campaigned vociferously) and interventionists (with whom Roosevelt was known to be sympathetic). Welles himself was very much a supporter of FDR, on the left and pro-European. It is in this highly emotional, politically charged, atmosphere that the allegorical aspect of Citizen Kane should be understood.

European immigrants in the United States were, by and large, ambivalent about the countries of their or their parents' birth. A certain nostalgia and idealization mixed with rejection and the desire to erase all memories of the past, often literally of poverty, hunger and persecution, in order to forge a new American identity and participate in the ultimate sign of American-ness, the consumer society. The Kane allegory would suggest an appeal to the American people to confront a collective amnesia, as fascism threatened Europe. In Kleinian terms, the early, pre-migration experiences of immigrants would combine a maternal, always-to-be-pined-for love with the deprivation of nourishment and external danger. These good and bad objects would have both psychic and historical realities. Kane ends his life literally isolated in a castle built out of the detritus of European history, the bits a hotch-potch of style, time and place. Welles may be suggesting, allegorically, that the American people re-order their psychic reality, not into the vertical time of chronology, but into a transformation of their 'good' and 'bad' objects into political understanding.

It is probably no more possible to verify this reading of Citizen Kane than for Thompson to decipher the Rosebud enigma. In his 1941 press release, Welles argued that for the purposes of his story, his central character had to have personal attributes that were so typical of a capitalist tycoon that similarities to Hearst were purely incidental. To reverse this position, it could be argued that the ideas and themes developed in Citizen Kane demand a psychoanalytic imagination whether the author actually adapted them from established sources or not. As these notes show, Melanie Klein had such an imagination.

Notes on Citizen Kane[9]

The film starts with death of Citizen Kane. His life story from two aspects – official one, which appears in the paper, describes the important events in his life.[10] From this point of view a very successful man, though his political ambitions never quite fulfilled. Enormously rich, one of the richest men in the world – most powerful through his press associations – many newspaper concerns, etc.

The story of two marriages shows failures. Nevertheless picture of a rich and successful, important life. Second version of life story worked out very cleverly through editor's wish to find out significance of Kane's dying word 'rosebud.' He wishes to know what sort of person Kane was. Various information gathered from a diary kept by Kane's guardian, from his second wife, his friends. We learn something about the real life of Kane. Nobody knows anything about the rosebud – only the butler, who was with him when he died.[11] Gives information.[12]

Interesting and amusing that this reporter, having finds [sic] that the whole enquiry wasn't worth while because it doesn't mean anything. However, that doesn't seem to be the opinion of the author, because in many ways he seems to know a great lot of the unconscious processes underlying and influencing Kane's development and life. It is obvious for us that Kane's dying word refers to the breast. The last thing he carries with him cherished and which, as the picture shows, he drops when dying while he speaks the word 'rosebud.'[13]

Kane not an ill man in clinical sense; no breakdown. To end of his life keeps his power to work, and though he finishes a lonely man, one could not call him actually ill. It is true both marriages are failures, and he never arrives at the high aims which he sets himself in politics. Here, however, is the point which I wish to discuss: depressive feelings overlaid and kept at bay by manic mechanisms in, as one might say, a normal person. How they influence the course of his life. In his youth Kane has strong social feelings and purposes; the under-privileged, the poor, are to be helped; he is going to devote his powers, his money, his capacities to this purpose. When he marries, he seems to prepare for a happy married life – his wife attractive, loves him, they have a charming child. For reasons unknown to Kane and un-understandable [sic] to his wife, he estranges himself more and more. Then comes his love affair. At this point again it seems as if love feelings would come to the fore, but as his second wife later on complains, Kane was actually only interested in her voice (which is not altogether true), but it becomes the predominant factor. Kane controls Susan, and through her, is going to control multitudes. As he says, he is going to make them think the way he wants. It suggests itself that the fact that Susan is poor, needs protection, stirs his feelings of a loving kind, possibly also that Susan's mother will not allow her to become a singer strikes a chord in him,[14] since his own mother so wilfully shaped his life away from her and his father, and with the design that he should be rich and powerful. But, however he struggles to love Susan – and he is tied to her through strong bonds – he has not got the capacity to love. He forces Susan to continue a career which, owing to her lack of talent, becomes a nightmare to her. Her attempt to commit suicide. Kane gives in, and now devotes himself to the grandiose plans of building the most luxurious and greatest castle which any private man ever had; the greatest private zoo since Noah's time – hundred thousand trees, 20 thousand tons of marble used. His collection of statues, which as time goes on becomes more and more manic. In this castle he keeps poor Susan, who, though she had wished to have a castle, is lonely and unhappy, in spite of being a great hostess. She doesn't realize that she is not actually, as she seems to think, out for entertainment, New York's pleasures, and so on but what she is starved in is love. She suddenly recognizes this through an expression he uses which shows her that there is nothing in him but selfishness; that he has no love to give, and that he ties people to him only because he wants them to love him.[15] Connections between love to internal objects can be selfishness in regard to external ones if the manic mechanisms of controlling etc. prevail.[16] Susan leaves Kane. The reaction to her parting is the rosebud. The only object he preserves from her room, ~~which he picks up~~, obviously unconsciou~~sly why he does it~~, of the motives for his picking it up and for his keep [sic] it. ~~The reference to~~

The only references to his mother are when he gets to know and like Susan, that he had been on a journey to visit his mother's grave and the place where she lived, and where he lived in his childhood.[17]

Somebody in the film, I think one of his 2 friends, says that he loves his mother.

Consider the reasons for his 'selfishness.' His incapacity to attach himself to the loved woman because of his fear of loss. Also the family life of his parents being destroyed when they sent him away. His father could not keep a son; Kane destroys the relation to his son when he allows his wife to divorce him. Again selfishness in regard to external people, while the fear of the death inside of the rosebud in himself increases as his life goes on.

Interplay between his incapacity to love people and to hold them and the fear of death inside, and of loved people inside. His collection of statues, predominantly women, growing as a means of reviving more and more assuming the nature of artificial inanimate things. Even the rosebud is an artificial thing – a glass bowl containing an artificial rosebud.[18] The more the incapacity to keep things alive inside him, and the incapacity of real contact with people increases, the stronger becomes his drive to control, to have power, – the manic mechanisms. [Speaking of the fear of death of the loved people inside him increasing: characteristic – the enormous hall in which poor Susan is occupied with her jigsaw puzzles, and Kane sitting at the other end of it, speaks to her at a distance in which they scarcely can hear each other distinctly. The communication between him and his objects is interrupted – the hall makes the impression of a mausoleum. At this point the break with Susan occurs, provoked by him, because he cannot keep up any longer the struggle.[19]]

Long-forgotten are his wishes to further the interests of poor people. These tendencies also soon changed into ways of controlling them, and of using these purposes for gaining power. It is pathetic how when he met Susan, her simple-mindedness, her poverty, her youth, etc. attracted him, and how he wished and struggled to love her. But soon he had to change her into an artificial object, an idealized person, clinging to talents in her which she actually did not possess – a means for gaining power. Interesting also the relation to men, and the changes in his rebellious attitude. His rebelliousness at his colleges in connection with the parents having forced them on him and given him up for the sake of making him rich and powerful. Then this rebelliousness, very much directed against his rich conservative, materialistic guardian, turns against capitalism and is used for the protection of the poor; but this he cannot carry through. The attraction and love for his youth as a poor child would imply keeping the love for his parents alive. But hatred and grievance seem to prevent this. He also seems to fulfil his mother's wishes in working out the kind of life which she seemed to have planned for him. This, however, is only possible by increasing his manic mechanisms and divorcing himself more and more from feelings of love, the wish to protect and help others, etc. Obviously the fact that he cannot hold the women he wishes to love becomes further proof of the failure in loving and keeping alive in his mind his mother and of reconciling himself with his parents. A happy family life would have meant renewing the past in a good sense, reviving the parents, etc. The more his capacity for love proves a failure, the more the manic mechanisms increase; control of inner objects because they have turned dangerous and injured respectively through his hatred, and cannot be kept alive. The necessity to be loved 'on his own terms' as a reassurance against his feelings of unworthiness because his guilt tells him that he is the cause of the death inside him. Nevertheless, the longing for the rosebud, for the good breast – carried always in his pocket – shows what he wished to preserve inside himself. Had he not been so gifted and had he not had the means to live out in activities and in actual life his drive to control and, in those activities also employed reparative tendencies, though they seemed obscured through his desire for power – had he not been able to do that – would he not have fallen ill, possibly a victim of manic-depressive states?

Somebody suggests that he got so much in life and always lost it. Perhaps is the rosebud, something which he always wanted and could not get, or also something which he had and lost again.

Notes

1 Laura Mulvey, *Citizen Kane* (London: BFI, 1992).
2 Melanie Klein, 'Mourning and its Relation to Manic-Depressive States' (1940), *Love, Guilt and Reparation and Other Works 1921–1945* (London: Virago, 1988), p. 352.
3 Melanie Klein, 'Notes on Some Schizoid Mechanisms' (1946), *Envy and Gratitude and Other Works 1946–1963* (London: Virago, 1988), p. 7.
4 ibid, p. 13.
5 ibid, p. 13.
6 See Melanie Klein, 'Infantile Anxiety-Situations Reflected in a Work of Art and the Creative Impulse' (1929), *Love, Guilt and Reparation*, pp. 210–18.
7 Melanie Klein, 'Mourning and its Relation to Manic-Depressive States', p. 353.
8 This volume, p. 26. LS
9 There are three variant manuscripts containing Klein's notes on *Citizen Kane* in The Melanie Klein Archives held at the Wellcome Medical Contemporary Archives Centre, The Wellcome Institute (PP/KLE/C.89). The most complete version is published here, unabridged and in its original form. LS
10 Kane's story is first told on the newsreel, 'News on the March', not in a newspaper. LM/LS
11 Kane dies alone. LM/LS

12 [Klein has inserted a hand-written marginal comment at this point which reads 'Tell the whole story, including rosebud.' With the manuscript, there is a free-floating page which tells some of the story. It reads ' . . . that he might even have become a candidate for the Presidentship. He becomes enormously rich. However none of his aspirations seem to come true. He sets out with a programme of sincere determination for social reform but drops it as time goes on. His hopes for political success also fail and as one of his friends describes it, he always remains a brides-maid and is never a bride. He marries a girl who seemed to have all the qualities as well as social advantages which could make for a happy marriage with him, but they get more and more estranged as time goes on. We get the impression that it is Kane's attitude is responsible for that, since his wife repeatedly appeals to him to devote more time and love to her. His son only appears once in the film, but obviously this relation too does not make for happiness and stability in him. He falls in love with a very simple girl, and his wife leaves him when his love affair is discovered. At this point we get the impression that Kane might now really develop a relationship which could give him happiness. LS]

13 [Klein has deleted the two sentences that follow. They read: 'The hypomanic nature of Kane's attitudes can be detected over and over again in the history of his life. He controls public opinion, and for this purpose, the newspaper concerns he brings under his direction grow constantly.' LS]

14 [There's no evidence for this in the film. LM/LS]

15 [The expression is 'You can't do that to me.' LM/LS]

16 [Klein has added this sentence by hand at the top of the page. LS]

17 [Kane is neither visiting his mother's grave nor his birthplace in the scene where he meets Susan. LM/LS]

18 [This is perhaps Klein's most interesting piece of misremembering. The glass bowl contains a snow scene which evokes Kane's childhood and the sled called 'Rosebud'. Klein has mistaken the word for a thing: she sees the literal rosebud in the glass bowl, maybe in the same way that the infant, in her theory, sees the literal breast in phantasy. LS]

19 [This passage appears on an unnumbered page in this version of the notes. LS]

Index

DAVID — 548-8634